BUDDHISM, POLITICS AND
THE LIMITS OF LAW

It is widely assumed that a well-designed and well-implemented constitution can help ensure religious harmony in modern states. Yet how correct is this assumption? Drawing on ground-breaking research from Sri Lanka, this book argues persuasively for another possibility: when it comes to religion, relying on constitutional law may not be helpful, but harmful; constitutional practice may give way to pyrrhic constitutionalism. Written in a lucid and direct style, aimed at both specialists and non-specialists, *Buddhism, Politics and the Limits of Law* explains why constitutional law has deepened, rather than diminished, conflicts over religion in Sri Lanka. Examining the roles of Buddhist monks, civil society groups, political coalitions and more, the book provides the first extended study of the legal regulation of religion in Sri Lanka as well as the first book-length analysis of the intersections of Buddhism and contemporary constitutional law.

BENJAMIN SCHONTHAL is Senior Lecturer in Buddhism and Asian Religions at the University of Otago. He received his Ph.D. in the field of History of Religions at the University of Chicago. His research examines the intersection of religion, law and politics in South and Southeast Asia, with a particular focus on Buddhism.

COMPARATIVE CONSTITUTIONAL LAW AND POLICY

Series Editors

Tom Ginsburg
University of Chicago
Zachary Elkins
University of Texas at Austin
Ran Hirschl
University of Toronto

Comparative constitutional law is an intellectually vibrant field that encompasses an increasingly broad array of approaches and methodologies. This series collects analytically innovative and empirically grounded work from scholars of comparative constitutionalism across academic disciplines. Books in the series include theoretically informed studies of single constitutional jurisdictions, comparative studies of constitutional law and institutions, and edited collections of original essays that respond to challenging theoretical and empirical questions in the field.

Books in the Series

Buddhism, Politics and the Limits of Law: The Pyrrhic Constitutionalism of Sri Lanka
Benjamin Schonthal

Assessing Constitutional Performance
Tom Ginsburg and Aziz Huq

Engaging with Social Rights
Brian Ray

Constitutional Courts as Mediators
Julio Ríos-Figueroa

Constitutionalism in Asia in the Early Twenty-First Century
edited by Albert Chen

Perils of Judicial Self-Government in Transitional Societies
David Kosař

Unstable Constitutionalism
edited by Mark Tushnet and Madhav Khosla

Social Difference and Constitutionalism in Pan-Asia
edited by Susan H Williams

Making We the People
Chaihark Hahm and Sung Ho Kim

Radical Deprivation on Trial
Cesar Rodríguez-Garavito and Diana Rodríguez-Franco

Presidential Legislation in India: The Law and Practice of Ordinances
Shubhankar Dam

Social and Political Foundations of Constitutions
edited by Denis J Galligan and Mila Versteeg

Magna Carta and its Modern Legacy
edited by Robert Hazell and James Melton

Constitutions and Religious Freedom
Frank Cross

International Courts and the Performance of International Agreements: A General Theory with Evidence from the European Union
Clifford Carrubba and Matthew Gabel

Reputation and Judicial Tactics: A Theory of National and International Courts
Shai Dothan

Constitutions in Authoritarian Regimes
edited by Tom Ginsburg and Alberto Simpser

Comparative Constitutional Design
edited by Tom Ginsburg

Consequential Courts: Judicial Roles in Global Perspective
edited by Diana Kapiszewski, Gordon Silverstein and Robert A Kagan

BUDDHISM, POLITICS AND THE LIMITS OF LAW

The Pyrrhic Constitutionalism of Sri Lanka

BENJAMIN SCHONTHAL
University of Otago

CAMBRIDGE
UNIVERSITY PRESS

One Liberty Plaza, 20th Floor, New York NY 10006, USA

Cambridge University Press is part of the University of Cambridge.

It furthers the University's mission by disseminating knowledge in the pursuit of education, learning, and research at the highest international levels of excellence.

www.cambridge.org
Information on this title: www.cambridge.org/9781107152236

© Benjamin Schonthal 2016

This publication is in copyright. Subject to statutory exception and to the provisions of relevant collective licensing agreements, no reproduction of any part may take place without the written permission of Cambridge University Press.

First published 2016

A catalogue record for this publication is available from the British Library.

Library of Congress Cataloging-in-Publication Data
Names: Schonthal, Benjamin, 1976- author.
Title: Buddhism, politics and the limits of law : the pyrrhic constitutionalism of
Sri Lanka / Benjamin Schonthal, University of Otago.
Description: New York NY : Cambridge University Press, 2016. | Series: Comparative
constitutional law and policy | Includes bibliographical references.
Identifiers: LCCN 2016018482
Subjects: LCSH: Constitutional law–Sri Lanka. | Buddhism and law–Sri Lanka. | Ecclesiastical
law–Sri Lanka. | Religious law and legislation–Sri Lanka.
Classification: LCC KPS2162 .S36 2016 | DDC 342.549308/52–dc23 LC record available
at https://lccn.loc.gov/2016018482

ISBN 978-1-107-15223-6 Hardback

Cambridge University Press has no responsibility for the persistence or accuracy of URLs for external or third-party Internet Web sites referred to in this publication and does not guarantee that any content on such Web sites is, or will remain, accurate or appropriate.

CONTENTS

Acknowledgments   viii
A Note on Translation and Language   xi
Abbreviations   xiii

1   Introduction: Religion, Law and the Pyrrhic
    Constitutionalism of Sri Lanka   1

    PART I   The Past Lives of the Buddhism Chapter   23

2   Managing Religion at the End of Empire   25

3   Contesting Constitutions in the 1950s and 1960s   60

4   Multivalent Solutions: Drafting the Buddhism Chapter   98

    PART II   From Creation to Implementation   147

5   Legal Battles for Buddhism   149

6   Battles within Buddhism   188

7   Constitutional Conversions   217

8   Conclusion: The Costs of Constitutional Law   261

References   274
Index   292

vii

ACKNOWLEDGMENTS

In 1996, I phoned my mother to tell her I was going to Sri Lanka to study Buddhism. I'll never forget her reply: "No you're not. And where is Sri Lanka?" Fortunately, she came around to the idea and since that time I have come to think of Sri Lanka as another home. This book owes everything to the many generous people there, who have helped me in more ways than I can say.

I owe a particular debt to Sri Lanka's legal community. This work was made possible by the support and patience of active and retired lawyers, judges, clerks, archivists, registrars and researchers. It has also been made possible by the willingness of litigants and lawmakers to share their stories. I cannot thank you all here, but this book would not be possible without you.

I would not have gone to Sri Lanka in the first place if it were not for John Holt, whose teaching made me want to pursue the study of South Asia instead of medicine. Once there, I was lucky to meet Rohan Edrisinghe, Udaya Meddegama, Tissa Jayatilleke (and the entire Fulbright family), Wickrama Weerasooria, Asanga Tilakaratne, Farzana Haniffa, Niran Anketell, Viran Corea, Liyanage Amarakeerthi, Kalana Seneratne, Chulani Kodikara, Uditha Egalahewa, Prasantha Lal de Alwis, Manohara De Silva, Ven. Prof. Kotapitiye Rahula, Savithri and R K W Goonasekera, Paikiasothy Saravanamuttu, Sharya Scharenguival, Lakshman Marasinghe, Deepika Udagama, V T Thamilmaran, Shibly Aziz, K M de Silva, M A Sumanthiran, Nihal Jayawickrama, Bradman Weerakoon, Sam Wijesinghe, Kandiah and Saravanan Neelakandan, Moahan Balendra, Ranga Dayananda, Damithe Karunaratne, and many others who spent long hours discussing the finer points of religion, law and politics in Sri Lanka. The staff of the National Archives, the Parliamentary Library, the Supreme Court Registry, ICES, SSA, AISLS, LSA, LST, the University of Colombo, the J R Jayewardene and Nadesan Centres were incredibly gracious in helping with (what must have felt like) endless, annoying requests for documents. At various points, the help of Ashan Munasinghe, Tilak Jayatilaka and Pubudu Senaratne proved vital. I will not forget the generosity shown to me in Kandy by Gananath and Ranjini Obeyesekere and the ISLE family. Paula and I remain grateful to the De Silva family of Kandy for their hospitality and ongoing friendship.

The groundwork for this book was laid during my time at the University of Chicago. One of the best things I did there was to ask Wendy Doniger to be my Ph.D. supervisor. Her advice and good humor kept me, like so many others, buoyant through what were, at times, rough seas. Steve Collins, Dan Slater, John Holt, Sascha Ebeling, Guy Leavitt, Jim Lindholm, Bruce Lincoln, Christian Wedemeyer, Richard Fox and Malika Zeghal gave me the linguistic and intellectual tools and the mentorship to do this work. Aside from the critical support given to me by the Divinity School, I must also thank the Departments of Political Science and the Law School (particularly Tom Ginsburg) at the University of Chicago for inviting me into their intellectual worlds so willingly. Disciplinary crossover can be bumpy; they made it smooth. I received formal training in Tamil, Sanskrit and Pali at Chicago, yet I have struggled with literary Sinhala on my own, a process made possible only by the selfless help of Jon Young, Asanga Tilakaratne, Udaya Meddegama, Habib Saleem and especially Bandara Herath, who gave their time generously on numerous occasions to help me make sense of political oratory, legal documents and other texts.

This book would still be half-written if it were not for the encouragement and counsel of Winnifred Sullivan and Beth Hurd. I cannot thank them enough for their critical feedback and generosity. If it were not for conversations with Asanga Welikala, I would not have enjoyed obsessing over Sri Lankan legal and political history quite so much; the pages that follow owe a lot to him and his astonishing intellect. The ideas contained here have also been enriched from conversations with Ben Berger, Frank Reynolds, Tamir Moustafa, David Fontana, Kristen Stilt, Erin Delaney, Jonathan Spencer, David Engel, Mitra Sharafi, Tomas Larsson, Anne Blackburn, Jeremy Morse, Lucas Carmichael, Amanda Lucia, Blake Wentworth, Dan Kent, Vivian Choi, John Madeley, Bill Kissane, Asli Bali, David Mednicoff, Nathan Brown, Peter Danchin, Saba Mahmood, Clark Lombardi, Melissa Crouch, Isaac Weiner, Matt Nelson, Mirjam Kuenkler, Christian Lammerts, Jolyon Thomas, Rick Weiss, Mara Malagodi, Harshan Kumarasingham, Jon Young, Neena Mahadev, Oshan Fernando, Noah Salomon, Molly Schonthal and others. If the writing in this volume shows any verve, it is probably because of the influence of Anne Mocko, who has been a trusted writing partner and friend for more than a decade.

H L Seneviratne, Kitsiri Malalgoda, Steve Berkwitz, John Rogers, Shylashri Shankar, Matt Nelson, Tamir Moustafa and Hanna Lerner have been extraordinarily generous with their time, reading large sections of this manuscript and giving critical feedback at critical moments. I am truly grateful to them. Aaron Glasserman, a remarkable scholar, read every chapter of this book closely and made several key interventions. I feel lucky to have worked with him before he becomes famous.

The research here benefitted from the generosity of numerous institutions, including the Fulbright-Hays Dissertation Research Fellowship, the American Philosophical Society, the US Institute of Peace, the Mellon Foundation, the Universities of Chicago and Otago, and the Center for Interdisciplinary Research (ZiF) at Bielefeld University.

Tom Ginsburg, Ran Hirschl and Zach Elkins supported this project since the beginning and have been instrumental in helping me to join together conversations in the study of religion with conversations in comparative constitutional law. I hope this book succeeds, at least some of the way, in its attempt to cross-fertilize the approaches of one discipline with the other. Thank you for taking a punt.

John Berger, Fiona Allison and Jeethu Abraham were generous with their time during the publication phase. Particular thanks go to Julia TerMaat and Deane Galbraith for their patience and efforts in editing.

Versions of Chapters 5 and 6 were previously published in *Modern Asian Studies* and the *Asian Journal of Law and Society*, respectively.

Finally, this book (like so much) would not have happened if it wasn't for the support of my family in Chicago and on Waiheke Island. I hope my two boys, Oliver and Henry, will like this book even though it doesn't have any pictures. Most of all, it is the love, strength, humor, generosity and patience of my amazing wife, Paula, that has made this – and everything else – possible. I dedicate this book to her. We did it together.

A NOTE ON TRANSLATION AND LANGUAGE

This book draws upon sources written in English, Sinhala, Tamil and occasionally Pali. Unless otherwise specified, the non-English words contained in this book are Sinhala and transliterated according to the standard conventions outlined in Gair and Karunatillake, with the exception that I use ae instead of ä.[1] Tamil words are transliterated according to the standard conventions described in Paramasivam and Lindholm.[2] Pali transliteration follows standard practices used by the Pali Text Society. Where the reader might be confused about the source-language of the non-English term, I use the following abbreviations to clarify: *S:* for Sinhala terms, *T:* for Tamil terms and *P:* for Pali terms.

In certain cases I use the anglicized versions (without diacritical marks) of Pali, Sinhala or Tamil words in order to replicate the conventions of the texts with which I am working. For example, the reader will encounter words like sangha, Eelam and Sasana. I also provide the anglicized names (without diacritics) of organizations that make legal or political submissions using their own English transliterations of their names (e.g., Bauddha Jathika Balavegaya).

When referring to Buddhist monks I use the standard convention of placing "Ven." before the name, meaning Venerable. In some cases, depending on how the name is referenced in the sources that I use, I also place "Thero" or "Thera" after the name. Thero and Thera are different forms of a Pali word that means elder monk. All of the monks mentioned in this book are fully ordained Buddhist monks, whether or not Thero or Thera is suffixed to their name.

As it relates to the name of the island, I use both Ceylon and Sri Lanka. Chapters 2 and 3 default to Ceylon, whereas all other chapters default to

---

[1] James W Gair and W S Karunatillake, *Literary Sinhala Inflected Forms with a Transliteration Guide* (Ithaca, NY: Cornell University, 1976).

[2] K Paramasivam and James Lindholm, *A Basic Tamil Reader and Grammar* (Evanston, IL: Tamil Language Study Association, 1987).

Sri Lanka. In general I refer to the island using its official name during the period under analysis.

For the sake of standardization, no diacritics have been used in the index of the book or in the list of abbreviations.

ABBREVIATIONS

ACBC	All-Ceylon Buddhist Congress
ACHC	All-Ceylon Hindu Congress
BBS	Bodu Bala Sena (Army of Buddhist Power)
BJB	Bauddha Jatika Balavegaya (Buddhist National Force)
BTS	Buddhist Theosophical Society
CBA	Commissioner of Buddhist Affairs
CMT	Commissioner of Motor Traffic
CNC	Ceylon National Congress
CP	Communist Party
DBR	Draft Basic Resolution
DWC	Democratic Workers' Congress
FP	Federal Party
INC	Indian National Congress
JHU	Jathika Hela Urumaya (National [Sinhalese] Heritage Party)
LSSP	Lanka Sama Samaja Party (Lanka Equal Society Party)
LTTE	Liberation Tigers of Tamil Eelam
MEP	Mahajana Eksath Peramuna (United People's Front)
MSV	Mavbima Suraekima Vyaparaya (Movement from the Protection of the Motherland)
SLFP	Sri Lanka Freedom Party
SLNA	Sri Lanka National Archives
SUCCESS	Secretariat for Upliftment and Conservation of Cultural, Educational and Social Standards of Sri Lanka
UF	United Front
UKNA	United Kingdom National Archives
UNP	United National Party
YMBA	Young Men's Buddhist Association

1

Introduction: Religion, Law and the Pyrrhic Constitutionalism of Sri Lanka

Courtrooms are not places that one expects to see Buddhist monks, which is why visitors to Sri Lanka are often surprised by newspaper images of saffron-robed men filing into or out of the island's courts of law. Although not an everyday occurrence, Buddhist monks in Sri Lanka visit courtrooms regularly, and for a variety of reasons. They attend hearings, give evidence and make civil suits. They file writ petitions and, on rare occasions, even face criminal charges.[1]

Visitors are not the only ones unsettled by the appearance of monks in court. For litigants, lawyers and judges, the presence of monks in Sri Lankan courtrooms can also generate unease due to an anticipated clash between civil and religious norms. Sri Lanka's rules of civil procedure require that all persons seated in a courtroom stand up when a judge enters. Yet Buddhist texts and customs (which are specially protected by Sri Lanka's constitution) dictate that monks should never rise to greet non-monks – judges included.[2] Therefore, when Buddhist monks go to court, a dilemma ensues: Do monks stand for judges or do judges stand for monks? Do civil or Buddhist norms prevail?

Sri Lanka's lawyers are aware of the clash and take steps to avoid it. When representing Buddhist monks, lawyers delay their clients' entry into courtrooms until *after* judges have taken their seats at the bench. In Sri Lanka today, virtually all cases involving Buddhist monks employ this tactic.[3] Rather than addressing the normative clashes directly, lawyers elect to avoid them by substituting one lapse in protocol (not standing) with another (arriving late).

---

[1] The most famous example of a monk facing criminal charges is described in detail in Lucian Weeramantry, *Assassination of a Prime Minister: The Bandaranaike Murder Case* (Geneva, Switzerland: S.A. Studer, 1969).

[2] None of Sri Lanka's civil court judges are ordained Buddhist monks; they are all laypersons.

[3] One important instance of exception will be discussed in the Conclusion, Chapter 8.

2   INTRODUCTION

To an outside observer, Sri Lanka's courtroom standoff might look like a minor procedural issue, a simple matter of symbolism and ceremony. For many in Sri Lanka, however, the dilemma – and its now-standard method of avoidance – strikes a more troubling chord. If protocols of courtroom etiquette prove so challenging, how can Sri Lanka's courts and constitution be expected to cope with more serious questions related to religion: Who is responsible for balancing religious and civil authority? Is it possible, in practice, to enforce constitutional obligations to "protect and foster" Buddhism while also guaranteeing religious freedom and equality?

Every time monks and judges perform their complicated dance of avoidance, refusing to perform the supremacy of either party, they call attention to the persistence of deeper uncertainties about law and religion in Sri Lanka, while also dramatizing a more unsettling fact: when it comes to religion, the very institutions to which citizens turn to resolve disputes – laws and courts – provoke new conflicts and conundrums that neither judges nor lawmakers nor lawyers seem willing or able to resolve.

*

Religion and Law in a Constitutional Age

Balancing law and religion is a challenge throughout the world. Sri Lanka's conundrums are culturally specific, but not unparalleled. In places like the United States and Canada, one finds similar difficulties trying to reconcile civil and religious authority in constitutional contexts that celebrate both the impartiality of law and the free exercise of religion. North American jurists argue over whether it is possible to prevent formally neutral laws (such as those banning the use of hallucinogens) from having substantively discriminatory effects on certain religious groups (such as Native Americans who use peyote for ritual purposes).[4] In places like India and South Africa, one finds similar

---

[4] Douglas Laycock, "Formal, Substantive, and Disaggregated Neutrality Toward Religion," *DePaul Law Review* 39, no. 4 (1990): 993–1018. Martha Nussbaum, *Liberty of Conscience: In Defense of America's Tradition of Religious Equality* (New York: Basic Books, 2010). Gerard Bouchard and Charles Taylor, *Building the Future: A Time for Reconciliation (Report Prepared for Commission de consultation sur les pratiques d'accommodement reliées aux différences culturelles, Province of Quebec)*, 2008. www.accommodements.qc .ca/documentation/rapports/ (accessed May 31, 2010).

RELIGION AND LAW IN A CONSTITUTIONAL AGE

challenges of trying to protect religious customs without officially endorsing those customs. The depth of these challenges can be seen in inveterate disagreements over whether state-recognized systems of religion-based family and customary law are compatible with otherwise secular legal cultures.[5] In places like Israel, Ireland and Malaysia, one finds analogous disputes over how a single constitutional system might simultaneously safeguard a majority religion (Judaism, Catholicism or Islam) while also protecting general religious rights.[6]

In recent years, these struggles to manage religion through law have taken on a new sense of urgency. One sees this urgency in the growing prevalence of contentious, high-profile legal disputes involving religion. These disputes touch on a vast range issues, from the display of religious symbols in public, to the teaching of religion in schools, to the use of special legal accommodations and exemptions for religious groups. One also sees this urgency in the growing attention given to the legal management of religion by scholars, governments and human rights organizations. In the past 15 years, the United States, Canada and the European Union have all created separate administrative offices charged with overseeing and extending legal protections for religion around the world.[7] A similar expansion has occurred in the non-governmental sector, where an increasing number of organizations have dedicated themselves to monitoring the regulation of religion domestically and abroad.[8] Today, the legal management of religion features as a key object of policy, advocacy and even international relations[9] – so much so that

---

[5] Gerald Larson (ed.), *Religion and Personal Law in Secular India: A Call to Judgment* (Bloomington, IN: Indiana University Press, 2001). Jean Comaroff and John L Comaroff, "Reflections on Liberalism, Policulturalism, and ID-ology: Citizenship and Difference in South Africa," *Social Identities* 9, no. 4 (2003): 445–473.

[6] Steven V Mazie, *Israel's Higher Law: Religion and Liberal Democracy in the Jewish State* (Lanham: Lexington Books, 2006). Bill Kissane, "The Illusion of State Neutrality in a Secularising Ireland," *West European Politics* 26, no. 1 (2003): 73–94. Tamir Moustafa, "Liberal Rights Versus Islamic Law? The Construction of a Binary in Malaysian Politics," *Law & Society Review* 47, no. 4 (2013): 771–802.

[7] Bouchard and Taylor, *Building the Future*. R Scott Appleby, Richard Cizik and Task Force on Religion and the Making of U.S. Foreign Policy, *Engaging Religious Communities Abroad: A New Imperative for U.S. Foreign Policy* (Chicago: Chicago Council on Global Affairs, 2010). Elizabeth Shakman Hurd, *Beyond Religious Freedom: The New Global Politics of Religion* (Princeton, NJ: Princeton University Press, 2015).

[8] Ibid. Allen D Hertzke and Pew Forum on Religion & Public Life, *Lobbying for the Faithful: Religious Advocacy Groups in Washington, D.C.* (Pew Forum, May 2012).

[9] Hurd, *Beyond Religious Freedom*.

4   INTRODUCTION

one scholar has characterized our current era as a time of unprecedented overlap between religion and law, a new age of "theo-legality."[10]

This age of so-called theo-legality has arisen alongside an age of constitutional law. In fact the growing interpenetration of religion and law is happening at a time when written constitutions have established themselves as the dominant form of law – "the norm" – for regulating societies throughout the world.[11] Only a handful of the world's countries have not developed codified constitutions; of that handful, all have produced some written body of basic laws.[12] Not only have constitutions become virtually omnipresent, they have also grown in influence. In many states, constitutional courts function not simply as jurisprudential bodies, but as extraordinarily powerful and active political and legal agents.[13]

Today, discussions about the legal management of religion are often discussions about constitutions. A well-designed and well-implemented constitution, many academics and policy-makers argue, holds the key to greater harmony and trust among groups with differing religious interests.[14]

[10] John L Comaroff, "Reflections on the Rise of Legal Theology: Law and Religion in the Twenty-First Century," *Social Analysis* 53, no. 1 (2009): 193–216.

[11] Zachary Elkins, Tom Ginsburg, and James Melton, *The Endurance of National Constitutions* (New York: Cambridge University Press, 2009), 49, no. 11. Justin Blount, Zachary Elkins, and Tom Ginsburg, "Does the Process of Constitution-Making Matter?," in *Comparative Constitutional Design*, ed. Tom Ginsburg (Cambridge: Cambridge University Press, 2012), 31.

[12] These include the UK, New Zealand, Saudi Arabia, and Israel. Even in these countries, however, the strong pull of written constitutionalism can be felt. Recently, the UK, New Zealand, and Israel have all undertaken formal inquiries to examine whether they *should* draft a written constitution. See, e.g., Hanna Lerner, "Constitutional Impasse, Democracy and Religion in Israel," in *Constitution Writing, Religion and Democracy*, ed. Asli Bali and Hanna Lerner (Cambridge: Cambridge University Press, 2016).

[13] Bruce Ackerman, "The Rise of World Constitutionalism," *Virginia Law Review* 83, no. 4 (1997): 771–797. Julian Go, "Modeling States and Sovereignty: Postcolonial States in Africa and Asia," in *Making a World After Empire: The Bandung Moment and Its Political Afterlives*, ed. Christopher Lee (Athens: Ohio University Press, 2010). Ran Hirschl, *Towards Juristocracy: The Origins and Consequences of the New Constitutionalism* (Cambridge, MA: Harvard University Press, 2004).

[14] On the promises of constitutional governance for the management of social and religious diversity see: Sujit Choudhry, *Constitutional Design for Divided Societies: Integration or Accommodation?* (New York: Oxford University Press, 2008). Jurgen Habermas, "Why Europe Needs a Constitution," *New Left Review* 11 (2001): 5–26. Donald L Horowitz, *A Democratic South Africa?: Constitutional Engineering in a Divided Society* (Los Angeles: University of California Press, 1991). Andrew Reynolds, *The Architecture of Democracy: Constitutional Design, Conflict Management, and Democracy* (London: Oxford University Press, 2002). Arend Lijphart, "Constitutional Design for Divided Societies," *Journal of Democracy* 15, no. 2 (2004): 96–109. Jennifer Widner, "Constitution Writing and Conflict Resolution," *The Round Table* 94, no. 381 (2005): 503–518.

THE COSTS OF CONSTITUTIONAL LAW 5

Debates about legal policies for religion therefore take the form of debates over *how* (rather than *whether*) to design or interpret constitutions.[15] Experts treat constitutional law as a form of "higher lawmaking" that supervenes over and structures all other state institutions. Accordingly, they treat constitutional provisions for religion as higher-order rules, which ought to trickle down to all aspects of governance. One can observe this emphasis on the constitutional management of religion not only in countries with long-standing, stable constitutional regimes, such as the United States, but also in debates over the world's newest constitutions, such as those of Tunisia, Egypt, Iraq, Afghanistan, Sudan and Nepal.[16]

The Costs of Constitutional Law

It is understandable why so many people trust in constitutional law's ability to reduce conflicts among (and within) religious communities and to address disputes about the proper relationship between religious and civil authorities. (In this book, I refer to all of these types of conflicts

---

[15] Haider Hamoudi, *Negotiating in Civil Conflict: Constitutional Construction and Imperfect Bargaining in Iraq* (Chicago: University of Chicago Press, 2013), 7. In a December 2013 speech to the United Nations General Assembly, the Special Rapporteur on Freedom of Religion or Belief, Heiner Bielefeldt, expressed this sentiment with striking directness: "[a]n open constitutional framework that allows free manifestations of existing or emerging religious pluralism on the basis of equal respect for all is a *sine qua non* of any policy directed towards eliminating collective religious hatred by building trust through public institutions" United Nations General Assembly, *Report of the Special Rapporteur on Freedom of Religion or Belief, Heiner Bielefeldt to the General Assembly of the UN*, 2013, www.iirf.eu/index.php?id=178&no_cache=1&tx_ttnews%5BbackPid%5D= 176&tx_ ttnews%5Btt_news%5D=1686 (accessed August 15, 2015), 11.

[16] Malika Zeghal, "The Implicit Shariah," in *Varieties of Religious Establishment*, ed. Winnifred Fallers Sullivan and Lori G Beaman (London: Ashgate, 2013). Ahmet T Kuru, *Muslim Politics Without an "Islamic" State: Can Turkey's Justice and Development Party Be a Model for Arab Islamists? (Policy Briefing)* (Washington, D.C.: Brookings Institution, February, 2013). B R Rubin, "Crafting a Constitution for Afghanistan," *Journal of Democracy* 15, no. 3 (2004): 5–19. Noah Feldman and Roman Martinez, "Constitutional Politics and Text in the New Iraq: An Experiment in Islamic Democracy," *Fordham Law Review* 75, no. 2 (2006): 883–920. J Alexander Thier, "The Making of a Constitution in Afghanistan," *New York Law School Law Review* 51 (2006): 557–579. Noah Salomon, "The Ruse of Law: Legal Equality and the Problem of Citizenship in Multi-Religious Sudan," in *After Secular Law*, ed. Winnifred Fallers Sullivan, Robert A Yelle, and Mateo Taussig-Rubbo (Palo Alto, CA: Stanford University Press, 2011). Mara Malagodi, "The End of a National Monarchy: Nepal's Recent Constitutional Transition From Hindu Kingdom to Secular Federal Republic," *Studies in Ethnicity and Nationalism* 11, no. 2 (2011): 234–251.

6   INTRODUCTION

as *conflicts over religion*.) Constitutions are, after all, documents that elaborate the guidelines according to which states agree to manage disputes. They are also documents that announce the principles of solidarity that are meant to join citizens together.[17] Governments often create constitutions after experiences of conflict (e.g., civil wars or revolutions) in an effort to assert a vision of national unity and to establish the institutional conditions for lasting peace. Moreover, even when constitutional practice fails to reduce the intensity of conflicts over religion, observers and activists frequently blame political, social and environmental factors outside of the constitutional system (e.g., political chauvinism or radical religious ideologies), or insist that the constitutional system was not designed or implemented properly in the first place.[18]

Yet this association of constitutional law with the reduction of conflicts over religion belies the fact that constitutional practice often coincides with the escalation, rather than the cessation, of these conflicts. This is true even in the world's most celebrated constitutional democracies. Though often held out as an epitome of democratic lawmaking, the U.S. Constitution's First Amendment and its judicial interpreters helped legitimate anti-Catholic discrimination in the United States for much of the nineteenth and twentieth centuries.[19] Similarly, in India, another country with a respected constitutional tradition, appeals to constitutional religious rights and secularism have permitted Hindu nationalists to justify complex forms of anti-Muslim politics.[20] In both cases, litigants, lawyers and judges acted as constitutional theorists would expect: they used the language, procedures and spaces of democratically designed constitutional law to advance and

---

[17] Sujit Choudhry, "Bridging Comparative Politics and Comparative Constitutional Law: Constitutional Design in Divided Societies," in *Constitutional Design for Divided Societies*, 3–40, 6.

[18] One can see vivid examples of both in discussions of Iraq's constitution. E.g., Hamoudi, *Negotiating in Civil Conflict*. Noah Feldman, "Review of Hamoudi, *Negotiating in Civil Conflict*," *International Journal of Middle East Studies* 47, no. 1 (2015): 177–178.

[19] Philip Hamburger, *Separation of Church and State* (Cambridge, MA: Harvard University Press, 2002). Sarah Barringer Gordon, "'Free' Religion and 'Captive' Schools: Protestants, Catholics, and Education, 1945–1965," *DePaul Law Review* 56 (2006): 1177–1220.

[20] Brenda Cossman and Ratna Kapur, "Secularism: Bench-Marked by Hindu Right," *Economic and Political Weekly* 31, no. 38 (1996): 2613–2617, 2619–2627, 2629–2630. Ronojoy Sen, *Articles of Faith: Religion, Secularism, and the Indian Supreme Court* (New Delhi: Oxford University Press, 2010).

arbitrate competing claims about religion. Nevertheless, in both cases, using constitutional law aggravated the very dynamics of exclusion and acrimony that most American and Indian constitution drafters had hoped to allay or avoid.

This book argues that, although unintended, the potential to deepen disputes over religion is not an aberration of constitutional law; it is one of constitutional law's intrinsic capacities. With respect to religion, the practice of constitutional law may strengthen the very lines of tension it purports to moderate. It can aggravate conflicts among those with differing religious commitments and opposing ideas about the proper relationship between religious and civil authority.

Understanding this conflict-intensifying capacity of constitutional law is important for scholars, activists and legal professionals. This is not because a better understanding of constitutional law might somehow help lawmakers craft the perfect constitution: these potentials for conflict are endemic to, and therefore not eradicable from, constitutional practice. Rather, understanding these capacities is important because it may help experts understand more clearly the potential costs of deploying constitutional law in the attempt to mitigate conflicts over religion. Investigating constitutional law's divisive capacities allows one to identify the limitations of constitutional solutions for existing (or anticipated) conflicts over religion, and to think holistically about whether to invest political, financial and other resources in creating and enforcing constitutional policies. It helps analysts to consider more critically the choice to promote constitutional law (rather than, e.g., civil society activities, bureaucratic institutions or grassroots initiatives) as a way of encouraging coexistence among diverse populations. It shines a light on the fact that, while constitutional law may be helpful for some goals of governance, it may be unhelpful for others.

The Case of Sri Lanka

Sri Lanka offers a particularly compelling case for understanding constitutional law's capacities to amplify conflicts over religion. A large portion of the world's constitutional systems operate in the former colonies of the global South, which often face social, economic and political challenges not unlike those faced by Sri Lanka. Nevertheless, with the notable exceptions of India and South Africa, these countries remain enormously underrepresented in the literature on comparative constitutional law – a literature that draws its theories and normative models disproportionately

8   INTRODUCTION

from a limited set of cases of mostly wealthy, mostly English-speaking, and mostly European (or European-settler) countries.[21]

To better understand constitutional law as a global practice, it helps to craft theory from places like Sri Lanka.[22] As in many parts of the global South, the history of constitutional law in Sri Lanka has been enmeshed with attempts to establish self-rule, design postcolonial economies, manage nationalism, and deal with political patronage and corruption. Moreover, like other former colonies, constitutional agents in Sri Lanka have addressed conflicts over religion in a context framed by the legacies of European control and Christian missionizing and by the ideological and institutional imprints of foreign laws.[23]

Sri Lanka's religious demography is also instructive. The constitutional management of religion has particular salience in countries like Sri Lanka, where religion, language and ethnicity intersect and show strong majority and minority contours.[24] Most Sri Lankans (70%) identify as Buddhists. Nevertheless, large proportions of Sri Lankans also identify as Hindus (12.7%), Muslims (9.7%) and Christians (7.6%).[25] These religious

---

[21] In his 2014 assessment of the state of comparative constitutional law, Ran Hirschl quotes several recent studies to indicate just how acute this selection bias is. According to one quote, from Rosalind Dixon and Tom Ginsburg, "90% of comparative work in the English language covers the same ten countries." Another assessment, by Sujit Choudhry, claims that for the last 20 years comparative constitutional law has been "oriented around a standard and relatively limited set of cases: South Africa, Israel, Germany, Canada, the United Kingdom, New Zealand, the United States and, to a lesser extent, India." As quoted in Ran Hirschl, *Comparative Matters: The Renaissance of Comparative Constitutional Law* (New York: Oxford University Press, 2014), 213–215.

[22] In making this claim, I echo the broader arguments made by Comaroff and Comaroff about the value of the theorizing from the South. Jean Comaroff and John L Comaroff, *Theory From the South: Or, How Euro-America Is Evolving Toward Africa* (Boulder, CO: Paradigm Publishers, 2012).

[23] Bernard S Cohn, *Colonialism and Its Forms of Knowledge: The British in India* (Princeton, NJ: Princeton University Press, 1996). Mahmood Mamdani, *Citizen and Subject: Contemporary Africa and the Legacy of Late Colonialism* (Princeton, NJ: Princeton University Press, 1996). M R Anderson, "Islamic Law and the Colonial Encounter in British India," in *Institutions and Ideologies: A SOAS South Asia Reader*, ed., David Arnold and Peter Robb (London: Curzon Press Ltd., 1993): 165–185.

[24] The following statistical estimates are based on the 2012 Census, Table 2.10 and Table 2.13, "Population by Ethnic Group and Census Year" and "Population by Religion and Census Year" respectively. Available at www.statistics.gov.lk/Abstract2015/CHAP2/2.10.pdf, and www.statistics.gov.lk/Abstract2015/CHAP2/2.13.pdf (Accessed February 16, 2016).

[25] Roughly 81% of Christians report to be Roman Catholic, leaving the estimated population of "Other Christians" (which includes Protestant sects and other newer Christian groups [see Chapter 7]) at approximately 1.5% of the total national population.

THE CASE OF SRI LANKA 9

affiliations overlap with ethnic and linguistic identities. Most Buddhists identify as ethnically Sinhalese (75% of total population) and Sinhalese-speaking. Most Hindus identify as ethnically Tamil (15% of the population) and Tamil-speaking.[26] Most Muslims identify their ethnicity as "Moor" or "Malay" (9.3% and 0.2% of the population respectively) and speak Tamil, Sinhala or both. Christianity alone crosscuts ethnic and linguistic backgrounds. In this way, the demography of Sri Lanka appears similar to that of other countries like India, Malaysia, Israel, Indonesia and Ireland.[27]

The case of Sri Lanka also recommends itself because of its long history of using constitutional law as a tool for managing the island's diverse population and the conflicts over religion that arise. Sri Lankans have convened constitution-drafting committees in each of the last eight decades. Sri Lanka's current constitutional policies for religion emerged from a popularly elected constituent assembly and were designed with reference to international law. These policies have been invoked in a legal culture in which public law remedies and protocols of judicial review are widely accessible[28] and have been interpreted by a Supreme Court that

[26] The census separates ethnic Tamils into two categories: "Up-Country" or "Indian" Tamils (4%), which refers to those who claim descent from plantation laborers who came from India, and "Ceylonese" or "Sri Lankan" Tamils (11%), which refers to those who claim descent from the island's long history of Tamil inhabitants. The ethnic designation Moor usually applies to the descendants of Muslim traders from the Arabian Peninsula. Other important categories of ethnicity on the census include Burghers (descendants of the Dutch) and Veddas (indigenous Sri Lankans). On these categories see: A J Wilson, "The Colombo Man, the Jaffna Man, and the Batticaloa Man," in *The Sri Lankan Tamils: Ethnicity and Identity*, ed. Chelvadurai Manogaran and Bryan Pfaffenberger (Boulder, CO: Westview Press, 1994). Qadri Ismail, "Unmooring Identity: The Antinomies of Muslim Elite Self-Formation in Sri Lanka," in *Unmaking the Nation: The Politics of Identity and History in Modern Sri Lanka*, ed. Pradeep Jeganathan (Colombo: Social Scientists Association, 1995). Dennis B McGilvray, "Dutch Burghers and Portuguese Mechanics: Eurasian Ethnicity in Sri Lanka," *Comparative Studies in Society and History* 24, no. 2 (1982): 235–263. Gananath Obeyesekere, "Representations of the Wildman in Sri Lanka," in *Beyond Primitivism: Indigenous Religious Traditions and Modernity*, ed. Jacob K Olupona (New York: Routledge, 2004).
[27] Scholars of comparative nationalism have tended to group Sri Lanka alongside other "ethnocracies," countries in which one ethnic group dominates the institutions of state power. The grouping above is meant to encompass these countries while also suggesting a broader collection of comparative cases in which religious identity and ethnic identity do not correlate as closely. That is, I believe that the relevance of the analysis to follow pertains not only to ethnocracies but also to many other democracies. See, e.g.: Sammy Smooha, "The Model of Ethnic Democracy: Israel As a Jewish and Democratic State," *Nations and Nationalism* 8, no. 4 (2002): 475–503.
[28] I refer here to pre-enactment (abstract) judicial review. For further descriptions, see Chapters 4 and 7.

10   INTRODUCTION

(despite its acknowledged faults and its descent into disrepute during the years surrounding the end of Sri Lanka's civil war in 2009) has been seen as relatively independent in its rulings on fundamental rights.[29] (In 2014, the World Justice Project ranked Sri Lanka as first among all South Asian countries in its Rule of Law Index.)[30]

This book documents the history of using constitutional law to address conflicts over religion in Sri Lanka by investigating the development and effects of the island's most consequential constitutional policy regarding religion. This policy is contained in the second chapter of the constitution, entitled "Buddhism":

> The Republic of Sri Lanka shall give to Buddhism the foremost place and accordingly it shall be the duty of the State to protect and foster the Buddha *Sasana*, while assuring to all religions the rights granted by Articles 10 and 14(1)(e).

Like nearly half of the world's basic laws, the Buddhism Chapter of Sri Lanka's constitution gives to the majority religion a privileged status ("the foremost place") while also guaranteeing general religious rights for all citizens, in the form of "Fundamental Rights" contained in Chapter III of the constitution:[31] the rights of individuals to "freedom of thought, conscience and religion, including the freedom to have or to adopt a religion or belief of his choice" (Article 10) and the rights

---

[29] While not seen as exercising independent judgment in all issues, when it comes to decisions involving individual fundamental rights, Sri Lanka's courts, particularly its Supreme Court, have been seen as relatively neutral arbiters. Deepika Udagama, "The Sri Lankan Legal Complex and the Liberal Project: Only Thus Far and No More," in *Fates of Political Liberalism in the British Post-colony: The Politics of the Legal Complex*, ed. Terence C Halliday, Lucien Karpik, and Malcolm M Feeley (New York: Cambridge, 2012). Viveka S De Silva, *An Assessment of the Contribution of the Judiciary Towards Good Governance* (Colombo: Sri Lanka Foundation and Friedrich Ebert Stiftung, 2005), 96.

[30] Sri Lanka, WJP Rule of Law Index, 2014, http://data.worldjusticeproject.org/#/index/LKA (accessed August 19, 2014). There are, of course, many problems with this index. However, I use it here as a rough indication of certain expert perceptions of Sri Lanka's legal system.

[31] According to a 2009 Pew Forum report 45% of the world's basic laws and constitutions "recognize a favored religion or religions," and, of those, most also "specially provide for 'freedom of religion' or include language used in Article 18 of the United Nations Universal Declaration of Human Rights." Pew Forum on Religion and Public Life, "Global Restrictions on Religion," 2009. http://pewforum.org/docs/?DocID=491 (accessed June 14, 2011), 60. By another measure, approximately 40% of the world's constitutions combine special protections for a particular religion with general religious rights. Email communication with Dr. Jonathan Fox, January 2011; the measurement is based on his RAS (Religion and State) Dataset.

of citizens to "manifest" religion in "worship, observance, practice or teaching" in a group or alone, in public or in private (Article 14(1)(e)).[32]

Those who drafted the Buddhism Chapter believed they were carefully representing and balancing the demands of large populations within Sri Lanka's electorate (see Chapter 4). In particular, they were committed to using deliberately ambivalent rhetoric to create a two-part bargain over religion: on the one hand, mediating between those who wanted to entrench special prerogatives for Buddhists and those who wanted to ensure equal religious rights for all; and, on the other hand, mediating between those who wanted greater state authority over Buddhism and those who did not. For this reason, the Buddhism Chapter can be seen as a constitutional success story, an "incompletely theorized agreement" designed to serve as the basis for shared political life, reached by people with conflicting interests in an atmosphere marked by political, ethnic and religious divisions.[33]

Pyrrhic Constitutionalism

Constitutional law did not create Sri Lanka's conflicts over religion.[34] (As I discuss in subsequent chapters, these conflicts have complex roots that intertwine closely with politics, economics, geography, history, and the island's 30-year civil war.) But constitutional law has not played a neutral or ameliorative role either. This book argues that constitutional practice – the acts of drafting, debating, implementing and invoking constitutional law – has rendered existing conflicts over religion in Sri Lanka more intractable and acrimonious. It insists that, in turning to constitutional law to manage religious life, Sri Lankans have hardened religious divisions, perpetuated disputes and, in some cases, amplified the perceived religious dimensions of social conflicts. At its core, this book explains why, when it comes to matters of religion, constitutional law has damaged, rather than promoted, harmony in Sri Lanka.

---

[32] Although not mentioned explicitly in the Buddhism Chapter, Article 12(2) protects citizens from discrimination on the basis of language, race, caste or religion.

[33] On the idea of "incompletely theorized agreements" see: Cass R Sunstein, "Incompletely Theorized Agreements," *Harvard Law Review* 108, no. 7 (1995): 1733–1772.

[34] For good summaries of these conflicts in recent years, and their increase, see the following reports: Gehan Gunatilleke, *The Chronic and the Acute: Post-war Religious Violence in Sri Lanka* (Colombo: International Centre for Ethnic Studies and Equitas, 2015). Centre for Policy Alternatives, *Attacks on Places of Religious Worship in Post-War Sri Lanka* (Colombo, CPA Publications, 2013).

12   INTRODUCTION

The persistence of conflicts over religion in Sri Lanka should not be attributed to the systematic failure of constitutional law as a legal project – an absence of viable constitutional institutions, a lack of sagacity or goodwill among drafters or judges, or an unwillingness to implement or enforce constitutional law. Rather, I argue that the endurance and depth of conflicts over religion are, counterintuitively, the partial consequence of creating and relying on constitutional law in the first place. Law-makers' achievement in creating a constitutional bargain over religion and judges' willingness to hear legal claims about religion have come at the cost of deepening social disharmony. Functioning constitutionalism has unwittingly aggravated the very grievances and tensions it was designed to mediate. This is not an example of failed constitutionalism; it is an example of what I call *pyrrhic constitutionalism*.[35]

Pyrrhic constitutionalism describes a discordant relationship between the goals and the effects of constitutional law. It occurs when the serious practice of constitutional law undermines the perceived purposes of that law, and where the effects of implementing constitutional policies under-cuts the stated aims of those policies or the aims of the lawmakers who designed them. By effects, I refer not only to constitutional law's formal legal effects – the consequences that follow from its interpretations by judges or its use in justifying administrative orders – but to the total ways in which constitutional institutions, discourse and procedures influence social life.

On the one hand, pyrrhic constitutionalism derives from the competing incentives and goals that define the processes of designing and implementing constitutional law respectively. As we will see in Chapter 4, constitution drafters use vague language to avoid disagreements over contentious issues and to ensure that a final text can be produced, even when there is an absence of consensus.[36] In the magical moment of

---

[35] I use the term constitutionalism in a narrow sense to refer to the practices of drafting and adjudicating constitutional law, rather than in the broader sense (which scholars some-times have in mind) of government limited by law. In most parts of the book, when not directly theorizing about pyrrhic constitutionalism, I use the phrase "constitutional practice" (previously defined in the main text) to avoid any confusion between the subject of this book – historical practices of arguing about, creating and invoking constitutional texts – and the understanding of constitutionalism as limited government.

[36] Hanna Lerner, "Permissive Constitutions, Democracy, and Religious Freedom in India, Indonesia, Israel, and Turkey," *World Politics* 65, no. 4 (2013): 609–655. Hanna Lerner, *Making Constitutions in Deeply Divided Societies* (New York: Cambridge University Press, 2011). Michael Foley, *The Silence of Constitutions: Gaps, "abeyances," and Political Temperament in the Maintenance of Government* (New York: Routledge, 1991).

constitutional ratification, however, these same ambiguous turns of phrase come to be treated as authoritative categories for managing contentious disputes.[37] Post-enactment, words that were once expressions of political impasse reappear suddenly as weighty principles, guidelines for ordering or harmonizing society in courtrooms, parliaments and public squares. This constitutional magic does not transcend the underlying disputes. Instead, it suspends those disputes in law, like solids in a liquid, making them ready for legal activation at any moment.

On the other hand, pyrrhic constitutionalism stems from the power of constitutional discourse to shape the ways in which citizens express, conceive and deal with their differing claims about religion.[38] Law, as the legal theorist Benjamin Berger argues, is not a neutral and benign curatorial tool, impartial to and aloof from the social relations it addresses. Legal discourse has its own epistemology, interpretive horizons, symbols, practices, commitments, categories and frames of experience.[39] In Sri Lanka, as in most parts of the world, the constitutional management of religion draws heavily upon the language of rights, freedoms and protections – a language that represents complicated

---

[37] It is not coincidental that moments of constitutional ratification are accompanied by elaborate and (one could say) quasi-religious ceremonies, the purposes of which are to enable this epistemic transformation from texts of political settlement to "sacred" national charters. Legal theorist Paul W Kahn describes a similar process of sacred transformation in the confirmation of a new Supreme Court justice in the United States: "Confirmation is literally a ritual of transformation – a rite of passage – whereby an individual who had been a political being becomes an instrumentality of the rule of law. Nothing is allowed to survive that breaks from one world into the other. The appointee will be born again, stripped of her old party attachments, institutional affiliations, contacts, and even friendships. Elected officials bring their political advisors with them; a Justice is not even supposed to accept a phone call from the very people who helped her obtain office. Once she enters the Temple of Justice, she is literally on her own – with the exception of a few law clerks, who are themselves characterized by their political innocence – standing before that *mysterium tremendum* of our civic order: the Constitution." Paul W Kahn, "Comparative Constitutionalism in a New Key," *Michigan Law Review* 101 (2003): 2677–2705, 2687. On ritual practices in legal culture generally, see: Peter A Winn, "Legal Ritual," *Law and Critique* 2, no. 2 (1991): 207–232.

[38] I take the idea of the "culture of law" from: Benjamin L Berger, "The Cultural Limits of Legal Tolerance," *Canadian Journal of Law and Jurisprudence* 21, no. 2 (2008): 245–277; and Paul W Kahn, *The Cultural Study of Law: Reconstructing Legal Scholarship* (Chicago: University of Chicago Press, 2000).

[39] Benjamin L Berger, *Law's Religion: Religious Difference and the Claims of Constitutionalism* (Toronto: University of Toronto, 2016).

context-based social facts in more rigid terms.[40] When recoded through the culture and lexicon of constitutional law and legal rights, real-world disputes among persons with complex motivations frequently take on the flavor of a clear-cut contest between rights and wrongs. A reductive economy of language also prevails: those who rely on the language of constitutional law tend to discard over time other idioms of difference (often with more flexible notions of religious identity) for a strict grammar of discrete rights and fixed communities (see Chapter 7). The rigidity of constitutional language gains a further combative quality in the standard protocols of litigation seen in most contemporary legal systems, which place court-goers in an agonistic battle between would-be winners and losers, plaintiffs and defendants, petitioners and respondents – or, as the opening anecdote dramatized, sitters and standers.

The effects of this reductive linguistic economy emerge not only in courtrooms, but also in the spread of constitutional discourse outside legal institutions. Law's role as a technical tool of governance should not be considered apart from the broader social worlds it acts upon. In addition to the *legal* life of law, one must also interrogate the *societal* life of law – the influence of legal language and imaginaries on teachers, politicians, religious leaders, civil servants, shopkeepers and others. The language of constitutional law spreads into everyday discourse through a variety of conduits: newspapers, political speeches, novels, television dramas, radio and so on. In so doing, the very constitutional terms that harden disagreements in the legal sphere come to do the same in the societal sphere. This is certainly true in Sri Lanka, where the conduits for disseminating constitutional law include the coverage of court cases by Sri Lanka's television and print news, the constitution-related activism of political groups, and periodic high-profile government campaigns to rewrite or revise the island's constitution. In recent years, this diffusion of constitutional discourse has also flourished on account of a growing culture of religion-related legal activism and the regularity of Supreme Court cases in which litigants cite as a key rationale for legal action the protection of Buddhism's "foremost place" (see Chapter 5).[41]

---

[40] Mary Ann Glendon, *Rights Talk: The Impoverishment of Political Discourse* (New York: Simon and Schuster, 1993).

[41] It is important to note that, throughout this book, when discussing the activities of litigants, I am discussing complex agents. Litigants are, at once, the agents and products of legal action. They are citizens represented by, and mediated through, the language and arguments of lawyers. I use the term advisedly in this respect.

While pyrrhic constitutionalism may occur with reference to a variety of issues, religion is particularly susceptible to its effects. Virtually all constitutions mention religion, and most give an elevated legal status to protections for religion (and/or a particular religion) by assigning to it special protocols of entrenchment and justiciability. Equally important is the unique polysemy of religion as a legal category. Unlike other polysemous legal rubrics (such as equality or freedom), constitutional actors invoke religion not only as an abstract entity, a general term of classification, but as a concrete thing in the world, a tangible object of state action. Litigants, drafters, judges, lobbyists and others use the category of religion – or particular religions such as Buddhism – to denote a range of objects: institutions, texts, beliefs, property, individuals, groups, customs, rituals, economic activities, charities and numerous other things (see Chapter 6).[42] Religion's particular form of polysemy – its manifold abstract *and* concrete meanings – generates both conflict and concord among constitutional agents. On the one hand, clashing views about who or what should be protected under the category of religion exacerbate disputes over how to design and enforce constitutional policies for religion. On the other hand, the same categorical flexibility that makes religion an object of interpretive clashes also permits constitution drafters and judges to sidestep those clashes by referring to religion without defining it (or by defining it in broad and ambiguous ways). Religion is prone to pyrrhic constitutionalism because of this distinctive combination of legal weightiness and semantic lightness: virtually all constitutions give special status to the category of religion, yet the agents of constitutional law use this important category in diverging ways to serve differing purposes.[43]

Where they appear in this book, "religion" and "Buddhism" suggest two referents: they refer, in one way, to a shifting and unstable assemblage of material and discursive items in the world (doctrines, institutions,

---

[42] The same polysemy often accompanies vernacular terms for "religion" insofar as these terms – such as *āgama* in Sinhala, or *matam* in Tamil, or *shukyo* in Japanese or *zongjiao* in Chinese – are, in many cases, neologisms and back-translations of "religion" from English or other European languages. See, e.g., Jason A Josephson, *The Invention of Religion in Japan* (Chicago: University of Chicago Press, 2012); and Rebecca Nedostup, *Superstitious Regimes: Religion and the Politics of Chinese Modernity* (Cambridge, MA: Harvard University Press, 2009).

[43] One might even say that the unique polysemy of religion as a constitutional rubric serves, simultaneously, as a *source of* and *solution for* the very conflicts that constitutional law is called upon to manage.

persons, and practices); and, in another way, they refer to *the act of categorizing* those items *as* religion or Buddhism. Pyrrhic constitutionalism unfolds, in part, through the collapsing together of these two referents. As states and citizens turn to constitutional law to manage religion, they narrow the divide between legal categories and the diversity of lived experience, between constitutional rubrics and the embodied ways of being which those rubrics imperfectly represent. They remake life in the image of law by encouraging citizens to treat constitutional discourse as a type of natural language,[44] and to view their circumstances through the lexicon of religious rights, religious freedoms or Buddhism's "foremost place." This process renders ordinary social grievances more inflexible and uncompromising. It obscures principles of commonality, shared interests and alternative modes of compromise or coexistence. It authorizes people to speak artificially on behalf of "Buddhism" or "Christianity," while at the same time denying or neglecting the widespread existence of subjectivities, practices, beliefs, places, institutions and socialities that blur the boundaries between religion and non-religion, Buddhism and non-Buddhism.

To some extent, the dynamics I describe pertain to many different types of modern law. Other scholars have written about the harmful consequences of "juridifying" disputes or the negative effects of "rights talk," "lawfare" and legal "adversarialism."[45] While pyrrhic constitutionalism is fortified by some of these processes, it cannot be reduced to any one of them. At the center of pyrrhic constitutionalism lie deeper conundrums that are unique to the production and application of constitutional law. In the same way that religion is a unique category of constitutional concern, so too is constitutional law a uniquely important form of law.

---

[44] As de Tocqueville would have it: "The language of the law thus becomes, in some measure, a vulgar tongue; the spirit of the law, which is produced in the schools and courts of justice, gradually penetrates their walls into the bosom of society, where it descends to the lowest classes, so that at last the whole people contract the habit and tastes of the judicial magistrate." As quoted in: Stuart A Scheingold, *The Politics of Rights: Lawyers, Public Policy, and Political Change* (Ann Arbor, MI: University of Michigan Press, 2004), 18.

[45] Scheingold, *Politics of Rights*. Glendon, *Rights Talk*. Jerold S Auerbach, *Justice Without Law? Resolving Disputes Without Lawyers* (New York: Oxford University Press, 1986). Comaroff, "Reflections on the Rise of Legal Theology." Winnifred F Sullivan, *The Impossibility of Religious Freedom* (Princeton, NJ: Princeton University Press, 2005). Benjamin Schonthal et al., "Is the Rule of Law an Antidote for Religious Tension? The Promise and Peril of Judicializing Religious Freedom," *American Behavioral Scientist* 60, no. 8 (2016): 966–986.

Constitutions are treated as the source and prototype of modern legality. As structurally positioned and imaginatively conceived, the ideal constitution reigns over all other forms of governmental power, while also representing the people over which it reigns.[46] Pyrrhic constitutionalism grows out of this dual role of constitutional law. It emerges from the tension between representation and regulation, identity and governance. The story of pyrrhic constitutionalism is, at its core, a story about the fraught nature of constitutional mediation, in both senses of the phrase: it is a story about the unintended consequences that come from using law as a vehicle for both representing and reconciling citizens' claims about religion.

Constitutional Microhistory and the Expanded Archive of Sri Lankan Law

Rethinking the work of constitutional law requires rethinking the archive used to examine it. Despite the "tremendous renaissance" of comparative constitutional law over the last two decades,[47] a great deal of comparative constitutional scholarship remains bound by a reliance on constitutional law's official archive of ratified and published constitutional drafts and public court decisions, and even more so by those that are available in English, and in electronic form.[48] Although important, relying on this official archive offers only a limited view of law's complex intermeshing with politics and society, one disproportionately marked by a kind of Hegelian master-narrative that portrays constitution drafters and judges as collaborating in a project of progressively realizing and refining constitutional principles, of working out and perfecting the rule of constitutional law over time.

Understanding pyrrhic constitutionalism requires that one question this master-narrative, and, therefore, move beyond the official archive of

---

[46] Choudhry, "Bridging Comparative Politics." Gary J Jacobsohn, *Constitutional Identity* (Cambridge, MA: Harvard University Press, 2010). Michel Rosenfeld (ed.), *Constitutionalism, Identity, Difference, and Legitimacy: Theoretical Perspectives* (Durham, NC: Duke University Press, 1994).

[47] Hirschl, *Comparative Matters*, 3.

[48] Jeffrey A Redding, "Invisible Constitutions: Culture, Religion, and Memory: Secularism, the Rule of Law, and Sharia Courts: An Ethnographic Examination of a Constitutional Controversy," *Saint Louis University Law Journal* 57 (2013): 339–376. Hirschl, *Comparative Matters*.

18   INTRODUCTION

constitutional law. For this reason, this book engages deeply with sources beyond the normal canon of ratified constitutions and published judicial decisions. This expanded archive includes a variety of unpublished and/ or not-widely-available texts relating to the design and application of constitutional law in Sri Lanka: political pamphlets, reports from governmental and non-governmental commissions, submissions made to constituent assemblies and courts, transcripts from the meetings of various constitutional bodies, judges' journals, letters written by religious groups, civil society organizations and lobbyists, and a variety of other sources. This expanded archive also includes interviews and oral histories with a variety of agents, both elite and ordinary. Adding to the diversity of sources used in this book is a diversity of languages. The story of Sri Lankan constitutional law unfolds in three languages: Sinhala, the "Official Language of Sri Lanka"; Tamil, which is, constitutionally, "also ... an official language [not capitalized]";[49] and English, the island's official "link language" and, in practice, the language that serves frequently as the medium for drafting and adjudicating law at the highest levels.[50]

This book uses this unofficial, expanded and multilingual archive to engage in an unconventional method, called constitutional microhistory. The approach is inspired by the work of a group of historians that, in recent decades, has begun to think about major historical forces through

---

[49] Articles 18(1) and (2), Government of Sri Lanka, *Constitution of the Democratic Socialist Republic of Sri Lanka* (1978). On the history of language laws in Sri Lanka see: Neil DeVotta, *Blowback: Linguistic Nationalism, Institutional Decay and Ethnic Conflict in Sri Lanka* (Palo Alto, CA: Stanford University Press, 2004).

[50] Although evidence presented in Supreme Court cases may be in any language (Sinhala being the most common), written petitions are mostly made in English; and all statutes, whether drafted in Sinhala or Tamil, are required to have English translations. When one looks at the history of managing religion in Sri Lanka, one finds that many of the primary drafts of religion provisions are produced in English, with Sinhala and Tamil translations being back-translations from the English (problematic ones, as I demonstrate in Chapter 4). Despite the preponderance of English in the state-level production and adjudication of law, debates over law take place in all of the island's recognized languages, whether in parliament, constituent assemblies, newspapers or roadside tea-and-sundry shops. Testimony to parliamentary commissions, letters to legal draftspersons, supporting evidence in court cases all occur in the vernaculars of Sinhala and Tamil more than in English. Official transcripts from constitutional committees, the 1970–1972 Constituent Assembly and parliamentary proceedings also reflect this. In most cases, speeches are transcribed in the language in which they were given, with simultaneous translations into other languages given by state-appointed translators at the time of oration. Those translations are not included in legal and political records.

the lives of ordinary persons or isolated events.[51] In an analogous manner, I think about the power of constitutional law by focusing on the life of a particular constitutional provision, the Buddhism Chapter of Sri Lanka's constitution.

This emphasis on particularity and empirical specificity shares much with other qualitative methods used in socio-legal studies and comparative constitutional law, particularly legal anthropology and constitutional ethnography.[52] Like these methods, constitutional microhistory employs interviews and archival research; it uses local languages and investigates how constitutionalism looks on the ground; it engages in the task of comparison from the inside-out, using an extended case study to reassess broader theories about the nature and functions of law.

Two aims, however, distinguish constitutional microhistory. First, constitutional microhistory considers the legal, political and societal lives of particular constitutional provisions *over time* by paying special attention to the relationship between drafting and deploying those provisions. Second, constitutional microhistory takes especially seriously the agency of actors whose voices have been occluded or elided by the official record. These actors include opposition politicians, lobbyists, unsuccessful constitution drafters, unacknowledged petitioners and submission-makers, and ordinary citizens who write to constitutional committees or make statements before constituent assemblies. Through pursuing these two aims, constitutional microhistory casts light on specific disjunctions between the public story of constitutional law (its depiction in official sources) and the unrecognized or unintended effects that constitutions have on society.

Outline of Chapters

This book proceeds in two parts. Part I – Chapters 2, 3 and 4 of the book – documents Sri Lankans' attempts from the 1940s to the early 1970s to create a constitutional settlement on religion, one which represented and reconciled the interests of political conservatives and radical reformers, secularists and nationalists, Buddhist monks and lay organizations, Sinhalese politicians and politicians representing the island's

---

[51] Sigurður G Magnússon and István Szíjártó, *What Is Microhistory?: Theory and Practice* (New York: Routledge, 2013).

[52] E.g.: Kim L Scheppele, "Constitutional Ethnography: An Introduction," *Law & Society Review* 38, no. 3 (2004): 389–406.

Muslim, Hindu and Christian communities. Chapters 2 and 3 analyze the consolidation of two broad paradigms for thinking about the legal management of religion in Sri Lanka: a *promotional paradigm* concerned with promoting rights and protections for Buddhism and a *protectionist paradigm* concerned with protecting fundamental rights for all citizens. These two chapters also show how the promotional and protectionist paradigms rose to prominence in the atmosphere of religious activism and constitutional reform that dominated Ceylonese politics in the 1940s, 1950s and 1960s.

Chapter 4 examines the process of drafting the religion policies of Sri Lanka's First Republican Constitution of 1972. It documents closely the process of designing, debating and ratifying the Buddhism Chapter, a chapter that has endured (with one very small exception) unchanged from 1972 to the present. The analysis considers the complex religious interests and politics behind the chapter and shows how its drafters relied on ambiguous rhetoric to bridge disagreements and to generate the two-part bargain described earlier.

Part II of the book – comprised of Chapters 5, 6 and 7 – examines how Sri Lanka's constitutional bargains over religion affect the ways in which citizens articulate, understand, advance, negotiate and (attempt to) resolve differing claims about religion. These chapters highlight three different ways in which the act of invoking constitutional law – both inside and outside of courtrooms – worked to perpetuate and deepen disagreement over religion. Chapter 5 analyzes approximately a dozen court cases – most of them unexamined in the academic literature – in which the Buddhism Chapter was invoked. It shows how constitutional provisions mandating that the state protect and foster Buddhism were recruited into a wide variety of legal matters. It argues that, rather than addressing concerns about the welfare of Buddhism, constitutional mandates to "protect and foster" Buddhism have projected threats to Buddhism into diverse domains of social and political life.

Building upon this insight – that constitutional protections for religion might amplify and validate perceived threats to religion – Chapter 6 documents how, by privileging a specific religion, constitutional law actually damages the well-being of those who claim affiliation to that religion. It makes this point by looking closely at an important legal case concerning whether or not Buddhist monks should be permitted to hold driving licenses. This chapter shows how, in this and other cases, the invocation of special constitutional prerogatives for Buddhism actually deepened conflicts among various Buddhist parties, while, at the same time, drawing the state unwittingly into tangled ecclesiastical disputes over who has the authority to speak for Buddhism.

Chapter 7 argues that even when appeals are made to fundamental rights (rather than Buddhist prerogatives), the protocols and terms of constitutional litigation tend to further polarize already-fractious conflicts. Here I examine the mechanics of constitutional litigation as applied to the highly contentious issue of religious conversion. Between 2000 and 2004, Sri Lankans found themselves divided over whether the state should place limits on religious conversion. Initially the conflict developed in somewhat general terms, as a debate over the ethics of religious proselytizing. However, when the issue went to court, debates eventually took the form of a clash between Buddhists and non-Buddhists. This chapter argues that, in relying on constitutional law to settle disputes about conversion, Sri Lankans distilled a complex and multidimensional set of issues and questions into a series of sharp, binary contests.

These chapters give historical flesh to the bones of the argument advanced earlier, namely that the process of managing religion through constitutional law in contemporary Sri Lanka has rendered conflicts over religion more rigid, uncompromising and agonistic while, in some cases, also thrusting religion into a variety of other disputes. They illuminate how pyrrhic constitutionalism works by highlighting a critical disharmony between the projects of making and implementing constitutional policies for religion in Sri Lanka. In the first movement of constitutional law – drafting law – political elites colluded in the submerging of disagreement in ambiguous legal rhetoric. In the second movement – interpreting law – religious interest groups used that ambiguous language to justify and deepen disagreement. The same frictions that provoked the need for vague constitutional rhetoric in the first instance reemerge in constitutional litigation, in a more severe form. When one looks over time at the constitutional management of religion, one sees not a Hegelian story but a Freudian one: a constitutional return of the repressed.

This book does not argue that constitutions, as a whole, are a bad thing. As someone who has followed Sri Lanka for many years, I am acutely aware of the importance of constitutional practice as a bulwark against the most egregious instances of political violence and injustice, including torture, detention, land alienation, corruption and other crimes. I do not reject the promises of constitutional law altogether, as though I were replacing one total map of constitutional life with another one, in which everything was turned upside-down. This book aims, instead, to add greater sophistication to our existing understandings of the ways in which constitutions manage religion by calling attention to the unexpected and unfortunate things that constitutional law might be doing, often unwittingly, even as it changes our lives in so many other ways.

PART I

The Past Lives of the Buddhism Chapter

Among scholars of microhistory, one finds two strands of thinking, which lead in opposite directions. One strand moves from the general to the particular. Scholars of microhistory tend to focus their inquiries on specific persons or events rather than on grand historical processes. The defining feature of microhistory, for many of its proponents, is its enthusiastic embrace of the idiosyncratic and the quotidian.[1] A second strand of microhistorical thinking moves the other way, from the specific to the general. Although focusing on small specimens, scholars of microhistory consider how those specimens reflect and engage with broader historical forces.[2]

Constitutional microhistory also engages in this bidirectional thinking; the play between particularity and generality can be seen especially in Part I of this book. Pursuing the first strand of microhistorical thinking, Part I stresses the importance of looking closely at what many would consider to be minor details in law's expanded archive: diverse understandings of religion implicit in the writings and speeches of politicians; strategies of legal borrowing evident in unpublished constitutional submissions; implied definitions of democracy visible in the pamphlets of Buddhist lay organizations; and many other things. Pursuing the second strand of microhistorical thinking, Part I uses these details to illuminate two larger trends. First, it offers an explanation for *why* Sri Lanka came to adopt its particular constitutional arrangements for managing religion along with an exploration of *how* those arrangements reflected and intersected with forces beyond Sri Lanka – colonialism in Asia and Africa, human rights movements in Europe, nationalism in India and trends in British legal theory. Second, Part I paints a picture of

---

[1] Carlo Ginzburg, *The Cheese and the Worms: The Cosmos of a Sixteenth-Century Miller* (Baltimore, MD: Johns Hopkins University Press, 1980).

[2] G Levi, "On Microhistory," in *New Perspectives on Historical Writing*, ed. Peter Burke (Cambridge: Polity Press, 1991), 98.

the seriousness and intensity with which Sri Lankans engaged in constitutional reform from the 1940s to 1972.

Microhistory looks closely at the lives of specific individuals. Constitutional microhistory does too. The life that stands at the center of this book is that of the Buddhism Chapter of Sri Lanka's current constitution. The Buddhism Chapter's *official* life begins in the 1970s, when it first appeared in the island's law books. However, Part I of this book gives to microhistory a Buddhist twist: the chapters that follow proceed from the premise that, like Buddhists, constitutional provisions have past lives. The stories of constitutional policies begin well before they are embodied in official, ratified legal charters. In their past lives, constitutional policies appear in the forms of demands made by lobby groups, promises contained in political manifestos, slogans advanced by reform movements, and the borrowed language of foreign laws. Part I explores the past lives of the Buddhism Chapter. It contends that, to understand the form, function and consequences of Sri Lanka's constitutional policies towards religion, one must begin not in the present but in the past.

2

Managing Religion at the End of Empire

The story of pyrrhic constitutionalism in Sri Lanka begins in the 1940s, in the twilight years of British colonial control. The core demands about religion that find expression in the Buddhism Chapter – demands to give Buddhism a special place and to ensure fundamental rights – took shape initially as reactions to the 1948 Constitution, under which Ceylon was granted self-rule.[1]

This fact is not obvious if one simply compares the official versions of the 1948 Constitution with official versions of the island's First and Second Republican Constitutions of 1972 and 1978. When it comes to religion, the Republican Constitutions retain virtually nothing from their 1948 predecessor. The influence of historical forces is also invisible when one looks solely at the final version of the 1948 Constitution. Like other texts in the official archive of constitutional law, the final version of the 1948 Constitution bears the marks of only a few powerful agents, and largely effaces the voices of others. When one looks beyond the official archive, however, another story appears.

Looking at the expanded archive of constitutional law, one sees clearly the intensity of contests over the 1948 Constitution as well as the importance of three paradigms for managing religion that rose to prominence during this time. One paradigm, supported by a small cohort of Ceylon's political leaders and legal experts, aimed to *prevent* partisan religious sentiments from influencing politics by prohibiting legislators from passing religiously discriminatory laws. A second paradigm, supported by a cohort of young, nationalistic politicians within the ruling political alliance, sought to *protect* the religious rights of individuals by creating a

---

[1] This book uses the official conventions of the times in naming the island. From 1948 to 1972, the island was officially known as Ceylon; therefore Chapters 2 and 3 of this book refer to the country as Ceylon. The 1972 Constitution officially changed the island's name to Sri Lanka, literally the resplendent (island of) Lanka. I refer to the country as Sri Lanka starting in Chapter 4 of this book.

constitution that made religious freedom a positive, fundamental right. A third paradigm, advocated by Buddhist groups on the island, hoped to *promote* Buddhism, over and above the island's other religious traditions.

In advancing these paradigms – which I refer to respectively as the *preventative, protectionist* and *promotional* paradigm – would-be constitution-makers mixed narrow questions of government policy with broader questions about law, religion and politics: Should the island's new charter borrow from the legal traditions of Ireland, India or Burma? Should it render religious freedom a positive or a negative liberty? Should it treat all religions equally? Should Ceylon enact a radical break with its colonial past or undertake a more gradual transition to self-rule? Advocates of these paradigms were also making history. Although unknown to them at the time, these paradigms would set the terms for constitutional discussions for decades to follow.

This chapter documents this story in three sections. Section I considers the history, events and key figures that contributed to the drafting of Sri Lanka's 1948 Constitution, with its *preventative* paradigm, focusing both on the 1940s and, briefly, on the longer colonial history of managing religion that preceded it. Sections II and III look, respectively, at the constitutional struggle waged against what would become the 1948 Constitution by those advocating *protectionist* and *promotional* paradigms.

SECTION I

Constitution-Making in 1940s Ceylon

Although it had revolutionary significance, the making of Ceylon's first independent constitution was not a revolutionary event. Unlike India and Burma, where violent protests accompanied the process of decolonization, Ceylon achieved self-rule through slow, incremental negotiation, on colonists' terms and timetables.[2]

---

[2] As S W R D Bandaranaike put it, "Then came freedom. But how did freedom come? ... [I]t came in the normal course [of] events ... in attempts to persuade commissions sent from England to grant this little bit or that little bit extra ... There was no fight for that freedom which involved a fight for principles, policies and programmes which could not be carried out unless that freedom was obtained. No. It just came overnight. We woke up one day were told, 'You are a Dominion now.'" Address during debate on Appropriations Bill of 1951–1952, in Solomon West Ridgeway Dias Bandaranaike, *Towards a New Era: Selected Speeches of S. W. R. D. Bandaranaike, Made in the Legislature of Ceylon 1931–1959*, 2nd ed. (Colombo: Government Information Department, 1976), 680.

In many ways, it was the British colonial government that set the agenda for constitution drafting. In May 1943, His Majesty's Government conveyed to Ceylon's politicians a letter "inviting" them to draft a constitution under which it would consider issuing a grant of self-rule. The invitation, however, came with conditions. The Crown would accept the constitution only if it included certain non-negotiable guarantees: Britain must be given continuing influence over Ceylon's trade, defense and foreign affairs;[3] three-fourths of the island's elected lawmakers must endorse the document;[4] and the final version must "satisfy" an unspecified audience of lawyers in Whitehall, British administrators in Colombo and multiple, yet-unnamed members of a parliamentary commission that would be sent to Ceylon. The letter also included a stipulation pertaining to religion: the new constitution must give the Governor, as the Crown's representative in Ceylon, the right to veto any bills which "have evoked serious opposition by any racial or religious community and in the Governor's opinion are likely to involve oppression or unfairness to any community."[5]

Colonial Legacies of Managing Religion

The 1943 letter is a final episode in a much longer story of British colonial attempts to regulate religion.[6] British rule in Ceylon lasted

---

[3] Colonial Government of Ceylon, "Reform of the Constitution," in *Ceylon Sessional Paper XVII* (Colombo: Ceylon Government Press, 1943), 3–4. Among the stipulated requirements for such a constitution are the conditions that the British would retain supervisory powers over Ceylon's foreign policy, its military bases, its shipping policies, its trade agreements and its currency.

[4] This figure was calculated to ensure that the constitution garnered some support from minority ethnic (non-Sinhalese) representatives in the legislature.

[5] Ibid., 1.

[6] From 1802 onwards, Ceylonese colonialism was controlled directly by the Colonial Office, not by the British East India Company. While religion never served as a primary rubric of social classification for British colonists in Ceylon, as it did in India, colonists regarded religion as an important subcomponent of "race" (or "community"), which they took to be the island's most basic social grouping. The number of "racial" groups identified by the British shifted over time. In the late colonial period, these groups included Sinhalese, Tamils, Muslims/Moors and Eurasians/Burghers. There were also debates as to whether "Up-country" and "Low-country" Sinhalese should be considered distinct or not. John D Rogers, "Post-Orientalism and the Interpretation of Premodern and Modern Political Identities: The Case of Sri Lanka," *The Journal of Asian Studies* 53, no. 1 (1994): 10–23. John D Rogers, "Early British Rule and Social Classification in Lanka," *Modern Asian Studies* 38, no. 3 (2004): 625–647.

28 MANAGING RELIGION AT THE END OF EMPIRE

from 1798 to 1948. In the earliest periods, British ordinances and proclamations relating to religion announced the Crown's intentions to accommodate local worship practices, within certain limits. For example, after formally assuming control over Ceylon from the Dutch in 1798, the Crown issued the "Proclamation of September 1799," declaring that it would "allow" Ceylonese inhabitants "liberty of Conscience" and "free exercise of Religious worship," provided that religion would be practiced "quietly and peaceably" and "without offense or scandal to the government," and provided that no new places of worship would be constructed without Crown permission.[7] Two years later, the "Charter of Justice," which would guide colonial courts from 1801 to 1833, enjoined judges to pay "an especial Attention to the Religion, Manners, and Usages of the native Inhabitants" and to "accommodat[e]" their "Religion, Manners, and Usages ... as the same can consist with the due Execution of the Law and the Attainment of substantial Justice."[8] Attempts at such accommodation appeared, among other places, in the diverse methods of oath-taking employed (often ineffectually) by British colonial courts during the first half of the nineteenth century: Crown courts encouraged Muslims, Hindus and Buddhists to take their oaths respectively on a Koran, holy water (symbolizing the Ganges) or *tulsi* leaves, and a set of rings symbolizing the Goddess Pattini.[9]

In 1815, British policies of accommodating local religions took on a new, more active form with respect to Buddhism. In that year, the Crown signed a convention annexing the island's last independent kingdom, the Kingdom of Kandy. Although the "Kandyan Convention" placed the territory of Kandy under British domination, it also promised the Kandyan chiefs that the British Crown would safeguard "the Religion of Boodhoo ... and its Rites, Ministers and Places of Worship."[10] Starting

---

[7] The Proclamation of the 23rd of September 1799 in W M G Colebrooke, *The Colebrooke-Cameron Papers: Documents on British Colonial Policy in Ceylon, 1796–1833*, ed. G C Mendis (London: Oxford University Press, 1956), ii, 161.

[8] Colonial Government of Ceylon, "1801 Charter of Justice," in *A Collection of the Legislative Acts of His Majesty's Government of Ceylon* (Colombo: Printed at the Government Press by N. Berbman, 1821).

[9] Vijaya Samaraweera, "An Act of Truth in a Sinhala Court of Law: On Truth, Lies and Judicial Proof Among the Sinhala Buddhists," *Cardozo Journal of International and Comparative Law* 5 (1997): 133–163. See also "1801 Charter of Justice," Section XXXIV.

[10] Article 5 Kandyan Convention of 1815 in *The Colebrooke-Cameron Papers*, i, 227–231, emphasis mine. Following a revolt, in 1818, this was superseded by the Declaration of British Sovereignty, which stated in Article 16: "As well the Priests as all the Ceremonies

in 1815, and for nearly two decades, British administrators acted as protectors of Buddhism, in a manner similar to Kandyan kings: they paid small monthly salaries to 42 senior monks and funded annual religious celebrations in the center of Kandy; they made official acts of appointment to recognize the high clerical office of senior Buddhist monks; they even arranged for British infantry to provide armed sentry outside the region's most important Buddhist temple to guard the sacred tooth relic of the Buddha contained within.[11]

By 1840, British civil servants in Ceylon and London began to face pressure from Christian lobbyists and missionaries to withdraw these special acts of sponsorship for Buddhism. For most of the following century, British governors intervened in Ceylonese religious life in inconsistent ways. When governors did authorize new ordinances or enforce new policies relating to religion, the goals appear to have been threefold: to prevent disturbances to "public order" caused by religious rituals; to prevent conflicts caused by one group "offending" the religious sensibilities of another group; and to wean the colonial state gradually from any direct responsibility for supporting or administrating religious rites, institutions or properties.[12] Governors used the Police Ordinance to list

---

and Processions of the Budhoo Religion shall receive the Respect which in former times was shewn them; at the same time it is in no wise to be understood that the protection of Government is to be denied to the Peaceable exercise by all other Persons of the Religion which they respectively profess or to the erection under due License from His Excellency of places of Worship in proper Situations." Donoughmore Commission, *Report of the Special Commission on the Ceylon Constitution* (Colombo: Ceylon Government Press, 1929), 137. See also: Lee Godden and Niranjan Casinader, "The Kandyan Convention 1815: Consolidating the British Empire in Colonial Ceylon," *Comparative Legal History* 1, no. 2 (2013): 211–242.

[11] K M De Silva, *Social Policy and Missionary Organizations in Ceylon: 1840–1855* (London: Longmans, 1965), 94–95. Guarding the sacred tooth relic also served another function: according to Kandyan political thinking, possession of the relic was a *sine qua non* of legitimate rule, something the British aspired to. Thank you to John Rogers for calling my attention to this further explanation.

[12] These were goals of legislation, but they were not always the effects. In certain cases, the creation of religion policies actually entangled the colonial state more in religious affairs. For example, when it came to colonial policies regarding the management of temple property, attempts to devolve control of property to local committees (rather than the colonial government) led to greater involvement with temple property by the colonial state. Moreover, it is important to point out that the goals mentioned above existed alongside other goals, including the maximizing of tax revenue. John D Rogers, *Crime, Justice, and Society in Colonial Sri Lanka* (London: Curzon Press, 1987). Steven Kemper, "The Buddhist Monkhood, the Law, and the State in Colonial Sri Lanka," *Comparative Studies in Society and History* 26, no. 3 (1984): 401–427.

general rules for conducting the island's many religious processions.[13] They also established a regular calendar of weekly and yearly religious holidays, on which the island's laborers would be given mandatory leave so that they could fulfil ritual obligations.[14] Over the course of the nineteenth century, British legalists drafted separate codes of personal law for Muslims, Jaffna Tamils (most of whom were Hindu) and Kandyans (most of whom were Buddhists).[15] In 1883, the British promulgated a unified Penal Code (modeled on the Indian Penal Code of 1860), which included an entire chapter enumerating "Offences Relating to Religion." These included offenses for "defiling" a place of worship, disturbing "an assembly engaged in religious worship," trespassing on a place of worship or graveyard, or "uttering any word or making any sound in the hearing, or making any gesture, or placing any object in the sight of any person, with intention to wound his religious feeling."[16] During this same period, governors transferred control of Buddhist temples and Muslim mosques from the state to appointed or elected committees of lay trustees.[17] In the case of Buddhist properties, colonial courts gradually formalized a body of case law, which came to be known as "Buddhist Ecclesiastical Law," through which judges could adjudicate competing claims among rival Buddhist monks as to who should be recognized as the legitimate chief incumbent of a temple and, therefore, the rightful possessor of its assets.[18]

---

[13] Michael Roberts, "Noise as Cultural Struggle: Tom-tom Beating, the British, and Communal Disturbances in Sri Lanka, 1880s–1930s," in *Mirrors of Violence: Communities, Riots, and Survivors in South Asia*, ed. Veena Das (Studies in Society and Culture; New Delhi: Oxford University Press, 1990).

[14] E.g.: The Police Ordinance of 1834, Section 4; The Police Ordinance of 1843 Section 31; The Public Holidays Ordinance No. 4 of 1886.

[15] When it came to Muslim personal law and Jaffna Tamil customary law (*Tesavalamai*), the British worked from codes that had been created by the Dutch. Kandyan personal law was never codified as such, but existed as a collection of case law. The most thorough and helpful source on Sri Lanka's history of legal pluralism is T Nadaraja, *The Legal System of Ceylon in Its Historical Setting* (Leiden: Brill, 1972). On Muslim Personal Law in particular see: Benjamin Schonthal, "Environments of Law: Islam, Buddhism, and the State in Contemporary Sri Lanka," *The Journal of Asian Studies* 75, no. 1 (2016): 137–156.

[16] Chapter XV, Sections 290–292. I transposed Sections 291 (offensive speech or gestures or objects) and 292 (trespass) in the order of my presentation. All offenses were subject to imprisonment for two years or fine or both. Not many cases, however, appear in Ceylon law reports. Reginald F Dias, *A Commentary on the Ceylon Criminal Procedure Code* (Ceylon: Colombo Apothecaries Publishers, 1935), 1300–1301.

[17] For example: The Buddhist Temporalities Ordinances of 1889 and of 1931; The Muslim Intestate Succession and Wakfs Ordinance of 1931; The Public Trustee Ordinance of 1930.

[18] Kemper, "The Buddhist Monkhood."

Beginning in the 1920s, and culminating in 1931, British officials changed their approach to managing religion, as part of a larger set of changes made to the logic and structure of local government. Nineteenth-century laws governing religion continued to be enforced. However, the temperament of regulation moved from one of accommodating religious practices and identities, however reluctantly, to one of preventing religious sentiments from affecting political life.

Central to these changes was a transformation in representative government. Since the nineteenth century, the British had determined Ceylonese members of an island-wide Legislative Council, which nominally advised Crown administrators, according to the "racial" communities that they represented.[19] However, in 1928, an official review of this system requested by the Secretary of State for the Colonies reported that so-called communal representation had produced a "wholly pernicious" effect on society and "an ever widening breach between communities ... [that] obscure[d] the national interests in the clash of rival races or religions."[20] On the recommendation of the special commission, in 1931, an Order-in-Council was passed to replace Ceylon's existing legislature (with its designated seats for Muslims, Burghers, Tamils and its highly restricted voting rights) with a new one based on territorial constituencies elected according to universal adult franchise.[21] Representation by numbers rather than religious or communal identity, the Commission insisted, would help "promote the assimilation of the different races in Ceylon" and "stimulate the development of a national and not a sectional outlook."[22] The legislation that affected this change also gave the Governor greater duties of surveillance over the reconstituted legislature. In particular, they empowered him to nullify "any Bill whereby persons of any particular community or religion are made liable to any disabilities or restrictions to which

---

[19] For example, in 1910, special seats were allocated for Muslims, Tamils, Low-country Sinhalese and Kandyan Sinhalese, Europeans and Burghers (Dutch descendants).

[20] Donoughmore Commission, *Report of the Special Commission on the Ceylon Constitution*, 79.

[21] Ceylon (State Council) Order-in-Council 1931, which came into force April 15, 1931. See also: David Scott, "Community, Number, and the Ethos of Democracy," in *Refashioning Futures: Criticism after Postcoloniality* (Princeton, NJ: Princeton University Press, 1999), 158–189. Nira Wickramasinghe, *Ethnic Politics in Colonial Sri Lanka* (New Delhi: Vikas, 1995).

[22] Donoughmore Commission, *Report of the Special Commission on the Ceylon Constitution*, 79.

32   MANAGING RELIGION AT THE END OF EMPIRE

persons of other communities or religions are not also subjected or made liable, or are granted advantages not extended to persons of other communities or religions."[23]

British administrators presented these policy changes as responses to what they perceived as growing racial and religious tensions in Ceylon.[24] At the same time, the policies themselves had their origins beyond the colony as part of a growing field of knowledge in Britain relating to "dominion constitutions." The 1931 Donoughmore Commission report looked at the administration of Ceylon from a comparative perspective, as similar to "various overseas countries of the Empire."[25] Describing

---

[23] Ibid., 55. For a discussion of the earlier types of restricted bills see: W Ivor Jennings and H W Tambiah, *The Dominion of Ceylon: The Development of Its Laws and Constitution* (Westport, CT: Greenwood Press, 1970), 18–24.

[24] Between 1883 and 1915, several religious processions become occasions for riots, pitting Buddhists, Catholics and Muslims against one another. For the British, these riots threatened all three governing objectives: they not only posed problems of "public order" and "offense," they also threatened to entangle the colonial administration further in religious polemics by involving colonial courts and officials in determining culpability and damages for the riots. In several cases, unsatisfactory legal outcomes gave way to coordinated lobbying efforts on the part of religious groups to pressure Crown officers in London and Colombo for greater legal protections. These included special protection for Christian rituals and churches, official recognition for Buddhist holidays and sacred sites, and special protections for Muslim mosques in Kandy and Gampola. Rogers, *Crime, Justice, and Society in Colonial Sri Lanka*, 176–202. George Bond, *The Buddhist Revival in Sri Lanka* (Columbia, SC: University of South Carolina, 1988). Vijaya Samaraweera, "Muslim Revivalist Movement, 1880-1915," in *Collective Identities, Nationalisms, and Protest in Modern Sri Lanka*, ed. Michael Roberts (Colombo: Marga Institute, 1979). Richard F Young and S Jebanesan, *The Bible Trembled: The Hindu-Christian Controversies of Nineteenth-Century Ceylon* (Vienna: Inst. für Indologie der Univ. Wien, 1995). Richard F Young and G P V Somaratna, *Vain Debates: Buddhist-Christian Controversies of Nineteenth-Century Ceylon* (Wien: Institut für Indologie der Universität Wien, 1996). Roberts, "Noise as Cultural Struggle."

[25] The Crown commissioners who recommended the 1931 reforms framed the situation in Ceylon in the following comparative terms: "One of the most difficult problems in connection with the formation or alteration of constitutions for the various overseas countries of the Empire is that of communal representation. The populations are made up of diverse elements, often with fundamental racial and religious differences. Even within with same racial or religious community caste distinctions may be responsible for rigid division of classes. These diverse elements and distinct classes, even if not antagonistic to each other, are in more or less separate compartments, this resulting in a lack of homogeneity and of corporate consciousness which make it difficult to achieve any national unity of purpose. Communal representation was devised with a view to assisting the development of democratic institutions in countries of different races and religions and in the hope of eliminating the clash of these various interests during elections. It was expected to provide, peacefully, an effective legislative assembly that would give a fair representation of the different elements in the population and would also tend to

ORIGINS OF THE PREVENTATIVE PARADIGM 33

Ceylon as "a characteristic example" of a colony that struggled to achieve "unity of purpose" in the context of multiple, competing communities,[26] the report recommended adopting other commonwealth laws to solve Ceylon's problems. It used the London County Council's system of executive committees[27] as the template for Ceylon's State Council and drew directly from the Government of Ireland Act of 1920 the wording for the Governor's supervisory powers over the legislature.[28]

Senanayake, Jennings and the Origins of the Preventative Paradigm

When, in 1943, the Crown invited Ceylon's political leaders to draft a constitution, it required them to heed these late colonial policies regarding religion – the same policies that the Colonial Office had implemented to prevent "communalism." Those policies found their way into Ceylon's independence constitution largely through the work of two men, who would serve as the key architects of the 1948 charter: D S Senanayake, the leader of the island's State Council; and William Ivor Jennings, Vice Chancellor of the newly established University of Ceylon, and ex-professor of constitutional law at the London School of Economics. While Senanayake and Jennings cannot take all the credit for drafting the 1948 Constitution, their influence remains paramount, particularly in regards to its provisions for religion.[29] Senanayake played the role of

promote unity. Unfortunately the experiment has not given the desired results, but has had, if anything, the opposite effect. The representatives of the various communities do not trust one another." Donoughmore Commission, *Report of the Special Commission on the Ceylon Constitution*, 67.

[26] Ibid., 67–68.

[27] The other model for this was the League of Nations' administrative committee system.

[28] Charles J Jeffries, *Ceylon: The Path to Independence* (London: Pall Mall Press, 1962), 53. Thomas J Baron, "The Donoughmore Commission and Ceylon's National Identity," in *Constitutions and National Identity: Proceedings of the Conference on "The Makings of Constitutions and the Development of National Identity" held in Honour of Professor George Shepperson at the University of Edinburgh, 3–6 July 1987*, ed. Thomas J Barron, Owen D Edwards and Patricia J Storey (Edinburgh: Quadriga Publishers, 1993). One committee member, Matthew Nathan, had been under-secretary to the Lord Lieutenant in Ireland at the time of the Easter Uprising.

[29] Also important were advisors to Senanayake, Oliver Goonatileke and A G Ranasinghe. W Ivor Jennings, "D. S. Senanayake and Independence," *Ceylon Historical Journal* 5, no. 1–4 (1955): 16–22. H A I Goonetileke and W Ivor Jennings, *The Road to Peradeniya: An Autobiography* (Colombo: Lake House, 2005), 162–177. K M De Silva, *British Documents on the End of Empire: Sri Lanka* (London: Institute of Commonwealth Studies, University

34   MANAGING RELIGION AT THE END OF EMPIRE

chief negotiator, consulting with Ceylonese lawmakers and British officials; Jennings played the role of chief draftsman.[30]

Neither Senanayake nor Jennings objected to the Crown's specific conditions pertaining to religion. In his communications with the Crown, Senanayake assented readily to the conditions included in the letter of May 1943. Replying to the letter, he declared that it "ha[d] not been necessary to use [the Governor's supervisory powers over religion] in the past and there is no reason to suppose that it will be necessary in the future."[31] Nevertheless, he conceded, "it gives the various communities in the Island a protection of which we would not wish to deprive them, though we do not think they will ever need it."[32] Ceylon, Senanayake was eager to suggest, was not a religiously divided society, but one prepared for orderly and peaceful self-rule.[33]

Jennings's assent to the terms of the 1943 letter owed as much to his understanding of legal theory as to his sense of political pragmatism. For Jennings, the letter's stipulations pertaining to religion cohered nicely with a larger paradigm of constitutional governance about which he had lectured and written for over 20 years – one that sought to eliminate communalism in politics by severing the links between representative

---

of London, 1997), Vol. I, lxii. Harshan Kumarasingham (ed.), *Constitution-Maker: Selected Writings of Sir Ivor Jennings* (Cambridge: Cambridge University Press, 2014).

[30] According to one of the leading constitutional historians in Sri Lanka: "Undoubtedly, the political input was given by the Ministers, but the drafting of the clauses of the First Constitution was a matter left to Jennings." M L Marasinghe, "Sir William Ivor Jennings," in *Legal Personalities: Volume 1* (Colombo: Law and Society Trust, 2005), 297.

[31] Ceylon Board of Ministers, "Statement by the Ministers on the Reforms Declaration by His Majesty's Government," in *Sessional Paper 19* (Colombo: Ceylon Government Press, June 1943).

[32] Ibid. This assessment was not entirely accurate: Senanayake had certainly witnessed tensions among the island's religious communities in the 1910s and 1920s. The British had imprisoned Senanayake as a suspected agitator in the aftermath of Muslim-Buddhist riots in 1915. In the 1920s, in his first years in the legislative council, he often spoke on behalf of Buddhists, defending their interests so that they would not be "trampled down" by the demands of Hindus, Muslims or Christians. Stanley Jeyaraja Tambiah, *Leveling Crowds: Ethnonationalist Conflicts and Collective Violence in South Asia* (Berkeley: University of California Press, 1996), 79. Government of Ceylon, *Ceylon Legislative Council Debates* (Colombo: Government Printers, 1928), 159.

[33] Marasinghe, "Sir William Ivor Jennings," 296. The "fundamental problem" that Senanayake and his advisors wrestled with was not how to produce a perfect charter that would satisfy all majority and minority politicians and religious communities but how to settle on "a short and simple draft [constitution] which they could persuade the Government of the United Kingdom to accept." W Ivor Jennings, "The Making of a Dominion Constitution," *Law Quarterly Review* 65 (1949): 456–479.

government and group identity. In language strikingly similar to that of the 1931 report,[34] Jennings reflected (some years later) that the "ultimate objective" of constitution-making, in Crown colonies as well as self-governing dominions, was ". . . remov[ing] communalism as a political motive" and persuading politicians of a particular country "to look at [its] problems . . . from a national point of view."[35] For Jennings, a well-functioning constitution, like a well-functioning colony, was one that encouraged politicians to "ignore all sentimental interests, whether they are based on race, religion, caste, language or any other social grouping."[36] Giving the Governor veto-powers over religiously prejudicial laws was for Jennings, as it was for the drafters of the 1931 report, one aspect of a broader constitutional strategy: by restricting lawmakers' abilities to legislate about religion, one could prevent religious identity from creating divisions in politics.[37]

The Preventative Paradigm and Section 29(2) of the 1948 Constitution

On February 2, 1944, Senanayake submitted to the Crown, on behalf of the Board of Ministers, the draft constitution that he and Jennings had produced.[38] While the "Ministers' Draft" (as it came to be known) would undergo scrutiny and alterations between 1944 and 1948, its two sections pertaining to religion would remain largely unchanged

---

[34] Cf. Donoughmore Commission, *Report of the Special Commission on the Ceylon Constitution*, 79.

[35] It should be noted that although Jennings referred to a "national point of view," he was a fierce critic of nationalisms of all kinds, which he interpreted as types of communalism, writ large. W Ivor Jennings, *The Approach to Self-Government* (Cambridge: Cambridge University Press, 1956), 85. Marasinghe, "Sir William Ivor Jennings," 310. Mara Malagodi, "'The Oriental Jennings': An Archival Investigation into Sir Ivor Jennings' Constitutional Legacy in South Asia," *Legal Information Management* 14, no. 1 (2014): 33–37.

[36] Donoughmore Commission, *Report of the Special Commission on the Ceylon Constitution*, 85.

[37] Regarding the relationship of politics and religion in Ceylon, Jennings wrote: "[T]he nationalist movement harnessed religion to their [sic] chariot. Hinduism and Buddhism became aggressive not through the priests but through the politicians." W Ivor Jennings, *Nationalism and Political Development in Ceylon (Institute of Pacific Studies Secretariat Paper, Series 9, Number 10)* (New York: Institute of Pacific Relations, 1950).

[38] "Ministers' letter of 2nd February 1944" in Ceylon Board of Ministers, "Reform of the Constitution (Memorandum From Ministers to HMG from 11 Sept 1944)," in *Sessional Paper 14 of 1944* (Colombo: Ceylon Government Press, September, 1944).

36 MANAGING RELIGION AT THE END OF EMPIRE

(with one small but important exception discussed later).[39] Under one section, the Minister's Draft included verbatim the clause concerning the Governor's veto powers over religiously discriminatory bills.[40] In another section, it integrated the same language into limiting conditions on the lawmaking powers of parliament. This section, which would become Section 29(2) of the final constitution, mandated that "[P]arliament shall make no law":

Section 29(2)
    (a) to prohibit or restrict the free exercise of any religion; or
    (b) to make persons of any community or religion liable to disabilities or restrictions to which persons of other communities or religions are not made liable; or
    (c) to confer on persons of any community or religion any privileges or advantages which are not conferred on persons of other communities or religions; or
    (d) to alter the constitution of any religious body except with the approval of the governing authority of that religious body.[41]

Section 29(2) broadened the restrictions on religiously prejudicial laws (contained in the Governor's veto-powers) to apply as guiding parameters for legislating by parliament. The section not only prohibited parliament from making laws that conferred unequal advantages or disadvantages on "persons of any community or religion," but also prohibited the island's lawmakers from passing legislation that infringed upon the "free exercise" of religion or that "alter[ed] the constitution of any religious body" without consent from religious leaders.

The language of the Ministers' Draft would have been familiar to British administrators and legal theorists in London. Paragraphs (b) and (c) reiterated word-for-word the language of the Donoughmore Commission report of 1931.[42] To that, the draft added additional passages from the same law that the Donoughmore Commission

---

[39] The final version of the document that would become the 1946 Ceylon (Constitution) Order in Council and the 1948 Constitution was an official re-drafting, by the Crown's own legal draftsman, of the Senanayake-Jennings version. W Ivor Jennings, "Limitations on a 'Sovereign' Parliament," *Cambridge Law Journal* (1964): 177–180.

[40] Section 38(1)(d): These powers were to be transferred to the Governor-General, appointed by the King, once Ceylon was granted self-rule.

[41] Section 8, "The Constitutional Scheme Formulated by the Ministers" (1943).

[42] Donoughmore Commission, *Report of the Special Commission on the Ceylon Constitution*, 55.

members had used as *their* legal model[43] – the Government of Ireland Act of 1920.[44] This double constitutional borrowing had been suggested by Jennings, who deemed the Ireland Act a good "precedent" for Ceylon, specifically the parts that "sought to protect the Protestants from discriminatory legislation in Southern Ireland and the Roman Catholics from discriminatory legislation in Northern Ireland."[45]

In choosing an Irish act as a template, Jennings analogized the situation of Catholics and Protestants in Ireland to the situation of Buddhists and non-Buddhists in Ceylon. Yet, by selecting in particular the Government of Ireland Act of *1920* – a defunct law at the time – Jennings also affirmed a more general principle of how constitutions ought to approach the state management of religion. Rather than require governments to actively protect religious freedom as a positive right, constitutions ought to *prevent* legislatures from intervening unfairly in the religious lives of citizens.[46]

SECTION II

Protectionist and Promotional Objections to the 1948 Constitution

Between 1944 and 1948, the document produced by Senanayake and Jennings progressed from a draft constitution (in 1944), to a colonial legal charter (in 1946), and then to the first independence constitution of

---

[43] Here, I refer only to the constitutional borrowing with respect to religion. In recounting the drafting process, Jennings points out that the bicameral design of the legislature was based on that of Burma, the design of the electoral constituencies was based on that of South Africa and the design of the cabinet system was based on that of Australia. Jennings and Tambiah, *The Dominion of Ceylon*, 65–66.

[44] Jennings, "The Making of a Dominion Constitution." Section 5(1) of the Government of Ireland Act reads: "... neither the Parliament of Southern Ireland nor the Parliament of Northern Ireland *shall make a law* so as either directly or indirectly to establish or endow any religion, or *prohibit or restrict the free exercise thereof, or give a preference, privilege, or advantage, or impose any disability or disadvantage, on account of religious belief or religious or ecclesiastical status, ... or alter the constitution of any religious body except, where the alteration is approved on behalf of the religious body by the governing body thereof ...* " (emphasis mine).

[45] W Ivor Jennings, *The Constitution of Ceylon* (Bombay: Oxford University Press, 1949), 77.

[46] W Ivor Jennings, *Law and the Constitution* (London: University of London, 1933), 257.

Ceylon (in 1948).[47] Although there had been frustrations along the way,[48] by the standards of the Crown's 1943 letter the document was a success: it had satisfied Crown representatives in London; it had been approved, with some minor alterations, by a special commission (led by Lord Soulbury) appointed by the Secretary of State for the Colonies;[49] and it had garnered the requisite three-fourths majority in the State Council.[50]

However, not everyone was happy with the new constitution, especially with its provisions relating to religion in Section 29(2). Even while the new constitution was being drafted, there were many who objected to its form, content, and the conditions under which it was produced. Between 1943 and 1956, two main factions – one led by politicians, the other by lay Buddhists – expressed deep misgivings about the religion provisions of the 1948 Constitution and the drafts that preceded it. The first group consisted of young politicians in the island's largest political organization, the Ceylon National Congress, who argued that, along with many other things, the new constitution did not adequately defend the

---

[47] The constitution was enacted primarily through two Orders-in-Council even before the transfer of power in 1948 February. The earliest iteration, which included almost all the provisions of the new constitution, appeared as the Ceylon (Constitution) Order-in-Council of May 15, 1946. For the purposes of this book, I also refer to this constitution as the 1948 Constitution.

[48] Perhaps the most significant index of this was the Board of Ministers' decision to withdraw the proposed draft constitution in 1944. They did this in protest to a statement issued by the Crown on July 5, 1944, shortly after the first constitution draft had been submitted. The statement announced the Crown's intention to appoint an external commission to review the constitution, led by Lord Soulbury. According to the ministers, the Soulbury Commission's inquiries would not only delay the process of the transfer of power, it would undermine local politicians' authority to negotiate on behalf of Ceylon's inhabitants. When the Soulbury Commission arrived, Senanayake and the Board of Ministers boycotted the public sittings and refused to make official submissions. (By most accounts, however, they spoke unofficially with the commissioners and acted as hosts during the commission's stay on the island.)

[49] The mandate for the Soulbury Commission was: "To visit Ceylon in order to examine and discuss any proposals for constitutional reform in the Island which have the object of giving effect to the Declaration of His Majesty's Government on that subject dated 26th May, 1943; and, after consultation with various interests in the Island, including minority communities, concerned with the subject of constitutional reform, to advise His Majesty's Government on all measures necessary to attain that object" (p. 1). The commission received 165 written petitions, and held 20 public sessions between January 22 and March 15, 1945 at the Colombo Town Hall. I reviewed these submissions, which are housed at the UK National Archives, in preparing this chapter.

[50] This political feat likely more reflected Ceylonese members' eagerness for independence than unqualified approval of the constitutional draft.

religious freedoms of citizens. The second group, represented by a Buddhist activist organization in Colombo, insisted that the island's new legal charter failed to acknowledge the demographic and historical importance of Buddhism, as the religion professed by the majority of the island's inhabitants and the religion with the deepest links to the island's culture and precolonial past. These critics challenged Senanayake and Jennings by proposing alternative ways of thinking about religion and alternative approaches to decolonization.

Origins of the Protectionist Paradigm: The Young Turks and Religion as a *Fundamental Right*

In advocating a preventative paradigm for managing religion, Jennings was not just choosing a favored model for constitutional governance. He was also rejecting a less favored model that had gained popularity in Europe and been championed by nationalist leaders in India. The paradigm that Jennings rejected aimed to actively *protect* the religious rights of individuals by making "religious freedom" a positive "fundamental right," which would be enshrined in a bill of rights.[51] Both in his scholarship prior to coming to Ceylon and in his work with Senanayake, Jennings argued against this protectionist paradigm.[52] He convinced Senanayake, who had originally favored the idea of a bill of rights, that Ceylon did not share the same religious and ethnic antagonisms as India and that "legal arguments over fundamental rights would [not] help much in the process of bringing a Constitution into operation or in the process of governing the country once it had come into operation."[53] By adopting a bill of rights, Jennings argued, Ceylon's lawmakers would further entangle the government with religion by making the government responsible for religion, as a guarantor of its well-being.[54] In taking this

---

[51] Jennings often referred to those constitutions that integrated a comprehensive bill of rights as following an American model. I did not use this categorization above to avoid any confusion based on the fact that the U.S. First Amendment also functions as a limit on lawmakers. Jennings, "The Making of a Dominion Constitution," 475.

[52] Jennings, *Law and the Constitution*, 257–267. Jennings, "The Making of a Dominion Constitution," 471–473.

[53] Jennings, *The Constitution of Ceylon*, 472.

[54] Jennings softened his views later in life. In 1956, while serving on the Reid Commission drafting the Constitution of Malaya, he advocated for and drafted a section on Fundamental Liberties for the Malayan Constitution. And, in 1961, in an interview with the BBC he admitted that a bill of rights might have been well suited to Ceylon. Joseph A L

stance, Jennings had the backing of the Colonial Office: at the time, it was official Crown policy to reject bills of rights for all dependencies.[55] Noting this policy, Jennings would later quip that, "an English lawyer is apt to shy away from [fundamental rights] like a horse from a ghost."[56]

Despite Jennings's protests, however, the idea of fundamental rights was popular among many politicians on the island. This included members of the island's largest political organization, the Ceylon National Congress (CNC). Those within the CNC who supported fundamental rights included lawyers, labor organizers, elected representatives to the State Council and members of the State Council's executive body, the Board of Ministers. Their support reflected both legal and political reasoning: in supporting fundamental rights, politicians not only supported a particular paradigm of constitutional governance, they also registered their opposition to the constitution-making efforts of Senanayake.

Tensions had been brewing since the late 1930s between Senanayake and this alternative group of would-be constitution drafters; these tensions hardened further in 1943. In the weeks and months that followed the reading of the Crown's letter of invitation, members of the State Council and the Ceylon National Congress gradually split off into two groups: those who supported Senanayake's tight control over the process of constitution-making and those who did not. (Senanayake would ultimately resign from the Ceylon National Congress in December 1943, ostensibly protesting the inclusion in the Congress of the island's Communist organizations, which he considered to be too radical.)[57]

Opposition to Senanayake consolidated around a group of younger politicians within the CNC. This group, which consisted largely of lawyers, came to be referred to (affectionately and derisively) as the "Young Turks," on account of their age and their advocacy of more

---

Cooray, *Constitutional and Administrative Law of Sri Lanka (Ceylon)* (Colombo: Hansa Publishers Ltd., 1973), 509.

[55] For a discussion of this see Charles Parkinson, *Bills of Rights and Decolonization: The Emergence of Domestic Human Rights Instruments in Britain's Overseas Territories* (London: Oxford University Press, 2007). S A De Smith, *The New Commonwealth and Its Constitutions* (London: Stevens and Sons, 1964).

[56] Quoted in: Ibid., 165.

[57] Frustrations had been brewing for some time over a range of other issues as well, including the question of whether the CNC should function as a singular, hierarchically structured political party or as a more loosely organized, federated, national political organization. *Documents of the Ceylon National Congress and Nationalist Politics in Ceylon 1929–1950* (Colombo: National Archives Dept., 1965), introduction.

aggressively anti-colonial policies. The Young Turks demanded broader participation in the drafting process, more attention to social reform and, most stridently, a shorter timetable for the transition to independence.[58] Where Senanayake favored an incremental approach to self-rule based on good-faith negotiation with the British, the Young Turks called for an immediate declaration of a "Free Lanka."[59] Where Senanayake sought to make Ceylon a dominion of the Crown, the Young Turks declared their intent to make the island an autonomous republic. In defiance of Senanayake and Jennings, the Young Turks insisted that negative limits on parliament were inadequate as civil rights protections. In their eyes, Ceylon needed a full palette of "fundamental rights" in its constitution in order to protect its citizens.

One of the earliest public expressions of support for fundamental rights by the Young Turks came in an article published in the *Times of Ceylon* several months after the May 1943 letter was publicized. The essay was written by J A L Cooray, a legal scholar, co-secretary of the Ceylon National Congress and an influential member of the Young Turks. In it, Cooray argued that any new constitution for the island must include "a chapter on Fundamental Rights," which, he observed, had become a central feature of "most of the modern constitutions." Such a chapter, he wrote, would "withdraw the sphere of political and individual liberty from the competence of the legislature and [fix] it in the form of a positive law," thereby rendering important "individual and civil rights" unalterable or undeniable.[60] Regarding religion he observed:

---

[58] On June 10, 1943, the Working Committee of the CNC, led by these younger members, drafted a resolution calling on Senanayake and the Board of Ministers to "take no action" regarding the 1943 letter unless the Crown would agree to "grant to the people of Ceylon the unfettered right to frame their own [new] constitution immediately after the cessation of [WWII] hostilities." Ibid., Vol. I, 778–9, cxli.

[59] Ibid., Vol. I, cxliii. By late 1943, the split between Senanayake and members of the CNC was sufficiently pronounced that Senanayake felt it necessary to resign from the CNC in order to signal his distance from the competing "forces of reaction." Regarding his decision, Senanayake wrote in a memo to the joint secretaries of the Ceylon National Congress that he objected to a change in the Constitution of the CNC that made "the attainment of freedom for Ceylon" the first objective of the body instead of obtaining Dominion Status. He also underscored that he rejected the CNC's attempts to declare itself free through appeals to the United Nations or by aligning with India, saying "I do not advocate the adoption of any method other than appealing to England itself." Ceylon National Congress, *25 Years – but Yet! (Pamphlet)* (Colombo: n.p., 1946), 31, 33.

[60] Joseph A L Cooray, "Constitution in the Making: Questions Which Our Ministers Will Have to Consider," *The Times of Ceylon* (October 16, 1943).

42   MANAGING RELIGION AT THE END OF EMPIRE

> There is invariably [in Fundamental Rights chapters] an Article dealing
> with religious liberty, which runs more or less on the following lines.
> Freedom of conscience and free profession and practices of religion are,
> subject to public order and morality, *guaranteed to every citizen,* and no
> law shall be made either directly or indirectly to establish or endow any
> religion, or impose any disability or make any discrimination on the
> ground of religious belief or status, or affect prejudicially the right of
> any child to attend a school receiving public money without attending
> religious instructions at that school, or make any discrimination between
> schools under the management of different religious denominations or
> divert from any religious denomination or any educational institution any
> of its property save for necessary works of public utility and on payment
> of compensation.[61]

Making religion a "fundamental right," according to Cooray, required
that the constitution not only prevent discriminatory lawmaking, but also
ensured government action in protecting religious rights. Although
Cooray included the caveat that such rights are typically limited by the
dictates of "public order and morality," he nonetheless sketched a model
of rights that portrayed the government as not just benignly aloof from
religion – concerned only with avoiding religious conflicts – but as
responsible for and receptive to the broader religious needs of citizens.
In making his point, Cooray chose as his exemplar of modern constitutions the Irish constitution that succeeded (and replaced) the 1920
Government of Ireland Act: the 1922 Constitution of the Irish Free State
and later the 1937 Constitution of Ireland. As will be seen below, this
choice was laden with significance.

   Cooray's advocacy of fundamental rights was not merely academic.
Beginning in August 1943, he worked actively to produce a constitution
on behalf of the constitutional "Working Committee" of the Ceylon
National Congress, led by members of the Young Turks. The committee,
in a special session, resolved to design its own "Draft Constitution for a
Free Lanka" separately from that of Senanayake and Jennings.[62] In the first

---

[61] Ibid., 2, Emphasis added.

[62] Rangita De Silva, "JAL Cooray: A Pioneer Lankan Constitutional Lawyer and Human
Rights Jurist," *Sri Lanka Journal of International Law* 6 (1994): 1–16. Ceylon National
Congress, *25 Years – but Yet!* , 28. K M De Silva and Howard Wriggins, *J. R. Jayewardene
of Sri Lanka* (London: Anthony Blond Quartet, 1988), Vol. I, 168–169. Joseph A L
Cooray, "Human Rights and Their Protection in Ceylon," in *Constitutional Government
and Human Rights in a Developing Society* (Colombo: Colombo Apothecaries Publishers,
1969), 34. For references to the Working Committee meetings of the CNC relating to

ORIGINS OF THE PROTECTIONIST PARADIGM   43

sections of the "Constitution for a Free Lanka,"[63] Cooray drafted eight discrete paragraphs of justiciable "rights" and "freedoms" that the state would guarantee to every citizen.[64] Among these was a section on "Freedom of Religion," which read:

> Freedom of conscience and the free profession and practice of religion, subject to public order and morality, are hereby guaranteed to every citizen. The Republic shall not prohibit the free exercise of any religion or give preference or impose any disability on account of religious belief or status.[65]

The clause differs from the draft constitution produced by Senanayake and Jennings in important ways. Rather than preventing damages to religion through placing limits on the legislature, the Constitution for a Free Lanka charges "the Republic" with protecting citizens' rights to religious belief, practice and teaching and with guaranteeing citizens' freedom from state discrimination or impositions on their religious practice. Religious rights were not merely preserved by preventing harmful legislation (an approach that assumes that those rights were already secure before legislative intervention); as a fundamental right, the protection of religious freedom applied to *all* agents and actions of the republic, including the civil service, police and judiciary.[66]

Cooray's constitution see *Documents of the Ceylon National Congress and Nationalist Politics in Ceylon 1929–1950*, Vol. I, 776–804.

[63] One should not confuse the Constitution for a Free Lanka that Cooray drafted with the Free Lanka Bill that was debated in the State Council between January and March 1945. The Free Lanka Bill was essentially a copy of the Minister's Draft (with all references to Dominion status replaced by references to a Republic) that was introduced to the State Council, in K M de Silva's words, as a sort of "political theatre" to dramatize the State Council's disapproval of the work of the Soulbury Commission. K M De Silva, *British Documents on the End of Empire*, Vol. I, lxv.

[64] These included statements of equality before the law, freedom from discrimination on the basis of "birth, sex, class, rank, caste, office, position, and religion," rights to a fair trial, rights to free education, rights to free expression and assembly, freedom of the press, and freedom of religion.

[65] J R Jayewardene, "J. R. Jayewardene's Draft Constitution 29 November 1944," in *Documents of the Ceylon National Congress and Nationalist Politics in Ceylon 1929–1950*, Vol. II, 2593.

[66] Whereas one year previously, the Young Turks had experimented with constitutional design based on certain core civil, political and economic "principles," these principles were now rebranded and reconfigured as a strong bill of rights. SLNA 60/144 (July 7, 1942) Letter announcing "Meeting of the sub-committee appointed to draft the new constitution," *Signed by J. R. Jayewardene* (as "convener"). *Copies to Dr. R. Saravanamuttu, Stanley de Zoysa, H. A. Koattegoda, Dudley Senanayake*. Based on archival examination, I suspect that the labeled date of this letter is incorrect and should be from July 7, 1943.

44 MANAGING RELIGION AT THE END OF EMPIRE

When it came to constitutional borrowing, Cooray's Constitution for a Free Lanka drew its religion policies, tellingly, not from the Government of Ireland Act of 1920 (as Senanayake and Jennings had done) but from the legal charter designed by Irish nationalists to replace it, the 1937 Constitution of Ireland. This choice further highlighted the opposition between Senanayake and Jennings, on the one hand, and the Young Turks of the Ceylon National Congress, on the other. Where Jennings based his religion provisions on a document that separated northern and southern Irish parliaments and gave each only limited "home rule" over internal affairs, the Constitution for a Free Lanka took its language from a document that aimed to establish total Irish independence from the Crown and that, in the words of Cooray, effected a definitive "break with the past, ... conduct[ing] what, in law, was a revolution."[67]

Legitimating the Protectionist Paradigm, Part I: Fundamental Rights as Human Rights

By insisting upon the inclusion of fundamental rights in the new constitution (in the form of a bill of rights), the Young Turks within the CNC not only marked their opposition to Senanayake and Jennings,[68] they marked their participation in a burgeoning human

---

Either way, the implication remains the same: the Young Turks gradually transformed a set of bill-of-rights-like guiding principles into a strong and clear list of positive fundamental rights.

[67] Joseph A L Cooray, "The Revision of the Constitution," in *Constitutional Government and Human Rights in a Developing Society* (Colombo: Colombo Apothecaries Publishers, 1969), 4. It should be noted that, for much of the 1920s and 1930s, politicians in Ceylon kept a keen eye on Ireland. Like Jennings, they likened the situation of British rule in South Asia with the situation in the British Isles. However, unlike Jennings, they viewed things from the Irish perspective, rather than the Crown's. See, e.g., K M De Silva, *A History of Sri Lanka* (Colombo: Vijitha Yapa Publications, 2005), 530. *Documents of the Ceylon National Congress and Nationalist Politics in Ceylon 1929-1950*, Vol. I, lvxii.

[68] There are ongoing debates over the relationship between the CNC leadership and Senanayake during this period (particularly 1945–1947). Some assert that the Senanayake remained influential in the CNC and, in fact, coordinated a behind-the-scenes political strategy with the CNC, encouraging the CNC to advocate a more aggressive vision of nationalism so that his demands appeared as a moderate alternative to British colonial officials. While Senanayake was undoubtedly influential

LEGITIMATING THE PROTECTIONIST PARADIGM, PART I   45

rights movement. Between 1941 and 1943, the affirmation of "fundamental freedoms" and "human rights" became a central ideological tenet of the allied "United Nations."[69] During this time, a number of activists and world leaders even began to call for an "international bill of rights" applicable to all countries. Members of the CNC used this developing discourse in their resolutions. They appealed to the rights and freedoms listed in Roosevelt's "four freedoms" speech (January 1941), the Atlantic Charter (December 1941) and the "Declaration by the United Nations" (January 1942).[70] In a manifesto from 1947, CNC drafters even outlined their own program (echoing Roosevelt's rhetoric) of "*five* freedoms," the first of which was the "Freedom from Foreign Rule."[71]

Using human rights discourse had the effect of aligning the Young Turks with an alternative source of international authority – one broader than, if not directly dominant over, the British Crown.[72] It also plotted

> during this period, even among the CNC, I maintain that the split between the Young Turks and Senanayake was, in fact, bona fide. Ceylon National Congress, *25 Years – but Yet!*, 41, 40.

[69] There are two convenient and commonly cited indices for the efflorescence of human rights discourse during this period. The first is President Roosevelt's January 1941 State of the Union Address, often referred to as the "Four Freedoms Speech" in which he identified freedom of speech, freedom to worship, freedom from want, and freedom from fear as the "essential human freedoms." The Address ends with Roosevelt glossing freedom as "the supremacy of human rights." The second is the "Declaration by the United Nations," the alliance treaty signed by 26 countries in opposition to the Axis powers, on January 1, 1942. The Declaration committed signatories to defend "life, liberty, independence, and religious freedom, and to preserve human rights and justice." Jan H Burgers, "The Road to San Francisco: The Revival of the Human Rights Idea in the Twentieth Century," *Human Rights Quarterly* 14, no. 4 (1992): 447–477. Susan Waltz, "Universalizing Human Rights: The Role of Small States in the Construction of the Universal Declaration of Human Rights," *Human Rights Quarterly* 23, no. 1 (2001): 44–72.

[70] Ceylon National Congress, *25 Years – but Yet!*, 19, 25, 41. *Documents of the Ceylon National Congress and Nationalist Politics in Ceylon 1929–1950*, Vol. III, 1870. See also: "Representation in the New Constitution" *Ceylon Daily News*, December 3, 1944.

[71] According to the manifesto, "Freedom from Foreign Rule" was "the necessary prerequisite to the obtaining of the other Freedoms." The four remaining freedoms of the CNC included: Freedom from Want, Freedom from Unemployment, Freedom from Ignorance, Freedom from Disease. Ibid., Vol. III, 1848–1850.

[72] At the time, it was unclear precisely what effect the Atlantic Charter or the Declaration by the United Nations would have on British colonial policies. This question would become particularly pertinent in the framing of the United Nations' Universal Declaration of Human Rights. Mark Mazower, *No Enchanted Palace: The End of Empire and the Ideological Origins of the United Nations* (Princeton: Princeton University Press, 2009). Mark Mazower, "The Strange Triumph of Human Rights, 1933–1950," *The Historical*

their constitution within an entirely different legal-philosophical terrain from that of Senanayake and Jennings. Senanayake and Jennings' draft constitution positioned rights in the context of a negotiation between states and citizens, as aspects of life into which states would not intrude. In contrast, in its evolving human rights discourse, the allied United Nations broadened the significance and context for understanding rights. According to this discourse, it was rights – not states – that were primary. That is, individuals gained rights, including religious freedom, not by virtue of their status as citizens, but by virtue of their very humanity. Governments did not legitimate rights; the protection of rights legitimated governments.

Using this alternative approach to rights, the Young Turks of the CNC linked together their call for a bill of rights with their demands for rapid and total independence from Britain. They relied on two arguments. On the one hand, propagandists criticized the colonial government's legitimacy by accusing it of failing to grant adequate fundamental rights to those who lived in Ceylon. As early as December 1941, in fact, members of the CNC called upon the British government to confirm its commitment to freedom as stated in the Atlantic Charter by extending those freedoms to "the subject peoples within the Empire."[73] On the other hand, members of the CNC simultaneously claimed *as* a fundamental right "the right to independence and a free constitution."[74] By outlining a schedule of fundamental rights they accused the colonial state of failing to guarantee those rights and, by extension, failing to meet international standards of political legitimacy.[75]

Journal 47, no. 2 (2004): 379–398. Mary Ann Glendon, *A World Made New: Eleanor Roosevelt and the Universal Declaration of Human Rights* (New York: Random House, 2001). Manu Bhagavan, "A New Hope: India, the United Nations and the Making of the Universal Declaration of Human Rights," *Modern Asian Studies* 44, no. 2 (2010): 311–347.

[73] *Documents of the Ceylon National Congress and Nationalist Politics in Ceylon 1929–1950*, Vol. III, 1870.

[74] "Twenty-sixth Annual Sessions of the Ceylon National Congress," January 27–28, 1945, in ibid., Vol. III, 1566.

[75] These anti-colonial implications were made explicit in discussions held prior to and during the first sessions of the nascent United Nations. Paul G Lauren, "First Principles of Racial Equality: History and the Politics and Diplomacy of Human Rights Provisions in the United Nations Charter," *Human Rights Quarterly* 5, no. 1 (1983): 1–26. Marika Sherwood, "India at the Founding of the United Nations," *International Studies* 33, no. 4 (1996): 407–428. Johannes Morsink, *The Universal Declaration of Human Rights: Origins, Drafting and Intent* (Philadelphia: University of Pennsylvania Press, 1999), Ch. 3.

Legitimating the Protectionist Paradigm, Part II: Fundamental Rights in South Asia

In pushing for a chapter on fundamental rights, the Young Turks looked not only to the human rights discourse emanating from Europe, but to the discourses of anti-colonial nationalism in South Asia. In particular, they looked to the Indian National Congress (INC), which had been working for many years to produce a Declaration of Fundamental Rights for India.

The CNC first established close relations with the INC in the 1920s. (In fact, the very idea to form the Ceylon Congress had come from India's Congress.) Members of the CNC attended important INC meetings (including those at Ramgarh in March 1940 and at Bombay in July 1942), and, following the INC model, they adopted "national dress" and campaigned for "home spun" fabrics as well as policies of "rural uplift."[76] In 1940, the CNC even considered joining the INC as a branch organization.[77]

During this period of close engagement between the two Congresses, the CNC watched as the INC formulated a statement of fundamental rights to be integrated into a new constitution, first in 1928, in the Nehru Report, then in the Karachi Resolution of 1931, and later, in 1944, in the recommendations of the Sapru Committee.[78] In pushing for fundamental rights, the Indian Congress had (mostly)

---

[76] De Silva and Wriggins, *J. R. Jayewardene of Sri Lanka*, Vol. I, 108, 126, 149. Ceylon National Congress, *25 Years – but Yet!*, 17. In a letter to Nehru dated 29 June 1945, J R Jayewardene, Joint Secretary of the CNC, wrote "we in Lanka feel that our fight for freedom is being fought largely in India, and India's freedom is Lanka's freedom too" and confirmed that "[t]he latest resolution of the Indian Congress Working Committee, demanding freedom for the colonies, has heartened us, for even the moral support of a powerful neighbor gives strength to our cause." *Documents of the Ceylon National Congress and Nationalist Politics in Ceylon 1929–1950*, Vol. IV, 2738–2739.

[77] See also: De Silva, *A History of Sri Lanka*, 480–481. K M De Silva and W Howard Wriggins, *J.R. Jayewardene of Sri Lanka: A Political Biography. 2 Vols* (Honolulu: University of Hawaii Press, 1988), Vol. I, 103. For a collection of correspondence between members of the INC and the CNC see: *Documents of the Ceylon National Congress and Nationalist Politics in Ceylon 1929–1950*, Vol. IV, 2701–2782.

[78] See: Tej B Sapru et al., *Constitutional Proposals of the Sapru Committee* (Bombay: Padma Publishers Limited, 1945). Neera Chandoke, "Individual and Group Rights a View From India," in *India's Living Constitution: Ideas, Practices, Controversies*, ed. Zoya Hasan, E Sridharan and R Sudarshan (London: Anthem, 2005). Granville Austin, *The Indian Constitution: Cornerstone of a Nation* (New York: Oxford University Press, 1966), 52–58.

48 MANAGING RELIGION AT THE END OF EMPIRE

unknowingly mounted their own challenge to the work of Ivor Jennings by drawing heavily on the ideas of one of Jennings's best-known interlocutors (and former colleagues at the London School of Economics), Harold Laski.[79] Laski disagreed stridently with Jennings on the matter of fundamental rights. Where Jennings opposed them, Laski insisted that a specially elaborated bill of rights was essential for any constitution in order to "canonize the safeguards of freedom" and to create "a rallying-point in the state for all who care deeply for the ideals of freedom."[80] In underscoring the importance of fundamental rights in the future Indian Constitution, the INC (which included some of Laski's former students) had presented the Ceylon Congress not only with an alternative template for constitution-making, but also with an alternative constitutional scholar from whose theories they might draw. This linkage was not lost on the CNC: many in the CNC (or with links to it) had, like their fellows in the INC, studied at LSE and even under Laski himself.[81]

In January 1945, facing what seemed to be the eventual ratification of Jennings and Senanayake's constitution draft, the CNC issued its own "Declaration of Fundamental Rights," one modeled directly on the work of the INC. In the introduction to the Declaration, the CNC stated – in a Laskiesque-sounding flourish – that in order to "enable the masses to appreciate what 'freedom' means" and to effect "political freedom," the Congress "declare[d] that in the Constitution of a Free Lanka the following fundamental rights and duties should be included." In the list that followed, the CNC reproduced virtually verbatim the list of "Fundamental Rights" contained in the Nehru and Sapru Reports. Even more than Cooray's Constitution for a Free Lanka, the CNC "Declaration of Fundamental Rights" elaborated the state's duties toward religion in active terms.[82]

---

[79] Ibid., 58–59. K D Ewing, "Law and the Constitution: Manifesto of the Progressive Party," *Modern Law Review* 67 (2004): 734–752.

[80] Harold J Laski, *Liberty in the Modern State* (New York: Harper, 1930), 49–50. Harold J Laski, *The Rise of European Liberalism* (New Brunswick, NJ: Transaction Publishers, 1997), xxxvii–xxxviii.

[81] Adrian Wijemanne, *War and Peace in Post-colonial Ceylon, 1948–1991* (Orient Black-swan, 1996), 25. Howard Wriggins, *Ceylon: Dilemmas of a New Nation* (Princeton NJ: Princeton University Press, 1960), 124.

[82] Differences from the Nehru Report are marked in *italics*. The Declaration read: "(1) *Every citizen* has the right to free expression of opinion, the right of free association and combination, and the right to assembly peacefully and without arms. (2) Every citizen shall enjoy freedom of conscience and the right freely to profess and practise religion.

THE ORIGINS OF THE PROMOTIONAL PARADIGM   49

SECTION III

The Origins of the Promotional Paradigm:
Religious Rights as Buddhist Prerogatives

At the same time that Senanayake and Jennings were defending their preventative paradigm and the Young Turks were advocating their protectionist paradigm, another movement in Ceylon began to argue for a third paradigm of managing religion. This movement grew out of the Buddhist reform and nationalist groups in the late nineteenth and early twentieth centuries and viewed Ceylon as an Island of Dhamma, chosen specially by the Buddha himself for the propagation of his teachings.[83] Advocates of this model rejected the idea that the new government should treat all religions equally: although all persons were entitled to practice their religions, they insisted, the independent state of Ceylon had an obligation to promote Buddhism especially.

Those who supported special protections for Buddhism did not justify their claims with reference to public order or universal rights, but by appeals to the island's unique demography, history and culture. According to their logic, Buddhism deserved to be promoted for four reasons: it was the religion professed by the majority of the population; it was the religion that had the longest historical connection with the island; it constituted a core cultural feature of the island's largest ethno-linguistic community, the Sinhalese; and it had suffered more than any other religion under colonial rule.[84] Viewed through this lens,

---

(3) The culture, language and script of the minorities shall be protected. (4) All citizens are equal before the law irrespective of religion, caste, race or sex and no disability attaches in regard to public employment by reason of such difference. (5) All citizens have equal rights and duties in regard to wells, tanks, roads, schools, *cemetaries* [*sic*] and places of public resort maintained out of state or local funds. (6) Every citizen has the right to keep and bear arms in accordance with regulations and reservations made in that behalf. (7) No person shall be deprived of his liberty nor shall his dwelling property be entered, segregated or confiscated save in accordance with law. (8) The State shall observe neutrality in regard to all religions. (9) The franchise shall be on the basis of Universal Adult Suffrage. (10) The State shall provide free, compulsory education." Ceylon National Congress, *25 Years – but Yet!*, 41.

[83] On these groups, see Bond, *The Buddhist Revival in Sri Lanka*. H L Seneviratne, *The Work of Kings: The New Buddhism in Sri Lanka* (Chicago: University of Chicago Press, 1999). Kitsiri Malalgoda, *Buddhism in Sinhalese Society, 1750–1900: A Study of Religious Revival and Change* (Berkeley: University of California Press, 1976).

[84] As one writer put it at the time: "Buddhism is the golden thread running through the history of the race and the land" and "the history of Lanka is the history of the Sinhalese

50   MANAGING RELIGION AT THE END OF EMPIRE

constitutional policies for religion appeared in a different light: rather than being indifferent to religion, the Ceylonese state should take steps to protect Buddhism over and above other faiths.

In the 1940s and 1950s, a number of Buddhist interest groups, both lay and monastic, argued for this promotional paradigm. The most organized, outspoken and influential was the All-Ceylon Buddhist Congress (ACBC).[85] The ACBC consisted largely of educated, middle-class lay Buddhists who lived in Colombo. It had been established as a coordinating body to promote cooperation among Buddhists and to encourage discussion on issues pertaining to the place of Buddhism in society. As it grew, the ACBC distinguished itself as a political and legal lobbying organization that would mediate between Buddhists and the government. The ACBC aimed to "represent the Buddhists and act on their behalf in public matters affecting their interests" and "to promote, foster and protect the interests of Buddhism and Buddhists and to safeguard the rights and privileges of Buddhists."[86]

Key to the ACBC's influence was its charismatic president, a well-known Buddhist scholar and professor of Pali at the University of Ceylon, G P Malalasekera.[87] Malalasekera was a forceful rhetorician. In orations and written articles he pointed to colonial history to legitimate

---

race." D C Vijayavardhana, *The Revolt in the Temple: Composed to Commemorate 2500 Years of the Land, the Race and the Faith* (Colombo: Sinha Publishers, 1953), 25.

[85] There were other Buddhist challenges to Senanayake and Jennings's constitution, aside from the ACBC-led challenge. A particularly important one came from the monks of a leading monastic college in Colombo, *Vidyalankara Pirivena*. Like the ACBC, these monks challenged the "the elitist, constitutionalist establishment" embodied by Senanayake and Jennings. Their response was to demand a more active role for Buddhist monks in the process of determining Ceylon's future. I do not focus on this movement – even though it came into direct conflict with Senanayake in 1947 – because its legacy, in my estimation, was less formative for the history of constitutional law on the island. Nonetheless it's important to mark it here. Seneviratne, *The Work of Kings*, 141. For further reading see: Ibid., 130–154. Ananda Abeysekara, *Colors of the Robe: Religion, Identity, and Difference* (Columbia, SC: University of South Carolina Press, 2002). Walpola Rahula, *The Heritage of the Bhikkhu* (New York: Grove Press, 1974).

[86] The ACBC operated in Ceylon since 1919. The quote above, however, derives from its "Act of Incorporation for All Ceylon Buddhist Congress Act No. 24 of 1955, Ch. 398, Government of Ceylon, *Ceylon Legislative Enactments* (Colombo: Ceylon Government Press, 1956).

[87] Stanley Jeyaraja Tambiah, *Buddhism Betrayed? Religion, Politics, and Violence in Sri Lanka* (Chicago: University of Chicago Press, 1992), 33.

THE ORIGINS OF THE PROMOTIONAL PARADIGM 51

the idea that the independent Ceylonese state should promote Buddhism. Malalasekera's narrative emphasized Buddhism's steady decline from an ideal past, beginning with Buddhism's flourishing as the "state religion" of Ceylon's precolonial kingdoms and devolving to a present-day state of deterioration.[88] In Malalasekera's description, colonization gradually destroyed Buddhism, particularly during the British era:

> Everything was done [by the British] sometimes openly but more often by devious and insidious ways to undermine the hold of Buddhism on the people's lives and to wean them away from the Bhikkhus [monks] who had been their teachers and leaders, in a word, to destroy Buddhism and put in its place a faith [Christianity] which was completely alien to the people's genius ... Buddhism [which] had entered in to the very marrow of the Sinhalese race as perhaps no religion had succeed in doing elsewhere ... gradually weakened and fell away – their [the Sinhalese] language and literature, their customs and traditions and their ways of life. .... The lands and perquisites attached to monastic establishments were taken away and given to others. Churches were erected on temple properties and padres received Government allowances for the propagation of their religion.[89]

During this period, according to Malalasekera, the British enervated Buddhism by denying support to the monkhood, expropriating temple property, giving preferential treatment to Christian missionaries and introducing alcohol. Through education in English at Christian schools, he argued, the British inculcated a new culture and morality based on "Christianity and European ways of life." Buddhists were made to feel "that [their] religion and [their] religious teachers belonged to an antiquated scheme of things" and should be abandoned for "the ways of life of the dominant races of the world."[90]

---

[88] Sinhalese kings, argued Malalasekera and the ACBC, were "the secular head[s] of Buddhism ... Defender[s] of the faith" who used royal decrees, state officials and treasury funds to protect Buddhist monks, maintain monasteries and ensure monastic discipline. Buddhism was not so much administered by the state in pre-colonial Ceylon so much as "the State itself existed but for the sake of Buddhism." The king, furthermore, ensured monastic discipline by administrating monastic courts and periodically disrobing monks deemed to be lax. All-Ceylon Buddhist Congress, *Buddhism and the State: Resolutions and Memorandum of the All Ceylon Buddhist Congress* (Maradana: Oriental Press, 1951), vi, ii, respectively.

[89] G P Malalasekera, "Congress Takes Stock of the Position of Buddhists," *The Buddhist*, February 1948, 130–132.

[90] All-Ceylon Buddhist Congress, *Buddhism and the State: Resolutions and Memorandum of the All Ceylon Buddhist Congress*, xv.

52 MANAGING RELIGION AT THE END OF EMPIRE

Pointing to this history of Buddhism's decline under colonial rule, the ACBC took it upon itself to promote Buddhism in independent Ceylon. In July 1951, Malalasekera led a small delegation from the ACBC to meet with then prime minister D S Senanayake to discuss their concerns. The delegation expressed frustration over the rhetoric of Section 29(2), insisting that it preserved Christian privileges and discriminated against Buddhism.[91] Members asked the prime minister to inquire into these matters by appointing a government committee to examine the condition of Buddhism on the island. When the prime minister failed to convene such a committee, the ACBC took matters into its own hands. In 1954, it established its own "Buddhist Committee of Inquiry" to survey "the present state of Buddhism in Ceylon" and to "report on the conditions necessary to improve and strengthen [its] position." Two years later, in the 300-page *Report of the Committee for Investigating the State of Buddhism* (herein ACBC report),[92] the ACBC confronted readers with a dire assessment of the island's new charter: "Christianity" they asserted, "was enthroned over Ceylon by our [1948] Constitution."[93]

Although the ACBC report included sections on education, economics, monastic comportment, social services and other topics, it gave special attention to criticizing the religion policies of the 1948 Constitution. Among the report's multifarious criticisms was a particularly long rebuke of Section 29(2)(d) and a last-minute alteration that Senanayake and Jennings made to the paragraph just before conveying the draft to the Secretary of State for the Colonies. The alteration pertained to the rights of incorporated religious organizations (and is marked in italics below):

> [No law shall...] 29(2)(d) alter the constitutions of any religious body except with the consent of the governing authority of that body: *provided that in any case where a religious body is incorporated by law, no such alterations shall be made except at the request of the governing authority of that body.*

According to the authors of the ACBC report, paragraph (d) and its late-added proviso gave already-incorporated "religious bodies"

---

[91] All-Ceylon Buddhist Congress, *33rd Annual Sessions, Kandy, December 29, 1951, English Translation of the Presidential Address by Dr. G. P. Malalasekera (Pamphlet)* (Borella, Colombo: The L.V. Press, December 29, 1951), 2.

[92] All-Ceylon Buddhist Congress, *Bauddha Toraturu Parīkṣaka Sabhāva Vārtāva* (Colombo: Visidunu Prakāśakaya, 1956 [reprinted 2006]).

[93] Ibid., 340.

THE ORIGINS OF THE PROMOTIONAL PARADIGM   53

(*āgamika āyatana*) – the majority of which were Christian[94] – complete autonomy from the state and almost total immunity from civil law because parliament could not revise their charters of incorporation. Those charters, the authors suggested, included special immunities and privileges given by the British during the colonial era (regarding tax exemption, owning and purchasing property, etc.)[95] Whereas the original (pre-alteration) version of paragraph (d) had given the parliament a *chance* to amend religious bodies' legal charters, and thereby amend those immunities and privileges, the final (post-alteration) version effectively robbed parliament of any power to do so.[96]

The problem was not just that the 1948 Constitution gave Christian groups too much power. Authors of the ACBC report argued that Section 29(2) also made it extremely difficult to incorporate Buddhist groups. This was because Section 29(2) presumed that each religious group had a single "governing authority" (*adhikāri*), a position that had no equivalent within Ceylonese Buddhism.[97] Buddhist monks were not organized into a single hierarchy, but were divided among several, competing monastic fraternities (*nikāya-s*). Even within specific fraternities, there were frequently multiple subsects, each of which affirmed a different line of monastic succession and different chief prelate.[98] Thus, the ACBC report pointed out, the act of declaring a "governing authority" would likely sabotage the legal incorporation of monastic fraternities

---

[94] The authors of the report asserted that "every Christian religious body" was incorporated in this manner and that no Buddhist religious body was. However, this was accurate only with respect to Buddhist monastic organizations. While the majority of corporations registered were Christian organizations, by the 1950s, a number of Buddhist groups had received acts of incorporation as well. The Young Men's Buddhist Association had received one as early as 1927 (Ord. 11 of 1927) and its branch organizations began incorporating in the 1940s, e.g., Nugegoda branch of YMBA in 1947. The ACBC received its incorporation in April 1955, during the course of preparing the ACBC Report (Ord. 24 of 1955). It is also interesting to note that certain Hindu and Muslim groups received acts of incorporation in the 1920s and 1930s as well: the Ramakrishna Mission, received an Act of Incorporation in 1929 (Ord. 8 of 1929); the *Saiva Paripalana Sabhāi* in 1931 (Ord. 17), the Maradana Mosque in 1924 (Ord. 18). Government of Ceylon, *Ceylon Legislative Enactments*, Ch. 319.

[95] All-Ceylon Buddhist Congress, *Bauddha Toraturu Parīkṣaka Sabhāvē Vārtāva*, 322–325, 355–360.

[96] Ibid., 358–359, emphasis mine.

[97] As far as I know, there was no *requirement* to name a governing authority in the document of incorporation that would be approved by parliament – although some smaller groups did so, particularly branch organizations of larger bodies, such as the Nugegoda Branch of the YMBA or the Batticaloa branch of the Saiva Paripalana Sabhāi.

[98] For more on this, see Chapter 6.

54 MANAGING RELIGION AT THE END OF EMPIRE

because it would provoke disputes among senior monks over who was the rightful governing authority![99]

In its conclusions, the ACBC report proposed a number of alterations to the constitution, including eliminating Section 29(2) entirely. This was necessary, it argued, in order to eliminate "the remaining vestiges of colonial powers and laws that had been put in place to protect Christianity"[100] and to remove "the chains of colonialism by which Buddhists in a free Lanka are still bound."[101] Also necessary was a redefining of religious freedom. The ACBC report called upon lawmakers to narrow and specify individual religious freedom in the constitution so that it would be applicable *only* to the "religious affairs" (*āgamika kaṭayutu*) of religious organizations (*āgamika āyatana*), and *not* to their financial, institutional or social activities. This change, the authors insisted, would permit the state to limit the abilities of Christian churches to use charitable (*puṇyādhāra*) funds for politics, commerce or agriculture.[102] Finally, the ACBC report recommended restricting the powers of government ministers to give money to religious organizations. Essentially, the report suggested that no government money be dispersed to religious groups without a comprehensive inquiry into their existing finances and numbers of adherents.[103] (The ACBC likely proposed this measure to curtail government support for Christian churches and to sanction government support for Buddhist religious bodies, which tended to be less wealthy by comparison.)

In addition to proposing changes to the constitution's religion clauses, the ACBC report also suggested that the government create new state institutions. It recommended appointing a special public commission to scrutinize the economic, social work and political activities of all religious bodies.[104] It advocated establishing a new ministerial position, the Minister of Religious Affairs (*āgamika kaṭayutu*), whose job it was to "remedy the situation of decline among religions that have [already] been destroyed during the era of foreign domination."[105] Most significantly, it insisted that the government should incorporate a separate Buddha Sasana Council (*buddha śāsana maṇḍalayak*) consisting of elected lay and monastic members, which would guarantee for Buddhism the same "special rights" (*viśēṣa ayitivāsikam*) that it enjoyed in the era of Buddhist kings. Through the Buddha Sasana Council, the state would

---

[99] All-Ceylon Buddhist Congress, *Bauddha Toraturu Parīkṣaka Sabhāvē Vārtāva*, 356–357.
[100] Ibid., 365.   [101] Ibid., 367.   [102] Ibid., 369–372.   [103] Ibid., 370–371.
[104] Ibid., 371.   [105] Ibid., 372.

essentially take over the duties to Buddhism previously exercised by kings, including responsibilities for overseeing temple lands, adjudicating disputes among monks, organizing Buddhist rituals and expanding Buddhist education.[106] Like Jennings and the Young Turks, the ACBC also engaged in its own form of legal borrowing. The report based its Buddha Sasana Council on a government body by the same name in Burma. To activate the recommended changes, the report even advised passing a statute nearly identical to the Buddha Sasana Act of Burma of 1950.[107]

Legitimating the Promotional Paradigm: Buddhist Privileges as Democratic Device

The ACBC's promotional paradigm did not define religious rights in abstract or universal terms. It placed religious rights in the context of a particular Buddhism-centric vision of Ceylon's past and present. The ACBC argued that constitutional protections for religion must take seriously the institutional and historical differences among religious groups on the island. They must also take seriously the differential impact of laws (that only *appeared* to be neutral) on those religions. In insisting that the state should take steps to support Buddhism, the ACBC was not looking to resurrect Buddhist kingship. Rather, they sought to make government support for Buddhism legitimate within the politics of a democratic, independent Ceylon. For that reason, the ACBC was at pains to show why Buddhist privileges were, in fact, coherent with secular democracy. To do so, they offered two arguments, one based on a populist vision of democracy, the other based on a liberal vision.

Populism featured prominently in many of the ACBC's publications. The ACBC asserted that democratic states should reflect the wishes of the majority of citizens. This involved a simple numerical calculation: the fact that Buddhism was the most populous religion justified the governmental measures to give it greater support. This argument was put forth clearly in an editorial that Malalasekera wrote to a prominent English-language journal in 1956, entitled "We Only Want Our Rights." In it, he insisted that Buddhists had a legitimate right to demand special status and legal concessions from the government:

---

[106] Ibid., 371.   [107] Ibid.

> The Buddhists wish – and quite rightly – that in this country, where they form 70 per cent, Buddhism should be recognised as the pre-dominant religion of the people. In the rest of the world, Ceylon is regarded as essentially a Buddhist country ... [Buddhists] want this claim established here as well. [Buddhists] will not be content to remain in the position of inferiority to which they had been reduced during 450 years of foreign occupation.[108]

According to Malalasekera, the terms of the 1948 Constitution prevented Buddhists from advancing their claims as a majority community. Rather, the provisions regarding religion in Section 29(2) "were interpreted to mean that the other religionists were allowed to do whatever they liked" while the "majority community was expected to give way to the requirements and prejudices of the minorities."[109] What was needed, suggested Malalasekera, was a set of laws that did not treat support for Buddhists as some sort of "'treason' and 'disloyalty' against the public weal."[110]

Malalasekera's first argument, that Buddhists' numerical predominance legitimated "preferential treatment" by the government, opposed diametrically the liberal vision of democracy and constitutionalism that animated the drafting of the 1948 Constitution and the Young Turk's Constitution for a Free Lanka. Senanayake, Jennings and the Young Turks in the CNC viewed constitutions as counterbalancing the majoritarian tendencies of democratic rule by giving minorities extra legal protection against the potential excesses of one-person-one-vote polities.[111] Constitutions, for them, were documents that protected less populous communities against more populous ones.

Buddhist lobby groups, like the ACBC, were well acquainted with this liberal position and made use of it themselves. They argued that Buddhist privileges were consistent with liberal interpretations of democracy because, although Buddhists dominated the electorate, Buddhism *as a religion* was uniquely vulnerable to harm. Unlike other features that defined communities, such as ethnicity, one's religion could be converted; and Buddhists, they insisted, were particularly susceptible to conversions because their religion was uniquely accepting of other worldviews. Buddhism's vulnerability also had a geographic dimension. Although Buddhism was the most populous religion in Ceylon, it was a minority religion in the wider setting of the subcontinent. As described

---

[108] G P Malalasekera, "We Only Want Our Rights," *The Buddhist* (1956).
[109] Ibid., 175–176.   [110] Ibid., 176.
[111] Ceylon National Congress, *25 Years– but Yet!*, 25–28.

AN ABORTIVE FOURTH PARADIGM? 57

by Malalasekera, the island of Ceylon was a fragile outpost for a tradition that had once flourished throughout India. These comparative disadvantages, he argued, meant that Buddhism, unlike Christianity, depended upon direct support from the government for its very survival. In Malalasekera's words, Buddhism "could not take a lasting hold on any soil, not even on the hallowed soil of Lanka, without the active support of the State."[112]

By underscoring the demographic, historical and institutional differences between Buddhism and other religious traditions, mainly Christianity, the ACBC argued that the promotional paradigm for managing religion actually upheld the principles of liberal democracy. Promoting Buddhist interests was not just reasonable, but necessary for independent Ceylon.[113]

An Abortive Fourth Paradigm?: Communal Representation

A brief word should be said about another paradigm for governing social difference that played an important role in debates about the 1948 Constitution, even if it was never broadly influential in politics after 1948. This paradigm was introduced by the head of the most influential Tamil political party at the time, G G Ponnambalam, and it involved a simple mathematical strategy for ensuring minority rights, one that was based on the representation of French Canadians in Canada, Maori in New Zealand, Muslims in Cyprus and Muslims, Sikhs and Christians in India (under the Government of India Act of 1935). Ponnambalam's system involved proportional representation based on "community,"[114] in which 50% of parliamentary seats would be reserved for Sinhalese and 50% for non-Sinhalese (Tamils, Muslims, Burghers, and Europeans).[115]

---

[112] All-Ceylon Buddhist Congress, *Buddhism and the State: Resolutions and Memorandum of the All Ceylon Buddhist Congress*, 3.

[113] Although Malalasekera spoke about Ceylonese Buddhism as a singular entity, he was well aware of the divisions within it. For Malalasekera, the unity of Ceylon Buddhism functioned in two ways rhetorically. It allowed the ACBC to speak on behalf of Buddhism, positioning the group as a small, active constituency representing an otherwise unified whole. Yet it also figured as a goal to be realized through the work of the ACBC: the imagined precolonial unity of Buddhism would be restored through action by the government.

[114] UKNA, FCO 141/2292 "Presidential Address from All-Ceylon Tamil Congress," 16.

[115] More specifically, Ponnambalam proposed that the country was to be divided into 100 territorial constituencies: 50 would be for minorities and 50 for Sinhalese. There would be 33 constituencies for Tamils, distributed as follows: 2 for Tamils residing in the

58 MANAGING RELIGION AT THE END OF EMPIRE

Ponnambalam's "50-50" plan never gained truly widespread support among Ceylon's political mainstream. Yet it offered an interesting alternative paradigm to the three described earlier. Rather than aiming to prevent, protect or promote religion, Ponnambalam's proposals ignore it, seeing religion as secondary or even epiphenomenal to one's ethnicity.[116] There is not a single reference to religion in Ponnambalam's draft proposals; in his writings, religion appears more as an instrument of (rather than motivation for) political action. Thus Ponnambalam reads demands for Buddhism to be made the "State religion" not as *bona fide* expressions of religious conviction, but as tactics of communal politics, a way for politicians to signal their Sinhalese-ness rather than indicating a "deep spiritual yearning."[117] Although abandoned soon after the 1940s, I include Ponnambalam's constitutional proposal here both because it figured prominently in the constitutional debates at the time and because it casts into relief something important about the preventative, protectionist and promotional paradigms of managing religion, which continue to influence politics after 1948: unlike Ponnambalam's proposals, each of these paradigms treats religion not simply as a concomitant of "community" or politics, but as something independently important, which ought to be addressed directly in constitutional law, even if only to ensure its separation from political life.

Conclusion: Paradigms of Managing Religion at the End of Empire

Three main paradigms for managing religion emerged in the context of debates over constitution drafting around 1948: a *preventative paradigm*, expressed in the Senanayake-Jennings draft (which eventually became the 1948 Constitution), which drew from existing colonial policies and

---

Western Province, 12 for Up-country (Indian) Tamils, and 19 for Eastern and Northern Province Tamils. Ponnambalam included Malayalis as Tamils. Among the remaining 17 minority seats, Ponnambalam left "to be determined" the exact number to be allocated to Muslims, Europeans and Burghers. In a draft of the proposal from 1945, Ponnambalam also specified that there should be one seat reserved to represent "Indian commercial interests in the Western province." UKNA FCO 141/2292, Schedule I, Section II(d). Recommendations to Soulbury Commission on Constitutional Reform tendered by G G Ponnambalam.

[116] Clearly, Ponnambalam seems to view the "communal" aspect of religion-based communal representation in India as more important than the "religion" aspect.

[117] UKNA, FCO 141/2292 "Presidential Address from All-Ceylon Tamil Congress," 10.

CONCLUSION

sought to avoid conflict among religious communities by preventing the legislature from passing religiously discriminatory laws; a *protectionist paradigm*, which drew from the discourses of the United Nations and the Indian National Congress and rendered religion as a "fundamental right" which governments were required to guarantee; and a *promotional paradigm*, expressed by the ACBC in particular, which positioned the government as a special supporter of Buddhism on account of its pre-eminent demographic, cultural and historical status and its weakened condition after colonialism. Each of these three paradigms, and the specific idioms of legal phrasing they incorporated or rejected, represented positions in much broader debates: over the function of national constitutions, the proper path to independent government, and the nature of rights and the goals of democracy.

Although honed and advanced by particular groups of politicians and activists, the paradigms were neither mutually exclusive nor immutable. As will be seen in the following chapters, some politicians and religious leaders, pre- and post-1948, were sympathetic to multiple models and a few even preferred to blend elements of all three. Equally, there were figures whose public support for Senanayake, the Young Turks or Buddhist activist groups would shift regularly. Members of the ACBC served in the Ceylon National Congress and on the Board of Ministers (led by Senanayake); and there were dissenters, half-supporters and indifferent parties in each group.

What is most significant about these three paradigms, and particularly the protectionist and promotional, is that they proved remarkably durable in the twentieth-century history of Ceylon/Sri Lanka. In fact, since the 1940s, they have served as the dominant idioms for debating constitutional policies for religion. As subsequent chapters will show, these paradigms function, like primary colors of a palette, as the basic modes for thinking about the legal management of religion in Ceylon; and their blending and contrasting would determine the contours of pyrrhic constitutionalism in the decades to follow.

3

Contesting Constitutions in the 1950s and 1960s

Constitutions often read like revolutionary charters. Using grand language, particularly in their preambles, they seem to mark the end of one epoch and the beginning of another.[1] The act of writing constitutions, however, does not always entail a moment of sudden social combustion. Constitution-making can be a common occurrence, a regular feature of domestic politics – an ongoing slow burn.

This slow-burn style of constitution-making characterizes postcolonial Ceylon/Sri Lanka. Since 1948, agendas for constitutional change have never been far from view. They have simmered away steadily in parliament, in newspapers, in the speeches of religious leaders, and in the reports of governmental and non-governmental commissions. Politics, itself, has frequently taken place in a constitutional register: political parties and candidates have defined themselves according to which models of constitutional reform they advocate. This kind of constitutional politics dominated Ceylon's first two decades of independence, the period between enacting the Constitution of 1948 and the First Republican Constitution of 1972.

During the 1950s and 1960s, protectionist and promotional paradigms of managing religion featured prominently in national politics.[2] The protectionist paradigm underwrote several attempts at drafting a fundamental rights chapter for the constitution. The promotional paradigm appeared clearly in campaigns to give Buddhism "its rightful place" in the island's legal system. During these two decades of slow-burn constitutional politics, politicians advocated constitutional reforms of these types

---

[1] Bruce A Ackerman, *We the People: Foundations* (Cambridge, MA: Belknap Press of Harvard University Press, 1991). Ulrich K Preuss, *Constitutional Revolution: The Link Between Constitutionalism and Progress* (Atlantic Highlands, NJ: Humanities Press, 1995). Asli Bali and Hanna Lerner (eds.), *Constitution Writing, Religion and Democracy* (Cambridge: Cambridge University Press, 2016).

[2] On these paradigms see Chapter 2.

CONTESTING CONSTITUTIONS IN THE 1950S AND 1960S   61

with such regularity that promises of protecting fundamental rights and promoting Buddhist interests become almost *de rigueur* in election manifestos and speeches. By the late 1960s it was difficult to find a major political group that did not advocate one or both of these positions. It is during this period that the pyrrhic constitutionalism of Sri Lankan gained its distinctive rhetorical structure.

While the topics of religious rights and religious freedom increasingly became common foci for political discourse in the 1950s and 1960s, the protections for religion listed in the 1948 Constitution did not become common instruments of litigation, as they would following the enactment of the 1972 Constitution. This lack of religion-related litigation reflects several factors: the importance of other urgent concerns such as language rights for Tamil-speakers, citizenship for Indian Tamil laborers and the nationalization of education (discussed later); and the growing perception that Section 29(2) was a weak instrument for making any type of religious claim.[3] When it came to contests over religion, the real action was in parliament, not in the courts.[4]

This chapter progresses in two sections. Section I focuses on S W R D Bandaranaike, one of the most important figures in Sri Lankan political history and prime minister from 1956 to 1959. Bandaranaike was a key agitator for constitutional reform in the early years of independence. During Bandaranaike's tenure as prime minister, he undertook programs both to promote Buddhism and to implement fundamental rights. It was through Bandaranaike's initiatives that Sri Lankan politics came to merge, popularize and institutionalize the major protectionist and promotional critiques of the 1948 Constitution's religion provisions.

---

[3] This perception spread in the years following independence as the island's courts proved unable or unwilling to use Section 29(2) to block laws that discriminated on the basis of ethnicity and language. There were two important, if unsuccessful, cases in which petitioners challenged legislation on the basis of discrimination against communities, but not with reference to religion. See *Kodakkan Pillai v. Mudanayake*, 54 *New Law Reports* 433 (1953) (challenging the Ceylon Citizenship Act of 1948) and *Attorney General v. Kodeswaran*, 70 *New Law Reports* 121 (1967) (challenging the Official Language Act No. 33 of 1956). See also C F Amarasinghe, "The Legal Sovereignty of the Ceylon Parliament," *Public Law* (1966): 73–81.

[4] During this period, questions about Buddhism did arise in courts. However, they did so in the form of property and succession disputes between Buddhist monks, as matters of Buddhist Ecclesiastical Law (see Chapter 2). For a helpful survey of these cases see W S Weerasooria, *Buddhist Ecclesiastical Law: A Treatise on Sri Lankan Statute Law and Judicial Decisions on Buddhist Temples and Temporalities* (Colombo: Postgraduate Institute of Management, 2011).

62   CONTESTING CONSTITUTIONS IN THE 1950S AND 1960S

Section II focuses on the politics of the 1960s and documents the challenges faced by successive governments in trying to implement the protectionist and promotional paradigms of governance. It documents a trend, from the late 1950s to the late 1960s, whereby politicians became more strident in their pledges to protect fundamental rights and promote Buddhism, while at the same time struggling to articulate how, precisely, the protectionist and promotional paradigms might be implemented in the everyday lives of Sri Lankans.

SECTION I: THE 1950s

Constitutional and Political Culture in the Wake of 1948

When it came to local politics, the years following independence in 1948 looked very similar to the years leading up to it. The same politicians who had run the colonial State Council now ran the postcolonial House of Representatives. The same man who had led the Board of the Ministers, D S Senanayake, now led the government as prime minister. The same group of elite, influential politicians that had shaped politics before 1948 continued to do so after, largely under the banner of the political party that D S Senanayake had formed in 1946, the United National Party (UNP). The same constitution that D S Senanayake had co-drafted in 1943 was now the supreme law of the island. In the first years of independence, it seemed as though political power in Ceylon had shifted from the British to the UNP.[5]

---

[5] The UNP's success during this period also resulted from the fact that there was very little organized opposition in the island's first two parliamentary elections. In the first election, held just prior to independence in 1947, almost all non-UNP candidates ran as independents. Despite some shared goals, these parties largely failed to form alliances. For example, although the Marxist parties all insisted on the need to redistribute the island's wealth, they fought bitterly over the correct interpretation of Marxist doctrine, dividing into supporters of Trotsky, Mao or Stalin. Similarly, although the Tamil Congress and the Indian Congress both represented Tamil-speaking populations, the two groups failed to align their interests on account of the different political agendas pursued by the "Ceylon Tamils" of Jaffna, Colombo and the East Coast and the "Indian Tamil" tea-estate workers of the up-country. With these organized opposition parties unable to collaborate, no coherent challenge to the UNP could evolve. In 1952, several opposition parties managed to form an alliance, however they failed to field a sufficient number of candidates for each electoral district. Wilson, "The Colombo Man." Ceylon Daily News, *The Ceylon Daily News Parliament of Ceylon 1960* (Colombo: Lake House, 1960), 12.

CONSTITUTIONAL AND POLITICAL CULTURE 63

In these early years of independence, tightly centralized political power discouraged constitutional reform. As the prime minister and head of the UNP, D S Senanayake was both the co-author of the 1948 Constitution and the most powerful man in Ceylon. He had recruited into his government many of the island's most outspoken critics of the 1948 Constitution, including the head of the Tamil Congress, G G Ponnambalam, and the man who in years to come would lead the opposition, S W R D Bandaranaike.[6] With these allies, Senanayake resisted calls by Tamil politicians to extend the ambit of Section 29(2) to guarantee citizenship rights, including religious rights, to Tamil tea estate laborers.[7] He also rejected demands made by the All-Ceylon Buddhist Congress to repeal or revise Section 29(2) of the constitution.[8]

In March 1952, Senanayake's control over politics and constitutional reform ended suddenly. While out on his regular morning horseback ride along Colombo's seashore, Senanayake was thrown from his horse. He died shortly afterwards. Without its leader, centrifugal tendencies within the UNP – which Senanayake had held together through charisma and patronage – began to take root.[9] The UNP's political dominance would not last much longer.

---

[6] De Silva, *A History of Sri Lanka*, 600–602.

[7] Senanayake is frequently criticized for disregarding the plight of stateless Tamil Indian tea estate workers in the up-country of Sri Lanka. Although domiciled in Ceylon, some for multiple generations, tens of thousands of workers could not vote or claim rights in either Ceylon or India. The reasons behind Senanayake's refusal to grant citizenship to this population were complex and reflected, among other things, his concern over the growth of labor unions and Marxist politics in the up-country. A J Wilson, "Minority Safeguards in the Ceylon Constitution," *Ceylon Journal of Historical and Social Studies* 1, no. 1 (1958): 73–95. I D S Weerawardana, "The General Elections in Ceylon, 1952," *The Ceylon Historical Journal* 2, no. 1–2 (1952): 109–178.

[8] Government of Sri Lanka, *Hansard Debates, House of Representatives* (Colombo: Government Press), July 24, 1951, 1550–1560.

[9] The factors that strained UNP unity in the early 1950s were captured nicely by two popular jokes that flowed through the capillaries of political satire during this period. The first joke mocked that the United National Party was – contrary to its acronym – neither united nor national nor a (single) party. This joke played upon the common observation that, outside of its shared allegiance to Senanayake, the UNP had not developed firm systems of party organization or discipline. For example, the UNP failed to coordinate the political agendas of its members, and UNP candidates for office regularly propounded their own reform programs at election rallies, ignoring the official party doctrine. In some cases, multiple UNP candidates had even run against each other on the same ticket. Similarly, when UNP members voted in parliament, they often flouted the wishes of party leaders.

64   CONTESTING CONSTITUTIONS IN THE 1950S AND 1960S

An enthusiasm for constitutional change was evident in the lead-up to the general elections of May 1952. Revising the constitution took a prominent place in the campaign manifestos of several opposition parties.[10] These calls for constitutional change resonated in a new culture of Ceylonese politics that emerged after Senanayake's death, one that Ivor Jennings characterized as having a new "undercurrent of opinion":

> It is aggressively nationalist and aggressively Buddhist. In language policy it is anti-English; in religion it is anti-Christian; in foreign policy it is anti-Western; and in economic policy it is both anti-capitalist and anti-socialist. Socially, it might be described as anti-Colombo, because it consists primarily of English-educated young men from the provinces, the sons of small cultivators, minor officials, shop-keepers, and the lower middle-class groups generally. It dislikes the cosmopolitan airs of the products of the big Colombo schools, who dominate Colombo society. It is not a [unified] political movement, but it is politically important because it has the support of the Buddhist *Sangha,* or priesthood, of the teachers in the Sinhalese schools, and of the *vedarala* or practitioners of indigenous medicine, all of whom have strong political influence in the villages ... it is aggressively nationalist: indeed, it is pro-Sinhalese rather than pro-Ceylonese.[11]

Politics in the mid-1950s in Ceylon reflected a new mood of populism, which cut in two directions. On the one hand, it was a populism directed at delivering greater power and political recognition to the

---

A second quip declared that the acronym UNP should not be read as United National Party, but "uncle-nephew party." This joke pointed out the widely recognized fact that, within the UNP, promotion and status seemed to derive less from credentials or performance than from familial links. While the rank-and-file UNP members came from exceedingly broad (and often conflicting) political backgrounds, the elite leadership of the party had a very narrow, nepotistic make-up. Senanayake's relations were well represented both in the senior leadership posts of the UNP and in his legislative cabinet. D S Senanayake's son was Minister of Agriculture. His nephew was leader of the House and the Minister of Transport. Another close relation, J R Jayewardene, was Minister of Finance. Thus, within the UNP, political fealty blurred with familial loyalty, creating a deep divide between the party's central organizing committee and its ordinary members. Amita Shastri, "The United National Party of Sri Lanka: Reproducing Hegemony," in *Political Parties in South Asia,* ed. Subrata Mitra, Mike Enskat and Clemens Spiess (Westport, CT: Praeger, 2004), 238–239. Wriggins, *Ceylon: Dilemmas of a New Nation,* 108–109.

[10] Weerawardana, "The General Elections in Ceylon, 1952," 119, 120, 124.

[11] W Ivor Jennings, "Politics in Ceylon Since 1954," *Pacific Affairs* 27, no. 4 (1954): 338–352.

island's "village-level elites," a group that included village headmen, *ayurvedic* physicians, vernacular school teachers, Buddhist monks and small-holding farmers.[12] In this sense, the new political climate was opposed to the urban, wealthy, English-educated lawyers, plantation owners and industrialists who had dominated parliament since the 1920s.[13] On the other hand, it was a populism directed at giving greater influence to the largest ethnic and religious group on the island, Sinhalese Buddhists.

The 1950s and the Rise of S W R D Bandaranaike

No person better embodies the new populist culture of Ceylonese politics in the mid-1950s and the possibilities of constitutional reform that it presented than S W R D Bandaranaike. Although he came from elite origins, Bandaranaike routinely presented himself as a "man of the people." He was a prominent member of the Colombo Westernized elite, yet at public events he wore the plebian "national dress" of white cloth, banian and shawl.[14] Educated in English at the island's most elite Christian school and at Oxford, he nonetheless addressed audiences in well-practiced Sinhala. Although raised Anglican, he advertised his deep faith in Buddhism, the religion that he had come to adopt formally.[15] Bandaranaike was the son of one of Ceylon's most powerful landowners (and wealthy in his own right) but was prone to conspicuous demonstrations of modesty.[16] In the words of one keen observer,

---

[12] This phrase is borrowed from James Manor who uses it to signal the fact that the "revolution of 1956" does not signal the entrance of the "masses" into politics, but high-status villagers, something like a village "middle-class." James Manor, *The Expedient Utopian: Bandaranaike and Ceylon* (Cambridge: Cambridge University Press, 2009), 250.

[13] One journalist at the time mocked the UNP's wearing of Western clothes as follows: "The top hat and frock coat, which Mr. D. S. Senanayake incongruously affected in imitation of the previous British rulers were the visible ceremonial symbol of the broad community of interests and solidarity between the Ceylonese landowners and the British plantation owners." Denzil Peiris, *1956 and After: Background to Parties and Politics in Ceylon Today* (Colombo: Lake House, 1958), 4. See also: Marshall R Singer, *The Emerging Elite: A Study of Political Leadership in Ceylon* (Cambridge, MA: MIT Press, 1964).

[14] "The National Dress," in S W R D Bandaranaike, *Speeches and Writings* (Colombo: Government Press Ceylon, 1963), 305.

[15] "Why I became a Buddhist" in: Ibid., 287–291.

[16] Manor, *The Expedient Utopian*, 58–59.

66   CONTESTING CONSTITUTIONS IN THE 1950S AND 1960S

Bandaranaike was "[a]n aristocrat who came down from Mount Zion to usher in the age of the common man."[17]

For most of his political career, Bandaranaike was an occasional challenger to and occasional collaborator with D S Senanayake. At times, Bandaranaike vied with the UNP leader for political power and, at times, he acquiesced to his control. Following independence, Bandaranaike joined Senanayake's cabinet as the Minister of Health and Local Government. However in September 1951, ostensibly for having been passed over for leadership of the UNP, Bandaranaike broke away from Senanayake's UNP and formed his own political party, the Sri Lanka Freedom Party (SLFP).

Bandaranaike described his new party, using a Buddhist idiom, as the "middle way" between the Westernized, urban-dwelling, capitalist, established power politicians of the UNP and the radical socialism of the island's leftist political parties.[18] In his speech at the inauguration of the SLFP, Bandaranaike announced that the new party opposed not only the elitism of the UNP but also the 1948 Constitution that its former leader had co-produced. At the first meeting of the SLFP, Bandaranaike affirmed his commitment to producing a "new constitution framed with the approval of the people that will give full effect to both the concepts of freedom as well as democracy."[19] He also asserted that this new constitution would remedy the defects of the 1948 charter – a document "cut off to a great extent from the masses"[20] – both by protecting the fundamental social and political rights of all citizens and by helping to rehabilitate the island's main religion, Buddhism.

Bandaranaike and the Two Paradigms of Constitutional Reform

Bandaranaike, more than any other politician at the time, committed himself firmly to both the protectionist and promotional paradigms of managing religion. The new constitution that he envisioned obliged the state to protect fundamental rights as well as promote Buddhism. Bandaranaike developed these commitments over time, having had deep

---

[17] A J Wilson, *Politics in Sri Lanka 1947–1979* (London: Macmillan, 1974), 178.

[18] Ibid., 125. Wriggins, *Ceylon: Dilemmas of a New Nation*, 122.

[19] Quoted in Maithripala Senanayeke Felicitation Committee, "S.W.R.D. Bandaranaike, the Progenitor of the People's Constitution," in *Maithripala Senanayeke Felicitation Volume* (Dehiwala, Sri Lanka: Tissara Press, 1972), 85.

[20] Ibid.

links with both the Ceylon National Congress and with the All-Ceylon Buddhist Congress. He had been a vocal critic of the 1948 Constitution since its inception, criticizing Senanayake and Jennings severely (between 1943 and 1946) for their tight control over the drafting process. He accused Senanayake of ignoring popular concerns and relying on his "old gang" of loyalists to produce the new charter.[21] Bandaranaike also consulted with Jayewardene, Cooray and others in the development of the Young Turks' Constitution for a Free Lanka, which (as described in Chapter 2) included a section on fundamental rights.[22] In the 1930s and 1940s, Bandaranaike also actively promoted Sinhalese Buddhists' interests, and over the course of the 1940s and early 1950s he supported the All-Ceylon Buddhist Congress.[23]

In 1956, Bandaranaike was elected as the island's first non-UNP prime minister. Almost immediately upon taking office, he took steps to alter the island's constitution. He did so by appointing two government committees: one committee would (among other things) draft a constitutional chapter on fundamental rights; another committee would suggest administrative and legal actions to enhance the position of Buddhism in Ceylon, and give to it its "rightful place."

Bandaranaike treated fundamental rights and Buddhist prerogatives as complementary parts of a populist program of constitutional reform. He argued that the 1948 Constitution had enshrined elite interests, especially those of Senanayake and his close associates, whom he accused of "nepotism and cliquism."[24] In public speeches, Bandaranaike presented fundamental rights and Buddhist privileges as twin elements necessary for a more inclusive national charter, one that reflected and responded to the desires of "the masses."[25] Bandaranaike's proposed fundamental rights, therefore, included social and economic rights,

---

[21] Michael Roberts, "Problems of Collective Identity in a Multi-ethnic Society: Sectional Nationalism vs Ceylonese Nationalism, 1900–1940," in *Collective Identities Revisited (Vol. 1)* (Colombo: Marga Institute Press, 1997), 455.

[22] *Documents of the Ceylon National Congress and Nationalist Politics in Ceylon 1929–1950,* Vol. II, 2591–2594.

[23] Ananda Meegama, *Philip Gunawardena and the 1956 Revolution in Sri Lanka* (Colombo: Godage, 2009), 54–55. Jane Russell, *Communal Politics Under the Donoughmore Constitution, 1931–1947, The Ceylon Historical Journal 26* (Dehiwala, Sri Lanka: Tisara Prakasakayo, 1982), 141–144. Robert Kearney, *Communalism and Language in the Politics of Ceylon* (Durham, NC: Duke University Press, 1967), 35–37.

[24] "The Sri Lanka Freedom Party," in Bandaranaike, *Speeches and Writings,* 141–150.

[25] Ibid., 142–143.

68   CONTESTING CONSTITUTIONS IN THE 1950S AND 1960S

including "freedom from any and every form of agricultural, industrial and social serfdom."[26] In his election manifesto of the SLFP in 1956, Bandaranaike argued that supporting Buddhism was also a type of social reform:

> Buddhism has played a very important role in the lives, thoughts and actions of Sinhalese Buddhists throughout our history. It is woven into our culture, our way of life and our very thoughts and actions. So that in rebuilding our people in this new era of freedom, it is very essential to remedy the injustices done to Buddhism and to enable Buddhists to take the fullest advantage of their religion and culture.[27]

In Bandaranaike's rhetoric, promoting Buddhism, like protecting fundamental rights, would empower and rehabilitate a population whose historical ways of life had been damaged by colonialism.

By the mid-1950s, many of the island's minority political leaders were also articulating their demands using the rhetoric of fundamental rights. Catholic-interest groups framed their desires for greater institutional autonomy (particularly with respect to the administering of educational institutions) as demands for the inclusion of fundamental religious rights in the constitution.[28] Tamil politicians argued for the inclusion of a constitutional chapter on fundamental rights in order to protect specific religious and linguistic interests.[29] In fact, in the lead-up to the general elections of 1956, a "United Front" of Tamil politicians from the UNP and other parties responded to growing popular demands to make Sinhala the sole official language of the state by organizing a campaign to add a new chapter on fundamental rights to the island's constitution.[30] In January of 1956, the Tamil United Front produced a "Charter of Fundamental Rights," which detailed eleven paragraphs of rights for all Ceylonese citizens. These included the rights to life, free assembly,

---

[26] W A Wiswa Warnapala, *Sri Lanka Freedom Party: A Political Profile* (Colombo: Godage International, 2005), 91.

[27] SLFP election manifesto 1956, "Free Lanka," as quoted in I D S Weerawardana, *Ceylon General Election 1956* (Colombo: Gunasena and Sons, 1960), 58.

[28] Catholic Union of Ceylon, *Companion to the Buddhist Commission Report: A Commentary on the Report* (Colombo: Catholic Union Press, 1957), 155–157.

[29] One can see the agitation for fundamental rights in the 1950s as marking a new strategy of legal reform adopted by the Tamil political opposition in the wake of Ponnambalam's failure to gain traction with his 50–50 proposal. C Suntharalingam, *Eylom: Beginnings of the Freedom Struggle: Dozen Documents by C. Sunatharalingam with "Candid Comments and Criticisms by Lord Soulbury" (Pamphlet)* (Jaffna: īzam pancāyutam, 1963).

[30] For a full discussion of this very important legislation see DeVotta, *Blowback*.

equality before the law, equality of language, rights of ownership, equal access to legal remedy and others.[31] No fewer than 8 of the 11 paragraphs of the United Front charter referred to religious rights, including: freedoms to believe and exercise one's religion, freedoms from discrimination on the basis of religion, freedoms to assemble "for the purpose of furthering [religious] interests," "freedoms to claim an equal share of public funds and freedoms to control one's own ritual and educational facilities."[32]

At the same time, Buddhist groups were also demanding increased government support for Buddhism. This took place within an atmosphere of anticipation around the 2,500th anniversary of the Buddha's enlightenment. The date of the anniversary fell in 1956 and many Buddhists on the island viewed this significant event as an occasion for reconfirming the state's commitments to Buddhism. (In the years leading up to it, the government had initiated several large Buddhist projects, such as compiling a Buddhist encyclopedia and translating important Pali texts into Sinhala.)[33] By the mid-1950s, the All-Ceylon Buddhist Congress (ACBC) began to take a more active coordinating role, drawing together a broad spectrum of Buddhist groups into a semi-unified front dedicated to increasing government support for Buddhism.[34]

---

[31] Weerawardana, *Ceylon General Election 1956*, 29, 255–259.   [32] Ibid.

[33] The date had been agreed upon by a number of countries in the region, including Burma, Thailand and Cambodia. Buddhist leaders from all of these countries felt that national and regional celebrations should take place. Buddhists in Sri Lanka kept a particularly close eye on the preparations in Burma and hoped to match the grandeur of the Burmese pageant in Ceylon. In October 1954, the government established a Lanka Bauddha Mandalaya of over 300 members to orchestrate the activities for the celebration. The activities included: completing a Sinhala translation of the Pali Tipiṭaka, writing a compendium of Jataka stories, authoring a Buddhist encyclopedia in English and Sinhala, publishing a special magazine for the Jayanthi, establishing a Chair of Buddhism at the University of Ceylon, creating a series of commemorative postage stamps, renovating important Buddhist archeological sites, convening an international Buddhist conference and an all-Island conference of representatives from Buddhist associations, and establishing an exhibition of Buddhist art. Bond, *The Buddhist Revival in Sri Lanka*. Lanka Bauddha Mandalaya, *An Event of Dual Significance*, ed. Gerald Peiris and S W R de A Samarasinghe (Colombo: Ceylon Ministry of Home Affairs, 1955).

[34] K N O Dharmadasa, "Buddhist Interests, Activists and Pressure Groups," in *History and Politics, Millennial Perspectives: Essays in Honour of K. M. De Silva* (Kandy: International Centre for Ethnic Studies, 1999), 217, 221. Wriggins, *Ceylon: Dilemmas of a New Nation*, 157. In the 1950s, one can identify five major lay Buddhist organizations, each one with a slightly different specialty and focus. The All-Ceylon Buddhist Congress focused on legal-political mobilization; the YMBA was oriented toward young people, sports, and organizing worship programs in Colombo; the Maha Bodhi Society was particularly concerned

70   CONTESTING CONSTITUTIONS IN THE 1950S AND 1960S

Through the interviews and surveys it had undertaken for its 1956 report (described in Chapter 2), the ACBC connected together laity from around the island, along with monks from most of the island's major *nikāya*-s.[35] They also aligned their efforts with three Buddhist organizations that had become extremely influential in the provinces: the first was a network of local temple-based groups designed to coordinate the interests of lay devotees, temple trustees and resident monks, called Buddha Sasana Societies (S: *bauddha śāsana samiti*); the second was a system of monastic councils (S: *saṅgha sabhā*) that organized Buddhist monks at a provincial (and later national) level;[36] the third was a group designed to bring together Buddhist government employees, the Local Government Buddhist Organization (which would become the Local Government Servants Buddhist Association).[37] Not only did these networks link together government employees with lay Buddhists and monks, they also helped to link rural Buddhists with urban Buddhists. By drawing these groups together, the ACBC synchronized the work of what were (until then) largely separate organizations and temples.[38]

By invoking fundamental rights and Buddhist prerogatives, Bandaranaike spoke directly to two growing (and increasingly organized) movements for legal reform on the island: one oriented around the concerns of religious and ethnic minorities, and one oriented around the desires of the Sinhalese Buddhist majority. In his parliamentary addresses, campaign speeches and political manifestos, Bandaranaike blended the two agendas together. His typical synthesis was that, if elected, he would give to Buddhism its "rightful place" while ensuring that no religious groups

---

with training Buddhist missionaries and with the condition of Buddhism in India; the Buddhist Theosophical Society was involved in establishing Buddhist schools; the All-Ceylon Buddhist Women's Congress was involved in mobilizing Buddhist women. It was not uncommon for people in Colombo to be part of two or three of these organizations. Interview with former civil servant, Ananda Guruge, February 19, 2010.

[35] Urmila Phadnis, *Religion and Politics in Sri Lanka* (London: Hurst & Co., 1976), 179. Buddhist Committee of Enquiry, *The Betrayal of Buddhism* (Balangoda: Dharmavijaya Press, 1956), i.

[36] Phadnis estimates 3,500 Buddha Sasana Societies and 72 Monastic Councils. Phadnis, *Religion and Politics in Sri Lanka*, 175–178.

[37] Interview with Ananda Guruge, February 19, 2010.

[38] Dharmadasa, "Buddhist Interests, Activists and Pressure Groups". K N O Dharmadasa, "Buddhism and Politics in Modern Sri Lanka," in *Bhikshuva Saha Lankā Samājeya*, ed. Maduluvave Sobhita et al. (Colombo: Dharmadhutasrama Pirivena, 1997). Bruce Matthews, "Buddhist Activism in Sri Lanka," in *Questioning the Secular State: The Worldwide Resurgence of Religion in Politics*, ed. David Westerlund (New York: St. Martin's Press, 1996).

would be discriminated against or have their religious rights violated. In a speech to parliament in 1951, defending a resolution that established a government department to help support Buddhism, Bandaranaike argued:

> I *make no distinction between one religion and another* nor do I want particular favours for one religion as against another. ... But *I ask [on behalf of] the vast majority of the Buddhists in this country*, whose religion has been linked with their lives for two thousand years and is one which has *suffered more than any other religion under foreign rule, certain just things ... [for]* the establishment of a suitable Department to help in protecting and maintain Buddhism and the Buddhist institutions.[39]

Similarly, in the "ten policies" (*dasa panata*) which Bandaranaike and his coalition endorsed in the 1956 campaign – a formula that echoed the "ten duties of kings" expressed in traditional Buddhist literature (P: *dasarājadhammā*) – he promised to "give complete freedom of religion, *to treat all alike without consideration* of religion but at the same time *to place Buddhism in a position due to it* as the religion of the majority."[40] Thus, regarding religion, Bandaranaike made conflicting promises: he would treat all religions identically, while simultaneously distinguishing Buddhism as the religion that was most important, most in need of support, and most damaged by colonialism.

In his campaign rhetoric, Bandaranaike treated fundamental rights and Buddhist privileges as corresponding features of a new constitution. Yet, as prime minister, Bandaranaike pursued these constitutional reforms independently through two government committees. One committee, the Joint Select Committee on the Revision of the Constitution, was charged with drafting a chapter on fundamental rights; a second commission, the Buddha Sasana Commission, was charged with identifying and implementing an appropriate program for promoting Buddhism. Both committees responded in their own way to popular frustrations with the 1948 Constitution. However, in their findings, each

---

[39] Government of Sri Lanka, *Hansard Debates, House of Representatives*, July 24, 1951, p. 1514, resolution quoted on p. 1538, emphasis mine.

[40] Weerawardana, *Ceylon General Election 1956*, 146, emphasis mine. It is interesting to contrast this with the UNP's official campaign statement on religion, which made similar points: "Buddhism is the religion practised by the vast majority of the people of this country. We have always recognised this fact in all our actions and will continue to do so. Consistent, however, with the true principles of democracy we will continue to recognise the policy of nondiscrimination on religious grounds which is embodied in our constitution," United National Party, *General Election 1956 Manifesto* (Colombo: n.p., March, 1956), 7.

72 CONTESTING CONSTITUTIONS IN THE 1950S AND 1960S

committee effectively ignored the work of the other: Buddhist privileges did not find their way into the list of religious rights generated by the Joint Select Committee; fundamental rights to religious freedom were not mentioned explicitly in the findings of the Buddha Sasana Commission. Although Bandaranaike had imagined protectionist and promotional reforms as linked vectors of constitutional change, separate committees worked independently to enact them.

Implementing Fundamental Rights: The Joint Select Committee on the Revision of the Constitution

Bandaranaike pushed for constitutional reform from the beginning of his term as prime minister. Only one month after elections, in one of his earliest speeches as prime minister, Bandaranaike announced that he sought parliament's approval to convene a Joint Select Committee of the House of Representatives and the Senate to consider the revision of the constitution. Among the core revisions that Bandaranaike urged the committee to consider was the inclusion of a chapter on fundamental rights:

> In our present Constitution there is no adequate statement of fundamental rights; fundamental rights as affecting all citizens [and] ... the minority sections of the general community. There is no statement beyond Article [sic] 29 which itself is not very satisfactory.[41]

Bandaranaike pitched the Joint Select Committee as an opportunity to enhance the scope and adequacy of the constitution by adding fundamental rights to it.[42] This, he insisted, would create "a Constitution more fitted to mete out justice to all sections of the people, to secure machinery for the speedier achievement of our full stature as a free people, in whatever sphere it may be, politically, economically, socially, culturally."[43] Bandaranaike presented the work of the committee both as a concession to populist demands as well as a direct response to the frustrations and calls for reform offered by Tamil minority politicians

---

[41] S W R D Bandaranaike, "Revision of the Constitution (Speech Made as Prime Minister, 7 Nov 1957)," in *Towards a New Era: Selected Speeches of S.W.R.D. Bandaranaike*, ed. G E P De S Wickramaratne (Colombo: Government Press, 1961), 137.

[42] The committee's terms of reference included the following: (1) the establishment of a Republic, (2) the guaranteeing of fundamental rights, (3) the position of the Senate and Appointed Members of the House of Representatives, and (4) the Public Service Commission and the Judicial Service Commission. Hansard, House of Representatives, April 26, 1957, p. 2784.

[43] S W R D Bandaranaike, "Revision of the Constitution," 142.

IMPLEMENTING FUNDAMENTAL RIGHTS 73

(as described earlier). He further suggested that "even the question of federation" – the call for a federal state proposed by many members of the Tamil political opposition – would be considered.[44]

Bandaranaike's motion passed and the Joint Select Committee met for the first time on March 14, 1958. The 18-member committee was a remarkably diverse group, in its religious, ethnic, caste, geographical and political make-up. It included Christians, Buddhists, Muslims and Hindus; Up-country and Low-country Sinhalese, Ceylonese and Indian Tamils; and representatives from almost all of the major political parties, including the SLFP, the UNP, the LSSP, the Ceylon Communist Party, and the Federal Party. Only six members were Sinhalese Buddhists and only seven members represented Bandaranaike's government.[45]

The Joint Committee began their work by soliciting feedback from the public. They distributed written questionnaires, asking respondents which fundamental rights should be included and how those rights should be enforced.[46] After reviewing these questionnaires, the committee deliberated for several sessions. On March 5, 1959, the Joint Committee issued a statement indicating that it had finalized a list of fundamental rights that "were generally approved for inclusion in the Constitution, to be considered further in the form of draft legislation."[47] It further suggested that "officers possessing the necessary knowledge of constitutional law and practice" should begin to prepare "detailed material necessary in future deliberation."[48] A draft chapter on Fundamental Rights was produced soon after.

Although largely ignored in Sri Lankan historiography, the committee's recommendations for fundamental rights were substantial and extremely progressive. The committee produced a chapter on fundamental rights

---

[44] Ibid., 136, 139–140.

[45] Nihal Jayawickrama, "Human Rights: The Sri Lankan Experience 1947–1981," Unpublished Ph.D. Thesis, University of London, September, 1983, 55–56. The committee included S W R D Bandaranaike, Stanley De Zoysa, D P R Gunawardena, T B Ilangaratne, M D Banda, S J V Chelvanayakam, Colvin R. de Silva, Gate Mudaliya, M S Kariapper, P G B Keuneman, N M Perera, and R S V Poulier. Chelvanayakam withdrew from the committee in September 1958 following the failure of the Bandaranaike-Chelvanayakam pact. Government of Sri Lanka, *Hansard Debates, House of Representatives*, October 2, 1958, pp. 1002–1006.

[46] Government of Ceylon, *Report from the Joint Select Committee of the Senate and the House of Representatives Appointed to Consider the Revision of the Constitution Together with Minutes of Proceedings (Parliamentary Series No. 12)* (Colombo: Government Press, April 4, 1958), 9, 12.

[47] Minutes to meeting, date March 5, 1959, mimeographed copy in Jayewardene Centre Library in Colombo. Box # 000260.

[48] Jayawickrama, "Human Rights: The Sri Lankan Experience 1947–1981," 58.

74 CONTESTING CONSTITUTIONS IN THE 1950S AND 1960S

that reached far beyond the bills of rights suggested in the 1940s. Rather than basing its draft on European models, the committee replicated (with some minor changes) the extensive section on Fundamental Rights in the Constitution of India. The chapter included eight sections: "equality before the law," "protection of life and personal liberty," "protection of rights regarding property, professions, businesses, etc.," "freedom of conscience etc.," and "freedom to manage religious affairs," "protection of any distinct language, script or culture," and "right of citizens to establish and administer educational institutions." Religion was mentioned in a number of provisions, most of which followed the Indian model closely.

Below, I present excerpts from the draft chapter while also indicating the differences between the Ceylonese and Indian versions.[49] As presented, I take the Indian Constitution as a baseline: words added to the Ceylonese chapter (which are not found in the Indian Constitution) are marked in italics; other wording changes are indicated with brackets; all unmarked portions mirror sections from the Constitution of India exactly.

Equality before the law [based on Article 15 of the Indian Constitution]

4. (1) the State shall not discriminate against any citizen on grounds only of religion, race, caste, sex, place of birth, or any of them.

(2) No citizen shall on the grounds of only religion, race, caste, sex, place of birth, or any of them be subject to any disability, liability, restriction or condition with regard to:

a. Access to shops, public restaurants, hotels and places of public entertainment; or

b. The use of wells, tanks, bathing places [the Indian Constitution has "bathing ghats"], roads and places of public resort maintained wholly or partly out of state funds or dedicated to the use of the general public.

(3) Nothing in this section shall prevent the State from making any special provisions for the advancement of any socially or educationally backward

---

[49] A final copy was never published by the government or presented to parliament. However, I did manage to locate multiple copies of the draft chapter on fundamental rights prepared by Bandaranaike's Joint Select Committee in separate archives on the island. I found one copy appended to submissions made to the Ministry of Constitutional Affairs in 1971. SLNA MCA 73/2/117. I use this for the analysis below. I also found another draft, which appears to be a mimeographed original from the Committee, in the personal archives of former president J R Jayewardene, housed at the Jayewardene Centre Library in Colombo. This copy includes references to the relevant passages from the Indian Constitution on which each of the draft's provisions were based. I indicate these references in the text to follow. Date March 5, 1959. Box # 000260.

IMPLEMENTING FUNDAMENTAL RIGHTS

classes of citizen. [The Indian Constitution includes sections on women and children as well as scheduled castes and tribes.]

Freedom of Conscience Etc. [based on Article 25 of the Indian Constitution]

8. All persons are entitled to freedom of conscience and worship and worship [*sic*] and the right freely to profess and practise [the Indian Constitution says "and propagate"] religion. Provided that nothing in the preceding provisions of this Section shall affect the operation of any existing law or prevent the State from making any law regulating or restricting any economic, financial, political or other secular activity which may be associated with religious practice. [The Indian Constitution adds an additional section, Art. 25(2)(b), regarding the state's ability to "[throw] open" public Hindu religious institutions to "all classes and sections of Hindus."]

Freedom to Manage Religious Affairs [based on Article 26 of the Indian Constitution]

9. (1) Subject to public order every religious denomination or any section thereof shall have the right to establish and maintain institutions for religious and charitable purposes, to manage its own affairs in matters of religion [the Indian Constitution adds "to own and acquire movable and immovable property"] and to administer its property in accordance with the law.

(2) [Based on Section 29(2) of Ceylon's 1948 Constitution.] *No law shall alter the constitution of any religious body, except with the consent of the governing authority of that body, and in any case where a religious body is incorporated by law no such alteration shall be made except at the request of the governing authority of that body.*

(3) No law or administrative act shall – (a) prohibit or restrict the free exercise of any religion or (b) make persons of any religion liable to disabilities or restrictions to which persons of other religions are not made liable: or (c) confer on persons of any religion any advantage which is not conferred on persons of other religions.

Right of Citizens to Establish and Administer Educational Institutions [based on Article 30 of the Indian Constitution]

11. (1) *All citizens* [the Indian Constitution says "all minorities"], *irrespective of race* or language [the Indian Constitution says "based on religion or language"], shall have the right to establish and administer educational institutions [the Indian Constitution says "of their choice"] *if they conform to the educational standards and policy laid down by law: Provided that such establishment and administration shall not be deemed to confer on the citizens concerned any right or [to] receive any assistance financial or otherwise from the State except in accordance with the law.*

76   CONTESTING CONSTITUTIONS IN THE 1950S AND 1960S

> (2) The State shall not, in granting aid to educational institutions, discriminate against any educational institution on the ground that is under the management of any section of the citizens whether based on religion or language.

In some ways, the chapter drafted by Bandaranaike's Joint Select Committee was an accumulation and culmination of all the religion policies proposed previously by politicians in Ceylon. The Joint Select Committee integrated Section 29(2) of the 1948 Constitution into the chapter under "Freedom to Manage Religious Affairs" – and affixed to it a section preventing the execution of discriminatory "administrative acts" as well as laws.[50] The chapter added a further list of positive religious rights and freedoms, which the state would be responsible for guaranteeing: freedom of conscience, worship and practice; the right to establish and maintain religious institutions; and the right to manage one's own religious property, places of worship and religious affairs. In terms of implementation, the Joint Select Committee draft gave to the Supreme Court original jurisdiction over fundamental rights petitions.[51] The draft also introduced judicial review of legislation, specifying that legislation deemed "inconsistent" with the fundamental rights provisions would be declared void.[52]

Like the various drafts and manifestos written by the Young Turks, the Joint Select Committee's chapter borrowed extensively from the Constitution of India – so much so that one learns more by analyzing its deviations than by analyzing its consistencies. One important difference between the two versions, which will become important in later chapters, pertains to the terms of "Freedom of Conscience, etc." Where the Indian Constitution allowed citizens to "propagate" religion, the Joint Select Committee's draft did not. This difference reflected popular anxieties over Christian proselytism on the island (see Chapter 7). Similarly, the Joint Select Committee draft excluded the right, contained in the Indian version, for religious groups to "own and acquire movable and

---

[50] In the copy contained among J R Jayewardene's personal papers, a note specifies that "[t]he Committee agreed that for the purposes of Fundamental Rights the expression 'State' shall be defined to include the Government and Parliament of Ceylon and all local and other authorities within Ceylon." Date March 5, 1959. Box # 000260.

[51] Section 13. A note appended to the front of J R Jayewardene's draft reads as follows: "The Committee considered the question of the Privy Council as a final Court of Appeal, arising from Question No. A.6 of the Questionnaire. They were of the opinion that appeals to the Privy Council should be set up to adjudicate on constitutional issues as well as to entertain appeals from the Supreme Court." Ibid.

[52] Section 14(2).

immovable property." This omission likely reflected the influence of Buddhist groups, including the ACBC, who had called upon the government to audit, and even restrict, the wealth of Christian churches (see Chapter 2). Finally, the draft written by the Joint Select Committee included far fewer education rights than the Indian Constitution. This decision was likely made in order to allow the government to nationalize the island's school system – a goal that, as will be discussed later, was important to politicians and lobbyists at the time.

One can infer that Bandaranaike was pleased with the draft. Not long after receiving it, he took steps to commence a formal drafting process. He held talks with a former Attorney-General, T S Fernando, who was serving on the International Commission of Jurists in Geneva, Switzerland. He also consulted with a Lecturer of Constitutional Law at the University of Ceylon. The Lecturer, J A L Cooray, was the same legal scholar who had prepared the Young Turks' bill of rights.[53] By March 1959, the Joint Select Committee and Bandaranaike had given the push for fundamental rights in Ceylon unprecedented momentum.

Implementing Buddhist Rights: The Buddha Sasana Commission

Bandaranaike's efforts to introduce a constitutional chapter on fundamental rights gained significant traction in parliament. It was Bandaranaike's initiatives regarding Buddhism, however, that seemed to garner more attention in public. In appointing the commission on Buddhism, Bandaranaike responded directly to the concerns of many of the voters who had brought him into power – activist monks, Buddhist lay groups and rural village elites. These voters had expressed frustration with the condition of Buddhism in Ceylon, the damages done to it by colonialism and the perceived threats to its vitality by Christian groups.

Bandaranaike signaled his commitments to Buddhism soon after being elected. At the opening of parliament in 1956, Bandaranaike and his entire coalition arrived at the legislature wearing the traditional white shirts and white sarongs of Buddhist laity. Soon thereafter, he and his cabinet made a pilgrimage to Kandy to worship at the island's holiest Buddhist relic, at the famous Temple of the Tooth.[54]

---

[53] Jayawickrama, "Human Rights: The Sri Lankan Experience 1947–1981," 58.

[54] Josine van der Horst, *Who Is He, What Is He Doing?: Religious Rhetoric and Performances in Sri Lanka During R. Premadasa's Presidency (1989–1993)* (Amsterdam: VU University Press, 1995), 108–111.

78 CONTESTING CONSTITUTIONS IN THE 1950S AND 1960S

As with the Joint Select Committee, Bandaranaike appointed the Buddha Sasana Commission shortly after taking office in February 1957. The commission consisted of ten monks and six laymen. Five members of the new commission (three of the ten monks and two of the five laymen) had served on the previous Committee of Inquiry convened by the All-Ceylon Buddhist Congress.[55] The commission's mandate required the members "to inquire into and report on the following matters":

(1) Such [sic] of the proposals contained in the Report dated February 4 1956 of the Committee of Inquiry appointed by the All-Ceylon Buddhist Congress as relate to –
(a) the establishment of a Buddha Sasana Council for the purpose of promoting the welfare of the Buddha Sasana, and (b) the constitution of ecclesiastical courts having exclusive jurisdiction in matters relating to the Sangha;

(2) the measures that should be adopted –
(a) for securing the efficient management and supervision of Buddhist temporalities; (b) for providing facilities for the training and education of bhikkhus and the nature and extent of such facilities; and (c) for preventing persons who have not been duly ordained as bhikkhus from assuming the habit of bhikkhus;

(3) the registration of Buddhist places of worship for the purpose of control or recognition by the Buddha Sasana Council or such other body as may be established for the promotion of the welfare of the Buddha Sasana;

(4) any other matter, whether incidental to the matters aforesaid or not, which, in your opinion is necessary for the *purpose of according Buddhism its rightful place in Ceylon.*[56]

Looking at the terms of reference, one sees immediately the influence of Malalasekera and the ACBC's critiques. The first goal of the commission was to consider further the recommendations of the ACBC Committee Report (discussed in Chapter 2); and the three remaining objectives coincided closely with the problems and suggestions discussed in various chapters of the report.

[55] Government of Ceylon, *Interim Report of the Buddha Sasana Commission (Sessional Paper XXV of 1957)* (Colombo: Government Press, November, 1957), 2. Madihe Pannasiha Mahanāyaka Thero; Balangoda Ananda Maitreya Mahānāyaka Thero; Kotahena Pannakitti Thero; P de S Kularatne; C D S Siriwardena.

[56] Ibid., 2, emphasis mine.

The Buddha Sasana Commission deliberated for two years. It met with monks, lay Buddhist groups, and individuals. It also fielded letters from the public. In the end, the commission confirmed and added to most of the very same suggestions that had been offered by the ACBC Committee. In particular, it suggested that the government ought to set up a Buddha Sasana Council. That council would then oversee the ordination and registration of Buddhist monks, help generate and administer a code of conduct for the entire monkhood, promote the spread of Buddhism on the island and overseas, manage temple donations, standardize and regulate the building of temples and establish ecclesiastical courts so that monks would not have to take their disputes to civil courts. The commission also made suggestions for improving monastic education, for setting up Buddhist-run public schools and for establishing collective temple trusts in rural villages.[57]

While the Buddha Sasana Commission did not offer a revised version of Section 29(2) of the 1948 Constitution (something the Joint Select Committee had been working on), it did recommend a kind of constitutional statute that would give Buddhism its "rightful place" in the country. The statute, like the one proposed in the ACBC Report, was to be called the Buddha Sasana Act (*buddhaśāsana paṇata*). Through it, Ceylon's parliament would create a powerful, state-sponsored Buddha Sasana Council (*buddhaśāsana maṇḍalaya*, anglicized as Buddha Sasana Mandalaya) recommended by the commission.[58] Once the statute was passed, the commission reasoned, the Buddha Sasana Council could take charge of organizing and overseeing all necessary reforms. In short, the Council would be a national authority related to all Buddhist activities. As proposed, the Council would contain three limbs: a supreme monastic committee (*uttarasaṅghasabhāva*) comprised of 50 monks plus a president who would handle all affairs related to the monkhood, a *sāsana* assembly (*śāsanasaṅgamaya*) of no more than 101 lay and monastic members who would address broader Buddhist issues, and an executive working committee (*kṛtyavidhāyakasaṅsadaya*) to be elected from among them.[59] Appointments would be made according to a mixture of government selection and public elections. As with the ACBC's earlier suggestions, the entire system was to be modeled on Burma's 1950 Buddha Sasana Council Act.[60]

---

[57] Government of Ceylon, *Buddha Śāsana Komiṣan Vārtāva (Buddha Sasana Commission Report)* (Colombo: Government Press, 1959).

[58] Ibid., 245–270.   [59] Ibid., 246.

[60] The ACBC Committee of Inquiry had recommended that a similar Buddha Sasana Council (Mandalaya) be set up by statute.

80 CONTESTING CONSTITUTIONS IN THE 1950S AND 1960S

The Buddha Sasana Commission imagined the Act as more than normal legislation. This was to be a foundational law mandating special governmental obligations for Buddhism. In defending the need for such a statute, the commission echoed the earlier writings of the ACBC. It stressed the unique burdens placed on Buddhism as a result of colonialism. The Buddha Sasana Act would remedy the damages done to Buddhism by the Portuguese, Dutch and British, the commission argued, by requiring the government to specially safeguard Buddhist institutions and teachings, as well as by enhancing the organization, discipline and (therefore) prestige of the island's Buddhist monks.

In proposing these reforms, Bandaranaike and the authors of the Buddha Sasana Commission walked a fine line between stipulating state support for Buddhism and recommending state supervision over Buddhist monks, rites and places of worship. Bandaranaike had been clear that he did not want Buddhism to be a "state religion";[61] nevertheless, the reforms proposed by the Buddha Sasana Commission seemed to vest a significant amount of supervisory responsibility in government-appointed bodies rather than in the monastic fraternities themselves. As read by some monks, the arrangement subordinated monastic authority to state authority, making the government – not the monks – the chief authorities and protectors of Buddhism.

Even before Bandaranaike's Buddha Sasana Commission submitted a final report in June 1959, it came under strong criticism from a variety of groups. Some non-Buddhists saw the report as a containing a plan for the government to elevate Buddhism over and above the island's other religious traditions. For example, the Ceylon Catholic Union published in 1957 a critical commentary on the ACBC Report, entitled "Companion to the Buddhist Commission Report." In it, the writers railed against the ACBC report, and its would-be implementers.[62] The commission also offended Buddhists, particularly the leaders of the two main branches of the island's oldest and wealthiest monastic fraternity: the Malvatu and Asgiri branches of the Siyam Nikāya. In the absence of a universally recognized island-wide monastic hierarchy (see Chapter 6), the *mahānāyaka*-s, or great leaders, of the Malvatu and Asgiri branches

---

[61] Government of Sri Lanka, *Hansard Debates, House of Representatives,* July 24, 1951, p. 1414.

[62] Catholic Union of Ceylon, *Companion to the Buddhist Commission Report: A Commentary on the Report.*

had a wide reputation as being the *de facto* spokespersons for Buddhism in Ceylon. It was therefore highly significant that these Buddhist leaders saw the report as an assault on the autonomy and power of Buddhist monks.[63] In verbal and written plaints directed to the government, the *mahānāyaka*-s argued that the formation of a Buddha Sasana Council – with powers to audit temple funds, survey temple lands, register monks, and authenticate ordination records – would put Buddhist clerics under the control of government authorities. They forbade their junior monks from participating in the workings of the commission and publically repudiated the project as a perversion of the traditional Buddhist hierarchy: the proposed structures, they argued, would invidiously position lay persons as dictating the terms of Buddhist monasticism to Buddhist monks.[64] When the final report was tendered, the Siyam Nikāya monks rejected it out of hand.[65]

Routinizing and Rationalizing the Promotional and Protectionist Paradigms

Through politicking and government initiatives, S W R D Bandaranaike routinized constitutional reform as a mode of national politics. He transformed the protectionist and promotional criticisms of the 1948 Constitution from tropes of political opposition into discrete campaign promises and political initiatives. The protectionist paradigm of managing religion underwrote the strong protections for religion contained in the Joint Select Committee's draft. The promotional paradigm of managing religion underwrote the report of The Buddha Sasana Commission, which, although controversial, would become standard reading and reference for a growing number of politicians

---

[63] On the history of the Siyam Nikāya, see: Malalgoda, *Buddhism in Sinhalese Society, 1750–1900*. Anne M Blackburn, *Buddhist Learning and Textual Practice in Eighteenth-Century Lankan Monastic Culture* (Princeton, NJ; Oxford, UK: Princeton University Press, 2001).

[64] Donald E Smith, "The Sinhalese Buddhist Revolution," in *South Asian Politics and Religion* (Princeton, NJ: Princeton University Press, 1966), 477. Phadnis, *Religion and Politics in Sri Lanka*, 216.

[65] "Divergent Views on Sasana Report," *World Buddhism*, January 1960, p. 10. See also: C D S Siriwardena, "The Idea of A Buddha Sasana Council," in *University Buddhist Annual, Vol. 2*, ed. Tilak Gunasekere (Colombo: University Buddhist Brotherhood of Colombo, 1959).

82   CONTESTING CONSTITUTIONS IN THE 1950S AND 1960S

who sought to follow in Bandaranaike's footsteps in giving the majority religion its "rightful place."

As indicated earlier, Bandaranaike did not see these two vectors of constitutional reform as antithetical. Fundamental rights and Buddhist prerogatives were, for him, complementary constitutional projects. Bandaranaike saw deep philosophical links between democracy (which he defined as "an agglomeration of freedoms, individual and collective"[66]), human rights and Buddhist teachings. "I believe in democracy," he asserted in a speech to Buddhist lay organizations in 1950, "because I believe in the Buddhist Doctrine, that a man's worth should be measured by his own merit and not some extraneous circumstance, and also that human freedom is a priceless possession."[67] For Bandaranaike, Buddhism secured freedom of the mind in the same way that fundamental rights secured freedom of the body. In an undated speech transcript that Bandaranaike penned for a celebration of the Buddha's birthday, he mused:

> Let us also remember the essential freedom and nobility of Man that the Buddha teaches – freedom of thought, the fundamental supremacy of the human mind, liberation from the shackles of superstition and that ultimately self-respect frees us from dependence even on a God. Freedom of thought because He [the Buddha] does not wish us to accept any doctrine merely because it conforms to rules of logic or because it is propounded by some respected teacher, or because it appears in some ancient book of high repute, or for any such reason, but only because we ourselves feel convinced of its correctness.[68]

Thus, Bandaranaike concluded, Buddhism raised humanity from "that primeval abyss" in which it is "shackled and bound with many [mental] bonds" to the "ultimate pinnacle of human freedom."[69]

Yet neither this vision of human rights nor this vision of Buddhism conformed to those of Ceylon's minority politicians or monastic elites. Fundamental rights, for Sri Lanka's religious and linguistic minorities, meant not simply a disembodied commitment to "the essential freedom of Man," it implied concrete measures for guaranteeing the protection

---

[66] See "The Democratic Tradition" and "Democracy in Asian Countries," in Bandaranaike, *Speeches and Writings*, 401–404, 505–414, quote from 401.

[67] "Buddhism – A New Force in the World," in ibid., 308.

[68] Excerpt from the manuscript draft of a speech written by Bandaranaike, titled "Message to the Buddhists," SLNA 25.23/529, n.d.

[69] Ibid.

ROUTINIZING AND RATIONALIZING 83

of individuals and communities. Similarly, Buddhism, for Sri Lanka's monastic leaders, was not, as Bandaranaike envisaged, a tradition free from ritual, hierarchy and clerisy, one which relied solely on practitioners' "own conviction of [the *dhamma*'s] correctness."[70] In the eyes of the Malvatu and Asgiri *mahānāyaka*-s of the Siyam Nikāya, Buddhism was a rarefied system that needed to be administered and controlled by the *sangha* itself. It was also a system in which monks received "equal adoration with the Buddha and the Dhamma."[71]

Where Bandaranaike saw an obvious link between fundamental rights and Buddhist prerogatives, many in Ceylon – particularly members of minority communities – did not. An editorial from the leading Catholic journal at the time captures the differences in perspective very clearly:

> [I]n his presidential address the Premier spoke of incorporating fundamental rights in the Constitution so that there would be no discrimination against a person of a minority community or religion. But what we would like to know is how this can be done in the light of the Sinhala Only Act [which made Sinhalese the sole official language of the state][72] and the implementation of the recommendations of the Buddhist Commission report to which the Government is committed. A member of the present Government naively stated at the Conference that the recommendations of the Buddhist Commission would be implemented without doing any harm to the Catholics. I am still wondering how it can be done and whether the implications of the recommendations of the Commission have been fully realised by the persons who make such statements and give such categorical assurances. In the absence of clear statements of how these safeguards are to be provided, I do not think one can be blamed for not taking too seriously these pious protestations of justice and fair play.[73]

The author of the editorial, writing under the pseudonym "Scrutinator," pointed to what many felt was a core inconsistency in Bandaranaike's political platform: how could he advocate policies of non-discrimination

---

[70] Ibid. Bandaranaike carries on "when a religion begins to operate through an established church, the true spirit of the religion tends to be obscured and smothered in the glittering vestments of ritual observance, and dogma." See also Bandaranaike's introduction to Various Medical Men, *Ceylon's Uplift (Through Buddhism)* (Colombo: Lake House, 1940).

[71] As quoted in the pamphlet, *The Memorial of the Mahanayake Theros and Anunayake Theros of Malwatte and Asigiriya Viharas to His Excellency Sir Oliver Goonetilleke* (n.p., February 2, 1958), iv.

[72] On this see DeVotta, *Blowback*.   [73] *Catholic Messenger*, March 23, 1957, p. 5.

84   CONTESTING CONSTITUTIONS IN THE 1950S AND 1960S

with regards to religion while at the same time promote policies that favored one religion over another?

Bandaranaike never answered these questions. On the morning of September 26, 1959, he was assassinated. His killer was a Buddhist monk. When Bandaranaike knelt down to pay homage to him, the robed man shot him with a pistol hidden inside folds of saffron cloth.

SECTION II: THE 1960s

Buddhism and the Politics of the 1960s

Although unsuccessful, Bandaranaike's attempted constitutional reforms had lasting impacts on Ceylon's politics. In the elections of 1960, almost every contesting party promised to pursue some or all aspects of Bandaranaike's constitutional reforms. The minority and leftist political parties – such as the Federal Party, Tamil Congress, LSSP (*Laṅkā Sama Samāja Pakṣaya,* the Lankan Equal Society Party) and CP (Communist Party) – promised to work toward the incorporation of fundamental rights in the constitution. The Sinhala nationalist parties – such as the MEP (*Mahajana Eksath Peramuṇa,* the People's United Front, which broke with the SLFP in 1960) and the JVP (*Jātika Vimukti Peramuṇa,* National Liberation Front) – pledged to implement the recommendations of the Buddha Sasana Commission. The largest parties, the UNP and the SLFP, pledged to do both. They would introduce a constitutional chapter on fundamental rights as well as review and implement the recommendations of Bandaranaike's Buddha Sasana Commission.[74] By the end of the decade, it would become virtually standard practice for political parties to state publically their commitment both to constitutional fundamental rights and to securing the "rightful place" for Buddhism.

The political climate of the 1960s differed from that of the 1940s and 1950s in certain key respects when it came to managing religion. Following Bandaranaike's death, it was no longer enough to speak generally about fundamental rights or Buddhism. In the 1960s, politicians, interest groups and voters began to query what, exactly, was meant by these policies. Precisely, how would politicians determine

---

[74] Ceylon Daily News, *The Ceylon Daily News Parliament of Ceylon 1960.*

the composition of fundamental rights? What did it really mean to give Buddhism its "rightful place"?[75]

Giving Buddhism its "Rightful Place"

Of the two paradigms of constitutional reform, it was initiatives to promote Buddhism that were most prominent in the first half of the 1960s. In 1960, Bandaranaike's widow, Sirima, took control of the party that her husband had founded. In the SLFP election manifesto from March 1960, she declared:

> Mr. Bandaranaike's government, in fulfillment of its policy, appointed the Buddha Sasana Commission to make recommendations for the reform of the Sangha. We recognise that there is a need for such reform, and we are pledged to examine the report of the Sasana Commission with a view to implementing such reform in accordance with the principles of the Vinaya, and to give legislative sanction and authority to Sangha, for that purpose.[76]

As presented in the manifesto, Mrs. Bandaranaike's policies for Buddhism would simply continue her late husband's policies. She would carry on with the task of formally reviewing and implementing the Buddha Sasana Commission report. Immediately after taking office, in her announcement of policy on the first day of parliament, she declared her intention to create a Buddha Sasana Mandalaya.[77]

Despite this initial enthusiasm, Mrs. Bandaranaike found the practicalities of giving Buddhism its "rightful place" to be extremely thorny. During the period of 1960–1964, she and her government negotiated, with difficulty, an official position on Buddhism. In formulating that position, they had to balance the interests of three influential constituencies, each of which differed in its views on the proper role of the government in supporting Buddhism. First, they contended with the

---

[75] At the same time, there was growing popular participation in government with increasingly larger percentages of people voting at general elections, from 69% in 1956 to 76% in 1960 to 82% in 1965. A J Wilson, *Electoral Politics in An Emergent State: The Ceylon General Election of May 1970* (Cambridge: Cambridge University Press, 1975), 30.

[76] SLFP Election Manifesto 1960. The UNP made a similar promise to "guarantee of freedom of religion to all resident in Ceylon. Grant the Nikayas with consent, a corporate status by legislation. Establish a Sasana Mandalaya consisting of representatives of the Sangha and the laity to work for the welfare of both without the infringement of the autonomy of the Nikayas."

[77] "New Premier Promises to Help Buddhism," *World Buddhism*, August 1960, p. 6.

86   CONTESTING CONSTITUTIONS IN THE 1950S AND 1960S

desires of lay Buddhist organizations from Colombo – such as the All-Ceylon Buddhist Congress and the Young Men's Buddhist Association – that were calling for the whole-scale implementation of the Buddha Sasana Commission Report and the near-term creation of a Buddha Sasana Mandalaya. Concerned with (what they saw as) Buddhist monks' growing laxity, these groups demanded significant, government-led restructuring of the monkhood, including the legal enforcement of monastic codes of conduct and the creation of separate monastic disciplinary courts.[78] They also advocated measures to limit the abilities of monks to undertake non-religious occupations by banning them from salaried employment and forbidding them from participating in government. Second, Bandaranaike and her government had to contend with monastic and lay groups – including the *sangha sabhā* (monastic councils) of the Amarapura and Rāmañña Nikāya-s and the newly formed but very outspoken Bauddha Jathika Balavegaya (Buddhist National Force)[79] – that called for a partial and more cautious implementation of the report. These groups wanted to create a central monastic organization but to leave ultimate authority for monastic affairs with the chief prelates of the different *nikāya-s*.[80] Third, Mrs. Bandaranaike had to contend with the powerful *mahānāyaka-s* of the Siyam Nikāya in Kandy, who had rejected the Buddha Sasana Commission and the entire project of monastic reform. The *mahānāyaka-s* maintained that, while

---

[78] See the editorial, "The Problem of the Sangha in the Present Day," in the YMBA-published journal *The Buddhist*, February 1964, p. 1.

[79] This organization was created by L H Mettananda, former principal of the island's most prestigious Buddhist secondary school and active participant in the ACBC Buddhist Committee of Inquiry. Mettananda formed the BJB with the help of influential government officials in order to provide a more outspoken platform for promoting "Buddhists' rights" but also, particularly, toward combating what they saw as Catholic privileges in public life. Regarding monastic reform, the BJB specified: "We acknowledge and recognize the principle that the problems pertaining to the Sangha should be settled by the Sangha themselves according to the letter and the spirit of the Dhamma [the Buddha's teaching]. In accordance with this principle we urge the setting up of Sanghadhikaranas [monastic courts] – recognized by the Government – at which all disputes among the Sangha will be heard and settled. We urge that Sasana Mandalas [Sasana committees] be constituted which would comprise only the Maha Sangha [the entire Ceylonese monkhood] and which would deal with all matters and problems pertaining to Buddhism." "Bauddha Balavegaya Demands," *World Buddhism*, August 1964, p. 27. See also: Benjamin Schonthal, "Phases of Buddhist Nationalism" in *Buddhist Militants and Muslim Minorities in Sri Lanka*, ed. John C Holt (New York: Oxford University Press, forthcoming).

[80] "Divergent views on Sasana Report," *World Buddhism*, January 1961, pp. 10–11.

GIVING BUDDHISM ITS "RIGHTFUL PLACE" 87

the government could take steps to protect and promote Buddhism, it should *not* take *any* steps toward overseeing or administrating the affairs of monks. Reciprocally, the *mahānāyaka*-s insisted, monks must not participate in politics.[81]

Despite widespread calls to give Buddhism its "rightful place," Mrs. Bandaranaike's government could not design a single comprehensive program for promoting Buddhism that did not alienate one or more of these influential Buddhist groups. Bandaranaike managed to create a Buddhist advisory committee, which, she hoped, could implement some of the recommendations of the Buddha Sasana Commission. However, the committee identified few reforms capable of generating broad consensus among Buddhist organizations.[82]

For example, in consultation with the advisory committee, Bandaranaike took tentative steps to keep monks out of salaried employment. (This was a key recommendation of the Buddhist Commission Report.) In 1961, she instructed her cabinet that government offices should not employ clerics of any religion in a job that could be filled by non-clerics. Lay Buddhist organizations in the first aforementioned group applauded this action, seeing it as a way to keep monks out of worldly affairs and to ensure that they concentrated their attentions on the traditional activities of a Buddhist monk: ministering to the public, conducting rituals and pursuing the ultimate goal of enlightenment. Yet, among Buddhist monks, this move was met with vociferous opposition. Some monks accused the prime minister of attacking the autonomy and influence of the island's guardians of Buddhism.[83] Other monks accused her of seeking to claim Buddhist authority herself. In other words, what began as an attempt to support Buddhist reform was viewed soon after as an unacceptable act of usurpation of monastic authority. Mrs. Bandaranaike's exasperation was palpable in a radio address made only a year after taking office:

---

[81] "The Mahanayaka Thero's Statement," *The Buddhist*, March–April 1964, p. 1. "Should Buddhist Monks Participate in Politics," *World Buddhism* May 1964, p. 23. "Politics and Sangha," *The Buddhist*, June 1964, p. 1.

[82] "Views on Sasana Mandalaya Sought," *World Buddhism*, September 1960, p. 13. Senanayake eventually put together a task force that included four members of the Buddha Sasana Commission, including the chairman Ven. Kalukondayawe Pannasekera. Smith, "The Sinhalese Buddhist Revolution," 505.

[83] Phadnis, *Religion and Politics in Sri Lanka*, 222–224. An editorial in *The Buddhist* quipped: "It is pathetic to see the Buddhist monk today hankering after Government jobs and University certificates instead of leading a life of retirement from the world devoted to moral advancement of himself and others." *The Buddhist*, September 1961, p. 26.

88   CONTESTING CONSTITUTIONS IN THE 1950S AND 1960S

> It is wrong to say that the government is seeking to destroy the freedom of the Sangha by legislation. The government does not intend to interfere in any way with the rules of the *Vinaya* [Buddhist monastic code of conduct] or in matters relating to the different *nikayas*. All that we propose is to implement the recommendations of the Sasana Report in consultation with the Sangha for the preservation of the Sasana in the same manner as was done by the Buddhist kings of old.[84]

One of the few policies that garnered support from all three Buddhist constituencies was the restructuring of education. In 1960, Mrs. Bandaranaike decided to nationalize the island's education system – a step that both the ACBC Report and the Buddha Sasana Commission had described as absolutely essential.[85] Since the 1940s, both lay and monastic Buddhist groups had advocated the measure as a way to counter the influence of the island's prestigious Christian secondary schools. By nationalizing the schools, the thinking went, the government could help combat the perceived dominance of Christian persons in positions of power. In November 1960, only six months after taking office, Mrs. Bandaranaike began this process by passing the Assisted Schools and Training Colleges (Special Provisions) Act. The Act mandated that all schools that received even minimal funds from the government (which many of the private schools did) would, on December 1, come under a government-appointed Director of Education. Any schools that elected not to receive funds could remain independent, only if they fulfilled two extremely difficult conditions: they could not charge fees unless 75% of teachers and parents agreed to pay fees, and they could not admit any child whose parents did not profess the same religion as that of the school.[86] The passing of the Act was followed shortly by the appointment of a National Education Commission, to which some former members of the Buddha Sasana Commission were assigned. Within two years, hundreds of

---

[84] Taken from *Ceylon Observer*, July 27, 1961 as quoted in: Donald E Smith, "Political Monks and Monastic Reform," in *South Asian Politics and Religion* (Princeton, NJ: Princeton University Press, 1966), 506.

[85] Government of Ceylon, *Buddha Śasana Komiṣan Vārtāva (Buddha Sasana Commission Report)*, 280.

[86] Smith, "The Sinhalese Buddhist Revolution," 485. The 1960 Act was followed several months later by the Assisted Schools and Training Colleges (Supplementary Provisions) Act 8 of 1961, which nationalized the property of all schools that had been turned over to the government.

GIVING BUDDHISM ITS "RIGHTFUL PLACE"

schools and their properties came under the direct administration of the government.[87]

The consensus with which Mrs. Bandaranaike nationalized the schools was, in retrospect, unusual. Regarding other issues that the Buddha Sasana Commission Report had recommended – such as prohibiting monks from participating in politics, establishing centralized monastic courts, and incorporating a Sasana Council – Mrs. Bandaranaike found herself at the center of an impasse. The delicate predicament of government support for Buddhism in the 1960s is captured nicely in an official statement on religion given by the UNP, who were then in opposition. In a pamphlet entitled "What We Believe," the UNP asserted that it was "strongly opposed" to any elements of the Buddha Sasana Commission Report that "suggest any control of the Sangha by the Government or the Laity." Moreover, it asserted:

> Some suggest that Buddhism should be made the State Religion. If by making Buddhism the State Religion it means that the Government of the day can appoint and transfer *Mahanayake* Theras [chief monks of monastic fraternities] and *Viharadipathies* [head monks of monasteries]; control religious ceremonies in Temples and manage the Sangha as a State Department, our Party cannot agree to the Buddha Sasana being made subservient to the state. If, however, it means that the State will aid the Sasana; that the Sangha will be helped to re-organise itself, and the directives of State Policy should be based on the principles of Buddha Dhamma, we hereby pledge ourselves to adopt such a policy. In practice, since Independence, Buddhism has gradually been recognized by the State as its official religion and Buddhist ceremonies are performed at the chief State functions.[88]

One can see in this description the caution with which the UNP side-stepped the varied objections of Buddhist pressure groups. The UNP promised to make Buddhism the "state religion" (as groups like the Government Servants Buddhist Association had asked), provided that such a step would not entail giving the government authority over monastic affairs (which most of the island's monastic fraternities opposed). It would move forward with centralizing the sangha (as the ACBC and some non-Siyam-Nikāya monks desired) without taking charge of the process (which the Malvatu and Asgiri

---

[87] Ibid., 486–487.
[88] UNP Pamphlet: "What We Believe" Summary of meeting held on September 29, 1963, pp. 9–10.

90   CONTESTING CONSTITUTIONS IN THE 1950S AND 1960S

mahānāyaka-s opposed).[89] It would continue to "perform" Buddhist ceremonies at state functions without "control[ling]" religious ceremonies in temples.

Such was the tenuous nature of Buddhist advocacy in the 1960s. It was a far cry from the ostensibly unified Buddhist interests of the mid-1950s, where (with notable exceptions) most of the island's Buddhist groups were unified around the work of the ACBC Commission and the Buddha Jayanthi anniversary preparations. In the 1960s, promoting Buddhism in law was exceedingly tricky business. Most mainstream political parties wanted to signal their support for Buddhism. However few were willing to wholeheartedly embrace all the recommendations of the Buddha Sasana Commission or to offer a comprehensive legislative scheme for establishing Buddhism in its "rightful place." Fifteen years after G P Malalasekera had presented the ACBC memorandum to D S Senanayake requesting that the state "restore" Buddhism to its precolonial glory, there seemed to be few principles for managing religion on which all major Buddhist groups could agree. The few reforms that were widely endorsed appeared prominently in the election manifestos of both the UNP and SLFP. These included: giving state aid to Buddhist religious schools, making Buddhist full-moon holidays national holidays, setting up a Buddhist university at Anuradhapura and sending Buddhist missionaries abroad.[90] There was no mention of incorporating a Buddha Sasana Council, which had been a centerpiece of the promotional paradigm since the late 1940s.

New Governments, New Constitutional Committees: The UNP Joint Select Committee

In the 1960s, the push for constitutional change was a regular feature of politics. From 1959 to 1965, the powers for constitutional change were vested in governments that were controlled by the party that S W R D Bandaranaike founded, the SLFP, under the leadership of his widow, Sirima Bandaranaike. From 1965 to 1970, those powers reverted back to a government led by the political party that D S Senanayake founded, the

---

[89] In 1961, the *mahānāyaka*-s of the Malvatu and Asgiri branches of the Siyam Nikāya had advocated a program of *sangha* reform, but one engineered by themselves. Smith, "Political Monks and Monastic Reform," 507.

[90] Ceylon Daily News, *The Ceylon Daily News Parliament of Ceylon 1965* (Colombo: Lake House, 1965).

THE POLITICS OF FUNDAMENTAL RIGHTS   91

UNP, now directed by his son, Dudley Senanayake. The slow burn of constitutional reform in 1960s Ceylon smoldered alongside oscillating political dynasties.

Not long after winning the 1965 elections, the UNP put forward its own constitutional agenda. In November 1966 at its national conference, the leaders of the UNP declared their intentions to complete the unfinished business of S W R D Bandaranaike and amend the 1948 Constitution themselves. These amendments, they proposed, would make the country a "Democratic Socialist Republic." UNP leaders also promised to introduce new constitutional chapters guaranteeing fundamental rights and giving "Buddhism, the majority religion of the country, where the population is about 75% ... its rightful place."[91]

Soon thereafter, the UNP-led government appointed a new Joint Select Committee on the Revision of the Constitution. This new committee met for the first time on November 5, 1967 and commenced its work under the very same terms of reference as the 1957 Bandaranaike Committee.[92] Unlike the Bandaranaike Committee, the UNP's constitution-drafting body included no members of the opposition. This was not by design; Senanayake had invited participation from all parties. However, the opposition – a United Front coalition, consisting of the SLFP along with the leftist parties (the LSSP and CP) – opposed the process, maintaining that the island needed an entirely new constitution, not simply an amendment (see later in chapter).[93] The UNP-led committee carried on nonetheless. Between 1967 and 1968, it held numerous sittings, reviewed hundreds of questionnaires and heard oral testimony from dozens of individuals and interest groups.[94]

The Politics of Fundamental Rights

If the implementation of Buddhist privileges proved to be a tricky issue during the first half of the 1960s, so too was the issue of fundamental

---

[91] *World Buddhism*, November 1965, Vol. 14(4), 17.

[92] Government of Ceylon, *The Joint Select Committee of the Senate and the House of Representatives Appointed to Consider the Revision of the Constitution (Parliamentary Series No. 30, 3rd Session of 6th Parliament)* (Colombo: Government Press, June 6, 1968), 1.

[93] M S Alif, "Towards a Free Sri Lanka," *Daily News* (1972).

[94] Government of Ceylon, *The Joint Select Committee of the Senate and the House of Representatives Appointed to Consider the Revision of the Constitution (Parliamentary Series No. 30, 3rd Session of 6th Parliament)*.

92 CONTESTING CONSTITUTIONS IN THE 1950S AND 1960S

rights in the second half of the 1960s. Many politicians still favored introducing fundamental rights into the constitution. However, since S W R D Bandaranaike's time, few had spoken precisely about how this should happen. After 1965, however, debates over fundamental rights began to heat up.

Although Colombo provided the crucible for debates over fundamental rights, the key stimuli came from overseas. In December 1966, in Geneva, Ceylon's representative to the United Nations voted in favor of adopting two covenants designed to advance the principles articulated in the Universal Declaration of Human Rights. These were the International Covenant on Civil and Political Rights (ICCPR) and the International Covenant on Economic, Social and Cultural Rights (ICESCR). While Ceylon's government would not formally adopt the covenants until 1980, events in Geneva nevertheless stimulated discussion in Colombo about the nature and place of civil and political rights on the island.

A key forum for these discussions was a meeting of the island's major political parties held in 1968 by the United Nations Association. The Association asked participants at the meeting about their willingness to implement a chapter on fundamental rights in the country's constitution.[95] Responses divided along political lines. On the one hand, members of the UNP-led government, including representatives from the Tamil parties, stressed the urgent need for a strong and entrenched chapter on fundamental rights. This, they claimed, was an essential device for protecting the minorities because the provisions in the 1948 Constitution for minority rights were "absolutely inadequate."[96] On the other hand, representatives of the two main leftist parties, who were in opposition at the time, took a different position. They warned that a charter of fundamental rights might not be the unequivocal good that the UNP-led government made it out to be. Although they had helped to draft a chapter on fundamental rights as part of Bandaranaike's Joint Select Committee, the leaders of the CP and LSSP now questioned the idea that such a chapter could be truly impartial or universal. All lists of fundamental rights, they argued, would inevitably advance the agendas of some groups at the expense of others.

---

[95] In the section, I rely on the descriptions of Nihal Jayawickrama, who was at this meeting, tape-recorded it, and later described its proceedings in Jayawickrama, *Human Rights: The Sri Lankan Experience 1947–1981*, 74–80.

[96] M Tiruchelvam as quoted in ibid., 74.

One person who voiced this view with particular vigor was Colvin R De Silva, an experienced lawyer, legislator and leader of the LSSP. De Silva had been an important member of S W R D's Bandaranaike's Joint Select Committee on the Revision of the Constitution and would become the key architect of the island's 1972 charter (see Chapter 4). In an argument that looked startlingly similar to that of Jennings in the 1940s, De Silva insisted that no fundamental rights should be treated as "eternally inviolate"; all such rights were, in effect, value statements relative to a present state of affairs, summaries of those principles that were important and esteemed at the present political moment. By entrenching those values in a chapter on fundamental rights, politicians were "constrain[ing] a future generation ... within the confines of its own postulates."[97]

De Silva opposed the idea that the Ceylon might adopt, in its entirety, a regime of fundamental rights authored by the United Nations or, worse, the UNP. However, he worried not only about the wording or content of those rights but vexed especially over the possibility that including non-amendable rights of any type might undermine popular sovereignty.

> If you place a declaration as being fundamental, then you have to accept an authority outside the makers of laws with the task of deciding whether the law is in fact a law. Whether we have faith in the Supreme Court is not the issue. Do we want a legislature that is sovereign or do we not? This is the true question. If you say that the validity of a law has to be determined by anybody outside the law-making body, then you are to that extent saying that your law-making body is not completely the law-making body.[98]

For De Silva, then, the inclusion of fundamental rights not only constrained future legislators by holding them to an earlier generation's values, it undermined the legal basis of parliamentary rule itself. De Silva worried that if Ceylon revised the constitution to include an unchangeable bill of rights, it would limit parliament's ability to legislate freely and this, in turn, would subvert the foundation of popular sovereignty. De Silva's arguments about fundamental rights echoed those of several Ceylonese legal scholars at the time, who also expressed anxieties about the limits imposed on parliament by entrenched features of the constitution.[99]

---

[97] Colvin R De Silva as quoted in ibid., 75.   [98] De Silva as quoted in ibid., 75.

[99] To understand this anxiety, one must digress briefly into a legal controversy that arose over the course of the 1960s in relation to Section 29(3) and 29(2) of the 1948 Constitution. The controversy involved the interpretation of Section 29(3), which stated that

94 CONTESTING CONSTITUTIONS IN THE 1950S AND 1960S

Disputes over fundamental rights interlinked with other political disputes. In the context of the UNP Committee, support for fundamental rights intersected with support for the UNP's Joint Select Committee and its goal of reforming the 1948 Constitution through amendment. In contesting fundamental rights, opposition politicians not only disagreed on points of legal theory, they rejected the idea of a UNP-led reform process. For them, amendment was not enough; they promised Ceylon a completely new "autochthonous" constitution to be created by way of a completely new constitutional assembly.

Further Debates over Buddhism and Fundamental Rights

Without the participation of the opposition, the Joint Select Committee of 1967 had the odds stacked against it. This was constitutional debate; but it was also party politics as usual. Nevertheless, in the records from the 1967 Committee and the transcripts from the hearings, one sees new inflections to the protectionist and promotional paradigms of managing religion, which would become important in the making of the

> any law made "in contravention" of the limits placed on the legislature in 29(2) was to be "void." As seen in the previous chapter, these limits involved restrictions on the free exercise of religion, discrimination on the basis of community or religion, or altering the constitution of "religious bodies." Interpreted in this way, these sections of the 1948 Constitution seemed to imply that Ceylon's own legislature had no capacity to alter its constitution. This, in turn, implied that Ceylon's parliament (and the people who elected it) were not fully sovereign and self-determining. This alarming interpretation of Section 29 of the 1948 Constitution gained popularity particularly in the mid-1960s, in the wake of one comment made by the Privy Council (which was, at the time, the highest court of appeal in Ceylon) in the case of *Bribery Commissioner v. Ranasinghe*. For our purposes, the details of the case are irrelevant, other than to mention that in the reported judgment, one member of the Privy Council, Lord Pearce, referred to the provisions in Section 29(2) (in *obiter dicta*) as: "entrenched religious and racial matters ... [representing] the solemn balance of rights between the citizens of Ceylon, the fundamental conditions on which inter se they accepted the Constitution ... [sections which are] *unalterable under the Constitution.*" Lord Peace's dicta seemed to confirm critics' concerns: Ceylon's legislature was indeed incapable of fully altering its constitution and, therefore, the 1948 Constitution did not grant to the island's legislators (or its people) complete sovereignty. *Bribery Commissioner v. Ranasinghe* (1962) 64 *New Law Reports* 78, emphasis added. For a helpful explanation of these debates see: M L Marasinghe, "Ceylon: A Conflict of Constitutions," *The International and Comparative Law Quarterly* 20, no. 4 (1971): 645–674. One can also see this viewpoint articulated in the testimony of Prof. Amarasinghe, a constitutional legal scholar, given to the 1967 *Joint Select Committee on the Revision of the Constitution.* Government of Ceylon, *The Joint Select Committee of the Senate and the House of Representatives Appointed to Consider the Revision of the Constitution (Parliamentary Series No. 30, 3rd Session of 6th Parliament)*, 110–115.

FURTHER DEBATES   95

1972 Constitution. On the protectionist side, one sees a new emphasis on borrowing the language of religious rights from the United Nations' Universal Declaration of Human Rights, indicating a turn to international human rights instruments rather than the Constitution of India as guidelines for protecting fundamental rights.[100] On the promotional side, one sees an even stronger emphasis on the importance of including in the new constitution the terms of the Kandyan Convention of 1815, the colonial treaty that committed Ceylon's British governors to protecting Buddhism in the same manner as the Kandyan kings.[101]

More importantly, however, one sees for the first time in the transcripts of the abortive 1967 Committee a growing concern over how one might reconcile the act of giving to Buddhism a special place with ensuring equal rights and nondiscrimination for other religious groups. While not a dominant theme of the hearings, the potential conflict between these two ideas appeared clearly in the transcript of a tense and sustained exchange between G G Ponnambalam, a senior Tamil member of the committee and the leader of the Tamil Congress, and Ven. Palipanne Chandananda Thero, a senior monk representing the *sangha sabhā* (monastic councils) of the Malvatu and Asgiri branches of the Siyam Nikāya. Ven. Chandananda had requested that clauses from the Kandyan Convention be included in the text of the constitution in order to give Buddhism added recognition and protection. In addition, Ven. Chandananda had submitted a memorandum on behalf of the Siyam Nikāya that asked drafters to include, under the topic-heading "fundamental rights," the statement "Buddhism must be placed higher than other religions."[102] Regarding these points, Ponnambalam pushed the monk to clarify whether he objected to the inclusion of "one chapter on fundamental rights ... under which all people would be equal under the law." Ven. Chandananda, speaking on behalf of the entire Siyam Nikāya, responded by arguing that the demand for state protections and privileges for Buddhism did not contravene the creation of a single code of fundamental rights for all citizens. It merely extended a tradition that had been practiced since the days of the "Buddhist kings": "we [the Siyam Nikāya monks he represented] are not asking you to treat other religions differently" but to continue "protecting and maintaining" (*ārakṣā kirīma hā naḍattu kirīma*) Buddhism as has been a "duty of the state" (*rajayē vagakīmak*) for centuries.[103] According to

---

[100] Jayawickrama, *Human Rights*, 77, 95.   [101] Ibid., 91, 142.   [102] Ibid., 146.
[103] Ibid., 146.

Ven. Chandananda, just as ancient Sinhala kings had granted land to Catholics and Muslims while continuing to support Buddhism, so too should the modern Ceylonese state give patronage to Buddhism while also supporting other religions. Chandananda's model was thus one of religious hierarchy and conditional pluralism. The state would be obligated to Buddhism primarily, and to other religions secondarily. Ven. Chandananda, representing the island's oldest and most powerful Buddhist monks, proposed that the state could tolerate all religions, provided Buddhism was the preferred faith of the island.[104]

Conclusion

Ponnambalam's challenge and Chandananda's reply are significant in that they constitute one of the first publicly documented moments in which would-be amenders of the constitution took seriously the potential incongruence of promotional and protectionist paradigms of Buddhist privileges and fundamental rights. This question lingered in the background in the 1967 Committee testimonies, yet it would become more pressing in the period of constitutional change that was to follow.

By the late 1960s, questions that had been gestating in the political sphere for two decades began to take on new urgency in the legal sphere. Virtually all political groups called for a new constitution that could redress the grievances of both non-Buddhist minorities and Buddhist interest groups. Could such a document outline a scheme for promoting Buddhism that did not alienate large sections of the Buddhist community? Could it promote Buddhism while also giving to all religions equal, and equally actionable, rights? Politicians, religious leaders and civil society groups had spent more than 20 years calling for constitutional reform and arguing about how it should be done. They had rallied

---

[104] In Chandananda's memorandum he had urged that "the Buddhist religion should not be regarded as being of the same status as the other religions." In his testimony this became clearer. Buddhism was not only to be the most important religion (*āgama*), it was to be referred to in terminology distinct from that used to describe Christianity, Hinduism or Islam. Therefore legal regulations surrounding Buddhism should be made in language specific to the taxonomy of Buddhist places of worship, clerics and temple property. Common (ordinary) words (*podu vacana*), he contended, failed to capture the nuance of Buddhism. The English word "priest," for example, mistakenly suggested an intrinsic similarity between Christian ministers and *bhikkhus* (Buddhist monks) and *kapuralas* (those who make offerings to deities' devales) and *pujākas* (Hindu ritual officiants). Therefore, Buddhism should be governed using its own terms according to its own set of laws. *Ibid.*, 142, 147.

CONCLUSION 97

around key ideas: revising Section 29(2), giving Buddhism its "rightful place," protecting fundamental rights. Yet, even after sustained and vibrant political debate (along with numerous attempts at designing constitutional provisions) one could find little agreement on the details of how to embody the promotional or protectionist paradigms in constitutional policies. Future constitution-makers had to construct the state's relationship with Buddhism in such a way as to communicate a responsibility to the religion of the majority but not authority over it. At the same time, it had to reconcile this preferential treatment of Buddhism with a chapter on fundamental rights that outlined certain and common freedoms.

Like Bandaranaike's Joint Committee, the 1967 Joint Committee ended up ineffectual. Politically, the UNP-led coalition was growing increasingly precarious. By late 1968, there seemed to be little hope that constitutional amendments produced by the committee would have adequate parliamentary backing. Yet, the popular mood was clear: the slow burn was intensifying; there would be a change in Ceylon's constitution and it would happen as soon as one political coalition could muster the necessary votes in parliament.

4

Multivalent Solutions: Drafting the Buddhism Chapter

Chapter 3II, "Buddhism" §6: The Republic of Sri Lanka shall give to Buddhism the foremost place and accordingly it shall be the duty of the State to protect and foster Buddhism while assuring to all religions the rights granted by section 18(1) (d).

Chapter V, "Principles of State Policy" §16 (2): The Republic is pledged to carry forward ... objectives of which include (a) full realisation of all rights and freedoms of citizens including group rights. ... *§16 (4)*: The State shall endeavour to strengthen national unity by promoting co-operation and mutual confidence between all sections of the people of Sri Lanka including the racial, religious and other groups.... *§16 (9)*: The State shall endeavour to create the necessary economic and social environment to enable people of all religious faiths to make a living reality of their religious principles.

Chapter VI, "Fundamental Rights and Freedoms" §18 (1): In the Republic of Sri Lanka: (a) all persons are equal before the law and are entitled to equal protection of the law ... (d) every citizen shall have the right to freedom of thought, conscience and religion. This right shall include the freedom to have or to adopt a religion or belief of his choice, and the freedom, either individually or in community with others and in public or private, to manifest religion or belief in worship, observance, practice and teaching.

–The Constitution of the Republic of Sri Lanka, 1972

It is an obvious point, but it bears repeating: constitutions are multivalent texts; they can be read and interpreted multiple ways. This multivalence serves several functions. It helps citizens to apply constitutional principles to their lives. It gives judges greater interpretive flexibility in managing difficult disputes.[1] It ensures that it allows constitution drafters

---

[1] Benjamin L Berger, "The Virtues of Law in the Politics of Religious Freedom," *Journal of Law and Religion* 29, no. 3 (2014): 378–395. Sunstein, "Incompletely Theorized Agreements."

to sidestep highly charged legal questions that, if addressed in more direct language, might derail the constitution-making process.[2]

The value of, or need for, multivalent language is particularly acute when it comes to the category of religion.[3] In many polities, questions about religion, and the state's relationship to it, are among the most contentious issues addressed by litigants, judges and lawmakers.[4] This has certainly been true in Sri Lanka.[5]

When it comes to drafting Sri Lanka's 1972 Constitution, multivalent language made possible two key bargains over religion. The first was an *interreligious bargain* between those who demanded that the new constitution *protect* all religions equally and those who demanded that the new constitution *promote* Buddhism over the island's other traditions. The second was an *intrareligious bargain*, among Buddhists, between those who wanted to give the state oversight over the affairs of Buddhist monks and those who wanted to defend monastic autonomy from state interference. The outcome of these bargains is visible in Chapter II of the Constitution, entitled "Buddhism" (quoted at the beginning of the chapter).

In what follows, I analyze the process of drafting and debating the Buddhism Chapter, which was one of the most heavily discussed features of the new constitution. Using a variety of transcripts, drafting documents, written submissions and other sources (many of them unpublished and, to date, unexamined by scholars), I explain how drafters used multivalent language to appease multiple stakeholders: Buddhist government ministers, secularist coalition members, reformist lay-Buddhist organizations, traditionalist monastic elites, liberal lobby groups, and members of the island's Christian, Muslim and Hindu communities. I argue that the Buddhism Chapter, although occasionally imagined as the unmitigated product of Buddhist nationalist interests, was in fact the product of difficult compromises on several levels, both within and outside of the ruling coalition. The Buddhism Chapter drew together the two major critiques of the 1948

---

[2] Hanna Lerner, "Permissive Constitutions, Democracy, and Religious Freedom in India, Indonesia, Israel, and Turkey," *World Politics* 65, no. 4 (2013): 609–655. Lerner, *Making Constitutions in Deeply Divided Societies*. Tom Ginsburg and Rosalind Dixon, "Deciding Not to Decide: Deferral in Constitutional Design," *International Journal of Constitutional Law* 9, no. 3–4 (2011): 636–672.

[3] Lerner, "Permissive Constitutions, Democracy, and Religious Freedom in India, Indonesia, Israel, and Turkey".

[4] Bali and Lerner (eds.), *Constitution Writing, Religion and Democracy*.

[5] Keeping with its official designation starting in 1972, in this chapter I refer to the island as Sri Lanka rather than Ceylon.

Constitution, the protectionist and the promotional, which had been embedded in popular culture and politics since the 1940s. By giving to Buddhism "the foremost place" and affirming "fundamental rights" for all religions, the drafters of the Buddhism Chapter hoped to *mediate* popular demands about religion in both senses of the verb: they aimed not only to represent the demands of citizens, but to reconcile them.[6]

This chapter unfolds in four sections. Section I describes the processes of proposing and drafting the earliest versions of the 1972 Constitution and its chapter on Buddhism. Section II examines public responses to the proposed Buddhism provisions, as indicated in memoranda sent to the drafters by Buddhist and non-Buddhist interest groups and political organizations. Section III looks closely at debates in the Constituent Assembly regarding the early drafts of the Buddhism Chapter and analyzes the discussions surrounding three proposed amendments to it. Section IV looks at the process of finalizing the Buddhism Chapter after the Assembly debates had concluded.

SECTION I: THE POLITICS OF DRAFTING A CHAPTER ON BUDDHISM

In 1970, after two decades of slow-burn attempts at reforms, amendments and constitutional committees, Sri Lanka teetered on the verge of a new constitution. The first indications of this came on July 17, 1970, in a radio address by Sirima Bandaranaike, who had just become the prime minister of Ceylon for a second time. In the address, Bandaranaike pledged that she would guide her government in drafting a new constitution that would "build a nation ever more strongly conscious of its oneness amidst the diversity imposed on it by history."[7]

Bandaranaike's promises were predictable. In pamphlets and campaign addresses leading up to 1970, she had announced that, if elected, her United Front coalition would give the island a new constitution. On May 27, the UF won a sweeping electoral victory, securing 115 out of 151 parliamentary seats.

When it came to religion, the United Front (UF) was an unlikely alliance of Sinhala Buddhist populists and members of the "Old Left"

---

[6] See epigram for passages referred to.

[7] *Ceylon Daily News*, July 16, 1970, quoted in Cooray, *Constitutional and Administrative Law of Sri Lanka (Ceylon)*, 76.

MULTIVALENT SOLUTIONS

driven together more by shared opposition than by shared ideologies of governance.[8] The coalition had taken shape in the mid-1960s in opposition to the United National Party (UNP)-led government at the time. When the UNP convened its committee on constitutional reform in 1967 (see Chapter 3), the UF responded with its own constitutional promises: they would not pursue amendments to the existing constitution (like the UNP), but would work to draft an "autochthonous" republican constitution from scratch.

Since the late 1960s, the UF had placed the promise of a new constitution at the forefront of its political campaigning. Members of the UF argued that the existing constitution served the interests of colonial Britain, not postcolonial Ceylon: rather than declare Ceylon to be an independent republic, the 1948 Constitution made the island a dominion of the Commonwealth; rather than make Ceylon's Supreme Court the highest court of appeal, it deferred authority to London's Privy Council. Most egregiously, argued UF politicians, the island's current constitution prevented Ceylon's legislators from altering the charter's most basic features, including its provisions regarding religion.[9]

Shortly after the electoral victory, Bandaranaike announced that the UF's success at the polls signaled a "clear mandate" for constitutional change. The United Front would use its super-majority to generate an entirely new legal charter for the island, one designed by an already-independent parliament and reflecting the desires and aspirations of an already-independent people. Such a document, according to the UF election manifesto, would make the island a "free, sovereign and independent Republic," "secure fundamental rights and freedoms to [sic] all citizens," and give to Buddhism its "rightful place" in the country.[10]

---

[8] This phrase ("the Old Left") is used widely to refer to the members of the LSSP and CP in the late 1960s and early 1970s (and after), many of whom had been prominent politicians on the island since independence. The phrase was coined in contrast with the "New Left" that seemed to be emerging in the 1970s. The New Left included younger, more radical socialist thinkers who joined revolutionary-*cum*-political organizations such as the JVP (People's Liberation Front) and started splinter parties, such as the LSSP (R). In 1971, the JVP would lead members of the New Left in insurrection against the state. Kearney, *Communalism and Language in the Politics of Ceylon* 120–123. Nira Wickramasinghe, *Sri Lanka in the Modern Age: A History* (London: Oxford University Press, 2015), ch. 6.

[9] See Chapter 3; for more on this see: L J M Cooray, *Constitutional Government in Sri Lanka 1796–1977* (Colombo: Stamford Lake Publishers, 2005), 232–235.

[10] Election Manifesto, United Front, 1970.

102   MULTIVALENT SOLUTIONS

From Bandaranaike's July 1970 speech, it would be almost two years before the constitution of the new Republic of Sri Lanka was ratified. During that time, the document underwent four stages of drafting. During stage one (July 1970 to January 1971) a 12-member Drafting Committee of senior lawyers and government legal experts composed 38 core constitutional principles, called Draft Basic Resolutions (DBRs), which would form the rudimentary outline of the new charter.[11] Those DBRs were then sent for review to the prime minister's cabinet and to a 17-member Steering and Subjects Committee, composed of government and opposition parliamentarians.[12] During stage two (January 1971 to July 1971), the DBRs were debated by a Constituent Assembly, in sequence, over the course of five months. During stage three (from July 1971 to January 1972), the Drafting Committee rewrote the debated (and, in some cases, amended) DBRs as a draft constitution. During stage four (from January 1972 to May 1972), the Steering and Subjects Committee guided the Assembly in reconsidering the draft constitution

---

[11] The Drafting Committee included practicing or former lawyers and one political science professor. Among the lawyers was J A L Cooray, who (it will be recalled) had played a central role in drafting the Constitution for a Free Lanka in 1943 and helped engineer the Ceylon National Congress's proposed list of fundamental rights. Cooray had also been involved in finalizing the draft chapter on fundamental rights in the Bandaranaike Joint Select Committee on the Revision of the Constitution. For a list of others, see: Alif, "Towards a Free Sri Lanka." Nihal Jayawickrama, "Reflections on the Making and Content of the 1972 Constitution: An Insider's Perspective," in *The Sri Lankan Republic at 40: Reflections on Constitutional History, Theory, Practice*, ed. Asanga Welikala (Colombo: Centre for Policy Alternatives, 2012).

[12] Government and opposition members were included in numbers proportional to the numbers of government and opposition members in parliament: Of the 17 committee members, 13 were from the ruling coalition (9 from the SLFP, 2 LSSP, 2 Communist Party, 1 Tamil Congress), and 4 were from the opposition (2 from the UNP and 2 from the Federal Party). *United Front Coalition Members*: Chairman, Mrs. Bandaranaike (Prime Minister, SLFP), Colvin R. De Silva (Minister of Constitutional Affairs, LSSP), Maithrapala Senanayake (Minister of Irrigation, Power and Highways, SLFP), Badiuddin Mahmud (Minister of Education, SLFP), Felix Bandranaike (Minister of Public Administration, Local Government and Home Affairs, SLFP), T B Ilangaratne (Minister of Foreign and Internal Trade, SLFP), Pieter Keuneman (Minister of Housing, CP), Hector Kobbekaduwa (Minister of Agriculture and Lands, SLFP), N M Perera (Minister of Finance, LSSP), George Rajapakse (Minister of Fisheries, SLFP), T B Subasinge (Minister of Industries and Scientific Affairs, SLFP), T B Tennekoon (Minister of Social Services, SLFP), C Arulampalam (MP Nallur, TC). *Opposition members*: J R Jayewardene (Leader of the Opposition, UNP), Dudley Senanayake (UNP) C X Martyn (MP Jaffna, FP), S J V Chelvanayakam (leader of FP) *Secretaries*: Noel Tittawella (Secretary [he was also a member of Drafting Committee]), S S Wijesinghe (Co-Secretary). Alif, "Towards a Free Sri Lanka."

alongside memoranda and deputations from the public. A final draft of the constitution was ratified on May 22, 1972.

As with constitution-making efforts in most parts of the world, one can, in retrospect, critique certain aspects of Sri Lanka's 1972 process. By virtue of their dominant numbers in parliament, members of the majority coalition, the UF, had a decisive influence over the committees associated with the process.[13] As a result, the UF did not take seriously enough the grievances of the island's Tamil minority, as represented by the opposition Federal Party. These two factors were complicated further by the fact that, during the second half of the drafting process, the government found itself struggling to quell a local armed Marxist uprising.

These criticisms notwithstanding, the 1972 process also has its strengths. When it came to the matter of religion, constitutional deliberation took place in a spirit of seriousness in trying to balance competing interests.[14] Compared with other Constituent Assemblies, such as that of India, Sri Lanka's Constituent Assembly received considerable popular input:[15] members of the Assembly were members of parliament, chosen in island-wide elections that saw 85 percent voter turnout; the relative political composition of members of committees roughly paralleled that of the government-opposition proportions of the legislature, even if it did not reflect the popular vote tallies.[16] Public feedback was solicited widely, considered at several stages in the process and, in a number of cases, acted upon. When it came to fundamental rights, drafters used as their basic template the conventions of international human rights law,

---

[13] Ibid. Deepika Udagama, "The Fragmented Republic: Reflections on the 1972 Constitution of Sri Lanka," *Sri Lanka Journal of Humanities* 39, no. 1–2 (2014): 81–97.

[14] This cannot be said for the matter of language, which was debated after the Buddhism Chapter (as we will see later on).

[15] The Indian Constituent Assembly by contrast was elected indirectly, from state legislatures, which were, in turn, elected through an extremely limited franchise: an electorate of 30 million, less than one-tenth of the population, voted; franchise was significantly limited by education, property and tax restrictions laid out in the Government of India Act of 1935. Rochana Bajpai, "Constituent Assembly Debates and Minority Rights," *Economic and Political Weekly* 35, no. 21/22 (2000): 1837–1845.

[16] Wilson, *Electoral Politics in An Emergent State*, 123–126. C R De Silva, *Sri Lanka: A History* (New Delhi: Vikas, 1997), 227. The UF gained approximately 50 percent of the popular vote but three-fourths of parliamentary seats. The discrepancy between these two figures reflects the fact that general elections were contested according to a first-past-the-post system. This voting system was subsequently replaced with a proportional-representation-based system in 1978 by the UNP government at the time.

particularly the United Nations' International Covenant on Civil and Political Rights. As it relates to the Buddhism Chapter, there were powerful forces working against Buddhist majoritarianism. In fact, the Minister of Constitutional Affairs and the unofficial architect of the constitution, Colvin R De Silva, was a resolute secularist.

The Buddhism Chapter Stage One: Before the Assembly Debates

Important negotiations over the constitution's policies for religion took place early on, *within* the ruling UF coalition itself. These *intra*coalition negotiations proved to be among the most difficult, requiring considerable bargaining and compromise. Contrary to its propaganda, deep ideological divisions split the UF, particularly with respect to the subject of religion.[17] On the one side, the dominant faction of the UF consisted of Sinhala Buddhist members of the Sri Lanka Freedom Party (SLFP) many of whom were committed to giving greater state aid to Buddhism.[18] On the other side, a smaller, but powerful, faction of the UF consisted of two Socialist parties – the LSSP, or *Laṅkā Sama Samāja Pakṣaya* (the Sri Lanka Equal-Society Party), and the CP, or Communist Party – whose representatives and supporters were mainly committed leftists and whose key leaders opposed direct state sponsorship of religion.[19]

In the late 1960s, UF campaigners blended together the coalition's opposing positions on religion into a "Common Program" that promised:

> Buddhism [would] be ensured its rightful place as the religion of the majority, and the adherents of other faiths [would] be guaranteed freedom of worship and the right to practise their religions.
>
> . . .

---

[17] In propaganda, the UF declared that members were united and resolved in their commitment to give Buddhism its "rightful place," and, in a statement calculated to combat the anti-religious image of the LSSP and CP, the UF's socialist members had publicly declared their respect for the majority religion. Michael Roberts, *Exploring Confrontation: Sri Lanka, Politics, Culture and History* (Chur, Switzerland: Harwood Academic Publishers, 1994), Ch 1.

[18] Jayawickrama, *Human Rights: The Sri Lankan Experience 1947–1981*, 83.

[19] De Silva, in a speech given in 1987, asserted that he had been a secularist (see later). The LSSP Election manifesto from the previous election in 1965 included a promise of: "No discrimination in the field of education, employment or grant of any state aid or license, or in any other sphere against linguistic or religious minorities," LSSP Election Manifesto 1965.

THE BUDDHISM CHAPTER STAGE ONE 105

[T]he people, irrespective of race, caste, sex, religious belief or occupation [would be ensured the ability to] fully exercise their rights and have all opportunities to fulfill their responsibilities without restraint.[20]

In these policies, the UF integrated two separate statements on religion authored by the SLFP and the LSSP respectively: it linked the SLFP's promise of government support for Buddhism taken from its 1965 election manifesto with the LSSP's promise of non-discrimination with respect to religion taken from its 1965 election manifesto.[21] These two positions were further elaborated in the UF Election Manifesto of 1970, which declared:

> RELIGION: Buddhism, the religion of the majority of the people, will be ensured its rightful place. The adherents of all faiths will be guaranteed freedom of religious worship and the right to practice their religion. The necessary economic and social environment will be created to enable people of all religious faiths to make a living reality of their religious principles.
>
> . . .
>
> NATIONAL UNITY: We shall ensure that no citizen will suffer any disability or discrimination in the matter of employment, in his relations with the state, or in access to public institutions and places, on the grounds of race, religious belief or caste.[22]

The manifesto juxtaposed, in even more pronounced ways, the UF's paired commitments to special Buddhist prerogatives and guarantees of religious freedom and non-discrimination. The manifesto pledged further to foster a social and economic milieu that maximized the abilities of "people of all religious faiths" to "make a living reality of their religious principles."

Members of the UF negotiated fiercely among themselves on the topic of religion from the earliest stages of constitution drafting. One can see this clearly in the very first outlines of Sri Lanka's new constitution, written by Colvin R De Silva. De Silva, as mentioned earlier, was a leader in the UF, the Minister of Constitutional Affairs, the head of the Constitutional Affairs Subcommittee, a member of the Steering and Subjects Committee and a key member of the Drafting Committee. In short, he was the most influential figure in the entire drafting process.[23] De Silva's

---

[20] Ceylon Daily News, *The Ceylon Daily News Parliament of Ceylon 1970* (Colombo: Lake House, 1970), 10.

[21] See Election Manifestos of SLFP and LSSP from 1965.

[22] Election Manifesto, United Front, 1970.

[23] Walter Jayawardana, "Colvin and the Making of the Republican Constitution," *The Island* (2000). In the lead up to his work with Constituent Assembly, De Silva had convened a

106   MULTIVALENT SOLUTIONS

earliest constitutional drafts omitted any reference to Buddhism.[24] In fact, in De Silva's first two outlines, the only reference to religion at all appeared in a section entitled "Principles of State Policy." In that section, ignoring the SLFP's commitments to Buddhism, De Silva offered a watered-down version of his party's own secularist stance: "The State shall endeavor to create the necessary economic and social environment to enable people of all religious faiths to make a living reality of their religious principles."[25]

Despite De Silva's influential position in the constitution drafting process, however, the forces of coalition politics compelled him to compromise. In December 1970, responding to the concerns of other coalition members (and her constituents), Prime Minister Bandaranaike sent a letter to De Silva advising him as it pertained to religion that

> there appears to be a considerable demand in the country for Buddhism as a State Religion, and for the protection of its institutions and traditional places of worship. Some provision will have to be made in the new Constitution regarding these matters without, at the same time, derogating from the freedom of worship that should be guaranteed to all other religions.[26]

In her letter, Bandaranaike pointed to two basic political facts. First, although De Silva was a key member of the UF, his opinion did not represent the entirety of the UF. Therefore, he must respect the broader opinions of the coalition and the prime minister. Second, reform of the constitution must reflect popular desires and, as Bandaranaike observed, the populace desired that Buddhism be given special status as the state religion.[27] In other words, De Silva would have to find a way to pair

series of meetings between 1967 and 1970 (while the UNP Committee was convening) to discuss the new constitution. Alif, "Towards a Free Sri Lanka," 32. Wiswa Warnapala, "Colvin and the Constitution," *Lanka Guardian* 5, no. 9 (1982). Wilson, *Politics in Sri Lanka 1947–1979*, 211–213. Other members of the "Lawyer's Committee" included the following: Somarasa Dassanayake (SLFP), G D C Weerasinghe (CP), S W Walpita (SLFP) and M S Alif (SLFP).

[24] On De Silva's preferences for secularism, see: Colvin R De Silva, *Safeguards for the Minorities in the 1972 Constitution* (Colombo: Young Socialist Publication, 1987).

[25] Resolution 46(8), Working Draft, Drafting Committee of the Constituent Assembly, August 1970. Private archive of Nihal Jayawickrama. This phrase is also included in a Working Draft from October 1970.

[26] Letter from Prime Minister Bandaranaike to Colvin R De Silva, dated December 9, 1970. Private archive of Nihal Jayawickrama. See also Jayawickrama, "Reflections on the Making and Content of the 1972 Constitution: An Insider's Perspective."

[27] Several persons with whom I spoke suggested that Bandaranaike herself was also under considerable pressure from other politicians and senior members of the judiciary to

GIVING BUDDHISM ITS "RIGHTFUL PLACE" IN DBR 3   107

guarantees of religious freedom with special protections for Buddhism in a way that satisfied popular opinion, political necessity and (as best as possible) De Silva's own conscience. It was a dilemma that prompted De Silva to reflect a decade later: "I believe in the secular state. But you know when constitutions are made by Constituent Assemblies they are not made by the Minister of Constitutional Affairs."[28]

Giving Buddhism Its "Rightful Place" in Draft Basic Resolution Three

With this early compromise, the parameters of the new constitution's religion policy took shape. The policy would reflect the two major currents of public opinion since independence: the constitution would combine the protectionist and promotional paradigms; it would include special prerogatives for Buddhism and fundamental religious rights for all citizens. The question of *how* these prerogatives for the majority religion would be articulated – how the "rightful place" of Buddhism would be textually expressed – remained, however, heavily in dispute. As seen in previous chapters, the phrase "rightful place" had circulated widely in politics since the early 1950s. But, during the intervening two decades, no singular program of government action for implementing the "rightful place" had attracted widespread support.

One early attempt to define the "rightful place of Buddhism" and translate it into enforceable legal principles can been seen in an unsigned, undated draft of a constitutional policy toward Buddhism prepared by an anonymous member of the Drafting Committee. The draft divides state obligations to Buddhism into two sections. Under one section, entitled the "Directives of State Policy," Buddhism is integrated into a series of aspirational (but not justiciable) statements concerning the goals of government. In this section, Buddhism is "declared to be the State religion of the Republic of Sri Lanka." The draft also integrates protections for Buddhism into a chapter of "Fundamental Rights," which are to be enforced by the island's courts. Here the author lists a number of

---

include Buddhist prerogatives in the constitution. A version of this story appears in an editorial from the newspaper, *The Island*, March 12, 2011, entitled "Who Provided 'Buddhism the Foremost Place' in Sri Lanka's Constitution?" This does not negate the fact that popular pressures also existed.

[28] De Silva, *Safeguards for the Minorities in the 1972 Constitution*, 10.

measures that attempt to "prevent the Government from performing numerous acts which may be 'unbuddhistic.'"

Fundamental Rights
1. It shall be the duty of the Government to protect and maintain the Buddha Sasana.
2. The right of the Maha Sangha and of any person, whether individually or in community with others, in public or private freely to manifest, profess, practice and propagate the Dhamma [Buddha's teaching] is hereby guaranteed.
3. The Sacred Tooth relic and the Jaya Sri Maha Bo-tree at Anuradhapura and the Reverence, Worship, Observances, Rites and Practices connected therewith are declared inviolable.
4. The following Sacred Places of Worship and the Reverence, Worship, Observances, Rites and Practices connected therewith are declared inviolable:
    1. The Atmasthana [eight important Buddhist sites in the ancient city of Anuradhapura]
    2. Sri Padasthana
    3. Kirivehera at Kataragama
    4. Mahiyangana
    5. Kelani Vihare
    6. Seruvila
    7. Digavapi
5. Without prejudice to the foregoing provisions no sacred place of (Buddhist) worship including the objects of worship, shall be acquired, altered or in any way affected without the consent of the governing authority.

The draft does not clarify who would have legal standing to demand these Buddhist "fundamental rights." Nevertheless, the author lists these protections in a way that clearly obligates the government to aid and protect Buddhist monks, Buddhist doctrines and Buddhist places of worship. In the second provision, the author uses language from Article 18 of the Universal Declaration of Human Rights, yet he replaces the Declaration's generic protections for religious freedom with specific protections for Buddhist monks and laypersons to "profess, practice and propagate" the teachings of the Buddha. The draft also identifies nine Buddhist sites to be declared "inviolable," on account of their special ritual significance. Finally, in the fifth paragraph, the author clarifies that ownership rights over Buddhist temples and holy sites are given not to the state but to a Buddhist "governing authority."

GIVING BUDDHISM ITS "RIGHTFUL PLACE" IN DBR 3   109

This draft chapter on Buddhism brings together a number of desires expressed by various Buddhist groups since independence: that Buddhism should be declared the "state religion"; that Buddhist places of worship should be protected; that Buddhism should be free from government interference while also receiving government support. In addition, in its statement that Buddhist sites will be "inviolable," the draft echoes deliberately the language of Article 5 of the Kandyan Convention of 1815, which a number of Buddhist groups and politicians wanted to include in the constitution (see later in chapter). In this way the policy represents a kind of composite solution to the different demands regarding Buddhism.[29] It is a maximal constitutional privileging of Buddhism, one that contrasts dramatically – and perhaps deliberately – with the "secular" drafts produced by Colvin R De Silva.[30]

If one compares De Silva's early drafts with the policies on Buddhism just described, one sees in microcosm the deep disagreements over managing religion that polarized the ruling UF coalition: one side wanted to privilege Buddhism; the other side favored a religiously neutral constitution. In light of these disagreements, De Silva and the Drafting Committee decided, in the end, to fall back on the compromises that the SLFP and leftist parties had struck initially, while campaigning together. They would use the UF's official policy on religion, taken directly from the coalition's election manifesto.

As presented to the Constituent Assembly, the UF's Draft Basic Resolutions recapitulated, in fragments, the UF compromise on religion in the 1970 campaign manifesto. Resolution 4 on the "Principles of State Policy" (4(viii)) integrated the UF's commitments to calibrate economic and social objectives to enhance citizens' ability to follow their religions:

---

[29] Appended to the rights pertaining to Buddhism described earlier was the following section that applied to all religious groups:

"Subject to the provisions of the Constitution and to public order, morality and health, every religious denomination or any section thereof shall have the right–

(A) to establish and maintain institutions for religious and charitable purposes,
(B) to manage its own affairs in matters of religion,
(C) to own and acquire movable or immovable property in accordance with law, and
(D) to administer such property in accordance with law."

Untitled, Undated Memoranda (presumably from 1970) contained in personal files of Nihal Jayawickrama, relating to Draft Committee activities.

[30] De Silva, *Safeguards for the Minorities in the 1972 Constitution*, 10.

"The necessary economic and social environment will be created to enable people of all religious faiths to make a living reality of their religious principles." Resolution 5 on "Fundamental Rights" (5(iv)) echoed the UF manifesto's reference to the fact that "adherents of all faiths will be guaranteed freedom of religious worship and the right to practice their religion" while integrating virtually verbatim the provisions on religious freedom (Article 18(1)) contained in the United Nations' International Covenant on Civil and Political Rights:

> Every citizen shall have the right to freedom of thought, conscience and religion. This right shall include the freedom to have or to adopt a religion or belief of his choice, and the freedom, either individually or in community with others in public or private, to manifest his religion or belief in worship, observance, practice and teaching.

Finally, Resolution 3, which would become the Buddhism Chapter, paired together the UF election manifesto's reference to giving Buddhism its "rightful place" with its commitments to fundamental rights:

> In the Republic of Sri Lanka, Buddhism, the religion of the majority of the people, shall be given its *rightful place*[31] and accordingly, it shall be the duty of the State to protect and foster Buddhism, while assuring to all religions the rights granted by basic Resolution 5(4).[32]

SECTION II: THE BUDDHISM RESOLUTION AND MEMORANDA FROM THE PUBLIC

The earliest complete draft of the Buddhism Chapter was Draft Basic Resolution 3 entitled "Buddhism" (herein referred to as the Buddhism Resolution). The Buddhism Resolution spelled out the state's obligations to Buddhism in terms that had a historical ring to them – politicians had

---

[31] The resolution was drafted in English. The Sinhala translation was *nisitaena*; Tamil: *atarkuriya iṭam*. Although the English term "rightful place" seems to echo the language of S W R D Bandaranaike's Buddha Sasana Commission Report, the Sinhala term used to gloss the phrase is, in fact, different. In the Commission Report, the Sinhala term used is *yathātattvaya*, which has the connotation of proper condition. In the draft basic resolution, the term is *nisitaena*, which has the connotation of the appropriate *place*. The Tamil translation, as well, suggests a physical location for Buddhism, the phrase *atarkuriya iṭam*, connotating "a place that that is appropriate to it."

[32] Constituent Assembly, *Constituent Assembly Committee Reports* (Colombo: Ceylon Government Press, 1971), January 17, 1972, pp. 65–95.

MEMORANDA FROM BUDDHIST GROUPS 111

promised to give Buddhism the "rightful place" since the 1950s – but remained silent on what it meant practically to "protect and foster" the majority religion.

None of the Draft Basic Resolutions addressed the potential incongruities between Buddhist prerogatives and general religious rights. Drafters divided the original UF policies toward religion into three separate provisions, putting each within a different section of the constitution. In this way, drafters built multiple layers of multivalence into the constitution's policies toward religion. On the one hand, they wrote the Buddhism Resolution in a way that purposefully refrained from clarifying the links between Buddhism and the state. On the other hand, they deliberately remained silent regarding the links between promoting Buddhism and protecting the fundamental rights of all citizens.[33] This double-multivalence made the Buddhism Resolution the object of a large number of critical memoranda sent to the Constituent Assembly. These included letters from Buddhist and non-Buddhist vocational organizations, lay groups, clerical councils, regional associations, social service groups, labor unions, and a variety of other formal and informal groups and associations.[34]

Memoranda from Buddhist Groups[35]

As seen in earlier chapters, Buddhist groups and monastic sects disagreed over precisely what types of government action could be considered

[33] These included those ensuring for all citizens "equal protection of the law" (Resolution 5(i)) and the guaranteeing the rights of all communities to "enjoy and promote" their own culture (5(v)). They also included certain aspects of the "Principles of State Policy" suggested in Resolution 4, which, although not justiciable, were meant to serve as "objectives" to be pursued by the country's lawmakers. These included pledges to "strengthen national unity by promoting co-operation and mutual confidence between all sections of the people of Sri Lanka including the racial, religious and other groups" (4(iii)) and to "eliminate ... social privilege [and] disparity" (4(iv)).

[34] Alif, "Towards a Free Sri Lanka," 33.

[35] The memoranda examined were originally sent to the Ministry of Constitutional Affairs and were subsequently forwarded, in many cases with English and Sinhala translations, to various members of the Assembly. In what follows, I rely mostly on English language memoranda, official English translations of Sinhala memoranda (as marked) and my own translations of Tamil memoranda. My reliance on the official English translations of Sinhala memoranda derives from the limited time I had with these documents. After nearly six months of petitioning for permission from various government offices in a context of war-time security and suspicion of foreign researchers, I finally received permission to view these memoranda only two days before I was

supportive for Buddhism. One group, consisting primarily of lay Buddhist organizations with headquarters in Colombo, believed that government support for Buddhism required significant state control over Buddhist institutions and clerics. The government could best protect Buddhism, they argued, by using bureaucratic and legal structures to manage Buddhist places of worship, to unify disparate monastic sects and to inculcate Buddhist morals among the public. A second group, consisting primarily of the island's traditional monastic elites, argued that state support for Buddhism should take indirect forms. Rather than regulating Buddhist institutions (creating a "Buddhist state"), they argued, the government should help secure the autonomy of Buddhist monks and provide financial support for Buddhist ceremonies and places of worship.

The first perspective on the government's links to Buddhism can be seen forcefully in memoranda presented by the influential All-Ceylon Buddhist Congress (ACBC), the group that had championed the promotional paradigm in the 1950s.[36] Before a resolution on Buddhism had even been drafted, the Ministry of Constitutional Affairs received a long memorandum from the ACBC. In it, the organization called upon drafters to take seriously the island's "Buddhist Heritage." According to the ACBC, Sri Lankans had "cherished and protected the sublime teaching of the Buddha for over 2200 years" and the reign of Buddhist kings comprised the "Golden Age(s) of the Nation." The group demanded that drafters make the island a "Buddhist Socialist Republic," in which adherents of other religions could also practice their faiths.[37]

The ACBC recommended that four Buddhist principles should guide drafters in framing the constitution. These principles, the group argued, should also be included in the draft as "Directives of State Policy." These were:

---

    scheduled to leave Sri Lanka, having only a matter of several hours to work through numerous archives stuffed full of folders and files. I returned to the National Archives to re-examine these folders and files in 2014 but, on presenting the same file numbers, received different documents; for others, I was informed by staff that the documents could not be located. Recent shifting of the documents from one storage room to another may explain this.

[36] All documents mentioned in this section derive from the Sri Lanka National Archives, Ministry for Constitutional Affairs archive. MCA 25/2/33 "Proposals Submitted by the ACBC in Connection with the Proposed Constitution," September 1970. On the Buddhist Committee see Chapter 2.

[37] Ibid.

MEMORANDA FROM BUDDHIST GROUPS

(1) The Four Ways of Treating the World (*satara sangraha vastu*) viz. Charity (*dana*), Pleasant Speech (*priya vacana*), Equality (*samantamata*) and Performing Services to the World (*arthacaritya*);

(2) The ten principles of government (*Dasa Raja Dharma*) viz. Generosity, Morality, Selflessness, Rectitude, Mercy, Restraint, Freedom from anger, Non-violence, Patience and Tolerance;

(3) The four modes of noble conduct: loving kindness (*metta*), compassion (*karuna*), altruistic joy (*mudita*), and equanimity (*upekkha*);

(4) The middle way as taught by the Buddha.[38]

These principles, argued the ACBC, should sit alongside other constitutional provisions for "[restoring] to the Sangha the rightful place held by it during the time of the Sinhala kings . . . [and securing] the special relationship between the Sangha and the Buddhist laity."[39]

To ensure that Buddhism would retain a privileged status in the county, the ACBC proposed two limits to freedom of worship. The first limit was to prohibit proselytism undertaken through the "exploitation of poverty or by unfair means." This limit emerged out of earlier Buddhist criticisms of Christian missionary activities and, although unstated, would have been interpreted at the time as a legal measure for stemming Christian proselytizing in rural Buddhist villages (see Chapter 7). The second limit was to specify that freedom of religion

> shall not include the right to any economic, financial, political or other secular activities that may be associated with religious practice. For the achievement of this objective there shall be enacted a Charities Act.[40]

This limit was also designed to temper the power of Christian churches by giving the state authority to investigate their wealth and influence (see Chapter 2).

To unify Buddhists, the ACBC repeated its call for the creation of a Buddha Sasana Mandalaya (Buddhism Council) consisting of civil servants, Buddhist monks and lay leaders, who would be charged with "the protection and development of the *Sasana*." The ACBC memo specified further that the state should appoint a Ministry of Religious Affairs (with a specially designated Department of Buddhist Affairs) to support the work of the Mandalaya and coordinate the interests of other religious groups on the island with those of Buddhists. According to the memo,

---

[38] Note: all bracketed terms, some Sanskrit and some Pali, were included in the original memorandum.

[39] Ibid.   [40] Ibid.

114 MULTIVALENT SOLUTIONS

the Ministry and the Mandalaya should work together to oversee the use and transfer (where needed) of monastic property. They should also guarantee the regular performance of *perahera* (religious processions) and other important rituals.[41]

In the same month that the ACBC memorandum was received, a memorandum was also received from the head monks of the island's largest, oldest and wealthiest monastic fraternity, the Siyam Nikāya.[42] Like the ACBC letter, the Siyam Nikāya memo encouraged lawmakers to replace the phrase "rightful place" with clauses that more clearly specified the government's discrete obligations toward Buddhism. In its memo, the Siyam Nikāya argued that the government should protect Buddhism in the new constitution in the same manner as the island's ancient kings by including the phrase:

> It shall be the responsibility of the state to protect and maintain permanently as in the days of the Sinhala kings, Buddhism, its activities, the sangha, sacred objects of worship, temples and other means of continuing religious rituals uninterruptedly in the future.

Unlike the ACBC, the memo from the Siyam Nikāya argued that the government should *not* take charge of Buddhist affairs itself. Rather, the state should aspire to "protect and maintain" Buddhism without unnecessarily interfering in it.[43]

Central to the Siyam Nikāya's letter was the idea that the monkhood (*sangha*) ought to be autonomous. Therefore, while the state could act as a patron of the sangha, it could not function as an agent of monastic reform. In fact, the Asgiri and Malvatu *mahānāyaka*-s requested that drafters include a clause ensuring that:

> the state or the legislature shall not impose legislation, orders and regulations pertaining to the disciplinary activities of the sangha (*vinayakamma*), its ancient and traditional customs and manners, the administrative institution of the sect or the Board of Administration and its internal affairs.[44]

---

[41] Most of the ACBC's suggestions were drawn directly from the 1956 Buddhist Committtee of Inquiry Report (which it authored) and the 1959 Bandaranaike Buddha Sasana Commission Report (which was based rather closely on the ACBC's 1956 Report).

[42] Copy of Memo submitted September 10, 1970 in MCA 73/2/30, resubmitted February 22, 1971.

[43] Ibid.   [44] Ibid.

With this proposed provision, the Siyam Nikāya monks sought to inoculate themselves against any new forms of government oversight, particularly against the creation of island-wide monastic courts (*sanghādhikaraṇa*), which had been advocated by the ACBC since the 1950s.

The memoranda of the ACBC and the Siyam Nikāya illustrate important points of conflict and confluence among the broader Buddhist public regarding the meaning of Buddhism's "rightful place." The ACBC construed the phrase to mean a formalizing of the relationship between the state and religion, making the state a "Buddhist socialist republic" guided by Buddhist virtues.[45] It advocated a greater role for the government in organizing and administrating the practice of Buddhism; and, in certain cases, regulating the affairs of monks.[46] In contrast, the Siyam Nikāya believed that giving Buddhism its "rightful place" was an act of sponsorship, not supervision. The state should support Buddhist institutions on the island, including its places of worship, ritual celebrations, and pilgrimage sites, but refrain from intervening in the lives of those who were human embodiments of the Buddha's teaching, the island's monks.

An important common ground linked together the ACBC and the Siyam Nikāya's memoranda: both groups viewed the act of giving

---

[45] In advocating for Buddhism as the "state religion," the ACBC were supported by 23 other memoranda, only 2 of which were from monastic groups.

[46] In this view, the ACBC was supported by the Mahabodhi Society (MCA 73/2/123) and other lay organizations (e.g., MCA 73/2/8; 73/2/31). Most vocal about supervising the activities of the sangha was the *Sinhala Bauddha Sandvidhana*, which railed against monks taking paid employment in its memorandum (MCA 73/3/63):

"... no person while being a member of the noble order of the Sangha (who on entering the Order has solemnly and voluntarily vowed to refrain from owning or receiving money) shall be eligible for any such appointment ... It is well known that a Buddhist layman when entering the Order of the Sangha takes a solomn [*sic*] vow to refrain from owning or receiving money in any shape or form. It is, therefore, incumbent on the state which has undertaken to protect and foster Buddhism to ensure that it does not encourage or provide the opportunities for bhikkus [monks] to soil their Sila [morality] by obtaining employment in state institutions. On this matter Buddhist public opinion is very strong as the main pillar on which Buddhism rests is the Order of the Sangha [the monastic community] which must be maintained in adequate strength and purity, if Buddhism is to be preserved. This restriction should not be regarded as the denial of Fundamental Rights of a citizen in view of the circumstance that the vow is voluntarily taken at the time of entering the Order and it is always open to the individual at any time to leave the Order without any let [*sic*] or hindrance if he desires to regain his right of eligibility for employment under the State. It is should also be mentioned that the most potent cause of the deterioration of the Community of Bhikkus has been the opening of the door to Bhikkus for securing paid employment in state institutions in recent years."

116   MULTIVALENT SOLUTIONS

Buddhism its "rightful place" in the constitution as an act of continuity with the past. In the language of the ACBC memo, this was the "Golden Age(s) of the Nation"; in the Siyam Nikāya memo, it was the era of the Sinhala kings. This theme was also visible in memoranda from a number of smaller Buddhist organizations. Consider, for example, the memorandum written by Dr. T Vimalananda, a member of the 1956 ACBC Committee, professor of Archeology at Vidyalankara University and the vice president of the *Sinhala Bauddha Sandvidhana* (Association of Sinhala Buddhists):

> Fundamental to that solemn task of laying down the framework for the new constitution was the restoration to its rightful heirs of the sovereign authority which has resided in the Sinhala Buddhist people of Sri Lanka, which they had jealously and steadfastly guarded and preserved for over two thousand years and which they had temporarily ceded to the British crown, in terms of the carefully drawn up Kandyan Convention ... [I]t is therefore the fundamental and inescapable obligation of any new Constitution to begin by legally restoring that sovereignty to those by whom it was ceded, namely the Sinhala Buddhist people of Sri Lanka.[47]

According to Vimalananda (and other memoranda), by including protections for Buddhism in the constitution, drafters were not establishing a new situation of government patronage for Buddhism, they were *restoring* a situation that existed prior to colonial intervention.

Another idea linked together the submissions of the ACBC, the Siyam Nikāya and most other Buddhist group who sent memos: protections for Buddhism ought to take precedence over protections for other religions. This sentiment took different forms. Some memoranda demanded that the president, prime minister and chiefs of the armed forces should be Buddhists.[48] Others wanted politicians to swear an oath of office before the Buddha.[49] One organization[50] even requested that a more general limitation be placed on all state activities such that the government would be obliged to "refrain from the pursuit of policies repugnant to the basic tenets of Buddhism, for example, the five precepts or *pancha seela* [P: *pañca sīla*, five moral precepts of Buddhism] which is the minimum observance required of a Buddhist." That same organization also

---

[47] MCA 73/3/63.
[48] E.g., MCA 73/2/24 *Ruhuna Bhikkhu Peramuna*, February 3, 1971; MCA 73/2/25 *Samargi Bauddha Mandalaya*, January 31, 1971; MCA 73/2/151 Colombo Secretariat Buddhist Association and others.
[49] MCA 7/2/31 Lanka Dharmapala Youth Society.
[50] MCA 72/3/165 *Sasana Sanrakshaka Baudha Mandalaya*.

requested that the new constitution require "due license from the head of the State" before any non-Buddhist religious site could be constructed. Another organization, an important lay Buddhist group from Colombo, requested that a caveat be included in the chapter on fundamental rights that the rights of other religions to freedom of worship would be exercised "without prejudice and subject to the provisions contained in Basic Resolution 3 [on Buddhism]."[51]

Thus, while petitioning Buddhist groups debated the question of how the government might best support Buddhism, they universally agreed on the fundamental *inequality* of religions on the island. Buddhism, they assumed, deserved a higher constitutional status: while *citizens* might be granted equal protection before the law, *religions* should not.

Memoranda from Non-Buddhist Groups

Memoranda sent by non-Buddhist organizations ranged from mildly worded appeals to vituperative condemnations. Some groups assented to the idea that Buddhism should be given primacy but requested that Hinduism, Islam and/or Christianity should also be acknowledged as "national" religions. Other groups asserted that the very act of singling out the majority religion for special protections threatened the rights of minorities and undermined the purposes of democratic government. A third set of memoranda went even further, arguing not only that Buddhist privileges were anti-democratic but that they contravened the very tenets of Buddhism itself. A fourth set advocated for a secular state.

Rather than contest the primacy of Buddhism, one set of memowriters appealed to drafters to expand the list of religions receiving special privileges in the island's new constitution. The reformist Hindu group, the Vivekananda Vedanta Society, a Colombo-based organization popular among urban and middle-class Hindus,[52] argued, "we are of the opinion that Hinduism should also be given its rightful place and receive the protection of the state" insofar as "Hindus and Hinduism in Ceylon have also suffered under foreign rule."[53] Hinduism,

---

[51] MCA 7/2/23, February 5, 1971; MCA 73/2/7, n.d.

[52] MCA 73/2/3, December 16, 1970.

[53] The Democratic Socialist Party requested Resolution Three to read: "In Sri Lanka, Buddhism, the religion of the majority of the indigenous Sinhalese people and Hinduism, the religion of the majority of the indigenous Tamil people, shall be given their rightful place and accordingly it shall be the duty of the State to protect and foster Buddhism and Hinduism ... " MCA 72/3/37, February 4, 1971.

118 MULTIVALENT SOLUTIONS

the Society declared, should be specially protected by constitutional assurances that the state would "grant assistance ... for the carrying on of Hindu Religious and Cultural activities" and protect the "right of Hindu Temples, Organizations and Institutions, to own, possess and dispose of both movable and immovable property." Equally, the Society requested constitutional guarantees that the state would assist Hindu educational institutions and places of worship, represent Hindus in offices of state, support the Hindu priesthood and generally provide measures for the "promotion of the welfare of the Hindu community."

The Vivekananda Vedanta Society was not the only group to adopt this strategy of diluting the exclusivity of the Buddhism Resolution by including special protections for other religions. Several other organizations also pursued this angle, but in more ecumenical ways. The All-Ceylon Moors Association,[54] one of the island's largest Muslim political organizations, requested that drafters modify the Buddhism Resolution by changing the phrase, "it shall be the duty of the State to protect and foster Buddhism, *while assuring to all religions* the rights granted by basic Resolution 5(4)" to the phrase, "... *while assuring to Hinduism, Christianity, Islam and all other religions* ... " The Muslim Progressive Association of Kalmunai,[55] proposed a similar measure, requesting that the phrase be amended to read "... *while the religions of the minorities namely Hinduism, Islam, Catholicism and Christianity shall be given each its due place and protection and no religion shall interfere in the actions of the state.*" Similar recommendations for rewriting appeared in the submissions made by a political party that represented Tamil tea estate laborers, the Democratic Workers' Congress (DWC). The DWC pointed out in its memo that it would "be a good gesture [for drafters] to recognize [Hinduism, Islam, and Christianity] by name in order that every person belonging to these religions in the country may feel assured that his religion has been given a rightful place, while recognizing Buddhism as the religion of the predominant majority."[56]

Alongside the submissions described above were submissions that criticized the very idea of giving Buddhism preferential treatment, arguing that all religions should have equal status in the new constitution. The largest and most influential of the Hindu organizations on the island, the All-Ceylon Hindu Congress (ACHC),[57] rejected the idea that

---

[54] MCA 73/2/21.   [55] MCA 73/2/162, January 6, 1971.

[56] MCA 73/2/27, February 3, 1971.

[57] MCA 72/2/33, February 3, 1971, President A Sinnathamby.

MEMORANDA FROM NON-BUDDHIST GROUPS

some religions should be given greater support by the state. In its memorandum, the ACHC expressed "grave concern" regarding the language of the Buddhism Resolution:

> the adherents of other religions too form a part of the people of Sri Lanka and it is the duty of the state to extend its protections to the religions practiced by all its peoples. To foster and protect only the religion of the majority of the people will be discriminatory of the rest.

Rather than make reference to Buddhism, or any particular religion, the ACHC appealed that constitutional protections for religion should be guaranteed to "every religion practiced by an appreciable number of its citizens." This view was also endorsed by the National Christian Council, the island's largest Protestant Christian organization, which urged that the new constitution incorporate "the highest principles of all religions."[58] Similar sentiments also appeared in the submissions of the Ceylon Harijan Union, which represented the island's Hindu untouchables.[59]

A third group of memoranda argued that giving Buddhism a privileged place in the country was, in fact, "un-Buddhistic" and would damage the majority religion. In its submissions to the drafting committee, the Ceylon Tamil League, one of the island's oldest Tamil groups (if not a politically powerful one), warned that creating special protections for Buddhism in the constitution would "demean" the religion and would undermine its influence on society.[60] Similarly, the People's Forum of Jaffna,[61] a small society of social reformers in the island's largest Tamil center, argued that

> Buddhism is stated as a religion when actually it is not so [i.e., it is a philosophy]; authority (Rev. Narada-*Buddhism in a nutshell* [sic]). Further by stressing on "giving its rightful place," "Protection and fostering by the state" [it is] tantamount to declaring Buddhism as a state religion which ridicules Buddhism itself and makes Ceylon a Theocratic State and not a "socialist democracy."

Thus, according to the People's Forum (and its reading of *Buddhism in a Nutshell*, a text written by the popular Colombo monk, Ven. Narada Thera), through making Buddhism the "state religion" the Buddhism Resolution sabotaged both the SLFP's pledge to protect Buddhism and

---

[58] MCA 73/2/15, February 3, 1971.
[59] MCA 73/2/16, n.d. Similar requests for including all religions instead of Buddhism came from MCA 73/2/60, Trincomolee Tamil movement.
[60] MCA 7/2/4, January 18, 1971.   [61] MCA 7/2/26, February 1971.

120   MULTIVALENT SOLUTIONS

the LSSP's pledge to create a socialist democracy. A similar attack came from a small activist group in Batticaloa, the Eelam Self-Determination and Freedom Front, which called for a secular socialist state and criticized:

> The socialist democratic republic should be a secular state[;] there should be no state religion in a country daily clamouring for beef, more beef and better beef and therefore involving the colossal slaughter of animals in direct violation of the principles of ahimsa, sacred to Buddhism and Hinduism alike, it would be a sham and a mockery to have a state religion.[62]

A final set of memoranda implored the drafting committee to declare the country a secular state.[63] Various reasons were cited for this, all of which were articulated in a comprehensive memorandum from the Kalmunai Regional Council Meeting Group,[64] which represented Roman Catholic Parishes on the east coast of the island:

> We fail to understand why in a democracy one religion should be more equal than the others. The dialectic materialistic politician who drafted the resolution [Colvin R. De Silva] surely had not been guided by his own principles but by crafty pragmatic expediency when he drafted this one resolution. Obviously Buddhism the religion of the majority does not require any special place of protection in independent Sri Lanka. The resolution dutifully proclaims to protect and foster that religion with money from tax-payers who include the non-Buddhist minorities. It is cryptic that a religion which has stood the physical and philosophical assault of its enemies for well nigh 25 centuries should now, when it stands triumphant as the religion of the majority, require the protection of the state. And protection from whom? Further any modern progressive state leaves religion to the individual and it remains secular. The guarantees and protections provided in the resolution 5(iv) are enough for religion in the island to survive if it wants to do so. So resolution 3 is redundant and should be deleted.

The Kalmunai Group memorandum argued that the Buddhism Resolution not only violated the espoused secularist principles of Colvin De Silva and his LSSP party, it threatened the very egalitarian ethic on which democracy should be based. In the words of Kalmunai Group, the

---

[62] MCA 25/2/54, n.d.
[63] MCA 73/2/61 *ilagkai tamiḻiṉ capai*, Colombo, February 1, 1971; MCA 25/1/130 Council of Religions Batticaloa, which represented Buddhist, Catholic, Hindu, Anglican, Muslim and Methodist religious leaders.
[64] MCA 73/2/40, February 4, 1971.

Buddhism Resolution was undemocratic because it heaped protections on a majority that already dominated the government.

Reviewing these memoranda from Buddhist groups and other organizations, one can see precisely how the multivalence of the Buddhism Resolution (and, later, the Buddhism Chapter) worked as tool of evasion as well as compromise.[65] On the one hand, the multivalent language of "rightful place" avoided intervening in conflicts between Buddhist organizations that advocated greater direct state involvement in Buddhist affairs (such as the ACBC) and monastic organizations that emphasized the importance of keeping the monkhood completely autonomous (such as the Siyam Nikāya). On the other hand, by juxtaposing Buddhist prerogatives with general religious rights – in a way that did not clarify the priority of either one – drafters avoided answering the question (begged by Buddhist and non-Buddhist memoranda alike) of whether protections for Buddhism took precedence over, and could therefore limit, the state's duties to guarantee fundamental religious rights for all citizens.

SECTION III: THE ASSEMBLY DEBATES[66]

The multivalence of the Buddhism Resolution played a different function at each stage of the constitution-making process. At its inception, the multivalent language of the Buddhism Resolution served as a ground of compromise between the various factions within the UF coalition: those who pursued special privileges for Buddhism and those who favored a secular state. In its reception by the public, the language of the "rightful place" for Buddhism and its juxtaposition with guarantees of fundamental rights functioned as an impetus for

---

[65] They reached the Ministry of Constitutional Affairs at two stages in the drafting process: after August 1970 (when the process of constitution drafting began) and after March 1971 (when the debates regarding the Buddhism Resolution commenced in the Constituent Assembly).

[66] A note on languages and translations: The debates on Draft Basic Resolution 3, on Buddhism, extend over 330 pages in the Constituent Assembly transcripts, and they are conducted in three languages: Sinhala, Tamil and English. The language contained in the transcript is the language used by the member. (During the debates, there was concurrent translation into English and Tamil; however, these translations do not appear in the transcripts.) I indicate the language in which the quote was given in the footnotes. Where unspecified in the main text, I also indicate the speaker.

MULTIVALENT SOLUTIONS

Buddhists and non-Buddhists to send memoranda to the Ministry of Constitutional Affairs demanding clarification.

During the Constituent Assembly debates, these two responses to the multivalence of the Buddhism Resolution collided, with speakers both challenging and defending the need for multivalent language. In this section, I examine the formal debates within the Constituent Assembly concerning the Buddhism Resolution. In addition to analyzing key arguments, I highlight attempts by Assembly members to preserve what they saw as a fragile multi-sided agreement over religion by defending the multivalence of the Buddhism Resolution against political opponents who sought to rewrite it or eliminate it.

Introducing the Buddhism Resolution

On March 29, 1972, Resolution 3 on Buddhism appeared on the docket of the Constituent Assembly. The members of the SLFP who introduced the resolution described it as an important and central feature of the new constitution. The Buddhism Resolution, SLFP representatives insisted, would be *as* critical to the constitution as the resolutions that declared Sri Lanka to be a "free, sovereign and independent republic." Commitments to religion, one SLFP minister asserted, were no less essential to the future of the state than were commitments to democracy and economic reform: "Just as economics influence human life in this world (*melova*), religion is similarly crucial to securing benefit in the next-world (*paralova*)."[67]

Notwithstanding the lofty rhetoric, the ruling coalition insisted that Assembly members should look upon the Buddhism Resolution as a general statement of national principles rather than a concrete mandate for state action. SLFP minister T B Ilangaratne encouraged the Constituent Assembly not to focus on the specific administrative and legal arrangements implied, or not, by the resolution. Rather, he said, Assembly members ought to interpret the Buddhism Resolution in the broadest possible sense as a generic commitment to the "triple gem": the Buddha, his teaching (the *dhamma*) and his monastic followers (the *sangha*). According to Ilangaratne, Buddhism also included certain rules and institutions (*āyatana*) regarding donations, land grants and financial gifts.[68]

---

[67] Constituent Assembly, *Constituent Assembly Debates* (Colombo: Ceylon Government Press, 1971), March 29, 1971, T B Ilangaratne speaking, 622 in Sinhala.

[68] Ibid., March 29, 1971, 625, in Sinhala.

What was important in the Buddhism Resolution, he asserted, was not the bare meanings of the words themselves but the broad, if vague, ideas, commitments and principles (*pratipatti*) that they suggested.[69]

SLFP ministers underscored the links between the Buddhism Resolution and the island's history. According to the SLFP Minister of Cultural Affairs, S S Kulatilake, who seconded it, the resolution gave to Buddhism its "historical position" (*aitihasika sthānaya*), which had been articulated previously in Article 5 of the Kandyan Convention of 1815 and in the policies of the Lankan kings prior to that.[70] Like the island's ancient kings, he declared, the resolution both protected Buddhism and gave to all other religions a "place" (*taenak*) by permitting them to build places of worship and practice their faith.[71] According to Kulatilake and Ilangaratne, the Buddhism Resolution also built upon the ACBC Report of 1956 and Bandaranaike's Buddha Sasana Commission Report of 1959. In fact, they explained that the current resolution simply brought to fruition the recommendations of the ACBC Committee of Inquiry, specifically its proposals to repeal Section 29(2) of the current Constitution.[72] It also carried on the work of S W R D Bandaranaike, which had been arrested prematurely on account of his assassination.[73]

In introducing the Buddhism Resolution, SLFP ministers Ilangaratne and Kulatileke made a point of referring to memoranda requesting that Buddhism should be made the "religion of the state" (*rajyē āgama*). Ilangaratne, the Minister of Trade, dismissed those requests on account of their economic implications. Making Buddhism the state religion would interfere, he predicted, with the government's ability to certify industries like breweries and fisheries because those industries encouraged the consumption of alcohol and meat, behaviors that many Sri Lankans viewed as inconsistent with the teachings of the Buddha.[74] Moreover, Kulatilake pointed out, even if the state declared Buddhism the "state religion" (*rājyāgama*) as many people had requested, it would be no more or less significant than giving Buddhism the foremost place. What counted, he stated, was not the words chosen but the steps taken by individual governments to support Buddhism. Those steps were encouraged by, but not specified by, the Buddhism Resolution.[75] In dismissing

---

[69] Ibid., March 29, 1971, 624, in Sinhala.   [70] Ibid., March 29, 1971, 629, in Sinhala.

[71] Ibid., March 29, 1971, 629, in Sinhala.

[72] Ibid., March 29, 1971, 626, in Sinhala, Ilangaratne speaking.

[73] Ibid., March 29, 1971, 631, in Sinhala, Kulatilake speaking.

[74] Ibid., March 29, 1971, 626, in Sinhala.   [75] Ibid., March 29, 1971, 632, in Sinhala.

124   MULTIVALENT SOLUTIONS

the "state religion" proposals, both Ilangaratne and Kulatileke were careful to point out that drafters had not taken the expression "rightful place" (*nisitaena*) lightly; it had been decided upon only after considering many other possible options.[76]

Proposed Amendments

After introducing the Buddhism Resolution to the Constituent Assembly, UF ministers proceeded to defend it. In keeping with rules of procedure to which it had agreed at the outset, the Constituent Assembly oriented its debates around proposed amendments to the Buddhism Resolution. The Assembly debated three amendments in all, each of which echoed a particular reservation that had been expressed in the public memoranda described earlier. Unlike the memoranda, these amendments were drafted by, and proposed directly to, the Constituent Assembly by members of the Assembly. The first amendment, proposed by a politician within the government's ruling coalition, accepted the foremost place of Buddhism but requested that the resolution also refer specifically to the island's other religious communities. The second amendment, proposed by the largest opposition party at the time, the UNP, sought to strengthen the Buddhism Resolution by reframing its protections and privileges in more direct and forceful language. The third amendment, proposed by the largest all-Tamil political party at the time, the Federal Party, rejected the idea that Buddhism should have any privileged status at all, and proposed to replace it with a clause declaring the country a "secular" state.

Proposed Amendment One

The first amendment to the Buddhism Resolution was proposed by Abdul Aziz, the president of the Democratic Workers' Congress, a party that represented tea estate laborers and that had entered into coalition with the UF for the 1970 elections. Aziz represented the interests of

---

[76] It is noteworthy that immediately after the resolution was introduced by the SLFP ministers, members of the Assembly voiced concern over the precise relationship between Resolution 3 and the sections of Resolution 5 to which it referred. A UNP parliamentarian suggested that only after Resolution 5 was finalized, and its amendments fully considered, could a full discussion be had on Resolution 3. I will reflect more on this concern later. Ibid., March 29, 1971, 634.

mainly Indian Tamil plantation-workers. His amendment was a small and carefully worded one, which signaled concerns about the status of the island's other major religions of Hinduism, Islam and Christianity, without denying the central (Buddhist) promotional thrust of the resolution. Aziz requested that, in order "to give a certain measure of confidence to the followers of these three religions,"[77] the Buddhism Resolution should be amended to read (added language in italics):

> In the Republic of Sri Lanka, Buddhism, the religion of the majority of the people, shall be given its rightful place and accordingly, it shall be the duty of the State to protect and foster Buddhism, *while assuring to Hinduism, Islam, Christianity and all religions* the rights granted by basic Resolution 5(4).[78]

By including the names of other religions, Aziz claimed, the new constitution would signal the government's recognition of the "important part" that these religions played in the "cultural life" of the country. Aziz hastened to point out, however, that his amendment did not undermine the "fundamentals" of the Buddhism Resolution. Buddhism, he agreed, had been particularly damaged by colonialism. Moreover, he was confident that other religious communities would not suffer "at the hands of Buddhism."[79]

Aziz's amendment echoes many of the memoranda sent by non-Buddhist groups to the Ministry of Constitutional Affairs during the Constituent Assembly process. It sought not to challenge the primacy of Buddhism in the country, but only to secure some specific acknowledgment that other religions were also legitimate and important to the island's citizens.

Aziz's amendment failed to generate wide support, in large part due to an impassioned appeal by the chief architect of the Draft Basic Resolutions, Colvin De Silva. In a long speech, De Silva warned against tinkering with what he took to be a "very balanced" provision.

> It was after very careful consideration that the particular mode of reference to religions and Buddhism in particular was arrived at in respect of Basic Resolution 3. It is intended, and I think in all fairness it should be so stated, that the religion Buddhism holds in the history and tradition of Ceylon a special place, and the specialness thereof should be recognized in the Resolution. It was at the same time desired that it should be stressed that the historical specialness, the traditional specialness and the contemporary specialness which flows from its position in the country should not

---

[77] Ibid., March 29, 1971, 642, in English. [78] Ibid., March 29, 1971, 640, in English.
[79] Ibid., March 29, 1971, 640–642, in English.

be so incorporated in the Constitution as in any manner to hurt or invade the susceptibilities of those who follow other religions in Ceylon or the rights that are due to all who follow other religions in Ceylon. It is for that reason that, first of all, into the Resolution stating the place being assigned to Buddhism there was incorporated the reference to fundamental rights, Basic Resolution 5(iv). As would be, I think, generally accepted by all, Resolution 5(iv), if accepted by this House in due course as one of the basic principles of the coming Constitution, ensures as a fundamental right to all religions those rights which they should have, namely, the complete freedom of observing one's religion and taking it to others also.

As [sic] the same time, while the State protects all these religions, it is also pointed out that there is a special place, which is in terms of the phrase "its rightful place," that is given to Buddhism and that it is the duty of the State especially to protect, which I think is the correct English rendition of the [Sinhala] words *surakṣita koṭa*, and foster it. In other words, the State is assigned that task too in respect of Buddhism.

It is after very careful thought that every single word has been introduced into the Resolution, and, much as I would like to state that I yield to none in my respect for all religions which all peoples in this country and elsewhere follow, I would earnestly urge that any efforts to change the language or the content of what is a very carefully expressed Basic Resolution may result in, shall I say, some kind of unanticipated unbalancing of what is a *very balanced* Resolution.[80]

For the Minister of Constitutional Affairs, the Buddhism Resolution was a hard-wrought formula that acknowledged an important political reality at the time: the widespread feeling that some nod should be made to Buddhism's "specialness" in the constitution. At the same time, in De Silva's eyes, the resolution tried to guarantee that such an acknowledgment would not threaten the rights of non-Buddhists.[81] As evident in his speech, De Silva saw the Buddhism Resolution as a very delicately phrased – and painstakingly "balanced" – rhetorical bargain that managed to articulate Buddhist priorities and general rights in a single widely acceptable provision.

Proposed Amendment Two

Where Aziz's amendment and De Silva's reply generated only limited debate, the second amendment, proposed by the opposition UNP, led to

---

[80] Ibid., 643–644, in English.

[81] In a later comment, De Silva pointed out that *surakṣita* meant not just "protecting" but "well-protecting" Buddhism. Ibid., March 29, 1971, 723, in English.

PROPOSED AMENDMENT TWO 127

considerable dispute over multiple days. The UNP's amendment, in essence, expanded the language of Buddhist support and privileges in the resolution, by adding phrases taken from the Kandyan Convention of 1815 (added language in italics):[82]

> In the Republic of Sri Lanka, Buddhism, the religion of the majority of the people, shall be *inviolable* and shall be given its rightful place, and accordingly, it shall be the duty of the State to protect and foster Buddhism, *its rites, Ministers and its places of worship*, while assuring to all religions the rights granted by basic Resolution 5(4).

The existing Buddhism Resolution, the UNP charged, gave inadequate support to Buddhism and failed to reflect the longer history of Buddhism on the island. Its amended version, the UNP argued, strengthened the provision so that it stated more clearly the government's obligations to the majority religion.[83]

While the UNP amendment ostensibly aimed to bolster and clarify the Buddhism Resolution, the debates surrounding the amendment hinged, in large measure, on a different question: to what extent was it proper to use the Kandyan Convention of 1815 (which was, after all, a treaty with a former colonial power) as a template for a new constitution? Over two days, the debate over the UNP's amendment merged with discussions about the significance of the Kandyan Convention. In the debates, another point of controversy arose: while some members wanted the new constitution to signal a continuity with Sri Lanka's colonial and precolonial past, others argued that the constitution, and its Buddhism Resolution, should signal a break with the past. That is, built into the Buddhism Resolution, unintentionally, was another important ambivalence regarding the warrant and purpose of constitutional prerogatives for Buddhism: was the purpose of the Buddhism Resolution to restore an older form of Buddhist governance or to generate an entirely new religio-political order?

---

[82] The Kandyan Convention of 1815 was a treaty signed by Sinhalese nobles and British administrators, which formalized Britain's control of the last independent Sinhalese kingdom on the island. It included Article 5 that specified: "the Religion of Boodhoo professed by the Chiefs and inhabitants of these Provinces is declared *inviolable*, and its *Rites, Ministers and Places of Worship* are to be maintained and protected." (Also see Chapter 2.)

[83] In keeping with the UNP's 1970 Election Manifesto, it is likely that the innuendo here is that those future governments that would seek to harm Buddhism would be Communist ones. *UNP Election Manifesto* 1970. See also the exchange at ibid., March 30, 1971, 891.

128 MULTIVALENT SOLUTIONS

Assembly members offered conflicting answers to these questions by way of their dueling assessments of the Kandyan Convention of 1815 and its legacy. The UNP treated the Kandyan Convention as an authorized source-text on which to base the country's religious policy. UNP spokespersons presented Article 5 as a set of terms that the Kandyan chiefs dictated to the British as a condition of their cooperation.[84] By contrast, most members of the UF argued that the Kandyan Convention was a surrender arrangement that was drafted only after the British had already taken control of the region. Article 5, they contended, contained small and trivial concessions to Buddhism, which were included only in order to placate the sensibilities of new vassal rulers, and to hide other, more insidious, features of colonial domination.

On the first day of debates, it was the second perspective, that of the UF, that dominated. The Minister of Constitutional Affairs, Colvin De Silva, again, spoke most forcefully. Trained as a historian as well as a lawyer, De Silva had published a history of British colonialism in Ceylon several years earlier. In that history, he shed a tragic light on the signing of the Kandyan Convention.[85] Presenting evidence from his book, De Silva rejected strenuously the UNP's imputed equivalence between the new constitution and the Kandyan Convention and between the Buddhism Resolution and Article 5. The Kandyan Convention, argued De Silva, was a document imposed by the British on the Kandyans. He described the UNP's glorification of the Convention as "an effort to present a document by which our country was sold to the foreigner as a document of freedom."[86] De Silva further asserted that the circumstances of the Convention and the new constitution were far from comparable. The Kandyan Convention spelled out the legal conditions of colonial occupation, while the new constitution would be the charter of a sovereign state:

> The people of this country are sovereign. Seventy-four per cent of the people in this country are Buddhists and my Hon. Friend wants to make Buddhism inviolable by the people of this country, 74 per cent of whom are Buddhists![87]

---

[84] Ibid., March 30, 1971, 852, in Sinhala.

[85] This book was based on De Silva's Ph.D. dissertation at the University of London, where he studied History. Colvin R De Silva, *Ceylon Under the British Occupation, 1795–1833 (2 Vols)* (Colombo, Sri Lanka: Colombo Apothecaries, 1953).

[86] Constituent Assembly, *Constituent Assembly Debates*, March 29, 1971, 652, in English.

[87] Ibid., March 29, 1971, 663, in English.

According to De Silva, the contrast between the Kandyan Convention and the new constitution could not be greater: the new constitution would be produced and ratified by an independent people; the Kandyan Convention was "a document which [we] signed as slaves."[88]

In De Silva's narrative, the Kandyan Convention's protections for Buddhism were weak concessions, many of which Buddhists had already been granted by the Portuguese and the Dutch. The Convention, he inveighed, did not reflect the aspirations of the Kandyan populace, but the treacherous self-interest of a few Kandyan nobles.[89] As evidence of this, De Silva pointed to a series of rebellions that took place in Kandy between 1818 and 1848.[90]

Other UF ministers joined De Silva in his views. One representative argued that the history of the Convention was one of low-country Sinhalese collaborating with the British to destroy the Kandyan kingdom, a story of sabotage and treason – of Sinhalese traitors contributing to the British conquest of the island.[91] Another UF representative went even further in arguing that the Kandyan Convention was, in fact, part of a conspiracy by the British to destroy Buddhism, not to protect it.[92]

UNP members, particularly those who represented Kandyan electoral districts, repudiated these negative interpretations of the Kandyan Convention.[93] In their eyes, the Convention was not a treasonous agreement, but a heroic attempt by patriotic nobles to overthrow a cruel and unjust king. They asserted that the last king of Kandy was a Tamil Hindu who ignored the needs of Buddhists and consolidated power around his own relatives.[94] Sinhalese nobles, seeing this, struck a deal with the British so that they could overthrow a tyrannical king *and* help protect Buddhism. Rather than terms of surrender, as De Silva had suggested, the UNP speakers argued that the Kandyan Convention was a treaty where "two separate kingdoms were merged [the Kandyan Kingdom, and

---

[88] Ibid., March 29, 1971, 720, in English.

[89] Ibid., March 29, 1971, 713–7, in English and Sinhala, Colvin De Silva speaking.

[90] Ibid., March 29, 1971, 673, in Sinhala.

[91] Ibid., March 29, 1971, 671, in Sinhala, Ratna Deshapriya (R D) Senanayake speaking.

[92] Ibid., March 29, 1971, 729–6, in Sinhala, Ilangaratna speaking.

[93] Ibid., March 30, 1971, 759, in Sinhala, Gamini Dissanayake speaking.

[94] In fact, the island's kings had long intermarried with South Indian royalty and, when the last of the Sinhalese Kandyan kings died in 1739 without heirs, it was a Tamil-speaking Hindu-born king, Kirti Sri Rajasinha, who helped revive Buddhist monasticism and restore Buddhist temples on the island. John Holt, *The Religious World of Kīrti Śrī: Buddhism, Art, and Politics in Late Medieval Sri Lanka* (New York: Oxford University Press, 1996).

the United Kingdom]."[95] In this narrative, the Kandyan Convention emerged from an act of self-*sacrifice* by those who perpetrated a lesser evil (transferring power to the British) to protect against a greater evil (a Tamil king who allegedly threatened Buddhism). Thus, the UNP representatives insisted, the Convention was a document born from a courageous act of "taking back" the country, a triumph of Sinhala over Tamil, Buddhism over Hinduism, and righteous nobles over an evil king.[96]

According to UNP speakers, the Convention also provided clear legal guidelines for protecting Buddhism. They pointed out that Article 5 of the Kanydan Convention listed the state's duties to secure Buddhist places of worship, which was something that the original Buddhism Resolution did not do.[97] According to one member, if Article 5 of the Convention served to protect Buddhism in a context of British occupation, so too could it protect Buddhism from a potential dictator in Sri Lanka.[98]

If the debates over the first proposed amendment tested the balance between the two parts of the Buddhism Resolution (its privileging of Buddhism and its assurances to other religions), the debates over the UNP's second proposed amendment challenged the very relationship between the island's constitutional future and its colonial past. The UNP's amendment not only sought to render more explicit the government's duties toward Buddhism, it attempted to link present legal arrangements to historical ones, to "restore" the primacy of Buddhism through recapitulating the language of earlier legal documents. Thus, the leader of the UNP underscored the importance of direct, linguistic continuity with the Kandyan Convention:

> Now it is March 1971. 156 years later [after the Kandyan Convention was signed], instead of an English dynasty we are preparing to create a dynasty of the people (*mahajana vaṅśayak*) ... in order to defend the Buddha's legacy (*buddha śāsanaya*), which has existed for 2500 years, it is fitting that we include also in our new constitution the same words that the Kandyan chieftains had used in 1815 in the Kandyan Convention ... Inserting them [the words of the Kandyan Convention] is an obligation for us.[99]

---

[95] Constituent Assembly, *Constituent Assembly Debates*, March 30, 1971, 764, in English, Dissanayake speaking.

[96] Ibid., March 30, 1971, 744–747, 753–755, mainly in Sinhala with some English.

[97] Ibid., March 30, 1971, 749, in Sinhala.

[98] Ibid., March 30, 1971, 771–776, 880–892, in Sinhala with some English, Dissanayake speaking.

[99] Ibid., March 30, 1971, 851, in Sinhala.

PROPOSED AMENDMENT THREE 131

The new constitution, in this light, corrected history by restoring a link between the state and Buddhism that was thought to have existed for thousands of years. The UNP presented the amendment to the Buddhism Resolution as an attempt to realign the present with an idealized past – to remake a new Sri Lanka in the image of an ancient one.[100]

Proposed Amendment Three

The final amendment, introduced by the largest Tamil opposition party at the time, the Federal Party (FP), proposed to eliminate special protections for Buddhism altogether.[101] The amendment, whose

---

[100] It is notable that, in course of the debate, regional loyalties prevailed over party loyalties on two separate occasions: two members of the SLFP who represented up-country constituencies defended the UNP view of the Kandyan Convention. P B Unantenna, a representative from Hanguranketa (near Nuwara Eliya) argued that the Kandyan Convention emerged out of a struggle between indigenous Sinhalese, the people that the Buddha had identified as guardians of Buddhism, and "foreign" invaders who threatened to destroy Buddhism. The drafting of the Kandyan Convention, he felt, represented an important episode in this history. The Kandyan chiefs who signed the convention were thus to be viewed alongside the great mytho-historical Sinhala kings, including Vijaya, Dutugemunu and Parakramabahu. According to Unantenna, at the signing of the Convention it was the Kandyan chiefs who negotiated, and from a position of power (the British being unable to conquer the kingdom without their assistance). Kandyan nobles' primary objective in negotiating the treaty was, therefore, to do what the earlier Sinhala kings had done, namely to protect Buddhism. The chiefs, Unantenna declared to the assembly, were not nation-betrayers (*dēśadrōhi*), but national patriots (*dēśaprēmi*). Ibid., March 30, 1971, 782–783, in Sinhala.

D M Jayaratne, an SLFP representative from Gampola, took this idea even further, narrating the entire history of Sri Lanka with the Sinhalese as natives – analogous, in his reasoning, to the Australian Aborigines and New Zealand Maori – and all other groups, including Tamils, as invaders or would-be colonizers. He also gave a slightly different version of events in the final days of the Kandyan Kingdom and the lead up to the treaty. In this version, it wasn't so much the fault of the Kandyan king for betraying the kingdom, but the fault of English spies such as John D'Oyly who befriended and misled the king. Seeing his betrayal, and, on account of his failure to support Buddhism, the Kandyan chiefs plotted against him (between 1818 and 1848), but with the ultimate desire of installing a Sinhala king. Jayarante pointed out further that Buddhist monks were involved in singing the Convention and had expressed, at the moment of signing, the belief that the document would secure Buddhism. Ibid., March 30, 1971, 786–809, in Sinhala.

[101] The Federal Party would later walk out of the Constituent Assembly process (see later). During the debates on the Buddhism Chapter, however, the Federal Party remained present and, according to the speeches recorded in the transcripts, appeared to participate in good faith, hoping to influence the shape of the new constitution to make it more responsive to Tamil concerns.

132 MULTIVALENT SOLUTIONS

original version was in Tamil not Sinhala, virtually rewrote the Buddhism Resolution entirely:

> The Republic of Sri Lanka must be a secular State[102] (T: *oru matar cārpaṟṟa aracātal*) but must protect and foster (T: *pātukākkavum pēṇi vaḷarkkavum*) Buddhism, Hinduism, Christianity and Islam.[103]

According to the Federal Party amendment, the Sri Lankan state would be a state that, in a literal translation of the Tamil term, "did not lean towards [a particular] religion" and, instead, supported all of the island's four major religions of Buddhism, Hinduism, Christianity, and Islam. The amendment was introduced not merely as a proposal from the Federal Party, but as an amendment that had been affirmed unanimously by all major Tamil political groups at an "All-Parties" conference of Tamil political organizations[104] held in the northern province town of Valveṭṭitturai on February 7, 1971. According to the FP representatives, the amendment embodied the "demands of the united Tamil people who want to live in this country as brothers of the Sinhalese people in unity and on equal terms."[105]

The Constituent Assembly debated the Federal Party's amendment under tense conditions. In early April, a group of armed Marxist insurgents, known as the People's Liberation Front (*Janathā Vimukti Peramuna*, JVP), launched a series of coordinated attacks on police and military barracks around the island, very nearly gaining control of large sections of the country. Bandaranaike and the UF government hesitated and then responded forcefully, declaring a State of Emergency and rounding up hundreds of suspected insurgents. The Assembly meetings were cancelled for several weeks. By the time that the debates got back under way in mid-May, the government had taken 450 people into custody and the government found itself fighting

---

[102] In the official Sinhala translation of the Amendment seen in the committee reports, "a secular state" is translated as *lōkāyatta rājyayak*. This particular translational decision would become important over the course of the debates, as examined later. Constituent Assembly, *Constituent Assembly Committee Reports*, February 27, 1971, 210–232, in English, Sinhala and Tamil.

[103] Constituent Assembly, *Constituent Assembly Debates*, May 14, 1971, 923, in Tamil.

[104] Including the Federal Party, the All-Ceylon Tamil Congress, the "*Eallam Thamil Ottumai Munnai*" (Eelam Tamil Unity Front) and the "*Tamil Suadchi Kazagam* (Association for Tamil Self-Government), these were quoted in English transliteration in an English portion of the speech. More accurate transliterations from Tamil would be: *īḻa tamiḻ ottumai muṉṉai* and *tamiḻ cu-āṭci kaḷakam*.

[105] Constituent Assembly, *Constituent Assembly Debates*, May 14, 1971, 905, in English.

PROPOSED AMENDMENT THREE 133

a guerilla insurgency.[106] The idea of cancelling the Assembly was addressed on more than one occasion. Yet, a majority of members voted to continue the process, passing a resolution that confirmed members' unrestricted freedom to express political opinions, however unpopular or controversial.

Seemingly not intimidated by the political climate, Visvanathan Dharmalingam, a senior Federal Party member, introduced the amendment on behalf of all Tamil opposition parties. Dharmalingam declared that the Buddhism Resolution violated the founding principles of almost all of the island's major political parties. He argued that it contravened the intentions of the SLFP's founder, S W R D Bandaranaike, who hoped to create a secular government when he appointed his Joint Select Committee on the Revision of the Constitution in 1957.[107] He argued that it also violated the original policies of the UNP, which aimed at creating a "government that did not lean towards religion" (*mata cārparra aracāgkam*). Ignoring this founding creed, Dharmalingam said that the UNP now appeared to favor a "theocratic state."[108] Finally, Dharmalingam claimed that the Buddhism Resolution contravened the socialist foundations of the LSSP and CP. Those parties, he argued, had abandoned two core tenets of Marxism: the idea that politicians should sever "any kind of link between the government and religion" and that they should aim to "keep religion outside of the state."[109] If the Assembly were to pass the Buddhism Resolution un-amended, Dharmalingam insisted, they would be forfeiting the secular political tradition that had once dominated the island's politics.[110]

In Dharmalingam's eyes, giving Buddhism its "rightful place" was not simply a statement of general principles. It had direct legal consequences.

> If the constitution is constructed in the same way as in the Third Draft Resolution, no one will be able to change the fact that there is a place for only one religion in this country ... Buddhism. Some may think that because they have spoken about other religions in Resolution 5(iv), no

---

[106] Mrs. Bandaranaike's state of emergency would be extended six more years until she left office. Warnapala, "Colvin and the Constitution." S Arasaratnam, "The Ceylon Insurrection of April 1971: Some Causes and Consequences," *Pacific Affairs* 45, no. 3 (1972): 356–371.

[107] Constituent Assembly, *Constituent Assembly Debates*, May 14, 1971, 926, in Tamil.

[108] Ibid., May 14, 1971, 925, in Tamil but "theocratic state" quoted in English.

[109] Ibid., May 14, 1971, 939 in Tamil. *matattirkum aracāgkattirkum enta vitamāna campattamum; matattai aracāgattirku veḷiyē vaittu.*

[110] Ibid., May 14, 1971, 924–925, in Tamil.

134   MULTIVALENT SOLUTIONS

> objection should be voiced. I want to point out the fact that except the
> rights (*urimai*) that have been applied to individual persons, there are no
> rights that have been allocated to religions ... except for Buddhism, and
> Buddhism alone. No place is given to all other religions. For this very
> reason, just as this government has eliminated the language of the minor-
> ity people of this country, so too will they eliminate [the people's] religion
> by establishing this constitution.[111]

With this speech, Dharmalingam pointed to an important feature of the
Buddhism Resolution that had gone unacknowledged in the debates: the
Buddhism Resolution and the resolution protecting fundamental rights
did not, strictly speaking, offset one another. They were not "carefully
balanced," as Colvin De Silva had suggested. The resolution promoting
Buddhism gave state perquisites to a *religion* (*matam*), while the resolution protecting fundamental rights applied to *citizens*. There was,
therefore, a distorting linguistic inaccuracy within the Buddhism Resolution: the UF claimed that prerogatives for the majority religion were
counterbalanced by assurances of fundamental rights for "all religions"
contained in Resolution 5; yet those fundamental rights applied not to
"all religions" but to individual persons (*taṇippaṭṭa maṇitarkaḷukku*).[112]
According to the letter of law, as the UF proposed it, Buddh*ism* could
claim legal status, protections and privileges that Hinduism, Islam and
Christianity could not:

> [E]xcept for the right for them to worship according to the Hindu
> religion, the right for them to worship according to the Christian religion,
> the right for them to worship according to the Islamic religion, Christian-
> ity or Hinduism of Islam have no other rights.[113]

Dharmalingam pointed out that guarantees of freedom to worship
and belief for citizens did not limit the preeminence of Buddhism as

---

[111] Ibid., May 14, 1971, 929–930, in Tamil.

[112] Dharmalingam and others raised the issue of the incoherence of Buddhist privileges and
religious fundamental rights, as well, during the debates on the Fundamental Rights
resolution (Resolution 5). Here the argument took a slightly different shape. Dharmalingam pointed out that, as currently worded, the protections for religion in Resolution 5
(iv) were rendered as protections for citizens, rather than for all persons living on the
island. Such a provision would not protect the many Tamil tea estate laborers who lived
in the up-country of the island but who had not been granted formal citizenship by the
government. Dharmalingam argued, "does that mean that this Government thinks that
it is not their duty to give a constitutional guarantee [of religious freedom] to the ten
lakhs of Tamils and Hindus are stateless today?" Ibid., May 20, 1971, 1157, in English.

[113] Ibid., May 14, 1971, 930, in Tamil.

a religion; nor did it ensure rights or protections for minority religions, as De Silva had declared. Rather, he contended, according to the resolution, Buddhism remained the only officially recognized faith and, as a consequence, the only religion that would be guaranteed state support and funding by the new constitution.[114]

Members of the Federal Party argued further that, aside from the fact that the Buddhism Resolution failed to secure the rights of other religious groups, it also violated the very logic of democratic constitutionalism. "In no [democratic] constitution of the world's countries," contended Dharmalingam, "is a place reserved for clauses in order to protect the religion of the majority."[115] He continued:

> Are you afraid that they [Sri Lankan citizens] will destroy Buddhism? In the national census, 79% of the persons are Buddhists. Are you afraid that they will destroy Buddhism? Or, do you think that Buddhist ministers in this government will undermine Buddhism or will destroy Buddhism? Or, do you think that the Marxists who are in your coalition will destroy Buddhism? Why do you seek this protection ... why must protection be sought for the religion and language of the majority within a country?[116]

Another Federal Party leader, K P Ratnam, contended that Buddhism was already protected in the proposed resolutions, along with other religions, under the sections on the Directives of State Policy and Fundamental Rights: Resolution 4(3) directed the government to support national unity though fostering all religions; Resolution 4(8) directed the government to strive for economic and social conditions that made it easier for all persons to live according to their religious ideals; and Resolution 5(iv) guaranteed to all religious individuals freedom of belief and worship. Thus, Ratnam said:

> All these sections that I cited enable adherents of all religions to practice their religions from now on, in the way that they desire. It is somewhat appropriate to say that, if this country's government is a religiously neutral government, then all the religions of this country *can be* protected. If not, I wish to point out that it [would be] fair to say that Buddhism, the religion of the majority group in this country, will be the state religion (*araca matam*).[117]

Thus, for Ratnam, as for Dharmalingam, the Buddhism Resolution was unnecessary for protecting the majority religion. Buddhism would be

---

[114] Ibid., May 14, 1971, 939, in Tamil.
[116] Ibid., May 14, 1971, 932, in Tamil.
[115] Ibid., May 14, 1971, 931, in Tamil.
[117] Ibid., May 14, 1971, 947, in Tamil.

136   MULTIVALENT SOLUTIONS

protected both demographically, as the religion of the island's majority, and legally, through the proposed protections for religion outlined in other sections of the constitution. The role of the Buddhism Resolution, in their eyes, was to link the identity of the state to Buddhism and to give Buddhism, as a religion, superior legal privileges. Rebutting the claims of the UF ministers who introduced it, Ratnam argued that the Buddhism Resolution effectively made Buddhism a "state religion."

Despite their critiques, Federal Party members also recognized that they did not have the voting power to influence decisively the course of the Constituent Assembly. As one member put it "if it is to be purely a question of taking votes, there is no purpose in our wasting our lungs here."[118] Instead, Federal Party speakers appealed to members' sense of religious harmony and communal solidarity, and even to the principles of Buddhism itself. Dharmalingam urged:

> Buddhism is not the only religion of this country. In this country, there are a significant number of Christians. In this country, there are a significant number of Saivites. In this country, there a significant number of Muslims. I want to ask, under these circumstances: if you say that we arose from a religious foundation and therefore need to give an important place to religion, why give an important place to Buddhism alone? Is Buddhism alone the religion of this country? Is there not a place in this country for all the other religions? I conclude this speech by saying that if the people of this country must live on the basis of religion, then among the duties of the government of this country is the requirement to protect, foster and cultivate all the religions of this country.[119]

K P Ratnam, in turn, appealed to the teachings of Buddhism. He argued that by including the Buddhism Resolution, the government was making a constitutional distinction between "majority" and "minority" populations, a distinction that cut against the underlying principles of Buddhism itself: "it is very sad that Buddhism, a religion which should unify people and which is founded on the principles of kindness and mercy, should divide the people of this country into majority and minority."[120]

Members of the Federal Party also suggested that the resolution on Buddhism, as written, was not only discriminatory, but hopelessly vague. One FP representative commented:

---

[118] Ibid., May 14, 1971, 952, in English, K Jeyakkody speaking.
[119] Ibid., May 14, 1971, 940, in Tamil.   [120] Ibid., May 14, 1971, 947, in Tamil.

RELIGION, SECULARISM, AND THE CONSTITUENT ASSEMBLY 137

> When I read further, I wonder whether this clause is meant to deceive the
> majority people themselves. What does it say? ... ["Rightful place"] is a
> very vague term. "Rightful place" may be like the length of the foot of the
> chancellor. It may mean anything.[121]

This vagueness, K P Ratnam pointed out accurately, was designed for
political approval, not legal clarity:

> You have given a place only to Buddhism. It appears that you have given
> this importance to Buddhism to satisfy two factions [the SLFP and the
> LSSP]. If you do one thing to satisfy both factions, you will be unable to
> satisfy either faction. This Basic Resolution looks as if it has been made to
> pacify [on one side] the opinions of extremists who say "we don't want
> religion," "don't mix religion with politics," "religion is opium," "a drug,"
> and [on the other side] those religious extremists who say that religion
> alone must give life to the country and religion alone must give life to the
> people. ... Our party does not object to Buddhism. I say make Buddhism
> the state religion. I only ask that you do not play both angles. You're
> trying not to offend those who oppose religion by saying that it won't be
> our state religion. [And] you're trying to say to those who want religion
> that, without recognizing other religions, you will only give a place to
> Buddhism. I want to point out that this basic draft resolution takes a
> position between the two. Therefore, both will sour.[122]

Referring to the intercoalition compromises of the UF, K P Ratnam
called attention to a fact known, if not always publically stated, by most
Assembly members: the Buddhism Resolution was purposefully multivalent. De Silva and the UF called it compromise; Ratnam called it political
expediency.

Religion, Secularism, and the Constituent Assembly

In the course of the Constituent Assembly, and in the debates surrounding the proposed amendments, one sees a clash between two responses to
the multivalence of the Buddhism Resolution. One response was to seek
further clarity by redrafting the resolution using more concrete language
and detailing more precisely the state's relationship to religion. A second
response was to defend the rhetoric of the clause as politically necessary
and deliberately unclear. In proposing amendments to the Buddhism

[121] Ibid., May 14, 1971, 947, in English.
[122] Ibid., May 14, 1971, 945–946, K P Ratnam in Tamil.

Resolution, members of the Assembly responded in the first way: they sought to refine or alter particular meanings of the Buddhism Resolution, either advocating for the equal recognition of Hinduism, Islam and Christianity (as in Aziz's amendment), expanding its prerogatives for Buddhism (as in the UNP amendment), or underscoring a principle of egalitarian secularism (as in the FP's amendment). In introducing and defending the Buddhism Resolution, UF ministers responded in the second way: they appealed to Assembly members to think broadly about the underlying principles of the Buddhism Resolution and not its specific words. For the opposition UNP and FP, the process of challenging the Buddhism Resolution involved exposing and destabilizing the UF's rhetorical equipoise by pushing for the inclusion of language that would signal more explicitly which paradigm of religious governance would dominate: promotional or protectionist, Buddhist privileges or fundamental rights. For the UF, the processes of disambiguating was dangerous insofar as it threatened to expose the precarious "balancing" (to use De Silva's term) of the language designed to satisfy multiple, competing political interests and to signal, however imperfectly, two types of bargains over religion: an interreligious bargain (between demands for Buddhist privileges and demands for equal religious rights) and the intrareligious bargain (between demands for government control over Buddhist institutions and demands for monastic autonomy).

Yet, the debates over the Buddhism Resolution were not only marked by deliberate attempts to use or contest the multivalence of constitutional language. The debates were also marked by unintentional multivalence that resulted from the multilingual format of the Constituent Assembly, itself, in which members gave their speeches in one of the island's recognized languages – Tamil, Sinhala or English – while translators worked in real time to translate those speeches into other languages. While these translations do not appear in transcripts from the Constituent Assembly, multilingual readers can see clearly in the debates over the third proposed amendment the fact that Tamil and Sinhala members of the Constituent Assembly talked *past* each other on account of subtle differences in the connotations of Tamil, English and Sinhala terms. In the English version of the amendment that the Federal Party presented to the Assembly, government translators used the word "secular" to translate the Tamil term *matacārparra*, which, as I indicated earlier, means "not leaning towards a particular religion." When Sinhala speakers cited the amendment, they used the term *lōkāyatta* or "worldly." These particular translational decisions distorted the debate considerably by suggesting

RELIGION, SECULARISM, AND THE CONSTITUENT ASSEMBLY   139

to non-Tamil speakers that the Federal Party favored a model of religious governance in which the state rejected all support or involvement with religion. In the interpretations of UF members, the Federal Party seemed to be advocating a policy of active dissociation between the state and religious communities – interpreting the translated term "secular" as something like "mundane" or "anti-religious."

However, such a translation-*cum*-interpretation could not be farther from the truth. One can see this clearly in the explanation of the Federal Party's amendment by K P Ratnam. In a long Tamil speech, Ratnam explained to the assembly the nature of the FP amendment as follows:

> We cannot create a peaceful life or a fruitful life in this country if we make use of religion (*camayam*) or language or any other thing, saying '[this is] a law for a [particular] person, this is a law for a [particular] community.' Rather, this country, where people of many religions live, will flourish, if the constitution that is being shaped for it will be truly unbiased towards a particular religion [*matacārparra*]. The intention of our amendment is to pave the way for a new constitution that does not discriminate among religions.[123]

In Ratnam's Tamil prose, it is clear that by *oru matacārparra aracāgkam*, the FP was referring to a state that did not show favoritism among religions; that is, he advocated a polity that did not, as the literal translation suggests, *bend or lean toward* one religion. The Federal Party did not intend the state to be wholly unconcerned or uninvolved in religion. Rather, as Ratnam notes in another part of the speech:

> Under today's circumstances [i.e., the JVP insurrection, the Emergency, civil disunity], religious principles (*camaya nerikal*) should be cultivated in this country. People should live in decent and upright ways ... We welcome all sections [of the proposed constitution] that protect the religions of this country.[124]

Ratnam saw religion as a necessary and important part of public life. What the Federal Party desired was a constitution that supported all religions equally, not a constitution that isolated religion from government.

The subtleties of Ratnam's position, and of the meaning of *oru matacārparra aracāgkam*, were obviously lost in the translations into English and Sinhala. Reacting to the Federal Party appeals, Colvin De Silva contested: "a secular state which will also encourage religion! This is

---

[123] Ibid., May 14, 1971, 945, in Tamil.   [124] Ibid., May 14, 1971, 943, in Tamil.

140 MULTIVALENT SOLUTIONS

one of those contradictions which I do not understand."[125] "Secular," in De Silva's interpretation, suggested a religious policy of government indifference toward religion, at minimum, or of government actively limiting the role of religion in public life, at maximum. This interpretation was similarly suggested by the official Sinhala translation of the Tamil phrase *oru matacārpaṟṟa aracāgkam*, which was *lōkāyatta rājyayak*. Like the English word "secular," the Sinhala term *lōkāyatta* suggested a kind of non-religious – even materialistic – "worldly" orientation of the state.

SECTION IV: CHANGES MADE AFTER THE CONSTITUENT ASSEMBLY DEBATES

In the end, the UF's resolution passed without amendment. When the draft chapter on Buddhism was presented to the public in the Ceylon Government Gazette on December 29, 1971, the Buddhism Resolution was transformed into a Buddhism Chapter:

> Chapter II, Section 6: In the Republic of Sri Lanka, Buddhism the religion of the majority of the People, shall be given its rightful place, and accordingly, it shall be the duty of the State to protect and foster Buddhism, while assuring to all religions the rights granted by section 18 (1) (d).[126]

However, there was one last opportunity to amend the Buddhism Chapter. Between January and March 1972, the Constituent Assembly divided into eleven separate Subject Committees to consider, once again, the individual elements to be contained in the new constitution. One entire committee investigated the Buddhism Chapter and considered public memoranda relating to it. Called the Buddhism Subject Committee, the group met for four sessions from March 2 to March 20, 1972 and was chaired by the prime minister.[127]

---

[125] Ibid., May 14, 1971, 942, in English.

[126] Ceylon Government Gazette Extraordinary, Number 14990/11, Wednesday, December 29, 1971, Part I.

[127] Constituent Assembly, *Reports of the Committees of the Constituent Assembly to Consider the Draft Constitution* (Colombo: Department of Government Printing, 1972), 21. The attendees changed slightly from meeting to meeting. There were never less than five cabinet ministers attending, however. Those who were present at all or almost all meetings included: T B Ilangaratne, P B G Kalugalla, Hector Kobbekaduwa, S S Kulatileke, George Rajapaksa, Colvin De Silva. The secretary for the Committee

MULTIVALENT SOLUTIONS   141

The Subject Committee looked explicitly at whether the phrasing of the Buddhism Chapter ought to be altered to alleviate some of the confusion and dissatisfaction that lobbyists and Constituent Assembly members had voiced over the past 18 months.

A number of Buddhist groups gave oral evidence.[128] These included important lay Buddhist groups (the All-Ceylon Buddhist Congress, Young Men's Buddhist Association, the Mahabodhi Society,[129] *Sasana Sevaka Samitya,*[130] Asoka *Dharmadhuta* Society,[131] *Sinhale Prajatatravadi Sangamaya,*[132] *Samastha Lanka Sinhala Samithi Ekabaddha Bala Mandalaya*[133]), the leaders of the Malvatu and Asgiri chapters of the Siyam Nikāya, an assembly of monks representing the three major Buddhist fraternities on the island,[134] and the association of Basnayake Nilames (chief trustees) responsible for maintaining up-country *devales* (deity temples).[135]

Records of the testimonies given to the Subject Committee reveal that all delegations requested a strengthening of the language of the Buddhism Chapter. The ACBC requested that the term "rightful place" be strengthened to "proper place" and that a clause be added so that the chapter read (added language in italics):

> In the Republic of Sri Lanka, Buddhism the religion of the majority of the People, shall be given its *proper place* [no Sinhala term was given]. Therefore it shall be the duty of the state to protect and foster

---

was Nissanka Wijayeratne, who was then the permanent secretary to the Ministry of Cultural Affairs.

[128] All groups with Sinhala names were given in the transliterated forms mentioned, without diacritics. I use this diacritic-free form here in imitation of the original transcripts.

[129] This is a group formed by Anagarika Dharmapala and was originally dedicated to protecting Buddhist archaeological and worship sites. However, since its founding in the late 1800s, the group has also served as a general lay Buddhist interest group. (On the role of the Mahabodhi Society in the 1950s, see Section I of Chapter 3.)

[130] The Buddhism Assistance Society.

[131] This is an association dedicated to the spreading of Buddhism outside of Sri Lanka. Dharmadhuta means "messenger of the dharma."

[132] The Sinhala Democratic Association.

[133] The All-Lanka United Action Council for Sinhalese Associations.

[134] *Samastha Lanka Trinikayika Maha Sangha Sabha* (the All Lanka Monks' Council of the Three Monastic Fraternities, by which was meant the Siyam, Rāmañña and Amarapura Nikāya-s).

[135] *Udarata Vihara Devala Bharakara Sangamaya* (the Upcountry Temple and Devala Caretakers Association).

Buddhism while assuring to all religions the rights granted by section 18, sub-section (1), para (d). *Accordingly, Buddhism, the Maha Sangha, Buddhist places of worship, traditional Buddhist rituals, customs, practices and ceremonies and Buddhist institutions, should be protected and developed and Buddhism should be propagated for world peace.*[136]

As with its written memoranda described earlier, the ACBC wanted to outline broad parameters for what was to be protected under the category of Buddhism. In this demand, the group found support from the Young Men's Buddhist Association (YMBA), which had proposed a similar amendment, specifying further protections for Buddhist monks, rituals, places of worship, and other "customs and practices of the Buddhists."[137]

The delegation from the island's oldest monastic fraternity, the Siyam Nikāya,[138] insisted that it was "not necessary" to include the descriptive phase that Buddhism was "the religion of the majority of the people." Their proposed amendment, which differed significantly from the gazetted version of the Buddhism Chapter, read as follows:

> The pre-eminent place due to Buddhism in Sri Lanka is recognized. Therefore, while the government ensures the rights granted to all religions by section 18, sub-section (1), para (d), it shall be the duty of the government to permanently maintain and protect the Buddha Sasana, its activities and traditional arrangements made for the uninterrupted performance of rites and rituals. The government will ensure that no action, contrary to or contravening [this] is taken.[139]

The Siyam Nikāya proposed to expand the state's obligations to Buddhism by giving Buddhism "the pre-eminent place" and making the government's responsibility to it "permanent" and "uninterrupted." Like the ACBC amendment, the Siyam Nikāya proposal also specifies those aspects of Buddhism to be protected, including its activities and rituals.

Although the discrepancies in wording are minor, there is an important difference in the proposed amendments offered by the

---

[136] Constituent Assembly, *Reports of the Committees of the Constituent Assembly to Consider the Draft Constitution*, 23.

[137] Ibid., 24.

[138] The delegation from the Siyam Nikāya included the *mahānāyaka*-s and *anu-nāyaka*-s of the Malvatu and Asgiri Chapters.

[139] Ibid., 26.

ACBC and the YMBA versus that of the Siyam Nikāya. This difference reflects the distinct approaches taken by the two groups in their written memoranda (described in Section II of this chapter). The ACBC amendment gives the state direct responsibility for ensuring the welfare of Buddhism and its various aspects, including its doctrines, monks, rituals, and institutions; that is, it gives the state responsibility for Buddhism *and* the sangha. Moreover, ACBC submissions also request that the state set up a government organization to administrate Buddhism, a Buddha Sasana Mandalaya that would consist of laity and monks and would oversee the affairs of all Buddhists on the island. In contrast, the Siyam Nikāya version does not require the government to "protect and foster" the *sangha* directly; rather, it emphasizes the government's role in preserving the Buddha Sasana along with its "activities and traditional arrangements," a term that seems calculated to protect the autonomy of monks. The Siyam Nikāya version further buttresses the independence of the monkhood through the additional clause added, as Section 6, paragraph (a), which ensures that the government will not interfere in monastic affairs.[140]

Thus, in the final committee stage, the now-familiar contest between government support for Buddhism and government oversight over the monkhood once again played out. Lay Buddhist organizations advocated greater government oversight over the *sangha*, while the Siyam Nikāya continued to resist it, as they had before. Yet, there were three places where almost all groups agreed. Virtually every group requested that the term "rightful place" (*nisitaena*) be changed to another, stronger term: some requested terms like "chief place" (*pradhānataena*) or "primary place" (*multaena*);[141] a majority (including the Siyam Nikāya) requested the term "foremost place" (*pramukhastānaya*). Several of the deputations requested that the word Buddhism (*buddhāgama*) be replaced by the term "Buddha Sasana" (*buddhaśāsanaya*), which, they felt, was a more capacious phrase, suggesting not just religious doctrine, but institutions, persons, rituals, and property as well. Finally, almost every one of the

---

[140] In oral testimony, the Siyam Nikāya clarified even further that the government ought to secure for the monkhood "[the] property required for performance of rites and rituals." Ibid., 26.

[141] Ibid., 23.

144 MULTIVALENT SOLUTIONS

Buddhist groups requested that clauses of the Kandyan Convention be integrated into the constitution in some way, either by including language from the document in the Buddhism Chapter or by including Article 5 of the Kandyan Convention as an entirely separate chapter in the constitution.[142]

In the end, the Buddhism Subject Committee responded to the requests of the Buddhist groups by making minimal and, as much as possible, uncontroversial changes. The Committee deliberately avoided language that appeared to support or oppose the government's authority over the monkhood and it refused to include language from the Kandyan Convention. Doing the first would have embroiled the government in disagreements among Buddhist organizations; doing the second would have tipped the "balance" that De Silva had sought by giving even greater prerogatives for the majority religion. Ultimately, the Committee gave with one hand and took away with the other. It strengthened the language of Buddhist primacy slightly from "rightful place" (*nisitaena*) to "foremost place" (*pramukhastānaya*). At the same time, it cut the clause that preceded it, which had distinguished Buddhism as "the religion of the majority of the people."

Managing Religion in 1972

On May 22, 1972, the legal charter that the UF shepherded through two years of drafting, debates and committees became the constitution of a country newly dubbed "Sri Lanka." The Buddhism Chapter became the island's official religious policy. The constitution was ratified by a vote of 119 to 16: the UNP voted against it; the Federal Party members did not vote at all, having walked out of the proceedings in late June after Sinhala was made the sole "official language."

In its final multivalent language, the Buddhism Chapter embodied the UF's complex bargain among numerous parties: a bargain that appeared to promote Buddhism and protect religious rights and which

---

[142] E.g., the Sinhala Democratic Alliance led by Tennakoon Vimalananda, requested that Chapter II read as follows: "Subject to the express provisions of the Kandy Convention of the 2nd of March 1815, guaranteeing the rights and privileges of the Buddhist Religion and Buddhist institutions and places of worship, freedom of worship shall be accorded to the adherents of all religious faiths in the same manner and on the same conditions as existed at the time of the signing of the Convention." Ibid., 28.

appeased (however imperfectly) those who supported the idea of state influence over Buddhist monks and those who did not. The Buddhism Chapter was, in this way, a successful constitutional settlement, one that leveraged the power of ambiguity and "incompleteness" to produce a multivalent language of compromise over religion. The effects of this language were, however, yet to be tested.

PART II

From Creation to Implementation

Up to this point, this book has considered the development of constitutional law. It has examined the history of debating and drafting constitutional policies for religion from the 1940s to 1972 and given a microhistorical account of the past lives of the Buddhism Chapter. Part II of this book takes a different approach. Rather than focusing on constitutional design, it focuses on the use, application and interpretation of constitutional law. It asks, how have Sri Lanka's hard-wrought constitutional bargains over religion impacted the ways in which citizens articulate, understand, advance, negotiate and (attempt to) resolve claims and grievances about religion?

Chapters 5, 6 and 7 demonstrate how pyrrhic constitutionalism works. Drawing upon legal records, newspaper articles, interviews with judges, lawyers and litigants, and other sources, these chapters highlight three distinct ways in which Sri Lanka's "carefully balanced" constitutional bargain has, in fact, sustained and sharpened conflicts over religion. Chapter 5 shows how the Buddhism Chapter creates incentives for multiplying legal claims about what Buddhism is and how the state ought to protect it, rather than helping to preempt, smooth over or reconcile those claims, as drafters had hoped. Chapter 6 explains why special constitutional protections for Buddhism may actually harm Buddhist groups, instead of helping them, by raising the stakes and profile of intrareligious disputes over the nature of Buddhism. Finally, Chapter 7 illustrates how invoking fundamental religious rights may aggravate and sharpen conflicts over religion, despite the fact that drafters imagined those rights as coordinating religious interests.

These chapters reveal pyrrhic constitutionalism in action. They document how the processes of implementing Sri Lanka's constitutional policies for religion have, in fact, cut against the goals of those who drafted the constitution. In so doing, they challenge several influential ideas about how constitutions work. They challenge the idea that constitutions are tools of top-down regulation used by elites to limit and

147

moderate religious claims in the public sphere. They challenge the idea that religiously preferential constitutions empower and enable the followers of the preferred religion. And they challenge the idea that religious rights are helpful and effective instruments for addressing and mitigating competing claims about religion. These chapters bring into focus the limits of constitutional practice; they also call attention to its negative costs.

5

Legal Battles for Buddhism

Looked at historically, Sri Lanka's constitutional policies toward religion appear to be the product of a very particular political, religious and social context. As the previous chapters of this book have shown, the Buddhism Chapter evolved from the 1940s to the early 1970s in large part as a reaction to the perceived deficiencies of the 1948 Constitution and as a compromise among specific groups. However, when one compares Sri Lanka's constitutional policies toward religion with those of other countries in Southeast Asia, they seem less idiosyncratic and more typical.

With the exception of socialist Vietnam, the constitutions of all Buddhist-majority states in South and Southeast Asia give Buddhism special status or recognition. In their own ways, the constitutional texts of Myanmar, Thailand, Sri Lanka, Laos, Cambodia and Bhutan all affirm the importance of Buddhism as a tradition that deserves special attention, protection or patronage. At the same time, these texts also acknowledge the existence of other religions and grant to citizens general rights to religious freedom in a framework inspired by liberal constitutional paradigms.[1] For example, Thailand's Constitution of 2007 requires that the head of state, the King, be a Buddhist (Section 9) and obliges the state to "patronise and protect Buddhism as the religion observed by most Thais for a long period of time [as well as] other religions" (Section 79). It also grants to all citizens liberty to profess or observe their religion and to worship (Section 37). Myanmar's Constitution of 2008 recognizes "the special position of Buddhism as the faith professed by the great majority of the citizens" (Article 361), while also "recognizing Christianity, Islam, Hinduism and Animism as the religions existing in the Union at the day of the coming into operation of this Constitution" and specifying religious rights for all citizens (Articles 362, 34). Cambodia's Constitution of 2008 declares Buddhism to be the "the state religion" and requires the

---

[1] On this paradigm, see Hanna Lerner, "Permissive Constitutions, Democracy, and Religious Freedom in India, Indonesia, Israel, and Turkey."

149

150   LEGAL BATTLES FOR BUDDHISM

state "disseminate and develop the Pali schools and Buddhist institutes," and also ensures rights to freedom of worship and belief (Articles 43, 68). In this way, one can identify in Southern Asia a rough template, if not a fully elaborated prototype,[2] for a form of constitutional law that one might call Buddhist constitutionalism.[3]

Constitutional Practice from the Bottom Up

As a type of constitutional law that privileges a country's most populous religion, Buddhist constitutionalism looks very similar to the constitutional traditions of many other countries.[4] For example, Egypt, Tunisia,

---

[2] In recent years, scholars have described in detail paradigms of Islamic constitutionalism in other parts of the world involving, for example, a standard set of clauses making *Shariah* "a" or "the" source of law. Among others, see: Clark B Lombardi, "Designing Islamic Constitutions: Past Trends and Options for a Democratic Future," *International Journal of Constitutional Law* 11, no. 3 (2013): 615–645; Nathan J Brown *Constitutions in a Non-constitutional World: Arab Basic Laws and the Prospects for Accountable Government* (Albany: State University of New York Press, 2002).

[3] To remind the reader, I use the term constitutionalism to refer to the practices of drafting and adjudicating constitutional law, rather than in the broader sense (which scholars sometimes have in mind) of government limited by law. It should be said that these shared features of Buddhist constitutionalism apply only at a very general level. Certain constitutions (e.g., Cambodia) seem to privilege Buddhism to a greater degree than others (e.g., Myanmar). A broader ranking of constitutional privileges for Buddhism would depend heavily on what criteria one uses. For example, does Thailand's constitutional requirement that the head of state (the King) is Buddhist exert a more preferential impact than Sri Lanka's constitutional requirement that Buddhism be given "foremost place"? Laos's constitution moves the farthest from the principles described earlier in that it places the state in a managerial role over all religions. Nevertheless, Laos's most recent constitution does give Buddhists special recognition vis-à-vis "other religious followers" in that it mentions Buddhist adherents and clerics specifically: "The state respects and protects all lawful activities of the Buddhists and of other religious followers, mobilises and encourages the Buddhist monks and novices as well as the priests of other religions to participate in the activities which are beneficial to the country and people. All acts of creating division of religions and classes of people are prohibited" (Art. 9). Aside from Bhutan (and possibly the Tibetan government-in-exile), Buddhist constitutionalism appears to be a phenomenon that applies mainly to Theravada (rather than Mahayana) countries. On Bhutan, see Richard W Whitecross, "Buddhism and Constitutions in Bhutan," in *Buddhism and Law: An Introduction*, ed. Rebecca R French and Mark A Nathan (New York: Cambridge, 2014), 250–268.

[4] In some cases, these constitutional arrangements are not just similar but identical. For example, the special status given for Buddhism in the 2008 Constitution of Myanmar – and which was included originally in the Constitution of the Union of Burma of 1947 (Section 21(1)) – is modeled deliberately on the 1937 Constitution of Ireland. Section 44 (2) of that charter reads: "The State recognises the special position of the Holy Catholic Apostolic and Roman Church as the guardian of the Faith professed by the great majority of the citizens." Aung San had initially wanted a secular constitution. The provision on

CONSTITUTIONAL PRACTICE FROM THE BOTTOM UP   151

Malaysia and Israel all have basic laws that combine special prerogatives for the majority religion with rights and (sometimes) recognition for other religions. These types of constitutions are by no means marginal. By some estimates, approximately 40 percent of all constitutions explicitly favor a particular religion while also guaranteeing general religious rights.[5]

The only comprehensive study of these types of constitutions has been done by the scholar of comparative constitutional law Ran Hirschl. In his ambitious volume, *Constitutional Theocracy*, Hirschl considers the effects of drafting constitutions that combine special endorsement for one religion with general features of liberal constitutionalism. These general features include the separation of political and religious authority, protocols of judicial review, and appeals to general religious rights. Hirschl concludes that, by giving religion special constitutional status, states contain and weaken religion's influence on political life because they make religion a legitimate object of state regulation:

> Granting religion formal constitutional status ... neutralizes religion's revolutionary sting, co-opts its leaders, ensures state input in the translation of religious precepts into guidelines for public life, helps mutate sacred law and manipulate religious discourse to serve powerful interests, and, above all, brings an alternative, even rival order of authority under state control and supervision ... As a result, constitutional law and courts in virtually all such polities have become bastions of relative secularism, pragmatism, and moderation, thereby emerging as effective shields against the spread of religiosity and increased popular support for principles of theocratic governance.[6]

For Hirschl, then, constitutions of this type diminish the force of religion in politics by bringing religious ideas, agents and institutions within the routinized world of law and under the control of government elites, particularly judges, who, he argues, share "an inclination toward secularism and modernism."[7]

Interpreted in light of the evidence he provides, Hirschl's conclusions seem illuminating. However, they are also the product of a particular

---

Buddhism was added by Ne Win, after the former's assassination. Melissa Crouch, "Personal Law and Colonial Legacy: State-Religion Relations and Islamic Law in Myanmar" in *Islam and the State in Myanmar: Muslim-Buddhist Relations and the Politics of Belonging* (Delhi: Oxford University Press, 2016).

[5] Email communication with Dr. Jonathan Fox based on his RAS Dataset, January 2011. Hirschl, Constitutional Theocracy, 46.

[6] Ibid., 13.   [7] Ibid., 162–163.

approach to studying constitutional law. Hirschl's analysis, like many comparative accounts, tends to read the life of law primarily through the decisions and dicta of its most powerful agents, particularly the benches of apical courts. This is the story of law as told by the official archive of law. In this story, applying constitutional principles appears to be a top-down procedure through which national rules, generated by political elites and interpreted by expert professionals, are applied to the disputes of those who come *under* their jurisdiction. Constitutional law, in this story, descends into society to order and regulate religious life in a manner similar to the way it regulates political, familial and economic life.[8]

Descent is one way that constitutional law works, but it is not the only way. In addition to viewing constitutional practice as a top-down process of official regulation, one can also view it as a bottom-up process of popular mobilization whereby people appeal to constitutional language in order to elevate the status and legitimacy of their concerns.[9] Viewed in this way, courts and constitutions appear less as institutions that wait around to resolve or regulate already-existing religious grievances than as enabling partners in generating and publicizing specific types of grievances. That is, constitutional protections for religion (and, in the analysis that follows, Buddhism) do not simply enable judges to intervene in matters of religion; they also encourage citizens to bring certain kinds of claims about religion to the courts in the first place.

Examined from this perspective, the most important question to ask about the intersections of religion and constitutional law is not "What did the highest courts decide?" but "How did appeals to constitutional principles and litigation serve to make particular claims about religion persuasive and/or publically visible?"[10] To look at legal action in this way is to see constitutional law not simply as an institution for ordering and

---

[8] Benjamin Berger refers to this as the "conventional account" of law. See: Berger, *Law's Religion*.

[9] Examples of this sort of perspective include, among others: Rohit De, "Rebellion, Dacoity, and Equality: The Emergence of the Constitutional Field in Postcolonial India," *Comparative Studies of South Asia, Africa and the Middle East* 34, no. 2 (2014): 260–278. Hussein Ali Agrama, "Reflections on Secularism, Democracy, and Politics in Egypt," *American Ethnologist* 39, no. 1 (2012): 26–31. Lauren Leve, "'Secularism IS a Human Right!': Double-binds of Buddhism, Democracy, and Identity in Nepal," in *The Practice of Human Rights: Tracking Law Between the Global and the Local*, ed. Mark Goodale and Sally Engle Merry (New York: Cambridge University Press, 2007).

[10] On the idea of "public visibility" see Abeysekara, *Colors of the Robe*.

CONSTITUTIONAL PRACTICE FROM THE BOTTOM UP 153

managing social life, but as a mode of practice that provides incentives for the translation of societal concerns into constitutional terms.

Such a view of law is not so unfamiliar. Scholars regularly point to these features of legal practice in cases of public-interest litigation and "test cases." Public-interest litigation differs from regular litigation in that, when it comes to these cases, litigants and lawyers seem less concerned with winning a favorable verdict than with using legal action as a platform for calling attention to a particular set of issues. Transparent in instances of public-interest litigation is the fact that constitutional court cases do not sit above or outside of politics, but function equally as venues for political action. Also visible in test cases is the often-unacknowledged relationship between the procedural rules of constitutional law and the way constitutional law works on the ground: the very same legal protocols and principles that ensure widespread access to courts and legal rights – for example, broad rubrics of standing and justiciability – can also provide avenues, even inducements, for citizens to bring legal action.

When it comes to religion (or Buddhism) the possibilities for constitutional claim-making are wider than they would be for other categories in law. The polysemy of the category of religion permits its invocation in a wide variety of claims about rights and freedoms.[11] Appeals to one's religious rights or religious freedom accompany all sorts of legal claims: claims about land, education, taxation, incorporation, commercial conduct, and many other things. Indeed, in most modern constitutional contexts, legal authorities seem reluctant to pre-judge the *bona fides* or legitimacy of religious claims out of fear of violating the presumptively secular nature of state legal institutions[12] or encroaching on the authority and autonomy of religious clerics. This reluctance (which is not seen to the same degree when it comes to other constitutional categories) provides further scope for would-be litigants to make constitutional claims about religion.

[11] As many scholars have shown, religion is a broad and ambiguous category that can be invoked in reference to a vast variety of human and superhuman goods: ideas, persons, institutions, texts, regimes of exclusion, property, values, sacra, etc. To cite only a few works that make this point: Jonathan Z Smith, *Imagining Religion: From Babylon to Jonestown* (Chicago: University of Chicago Press, 1982). Talal Asad, *Genealogies of Religion* (New York: Johns Hopkins University Press, 1993). Sullivan, *The Impossibility of Religious Freedom.*

[12] Regarding the history and criticisms of modern law's claims to secularity, see: Winnifred F Sullivan, Mateo Taussig-Rubbo and Robert A Yelle, (eds.), *After Secular Law* (Palo Alto: Stanford University Press, 2012).

Buddhist Constitutionalism in Sri Lanka

In this chapter, I present an alternative story of how religiously preferential constitutions work, one that approaches the issue from the perspective of litigants.[13] I consider the opportunities for legal action produced by Sri Lanka's constitutional commitments to "protect and foster" Buddhism contained in the Buddhism Chapter. As noted in the previous chapters of this book, the Buddhism Chapter appears first in Sri Lanka's 1972 Constitution and endures (with one small change, which I discuss later) in Sri Lanka's 1978 Constitution, which is currently in force. I argue that the constitutional prerogatives for Buddhism contained in the Buddhism Chapter have had effects other than those suggested by Hirschl or imagined by Sri Lanka's constitutional drafters. Constitutional protections for Buddhism have not contained the spread of Buddhist claims on political life, nor have they authorized the state to act in the best interests of Buddhism. Rather the Buddhism Chapter has, more often than not, enabled and incentivized Sri Lanka's citizens – or, at least, those with adequate resources – to translate specific disagreements and political concerns into formal contests over the nature of Buddhism and the state's obligations to protect it. Constitutional protections for Buddhism have activated a culture of Buddhist-interest litigation, one that has increased both the number and the visibility of grievances about Buddhism, while also making those grievances matters of national concern. In short, constitutional protections for Buddhism have, counterintuitively, in pyrrhic fashion, amplified and multiplied – rather than allayed – public concerns over the well-being and status of Buddhism.

While special constitutional safeguards for Buddhism figure centrally in Buddhist-interest litigation, equally important is the liberal side of the constitutional equation.[14] A culture of Buddhist-interest litigation

---

[13] As stated in Chapter 1, in talking about the activities of litigants, I am talking about complex agents. Litigants are, at once, the agents and products of legal action. They are citizens represented by, and mediated through, the language and arguments of lawyers. I use the term advisedly in this respect.

[14] I do not mean to insinuate that constitutional law was the only stimulant for Buddhist claim-making. Politics, education, economics, nationalism and a variety of other factors influenced the tendency for Sri Lankan Buddhists to make public claims about Buddhism. There is a large and important literature that illuminates this history. To name only a few works: Tambiah, *Buddhism Betrayed? Religion, Politics, and Violence in Sri Lanka*. Bruce Kapferer, *Legends of People, Myths of State: Violence, Intolerance, and Political Culture in Sri Lanka and Australia* (London: Smithsonian Institution Press, 1988). Seneviratne,

has been fortified by the adoption, after 1972, of two new protocols for practicing constitutional law. Drafters included those protocols to add efficiency and accessibility to processes of judicial review and constitutional litigation. The first protocol, introduced in the 1972 Constitution, was the introduction of *pre-enactment* judicial review, which permitted citizens to challenge the constitutionality of legislation prior to its ratification, based on its anticipated (unconstitutional) effects. Although the window for challenging bills was brief (within one week of the bill being placed on the Order Paper of parliament), the incentives to do so were significant: challenges were heard directly by the island's highest administrative court;[15] decisions were final; bills deemed unconstitutional, while not nullified, were made to undergo very stringent and daunting ratification processes. The second protocol, adopted in 1978, gave the Supreme Court original jurisdiction over all fundamental rights claims against the state. According to this protocol, citizens who alleged that government actors had violated (or were likely to violate) their constitutional fundamental rights, including rights to freedom of religion, could now petition the Supreme Court directly without having to wend their claims through an upwards-spiral of higher-court appeals.[16]

The history of Buddhist-interest litigation in Sri Lanka cannot be studied through published court decisions alone. Despite a plethora of claims made by litigants, few published judicial decisions discuss the Buddhism Chapter directly.[17] This chapter, therefore, uses not only the records of court decisions (which I read against-the-grain), but a larger and more diverse collection of published and unpublished sources taken from the expanded archive of constitutional law. These sources include judicial opinions, affidavits, written submissions, petitions, newspaper articles and interviews with lawyers and litigants.

Work of Kings. Mahinda Deegalle, *Buddhism, Conflict, and Violence in Modern Sri Lanka* (New York: Routledge, 2006). Ananda Abeysekara, *Colors of the Robe.*

[15] *The Constitution of the Republic of Sri Lanka of 1972* (ratified May 22, 1972, herein: 1972 Constitution), Art. 54 and subparts. Under the 1972 Constitution, the highest court of administrative law was a specially designated Constitutional Court. Under the *Constitution of the Democratic Socialist Republic of Sri Lanka* (ratified September 7, 1978, herein the 1978 Constitution), it was the Supreme Court.

[16] 1978 Constitution, Arts. 17, 126.

[17] Of course the courts regularly discuss Buddhism in the disputes over property that form the core of the system of common law in Sri Lanka known as Buddhist Ecclesiastical Law (see Chapter 6 along with footnotes contained in Chapter 1).

156 LEGAL BATTLES FOR BUDDHISM

The remainder of this chapter unfolds in two sections. In the first section, I consider two major historical events that formed the salient background of Buddhism Chapter litigation from the 1970s onwards: the joint rise of militant Tamil separatism and "territorialized" Buddhist nationalism, and a change in the governing ideology of the state between the 1970s and 1980s from welfare socialism to economic liberalism. In the second, longer section, I turn from general historical considerations to a detailed examination of Buddhist-interest litigation, defined here as court cases in which litigants articulated grievances in terms of constitutional duties to Buddhism.[18] I analyze these cases according to four distinct idioms of litigation, each of which uses constitutional protections for Buddhism to advance and publicize particular claims about what Buddhism is, what or who threatens it and how the state should safeguard its well-being. While these idioms of litigation have not always been legally successful, they have been politically influential, giving grievances made in the name of Buddhism added visibility, importance and legitimacy.

Through these two discussions – the first oriented broadly around major trends in Sri Lankan political, social and economic history, and the second oriented more narrowly around Buddhist-interest litigation – it becomes clear that, thinking from the bottom-up, the work of constitutional law appears differently to the portrait painted by Hirschl. Invoking the Buddhism Chapter in Sri Lanka's courts has come to serve as a very powerful and very public method of making political claims religiously salient and religious claims constitutionally salient. In the process, Sri Lankans have multiplied, rather than reduced, perceived threats to Buddhism and intensified, rather than allayed, anxieties about Buddhism's protection.

Sri Lankan History and Sri Lankan Law

As with any legal history, the significance of law inside courtrooms reflects broader political, social and economic debates circulating outside courtroom walls. More than others, two historical events, a violent civil

---

[18] Unlike public-interest litigation in other contexts, the cases I classify as Buddhist-interest litigation in Sri Lanka do not always place Buddhism alone in the foreground of petitions and legal submissions. Buddhist-interest litigation often invokes the Buddhism Chapter alongside other elements of law, such as constitutional fundamental rights, penal code provisions, zoning ordinances, etc. I also distinguish Buddhist-interest litigation from disputes among Buddhist monks over incumbency, succession and temple property, which are collectively referred to in Sri Lanka as Buddhist Ecclesiastical Law (see Chapter 2).

war and a change in state ideology, have made debates about the Buddhism Chapter especially important and fraught. The first event, the civil war, gave constitutional duties to protect Buddhism distinct territorial overtones: both the Liberation Tigers of Tamil Eelam (the LTTE) and Sinhalese Buddhist nationalists interpreted the Buddhism Chapter as laying claim to the island for Buddhists alone. For the LTTE, this interpretation justified their demands for an independent, secular state. For Buddhist nationalists, this interpretation justified military offensives to "liberate" Buddhist temples, shrines, historic sites and villages from what they took to be hostile occupiers and to unify the country as a Buddhist island.

The second major event has been the transformation, starting in 1978, from a socialistic, managed economy to a liberalized economy, and the broad exposures to international trade, travel and foreign aid that accompanied it. In this context, the protection of Buddhism came to be associated, in some cases, with the protection of Buddhist monks from the unwanted intrusions of a socialistic government and, in other cases, with the protection of Buddhist institutions from the corrupting influences of industrialization and globalization. Before turning to the Buddhism Chapter's uses in legal action, therefore, it is important to consider the influence of these extra-legal conflicts and debates.

Secularizing Separatism, Territorializing Buddhism

The links between the Buddhism Chapter and Sri Lanka's civil war date to the mid-1970s, when Tamil nationalist groups began to oppose the policies of Sri Lanka's 1972 Constitution. The document that served as the main manifesto for Tamil nationalism, the Vaddukodai Resolution, explained the need for a separate state of Tamil Eelam in the island's North and East, in part as a response to the fact that Buddhism had been singled out for special privileges in the new constitution:

> Buddhism has been given pre-eminence in the constitution and declared to be the only religion that would enjoy state protection. Other faiths have no right to any protection except the right of being practised, in private. The Tamil nation comprises Hindus, Christians and Muslims, and the constitution has thus placed on them the stamp of second class citizens.[19]

[19] Tamil United Liberation Front (TULF), "The Vaddukoddai Resolution," *Logos* 16, no. 3 (1977): 10–25.

158 LEGAL BATTLES FOR BUDDHISM

In contrast, Tamil nationalists promised (using the same language as the FP amendment discussed in Chapter 4) that the desired state of Tamil Eelam would "not bend towards [any] religion" (T: matacārparra) but would give "equal protection and aid . . . [to] all religions practised by the people in the State."[20]

By the early 1980s, a number of Tamil militant groups echoed the Vaddukodai Resolution in demanding a religiously impartial state. The group that would come to dominate the armed struggle for a new state, the LTTE, publically committed itself to secularism. In written LTTE propaganda, Tamil Eelam was regularly defined as a "secular socialist state." In speeches, the LTTE's leader, Velupillai Prabhakaran, described the group as an a-religious force fighting against a Sri Lankan state in which "Sinhala Buddhist chauvinism was the national doctrine."[21]

From the late 1970s onwards, Tamil claims for a separate "secular" state were echoed in the claims of a growing number of nationalist Sinhalese politicians, religious leaders and activists, who used the language of the Buddhism Chapter to enjoin military action against the LTTE. In the discourse of Sinhalese Buddhist nationalists, the state's constitutional commitments to Buddhism required the government to defend Buddhist sacred sites in the Tamil-majority North and East of the island from alleged Tamil vandals. In testimonies before a special presidential commission that was convened in the late 1970s to investigate incidents of Tamil-Sinhalese violence,[22] Buddhist witnesses from the Young Men's Buddhist Association blamed hostilities in part on "the grave situation" endangering Buddhist "cultural objects":

> [a]ncient Buddhist sites excavated and conserved by the Department of Archaeology have either been unofficially handed over to or allowed to be taken over by the non-Buddhists (Particularly Hindu Tamils) . . . several sites in Jaffna Penninsula where ancient Buddhist ruins were found were completely converted to Kovils [Hindu temples] . . . At present there is hardly a trace of their Buddhist origin.[23]

---

[20] Ibid., 23.

[21] Liberation Tigers of Tamil Eelam (LTTE). *Heroes Day Speech 2006* (in Tamil), *Delivered by V. Prabhakaran,* in Tamil. www.eelamweb.com/leader/messages/herosday/2006/tamil (Accessed October 9, 2007, weblink now defunct).

[22] Government of Sri Lanka, "Report of the Presidential Commission of Inquiry into the incidents which took place between 13 August and 15 September, 1977," *Sessional Paper no. VII* (Colombo: Government Publications Bureau, 1980).

[23] As quoted in n.a., "Appalling fate of Buddhist antiquities," *The Buddhist* (October 1978).

SHIFTING STATE IDEOLOGIES 159

These charges built upon earlier accusations, made by Buddhists in the late 1960s, that Tamils in Jaffna and Batticaloa had sought to intimidate Buddhist monks and laypersons living in the area by building Hindu shrines adjacent to Buddhist temples and by cutting down sacred Bodhi trees.[24]

By the early 1980s many politicians, activists and Buddhist groups insisted that protecting Buddhism required protecting Buddhist holy places. Buddhist action groups mobilized Buddhist laymen and monks in defence of sacred sites. Prominent among these groups was the MSV (*Mavbima Suraekīma Vyāpāraya,* or the Movement from the Protection of the Motherland), a collection of Buddhist political leaders (including a former prime minister), professionals, lay Buddhist organizations and monks. The MSV opposed a government-backed proposal to devolve power to Tamil-majority areas. From 1986 through the early 1990s, the MSV and other similar groups staged rallies, wrote editorials and lobbied parliament, linking the recognition of Tamil political autonomy with the violation of the state's constitutional duties to protect Buddhism. The movements had militant overtones, calling on monks to take up arms to protect Buddhism by preserving the unity of the island.[25] Buddhist monks, Buddhist activists and prominent politicians continued to voice these arguments loudly in the public sphere during the 1990s and 2000s, using territorial interpretations of the Buddhism Chapter to oppose attempts by the government to negotiate with the LTTE.

Shifting State Ideologies

In addition to the spread of secular Tamil separatism and territorial Buddhist nationalism, competition over state ideology influenced the way Buddhists, in particular, read the Buddhism Chapter. From 1970 to 1977, the United Front (UF) government, led by Sirima Bandaranaike, committed itself to implementing policies of welfare socialism.

---

[24] Kemper, *The Presence of the Past,* 148–160. Bryan Pfaffenberger, "The Political Construction of Defensive Nationalism: The 1968 Temple-Entry Crisis in Northern Sri Lanka," *The Journal of Asian Studies* 49, no. 1 (1990): 78–96.

[25] Peter Schalk, "'Unity' and 'Sovereignty': Key Concepts of a Militant Buddhist Organization in Sri Lanka in the Present Conflict in Sri Lanka," *Temenos* 24 (1988): 55–87. Sarath Amunugama, "Buddhaputra and Bhumiputra?: Dilemmas of modern Sinhala Buddhist monks in relation to ethnic and political conflict," *Religion* 21 (1991): 115–139. Ananda Abeysekara, "The Saffron Army, Violence, Terror (ism): Buddhism, Identity and Difference in Sri Lanka," *Numen* 48, no. 1 (2001): 1–46.

160 LEGAL BATTLES FOR BUDDHISM

These policies increased state control over many aspects of economic and social life. Bandaranaike's government (1970–1977) extended state control over land, trade, industry, media, education and religion.[26] Between 1970 and 1976 her government nationalized over one million acres of privately held land, established over 100 state corporations to run vital sectors of the economy and passed legislation allowing the state take-over of many private businesses.[27] The government also introduced policies to manage religion, including laws mandating that all Buddhist monks should be issued with identity cards, that religious education come under closer state scrutiny and that all religious communities gain government approval before building or renovating places of worship (see later in this chapter).

Beginning in 1977, a new UNP-dominated government, led by J R Jayewardene, reversed Bandaranaike's policies and began a program of liberalization aimed at encouraging an open, modern, "righteous" (also *dharmistha*) society. With this reversal came new interpretations of the Buddhism Chapter. Under Jayewardene, the government aimed to reduce the state's reach into industry and society, making businesses more independent and citizens less reliant on public subsidies. It established Free Trade Zones on the south-western coast, privatized state cooperatives, encouraged foreign investment and used international loans to finance large development projects in the island's rural areas. In public addresses, Jayewardene suggested that what was good for the nation's industrial order was good for the nation's religious order. Jayewardene approached the promotion of Buddhism in free-market terms, insisting that "[t]he Buddha never for a moment thought that it was possible to reform society through legislation."[28] According to Jayewardene, government could not legislate Buddhist values or practices; the protection of Buddhism had to be undertaken independently, by individual Buddhists.

Both ideologies of government, Bandaranaike's state-centric socialism and Jayewardene's privatizing liberalism, found expression in the legal debates concerning Buddhism from the 1970s onwards. Each ideology implicated a different understanding of what it meant to protect

---

[26] K M de Silva, "Ivor Jennings and Sri Lanka's Passage to Independence," *Asia Pacific Law Review* 13, no. 1 (2005): 1–18. Deborah Winslow and Michael D Woost, *Economy, Culture, and Civil War in Sri Lanka* (Bloomington, IN: Indiana University Press, 2004).

[27] Patrick Peebles, *The History of Sri Lanka* (Westport, CT: Greenwood Press, 2006), 124–125.

[28] As quoted in: Kemper, *The Presence of the Past*, 176.

Buddhism. Defenders of these understandings clashed in courtrooms. The managed welfare state of the Bandaranaike government associated protecting and fostering Buddhism with a paternalistic act of state intervention, of using laws and state agencies to regulate Buddhist monks, sites and institutions. Jayewardene's liberalism appeared to treat the protection of Buddhism as involving indirect support for Buddhists. Jayewardene gave state money generously for Buddhist causes (e.g., for temple upkeep, monastic education and public Buddhist rituals), yet he was careful to place institutional boundaries between the state and religion, rejecting strenuously the idea of monks influencing politics and refusing to create ordinances that policed Buddhist morality through, for example, restricting alcohol or meat consumption.[29]

Also implicated in the political and ideological contest between the UF's socialism and the UNP's liberalism were competing ideas about the costs and benefits for Buddhism of Sri Lanka's integration into broader networks of global capitalism. Interpreted through Jayewardene's ideology, Buddhism benefited from an open economy because exposure to international markets and foreign investment enhanced national prosperity, and that prosperity increased resources available for promoting Buddhism. At the same time, global exposures also contributed to public anxieties over the malignant effects of foreign influences and organizations on Sri Lankan Buddhism.

Idioms of Buddhist-Interest Litigation

Since the 1970s, in this context of intermittent civil war and economic change, Sri Lankan litigants regularly appealed to the island's courts to enforce the state's constitutional duties to protect Buddhism. Through legal action, Sri Lankans expressed a range of concerns about religion, politics, economics, war and globalization using the language of protecting Buddhism. This Buddhist-interest litigation can be grouped into four types – four idioms of litigation – according to the major assertions made regarding what Buddhism is, how the state ought to defend it, and what or who threatens it. In the first idiom, litigants sought to protect Buddhism's autonomy from unwanted government interventions. In the second idiom, litigants sought to protect Buddhist orthodoxy against what they considered heterodox Buddhist monks. In the third idiom,

---

[29] Ibid., 177–180.

162   LEGAL BATTLES FOR BUDDHISM

litigants sought to protect Buddhist places from non-Buddhist inter-lopers. In the fourth idiom, litigants sought to protect Buddhism against foreign "profaners." In all cases, Buddhist-interest litigation, even when it failed to generate an affirmative judgment, provided potent opportunities for expanding the importance of religious claims in public life and potent incentives for litigants to rethink and reclassify complex social realities in terms of constitutional commitments to promote Buddhism.

Idiom One: Protecting Buddhist Autonomy from the State

Sri Lanka's constitution specifies special protections for Buddhism, but it does not specify the precise relationship between religious authority and civil authority. The language of protecting and fostering Buddhism was chosen because it neither implied nor denied the possibility of state oversight over Buddhist institutions and monastic life. In the context of the nationalizing and socialist policies of the Bandaranaike government, litigants used this evasive language to implicate Buddhism in broad debates about the appropriate aims and limits of state regulation. In particular, litigants invoked constitutional protections for Buddhism and for religion-in-general to challenge attempts to expand the state's management of religious life.

Constitutional duties to protect Buddhism, along with new protocols of judicial review, figured prominently in two important judicial review cases from 1973 and 1976. In these cases, litigants sought to compel the island's highest constitutional tribunal at that time, the Constitutional Court, to review the policies of Bandaranaike's UF government. The challenges related to two government bills. The first bill, entitled the "Places and Objects of Worship Bill," specified a list of registration and application requirements that all religious groups, including Buddhists, would have to fulfil in order to gain official approval to build or renovate a site of religious worship. The second bill, entitled the "Pirivena Education Bill," gave the government greater control over Buddhist schools (*pirivena*-s), where most of the island's monks were educated. An opposition minister of parliament and accomplished lawyer, Prins Gunasekera, challenged the first bill.[30] A much larger collection of petitioners challenged the second bill. These petitioners

---

[30] Gunasekera was elected on the United Front ticket, but crossed over to the opposition in October 1971. Ceylon Daily News, *Ceylon Daily News' Parliament of Sri Lanka, 1977* (Colombo: Associated Newspapers of Ceylon, 1978), 79.

IDIOM ONE: PROTECTING BUDDHIST AUTONOMY 163

included leaders from Colombo's major lay Buddhist organizations,[31] 11 senior Colombo-area monks and a senior civil servant.[32]

In using the Buddhism Chapter to petition for judicial review, petitioners framed their concerns about the centralizing ambitions of the Bandaranaike government in terms of the state's powers over Buddhist life. One can infer the importance of petitioners' political interests from the fact that the very persons and organizations that argued most fervently in favor of the state's supervisory powers over Buddhism during the constitution-making process now offered equally passionate arguments against such powers in court.[33] The petitioners argued that the proposed government bills violated the terms of the Buddhism Chapter because they subordinated Buddhist institutions to non-Buddhist (secular or anti-Buddhist) state authority.

In the first case, concerning the Places and Objects of Worship Bill, the petitioning politician from the opposition argued that requiring Buddhist groups to gain approval from the Ministry of Cultural Affairs to build a Buddhist temple would be to destroy "a historical right and freedom that has been enjoyed by Buddhists for over 2500 years, of freely practising and propagating the Buddha Dhamma."[34] He argued that the bill, in its requirement that Buddhists gain government approval, would subject Buddhism itself to "subtle, anti-religious, anti-cultural" influences.[35] This, he asserted, was because "anti-Buddhist" Trotskyite and Communist ministers (key coalition members in the UF government) controlled the relevant ministries.

The collection of petitioners in the second case, concerning the Pirivena Bill, made similar arguments regarding the proposed controls over monastic education. Any attempts by the state to extend regulatory powers over Buddhist schools, they argued, would be to "interfere with the autonomy of Buddhist institutions," to "usurp" monastic property

---

[31] The YMBA, ACBC, BTS, Mahabodhi Society and Sasana Sevaka Samithiya of Maharagama.

[32] L O H Wanigasekera was, during the 1970s and 1980s, a regular intervener in court cases and legislative committees that involved the status of Buddhism on the island.

[33] The YMBA, ACBC and Mahabodhi Society had all been advocates of creating a new government-run Buddhist Council to oversee Buddhist affairs on the island.

[34] Government of Ceylon, "Decision of the Constitutional Court on Places and Objects of Worship Bill," in *Decisions of the Constitutional Court of Sri Lanka* (Colombo: Registry of the Constitutional Court, 1973), 28.

[35] Ibid. Bandaranaike's UF coalition had, at that time, a strong Trotskyite and Communist Party presence.

164   LEGAL BATTLES FOR BUDDHISM

and to "take over effective control" of Buddhist education.[36] In making these arguments, petitioners deployed a capacious definition of Buddhism, which encompassed places, practices, persons, values, teachings and customs, all of which, they insisted, thrived solely in the absence of government involvement. The protection of Buddhism, they urged, required the withdrawal of the state from a broad zone of Buddhist institutional autonomy.

In two public and reported decisions, Judges of the Constitutional Court, many of them sympathetic to the government and appointed by Bandaranaike herself, defended the legality of the government's bills and, in so doing, offered differing definitions of Buddhism and how the state ought to protect it. In the first case, the court behaved in a manner consistent with Hirschl's predictions. It dismissed the Buddhists' religious concerns, rejecting claims that government ministers might execute an anti-Buddhist agenda. The court pointed out that the bill, which had been drafted in order to regulate *all* religions, did not specially disadvantage Buddhism *per se*. However, although it rejected Gunasekera's petition, the court unwittingly gave credibility and visibility to important aspects of Gunasekera's argument. Aside from the publicity generated by the petition, the petitioner gained an important affirmation of sorts. In the detail and length of the judges' arguments (discussed later) about why Buddhism was not damaged by the Places and Objects of Worship Bill, the court found itself affirming indirectly the need for Sri Lanka's judiciary to look closely at government policies' effects on Buddhism. Therefore, even though the Constitutional Court ultimately rejected the specific rationale behind Gunasekera's claims, it validated publically one of his larger claims: that the state had a special obligation to safeguard Buddhism, and that obligation could override and challenge the government's policies of nationalizing the island's institutions.[37]

The decision in the first case not only (re)affirmed the necessity of protecting Buddhism, it led the court to advance a particular definition of Buddhism. To make the case that the bill did not offend Buddhism, judges interpreted Buddhism through the lens of First Amendment

---

[36] Government of Ceylon, "Decision of the Constitutional Court on Pirivena Education Bill," in *Decisions of the Constitutional Court of Sri Lanka (Vol. IV)* (Colombo: Registry of the Constitutional Court, 1976), 6, 8.

[37] Government of Ceylon, "Decision of the Constitutional Court on Pirivena Education Bill," 6, 8.

jurisprudence in the United States. Citing U.S. Supreme Court decisions involving the religious "free exercise" rights of polygamous Mormons in Idaho and proselytizing Jehovah's Witnesses in Connecticut,[38] the Sri Lankan Constitutional Court insisted that, notwithstanding its privileged place in the country, Buddhism could be analyzed like any other religion, and therefore could be divided into two separable aspects: "religion," which the court glossed as religious conscience, and "religious practice," which the court glossed as an "expression" of religion "by overt acts." Where the state must not impede the first, it could justifiably limit the second. The court then advanced the argument (a specious one for many Buddhists) that building places of Buddhist worship was simply a form of religious practice rather than "religion" and could therefore be limited without impinging upon "Buddhism."

In the second, Pirivena Bill case, the Constitutional Court bisected Buddhism in a similar way to respond to petitioners' claims. In this case, the court majority invoked an almost identical contrast between a primary religious belief (which they termed "religion") and a secondary religious "manifestation." However, the relevant question here was not whether *pirivena* education should be classified as either religious belief or religious manifestation, but if *pirivena* education should be viewed as *religious* at all: did Buddhist monastic schools constitute a "manifestation" of "the Buddhist religion"? In a split opinion, the two-justice majority relied on another act of bisection to insist that Buddhist schools were not, in fact, part of Buddhism. It argued that one's religious beliefs were completely distinct from the creation and maintenance of religious institutions:[39] The first was a protected "religious right," the second was not.

In these early cases concerning the Buddhism Chapter, petitioners invoked constitutional duties to Buddhism as part of an effort to challenge the government and its policies. Arguments about Buddhism merged with, and served as proxies for, conflicts over political commitments and governing ideologies. Petitioners used legal arguments about protecting Buddhism as part of broader projects of resisting the Sirima Bandaranaike government and its managerial approach to governance. By using constitutional law, petitioners blended ideas about protecting

---

[38] *Cantwell v. Connecticut (1940) [310 U.S. 296 (1940)], Davis v. Beason (1890) [133 U.S. 333 (1890)] (incorrectly spelled as "Davies v. Beason").*

[39] Government of Ceylon, "Decision of the Constitutional Court on Pirivena Education Bill," 10.

166   LEGAL BATTLES FOR BUDDHISM

and fostering Buddhism with political calculations; they cast broader disputes as specific questions about what Buddhism was and how the state should conduct itself toward it: Did the state's constitutional duties to Buddhism permit or even require the government to actively intervene in the administration and oversight of Buddhist institutions, or did they require the state to carve out for Buddhism a zone of autonomy from state actions? Did Buddhism refer to a broad range of persons, places, properties, teachings and institutions or to a narrower core of essential beliefs (leaving a penumbra of less essential practices upon which the state could legitimately intrude)?[40] Was protecting Buddhism the same as protecting "religion"?

Answers to these questions not only implicated opposing conceptions of Buddhist temples and *pirivena*-s, they coalesced into larger opposing visions of religious governance, of religiosity, of Buddhist identity and of religious difference. Where petitioners rejected the binary splitting of religion into belief and practice, judges affirmed it. Where petitioners valorized the importance of religious autonomy, judges valorized the importance of formal neutrality. Where petitioners resisted the homology of Buddhism to other religions, judges assumed it. Where petitioners glossed Buddhism in broad terms, (most) judges chose narrower belief-centric definitions.

Arguments about Buddhism made political divisions religiously salient, and made religious divisions politically salient. In their invocation of the Buddhism Chapter, judicial review cases drew litigants and judges into asserting rival visions of Buddhism as part of challenging or supporting the constitutionality of the Bandaranaike government's policies. By invoking the Buddhism Chapter in the context of constitutional review, litigants required the country's highest administrative court to deliberate on – and to that extent, publically affirm – the state's constitutional duties to protect Buddhism as well as to judge the Buddhist character of the Bandaranaike government. Therefore, even if the petitioners' own vision of protecting Buddhism did not prevail, the use of constitutional law elevated their assertions about Buddhism (which were also assertions about politics) to matters of national concern. And, as matters of national concern, those assertions would be recorded in official documents, publicized through newspapers and discussed by legal

---

[40] There is a doctrine of "essential practices" in Indian jurisprudence on religion. Sen, *Articles of Faith*.

experts around the island.[41] As the petitioning lawyer in the first case explained, the goal was not so much to win the case; it was to "create public opinion on the issue."[42]

Idiom Two: Protecting Buddhist Orthodoxy

If some litigants invoked the Buddhism Chapter as a way to contest the Buddhist character of the government, other litigants invoked the Buddhism Chapter to compel the state to enforce Buddhist orthodoxy. In 1977, at the fulcrum moment between the welfare socialism of the Bandaranaike years and the economic liberalism of the J R Jayewardene government, Sri Lanka's highest court took up the case of Ven. Nakulugamuwa Sumana Thero.[43] Ven. Sumana was a Buddhist monk who, having completed his law degree in Colombo, decided to submit the necessary documents to enrol as an attorney. As a matter of procedure, Ven. Sumana's name appeared in the newspaper along with other candidates who had made application to take their oaths as lawyers. Seeing that a Buddhist monk was preparing to become a lawyer, several Buddhist lay organizations in Colombo lodged formal objections with the Supreme Court, which had jurisdiction over applications to the bar, requesting that his application be refused.[44]

The Buddhist groups' challenge initiated a highly public and controversial Supreme Court case. The Chief Justice referred the case to a full, five-justice bench, declaring it "the first case of its kind in the annals of our Courts."[45] Two groups of litigants appeared before the court, supporting and opposing with equal vehemence Ven. Sumana's right to apply to the bar. Ven. Sumana's application was opposed by virtually the same constellation of Colombo-based Buddhist lay organizations that challenged the Pirivena Bill, including the Young Men's Buddhist Association (YMBA), the All-Ceylon Buddhist Congress (ACBC) and

---

[41] Interestingly, these two cases continue to appear prominently in many textbooks on Sri Lankan constitutional law. E.g., R K W Goonesekere, *Fundamental Rights and the Constitution: A Case Book* (Colombo: Law & Society Trust, 2003).

[42] Interview with Prins Gunasekara by phone, September 5, 2014.

[43] As stated in the front matter, "Ven." Refers to Venerable, which is the honorific title used to refer to Buddhist monks in Sri Lanka.

[44] Although referring to the state's constitutional duties to protect and foster Buddhism, the objections were filed under the terms listed in the Administration of Justice Act of 1973.

[45] *In the Manner of the Application of Rev. Sumana Thero to be Admitted and Enrolled as an Attorney-at-Law* (2005) 3 *New Law Reports* 370.

168 LEGAL BATTLES FOR BUDDHISM

the Buddhist Theosophical Society (BTS). Ven. Sumana's application was supported by Prins Gunasekera, the same lawyer-politician who had challenged the constitutionality of the Places and Objects of Worship Bill. Gunasekera, in turn, had the support of several senior Buddhist scholars and monks, including the prelates from Ven. Sumana's monastic fraternity. If, in the earlier cases, Buddhist groups had united in criticizing the government, the question of monks in secular employment provided an occasion for new alignments, showing that the idea of protecting Buddhism could be used to support many different agendas and coalitions.

Although the matter before the court pertained to the specific activities of one monk, litigants used the case to advance much broader visions of Buddhism and the state's obligations to it. Those who opposed Ven. Sumana argued that protecting Buddhism required the state to ensure that monastic life remained aloof from worldly concerns. If one monk were to become a lawyer, they contended, he would encourage other monks to do so. This could lead, in turn, to widespread violations of the Pali code of monastic discipline (the Vinaya Pitika), which would threaten the "larger interests of Buddhism."[46] Those who supported Ven. Sumana's admission – including Ven. Sumana's monastic superiors and a leading Buddhist academic – also claimed to protect Buddhism. Protecting Buddhism for them meant securing the autonomy of head monks to supervise the conduct of the less-senior monks in their fraternities. To protect Buddhism, they argued, the Supreme Court must accept the decision made by prelates in Ven. Sumana's own monastic fraternity to permit his admission to the bar.

These competing visions of Buddhism split the judges on the court. A three-justice majority supported Ven. Sumana's application and affirmed the idea that the ultimate evaluator of monastic conduct ought to be the prelates of individual monastic fraternities, rather than state-court judges' interpretations of Pali texts or the opinions of monks from outside of that fraternity. In this case, they insisted, Ven. Sumana's direct monastic superiors must be regarded as "final arbiters" whose dicta "can hardly be questioned by this court and must be accepted by us . . . [as] the only evidence before us."[47] As with the aforementioned cases, Supreme Court justices justified their ruling according to a particular definition of Buddhism. In this case, the court majority divided Buddhism into a core

[46] Ibid., 370–371.   [47] Ibid., 373.

set of "doctrine and belief" that are "immutable," and a secondary system of "discipline and administration [that] are naturally subject to modifications."[48] Norms of monastic conduct – and even the Vinaya Pitaka itself – fell into the second category because, the majority insisted, monastic fraternities used different redactions of the Vinaya and thus followed slightly different sets of rules.[49] The majority opinion reasoned that because standards of monastic conduct changed from fraternity to fraternity (unlike Buddhist doctrine), devolving disciplinary authority over monks to those fraternities could not be avoided, nor would it "ruin" Buddhism as a whole. The majority also declared that the lack of a single source-text for assessing monastic comportment made any attempt to audit monks' behaviors a matter that was "purely ecclesiastical in nature" and "outside the pale of civil law." As "secular" authorities, they asserted, judges must not act as religious experts.

Through their petitions, opponents and supporters of Ven. Sumana made public claims about the importance of protecting Buddhism in the form of two competing ideas about what threatened Buddhism: supporters claimed that by assessing the piety of Buddhist monks, the state risked violating the autonomy of the *sangha*. It also risked improperly arrogating for itself "ecclesiastical" authority. Opponents claimed that by refusing to intervene in disputes over orthodoxy, the state risked a gradual degradation in monastic discipline and, thus, over the long term, a more general damaging of Buddhism. Like the petitioners against the government bills in the first idiom of litigation, petitioners against Ven. Sumana's application recruited the country's highest court into debates over the nature and valid sources of Buddhist authority. In discussing the ostensibly singular act of "protecting and fostering" Buddhism, litigants made questions over Buddhist orthopraxy and authority matters of state concern. In the years that followed, litigants would continue to do so in court cases involving, among other things, monks working in salaried employment as social workers and monks who wanted to drive cars (see Chapter 6).[50]

Looking only at published decisions,[51] one might conclude that the court ruling resolved the matter. (After all, it ruled that that monks could

---

[48] Ibid., 374.   [49] Ibid., 374.

[50] See *Warapitiya Rahula Thero v. Commissioner General of Examinations and Others* (2000) 3 SLR 344; *Paragoda Wimalawansa Thero and Others v. Commissioner of Motor Traffic* (2014) Unreported judgment with the author.

[51] In three years of trying, I was unable to locate the file for Ven. Sumana's case in Sri Lanka's Supreme Court archives. Filing challenges, along with the recent destruction of files from a variety of higher judiciary cases (for reasons of insufficient storage space)

apply to become lawyers.) Viewed through the expanded archive of constitutional law and from the perspective of litigants, however, these petitions appear to have had a different effect. Through litigation, petitioners raised the profile of debates over Sumana's conduct and the need to protect Buddhism. That is, they brought difficult, divisive questions into a highly visible and public arena. This had important consequences for Sumana himself. Although a majority of the Supreme Court affirmed Ven. Sumana's right to apply to the bar, ultimately negative public attention generated by the court case seems to have swayed things in the opposite direction. When Ven. Sumana returned to the Supreme Court to take his oaths as a lawyer, the same bench that approved his right to apply to the bar denied him entrance on account of technical, sartorial requirements: even if a monk could be admitted to the bar, the chief justice asserted, a saffron robe could not substitute for the customary black and white suit of an attorney.[52]

Idiom Three: Protecting Buddhist Places

One can see certain trends in the Buddhist-interest litigation cases examined so far: by invoking the Buddhism Chapter in court, litigants translated specific concerns into broad, public, consequential claims about what Buddhism is and who has the right to speak for it. Litigants also joined together political contests with interpretive contests over the state's duties to secure Buddhism.

One can extend these observations further by looking at a third genre of cases. In these cases, litigants interpreted the state's duties to protect and foster Buddhism as requiring state interventions to defend Buddhist temples, archaeological sites, buildings, properties or villages against non-Buddhists who, they insisted, might harm them. These cases have roots both in the context of Sri Lanka's civil war and in the context of

---

have made the submissions from court cases from the 1970s difficult, if not impossible, to obtain. This case proved particularly challenging insofar as the judgment lists only the number of Ven. Sumana's application to the bar and not a standard record number.

[52] According to the Chief Justice: "if [Ven. Sumana] appears before us, he must be clad in the correct attire. Otherwise we refuse to see him. Likewise if a lawyer comes here in a bush shirt we won't tolerate him in our Courts. Now that there are many members of the fair sex functioning as Attorneys-at-Law do you want us to allow them to sit at the Bar Table in bell-bottoms and tight skirts?" A R B Amerasinghe, *The Supreme Court of Sri Lanka: The First 185 Years,* (Colombo: Sarvodaya Book Pub. Services, 1986), 92. I am grateful to Dr. Wickrama Weerasooria for directing me to this passage.

increasing exposure to transnational agencies and actors in the 1990s and 2000s. In these cases, litigants treated the protection of Buddhism as requiring the protection of purportedly Buddhist spaces. Litigants' definitions of Buddhism in these instances, therefore, directly opposed those offered by the Constitutional Court in the first idiom: true Buddhism was not primarily a collection of doctrines, beliefs and states of conscience, nor was it a combination of distinct beliefs *and* manifestations; Buddhism, as a religion, depended equally upon temples, shrines, *bodhi* trees, gifted properties and villages of Buddhist patrons – in other words, on the spaces inhabited and visited by Buddhist laypersons and monks.

In these cases, litigants rendered constitutionally legible and made politically salient different types of conceptual, legal and political boundaries. Rather than using constitutional protections for Buddhism to advance the interests of a particular parliamentary bloc or a particular group of Buddhist monks, in these cases litigants used constitutional action to reify a stark distinction between Buddhism and other religions. They not only introduced to the country's apical courts arguments about the superior status of Buddhism, they advanced arguments about the incommensurability of Buddhism with other religions. This line of argument assumed that even the terms "Buddhism" and "religion," along with their Sinhala approximations (*buddhāgama* and *āgama*), should not be used to name the Buddha's dispensation because those terms suggested equality and isomorphism among all traditions:[53] by using those terms, Buddh-*ism* (*buddha* – *āgama*) appeared analogous to Hindu-*ism* (*hindu* – *āgama*) and Christian-*ity* (*kristiyāni* – *āgama*).

The idea that the Buddha's dispensation was more than simply a form of religion (*āgama*), in fact, influenced those who drafted Sri Lanka's Second Republican Constitution of 1978 (about which much has been written and more will be said in Chapter 6).[54] In the 1978 Constitution, a

---

[53] Kitsiri Malalgoda, "Concepts and Confrontations: A Case Study of Agama," in *Sri Lanka: Collective Identities Revisited (Vol. 1)*, ed. Michael Roberts (Colombo: Marga Institute Press, 1997), 60–63.

[54] The 1978 Constitution introduced an executive president (in a mixed executive, Gaullist-style, system), introduced proportional representation, strengthened fundamental rights and made other changes. Minimal alterations were made to constitutional policies toward religion, other than the procedures of justiciability relating to religious rights (to be discussed in Chapter 7). Among the important works on the 1978 Constitution, generally, see: A J Wilson, *The Gaullist System in Asia: The Constitution of Sri Lanka (1978)*

172   LEGAL BATTLES FOR BUDDHISM

UNP-dominated Select Committee of Parliament made one small but salient change to the Buddhism Chapter at the last possible moment: it altered the phrase "it shall be the duty of the state to protect and foster Buddhism" to read " . . . to protect and foster the Buddha Sasana (*buddha śāsanaya*)." Choosing "Buddha Sasana" rather than Buddhism (*buddhāgama*) highlighted the distinctiveness of the Buddha's dispensation; everything else was simply "religion."[55] Choosing "Buddha Sasana" also supported those who favored a territorialized definition of Buddhism because *buddha śāsanaya* implicated not only the Buddha's teachings but his entire legacy, which included properties, shrines, statutes, temples and other material objects and geographic spaces.[56]

Litigants rendered this view of protecting Buddhism – as explicitly including the protection of Buddhist spaces – nationally visible and legally influential in three cases from 1987, 2003 and 2008. In each case, Buddhists petitioned the Supreme Court, requesting that it require the government to guard Buddhist places (temples, historic sites, villages) from threats by Hindus, Christians and Muslims, respectively.

One of the most important instances of constitutional action of this type occurred in 1987 in a Supreme Court case that one justice referred to as "the most important and the most far-reaching that had ever arisen in the history of our courts."[57] In a climate of deepening political rifts[58] and escalating hostilities between the government and the LTTE (including a recent LTTE attack on Buddhist monks), a number of lawyers, politicians and Buddhist groups submitted judicial review petitions to the

(London: Macmillan Press, 1980). Asanga Welikala (ed.), *Reforming Sri Lankan Presidentialism: Provenance, Problems and Prospects* (Colombo: Centre for Policy Alternatives, 2015).

[55] This is unlike the Thai Constitution's use of the term, for example, which uses the vernacularized version of the Pali term *sāsana* to apply to all religions. Thank you to David Engel for pointing this out.

[56] On the meanings of *sāsana* see: John Ross Carter, "A History of Early Buddhism,"*Religious Studies* 13, no. 3 (1977): 263–287.

[57] *In the Matter of the Thirteenth Amendment to the Constitution and Provincial Councils Bill* (1987) 2 SLR 333 (Wanasundera J dissenting).

[58] These rifts primarily involved the role of the Indian government in brokering a peace between the government and the LTTE. By 1989, India would have 100,000 peacekeepers on the island acting as mediators in the conflict between the LTTE and the Sri Lankan government. For more on the complex history of this era see De Silva and Wriggins, *J. R. Jayewardene of Sri Lanka*, Vol. II, 656–660. Amita Shastri, "Sri Lanka's Provincial Council System: A Solution to the Ethnic Problem?,"*Asian Survey* 32, no. 8 (1992): 723–743.

IDIOM THREE: PROTECTING BUDDHIST PLACES   173

Supreme Court contesting the constitutionality of two pieces of legislation designed to give greater political autonomy to Tamil-majority regions of the island in the North and East.[59] Among the Buddhist petitioners, the Colombo-based lay organization of the YMBA filed a substantial petition. The YMBA argued that in order to fulfil its obligations to protect Buddhism, the state must guarantee the preservation, maintenance and restoration of Buddhist historical sites and temples in the northern and eastern parts of the island. By proposing to devolve political authority to provincial governments, the group argued, the state was not only reneging on that duty, it was placing control over those sites in the hands of non-Buddhists who had been engaged in a "studied and sedulous campaign ... to obliterate all traces of places of ancient Buddhist worship."[60] The YMBA's reading of the Buddhism Chapter failed to persuade a (narrow) four-justice plurality. However it was affirmed in two prominent dissenting opinions, one of which recognized explicitly the territorial implications of the term "Buddha Sasana," which was added to the 1978 Constitution:

> The expression "Buddha Sasana" was advisedly substituted for the word "Buddhism" which was used in the corresponding Article of the 1972 Republican Constitution. *The new expression is a compendious term encompassing all ancient, historic and sacred objects and places which have from ancient times been or are associated with the religious practices and worship of Sinhala Buddhists.* [61]

This interpretation of the Buddhism Chapter gave public expression and validation to the YMBA's territorial definition of Buddhism. Moreover, this definition and the text of the dissent continue to exert significant influence on legal specialists and politicians in Sri Lanka.[62]

In recent years, litigants have used the courts as forums for giving new inflections to this territorial understanding of Buddhism. These inflections

---

[59] The legislation included a parliamentary bill and a constitutional amendment designed to create nine Provincial Councils, including an Eastern and Northern Provincial Council.

[60] Written Submissions on behalf of Young Men's Buddhist Association of Colombo, *SC (Spl.) 15/1987*, Paragraph 9. Copy with YMBA, Colombo, Borella Branch Library.

[61] 1987 2 SLR 312. Emphasis mine.

[62] In my discussions with Buddhist groups and lawyers in Sri Lanka, I have found that this dissent is referred to frequently. Moreover, one sees this (dissenting) definition affirmed in subsequent legal judgments such as SC(SD) 1/1994 *In the Matter of the Antiquities Ordinance.* Hansard, May 3, 1994, 1–5. See also: Report of the Presidential Commission on Buddha Sasana (*buddha śāsana janādhipati komiṣan vārtāva*) (Colombo: Sri Lanka Government Printing Department, 2002), 6–15.

174 LEGAL BATTLES FOR BUDDHISM

stress the protection of Buddhist places while also imagining those places as threatened by Christian proselytizers (not only Tamil militants) and as including Buddhist villages (not only temples and archaeological sites). Since the late 1990s, litigants have used the Buddhism Chapter to challenge the building of Christian prayer centres in rural, predominately Buddhist areas. Even through the critical legal questions often pertain to zoning regulations, litigants foreground in their petitions appeals to protect the Buddhist demography and culture of villages. For instance, in one case, representatives from the lay Buddhist organization, SUCCESS (the Secretariat for Upliftment and Conservation of Cultural, Educational and Social Standards of Sri Lanka) challenged the building of a new church near the town of Polonnaruwa, insisting, among other things, that the construction was "obnoxious and/or repugnant" to the state's obligations to protect Buddhism, because "the objective of the construction and occupation of said building [is] the spreading and/or propagation of a religion other than Buddhism in the predominately Buddhist District of Polonnaruwa amidst villages that comprise about 97% Buddhists."[63] According to the petitioner, the protection of the Buddha Sasana required the state to protect Buddhist villages against non-Buddhists' attempts to build competing places of worship because this might lead to the spread of "a religion other than Buddhism."[64] In the logic of these submissions, general concerns for the protection of Buddhism extend even to the demography of remote villages.

Through Buddhist-interest litigation, Buddhist organizations in the island's major urban areas of Colombo or Kandy claimed a legitimate interest – and legal standing – in the religious lives of agrarian communities dozens or hundreds of kilometres away. Protecting Buddhism, in these cases, assumes a further spatial dimension. Litigants used constitutional protections for Buddhism to argue not only for the necessity of state actions, but to pursue formal judicial recognition that Buddhists from one part of the country have a legitimate interest in the affairs of Buddhists in other parts of the country. That is, in the very framing of their petitions, particular Buddhist groups presented themselves as acting for "the advancement and protection of economic, social and cultural standards of the *Sri Lankan Buddhists.*"[65] Moreover they averred implicitly the idea of Sri Lanka as a whole as a single, continuous space of Buddhism.

---

[63] Written Submissions of Petitioner S G De Silva (November 1, 2004), CA 2022/2003, *S.G. De Silva v. Lankapura Pradeshiya Sabha and others*, p. 2.
[64] Ibid., p. 11.   [65] Ibid., p. 3. Emphasis mine.

IDIOM THREE: PROTECTING BUDDHIST PLACES 175

Court cases such as the one described are often invisible in the official archive of constitutional law because they do not leave published judicial decisions. (In many instances, Christian or Buddhist litigants withdrew their petitions before any official decision was given, in order to avoid an anticipated unfavorable judgment.)[66] However, despite the lack of published records, cases like these frequently become vehicles for rallying public attention. According to Christian and Buddhist religious leaders and activist groups that I spoke with, as well as the lawyers who represented them, building non-Buddhist worship sites in Buddhist-majority areas remains a highly incendiary issue in modern Sri Lanka. Conflicts over church-building, in particular, have led to arson and vandalism against churches and physical attacks on church-goers. In these cases, legal appeals to the Buddhism Chapter enable litigants to treat local conflicts among religious communities as grand constitutional contests over Buddhism. Disagreements that emerge from contextual circumstances or local, personal acrimonies come to be interpreted in the framework of broad questions over how the state ought to act with respect to Buddhism: should the state take measures to control the building of non-Buddhist religious sites in areas with large Buddhist majorities in the interest of "protecting Buddhism"?

A lack of published rulings on these questions has not stopped litigants from provoking them. In 2008, the island's apical court heard a fundamental rights petition involving the protection of Buddhists living near a particularly important temple in the East of Sri Lanka, the *Dīghavāpi* (sometimes transliterated *Deeghawapiya*) *Raja Mahāvihāra*. In the opinion of the Chief Justice (and many others), the case had special "sensitivity ... from the perspective of Buddhists, not only in that area but in the entire country."[67] While the Supreme Court's decision did not mention violations of the Buddhism Chapter, arguments about Buddhism's "foremost place" were prominent in written submissions and courtroom arguments, and were absolutely central to the media attention surrounding the case.[68] The case involved the

---

[66] Interview with Rev. David Beiling, April 1, 2009; Interview with M A Sumanthiran, February 4, 2009.

[67] Determination SC (FR) 178/2008, Ven. *Ellawala Medananda Thero and Others v. Sunil Kannangara and Other* (copy obtained from office of Attorney General). The temple is an important pilgrimage site for Buddhists.

[68] Interview with lawyers involved in the case: M A Sumanitharan February 4, 2009; S. Aziz April 27, 2009. The legal bases for the judgment are complicated. The settlements were built on land alienated through executive order and *not* through the usual procedures of

building of 500 homes to house victims of the December 2004 tsunami. The homes were financed by the Saudi Arabian government and earmarked for Muslim displaced persons. While other housing settlements had been built for Tamils and Sinhalese in other parts of the island,[69] the Muslim dwellings were located 13 kilometres south of the Dīghavāpi temple, in a location halfway between the temple and a community of Buddhists who frequented the temple. In 2008, Ven. Ellawala Medhananda Thero, a Buddhist monk, and senior member of the JHU (*Jātika Heḷa Urumaya*) or National (Sinhala) Heritage Party – a political group well known for its pro-Sinhalese, pro-Buddhist politics – filed a petition to the Supreme Court claiming that, among other things, "the settlement of such a large number of Muslims within close proximity to the Raja Maha Viharaya would block further expansion of Sinhala Buddhist residents who are now living close to the Viharaya." This, in turn, would threaten the vitality of Buddhism and the existence of the temple.[70] The petition acquired the support of approximately 20 intervening petitioners including Buddhist monks (among them, the chief incumbent monk of the Dīghavāpi Mahāvihāra), government servants' associations and Buddhist lay organizations, many from Colombo.[71]

Most of the petitions submitted by Buddhists included a clear demand that the court should find the Muslim settlements illegal in large part because they violated the state's obligation to protect Buddhism. In a key interpretive move, petitioners associated protecting Buddhism with preserving the links between the temple and the surrounding Buddhist community. According to one petitioner, the settlements threatened to "encircle the *Deeghvapiya Bauddha Janapadaya* [Dīghavāpi Buddhist region] with Muslim settlements," and, in so doing, to squeeze out

---

land acquisition and distribution, which normally involve a land alienation committee plus oversight by the Provincial Council. In addition, the court found that the process of determining beneficiaries violated Articles 12(1) and 10 of the constitution insofar as it deliberately preferred Muslims.

[69] Interview with M A Sumanthiran, February 4, 2009.

[70] Determination SC (FR) 178/2008, *Ven. Ellawala Medananda Thero v. Sunil Kannangara and others.*

[71] A number of major lay Buddhist organizations from Colombo intervened as petitioners, including (in anglicized form, as included on their respective petitions): Dharmavijaya Foundation (Colombo), the Centre for Buddhist Action (Kotte), the Jathika Sanga Sammelanaya (Colombo), Government Servants Buddhist Association (Colombo), Buddhist Resource Centre (Colombo), Lanka Bauddha Sanrakshana Sabha (Colombo), the ACBC (Colombo), and SUCCESS (Colombo and Kandy).

Buddhists living in the area.[72] The petition argued, "it is the duty of the State to protect and foster Buddha Sasana [and] the Buddha Sasana cannot be protected if the appertaining village (*Goduru Gammanaya*) is not maintained and preserved."[73] In the words of another submission offered by the head of a Colombo-based Buddhist foundation:

> It is our respectful submission that as aforesaid the said 500 houses are constructed and/or are being constructed in Deegawapiya Bouddha Janapadaya which is in the proximity of the most sacred place of worship of Buddhists. Further it is as clearly established [that] the said area consists of various historically and archeologically valuable and important places of Buddhists and the other communities. Further your Lordship's Court be pleased to take in to consideration the fact that the temples in the said Bouddha Janapadaya including the connected institutions and the Buddhist monks survive and/or are being looked after by the members of the Buddhist community in and around the said Janapadaya. Therefore, the arbitrary colonization of the said areas with non Buddhists, undoubted would cause severe prejudice to such institutions and would cause severe harm to the archaeological and historical values of the Non-Muslims specially to Buddhists.[74]

In the arguments of the petitioners then, to protect Buddhism the state must protect Buddhist places; to protect Buddhist places the state must protect the networks of lay Buddhists who tend to the temple, donate money for its upkeep and offer support to the monks who live there. The arguments suggested that protecting the Buddha Sasana required defending broader social geography, a *goduru gammana,* or "sustenance village," upon which local monks can rely for food, work and material support:

> [A] Buddhist place of religious worship of the magnitude of Deeghavapiya cannot be maintained without a considerable segment of the population living close to the Vihara. It is respectfully submitted that historically every place of Buddhist religious worship had a *goduru gammana* ... It is the Petitioners most respectful submission that any

---

[72] Written Submissions, P Dayaratne (August 4, 2008), SC (FR) 178/2008 *Ven. Ellawala Medananda Thero v. Sunil Kannangara and others*, paragraphs 6–9. Dayaratne was a parliamentarian and government minister at the time (Minister of Plan Implementation). He was also president of the *Deeghavapi Prathisanskara Sabhawa* (the Dīghavāpi Reconstruction Council).

[73] Ibid., paragraph 20.

[74] Written Submissions, Dharmavijaya Foundation (November 24, 2008), SC (FR) 178/ 2008, *Ven. Ellawala Medananda Thero v. Sunil Kannangara and others*, paragraphs 13–14.

178 LEGAL BATTLES FOR BUDDHISM

decision taken in violation of the said policy is a violation of Article 9 and 10 of the Constitution.[75]

Litigants in the Deeghawapiya case, as in the church-building cases, construed the state's duties to protect and foster Buddhism as duties not only to secure places of worship but to preserve the broader (Buddhist) community in which those places of worship were situated. In this sense, they used constitutional law to present non-Buddhists as a particular kind of threat: by threatening to alter the religious demography of a particular area, they posed a risk to the existing reciprocity between Buddhist temples and lay devotees.

In the above cases, invoking the Buddhism Chapter in court generated public visibility for a particular social and religious geography. That geography divided the island into a network of Buddhist spaces. Litigants mapped the Buddha Sasana onto a distinct terrain, the location and boundaries of which corresponded to the sites of Buddhist temples, shrines, Bodhi trees and Buddhist communities, sites that were presumed to be physically distinct from other religious and non-religious sites and to be singularly Buddhist properties. Equally pronounced in these cases was the assumption and assertion of the unity of Buddhist persons and practices in Sri Lanka, a unity that was threatened by LTTE separatism, Christian evangelism and Muslim settlements, and that permitted Buddhists in Colombo to appear in court on behalf of Buddhists living across the island.

Idiom Four: Protecting Buddhism from Profanation

Litigants have also appealed to constitutional duties to protect Buddhism as a way to call attention to and to intervene against threats posed by globalization and neoliberalism. These cases can be thought to relate to the act of profaning religion, by which I mean the purportedly improper mingling and association of practices, ideas, motivations and objects deemed religious with those deemed economic or commercial.

---

[75] Written Submissions of Ven. Nannappurawe Buddharakkitha Thero (November 24, 2008), SC (FR) 178/2008, Vihāradhipathi of Dīghavāpi Raja Māha Vihāraya. *Ven. Ellawala Medananda Thero v. Sunil Kannangara and others*, "Conclusion," (no paragraph number indicated).

IDIOM FOUR: PROTECTING BUDDHISM FROM PROFANATION   179

In two sets of cases – the first, a series of writ petitions submitted initially in 2005, the second, a collection of three separate judicial review petitions against parliamentary bills, beginning in 2000 – Buddhist petitioners used the Buddhism Chapter to call upon the state to curb the profaning of religion. In the first case, the petitioner, a Buddhist monk, worried about the profaning of Buddhism itself and implored the court to prevent domestic and international retailers from selling clothing with the Buddha's image. In the second case, litigants used the Buddhism Chapter to demand that the state prevent the activities of profane Christian groups that threatened Buddhism. Here, petitioners asked the court to rule unconstitutional three bills that aimed to give legal incorporation to Christian groups that, they claimed, used financial inducements to gain converts. These cases show similarities with the Dīghavāpi and church-building cases described earlier in their concern with the ability of foreign agents to use superior wealth and political influence to interfere with local Buddhist practices and persons: in the case of Dīghavāpi it was overseas' (particularly Saudi Arabian) Muslim donors; in the case of Buddha images it was international merchandizers; in the case of church-building and proselytizing Christian organizations, it was global church networks.

In 2004 the Supreme Court heard the fundamental rights petition of Ven. Daranagama Kusaladhamma Thero, the head monk of a large Colombo temple. The petition requested that the court order the Inspector General of Police to arrest anyone involved in selling "merchandised Buddha images which defiles and defame[s] Lord Buddha."[76] The merchandise in question included swimwear manufactured by Victoria's Secret containing "the image of the Buddha displayed on the breasts and crotch areas,"[77] a pair of slippers with Buddha images on it, a candle made in the likeness of the Buddha, and a set of "Buddha Bar" compact discs (on sale in a Colombo music store). The monk petitioned that the products would cause Buddhists to be "emotionally hurt, annoyed and therefore offended," to be "gravely provoked" and to be made "emotionally turbulent."[78] This would, among other things, contravene the Buddhism Chapter's obligations to protect and foster the Buddha Sasana.

In his submissions, the monk publically affirmed a categorical opposition between Western capitalistic imperatives and local Buddhist sensibilities:

---

[76] Petition, Ven. Daranagama Kusaladhamma Thero (June 2, 2004), SC(FR) 237/2004, *Ven. Daranagama Kusladhamma Thero v. Indra de Silva and others*, p. 7.

[77] Ibid., p. 3. The Sinhala newspaper *Silumina* ran an article on the product in May 2004.

[78] Ibid., pp. 2–3.

180 LEGAL BATTLES FOR BUDDHISM

> [I]f the Buddha's image is continuously used publicly on bikinis, on slippers, as candles and on music compact discs etc. it would loose [*sic*] the impact as an image of honour and pilgrimage. Further it would be perceived as a brand like "Coca Cola," cream soda etc. ... Naturally the children, teenagers and youth of such religion who are exposed to religious images in such casual and merchandised manner would loose [*sic*] faith and sincere respect in the philosophy stated by such religious leaders.[79]

The petition accused global manufacturers of transforming the Buddha into a symbol for branding and marketing products. Ven. Kusaladhamma saw this as a significant threat to Buddhism. By using religious imagery as a marketing device, manufacturers (and those who sold their products) contributed to the "decline in worshiping or observing practices on such religious image or symbol ... [and] this would not only affect the individual *per se*, it would affect his or her religion in observing and worshiping in the long run."[80] According to Ven. Kusaladhamma's submissions, reproducing the Buddha's image on common items not only cheapened and degraded the image of the Buddha, it lead to the discrediting of Buddhism and therefore to a decline in membership and observance.

The submissions made by Ven. Kusaladhamma invoked the Buddhism Chapter in order to prevent a particular profaning effect of neoliberal commercialism: that of using Buddhist iconography for the selling of commercial products. This, he insisted, was an improper (and unconstitutional) mixing of religion and economics. Similar impulses appear in a second set of cases. In these cases, litigants invoked constitutional protections for religion to thwart a different kind of mixing between religion and monetary gain. In three cases that were heard by the Supreme Court between 2000 and 2003, petitioners opposed, as threats to Buddhism, the mixing of economic incentives and religious motives by Christian organizations. Here, however, it was not the commercial degrading of Buddhism that was at issue, but the "unethical" use of wealth (notably, wealth deriving from foreign sources) to promote conversion to Christianity.

The cases related to attempts by three separate Christian organizations to gain legal incorporation through acts of parliament.[81] (At the time,

---

[79] Ibid., p. 9.

[80] Written Submissions, Ven. Daranagama Kusaladhamma Thero (August 22, 2005), SC(FR) 237/2004, *Ven. Daranagama Kusladhamma Thero v. Indra de Silva and others*, p. 8.

[81] In each case, the bill was introduced as a Private Member's Bill. On this type of bill, and its importance, see Chapter 7.

IDIOM FOUR: PROTECTING BUDDHISM FROM PROFANATION 181

this was a common procedure for legally incorporating religious groups in Sri Lanka.) In each case, a petitioner, affiliated with a Buddhist organization,[82] challenged the proposed incorporation bill, claiming, among other things, that by recognizing the particular Christian group, the government would be contravening its constitutional duties to Buddhism. In 2001, a petitioner challenged the incorporation of an evangelical "Prayer Centre" that conducted regular services, faith healing and charity work.[83] In 2003, two separate petitioners challenged the incorporation of two other groups: one was an independent evangelical ministry whose stated aims included holding "deliverance meetings," building places of worship, organizing workshops, performing social service, and holding religious services;[84] the other was an order of Catholic nuns who ran schools, assisted in medical centres and undertook other social service activities.[85]

In all of the cases, petitioners advanced a particular argument concerning the links between religion, economic activity and Buddhism. Take for example, the first bill, entitled "Christian Sahanaye Doratuwa Prayer Centre (Incorporation) Bill." The bill aimed to give legal recognition to an organization in Colombo whose stated aims included the following:

(a) to encourage the active observance of Christianity;
(b) to promote the co-operation of the devotees who have faith in the prayer of God;
(c) to provide assistance and aid to needy Christians who seek assistance of the Corporation;
(d) to cure patients through prayer;
(e) to provide assistance to persons in order to solve their problems through prayer;
(f) to assist persons in various ways to enable them to obtain job opportunities.[86]

---

[82] These affiliations were not mentioned in the petitions or affidavits. Petitions were made as citizens of Sri Lanka.

[83] SC (SD) 2/2001 (June 8, 2001), *Regarding Christian Sahanaye Doratuwa Prayer Centre (Incorporation) Bill.*

[84] SC (SD) 2/2003 (February 18, 2003), *Regarding New Harvest Wine Ministries (Incorporation) Bill.*

[85] SC (SD) 19/2003 (August 5, 2003), *Regarding Provincial of the Teaching Sisters of the Holy Cross of the Third Order of Saint Francis in Menzingen of Sri Lanka (Incorporation) Bill.*

[86] "Christian Sahanaye Doratuwa Prayer Centre (Incorporation) Bill" (April 27, 2001), *Gazette of Democratic Socialist Republic of Sri Lanka*, p. II.

182   LEGAL BATTLES FOR BUDDHISM

The bill also specified that the proposed corporation should have the powers to raise and borrow money, to maintain bank accounts and draft checks, to enter into contracts, to administer trusts, to employ workers, to put money in investments,[87] to create corporate funds,[88] and to acquire, hold and sell property.[89] In the challenge to this bill, the petitioner pointed to the presence of both "material" and "religious" objectives in the proposed articles of incorporation to argue that the Prayer Centre intended to use "material rewards" and "economic assistance" to "induce" people to adopt Christianity:

> The cumulative effect of clause 3(a) to 3(i) is to convert people of other religions to Christianity by fraud and/or allurement. There is nothing objectionable in any institution helping people to find jobs, ease them from their problems or relieve them from any disease or pain quite legitimately, such objectives could be carried out through job agencies, hospitals, banks etc. What is objectionable is to provide material assistance in an attempt to convert the recipients to the Christian faith.[90]

According to the petition, neither the religious activities nor the "material assistance" specified in the proposed bill, alone, violated the terms of the constitution. The problem was the mingling of the two. By mixing material and religious imperatives, the petitioners insisted, Christian groups would be able to leverage one against the other, using promises of better jobs, improved health or increased wealth – promises that were underwritten by the perceived wealth and resources of related, international Christian organizations – to draw Buddhists to Christianity. The result was "unethical" proselytizing.

As with the aforementioned cases, litigants associated the profaned religion with distinct foreign threats. Petitioners pointed out that Christian groups represented not only an alternate faith (to Buddhism), but an alternate "culture" as well. The conversion of Buddhists to Christianity, in this view, threatened Sri Lanka's demographic, cultural and religious uniqueness, exposing vulnerable local persons to powerful "international" forces.

In 2003, the Supreme Court itself affirmed some of these claims, albeit in terse and evasive language. In the second incorporation case (relating to the incorporation of an evangelical ministry) a Supreme Court majority opinion insisted, without further explanation, that because the

---

[87] Ibid., Section 4.   [88] Ibid., Section 7.   [89] Ibid., Section 8.
[90] Written Submissions, P A Amarasekera (May 16, 2001), SC (SD) 2/2001 *Regarding Christian Sahanaye Doratuwa Prayer Centre (Incorporation) Bill*, p. 8.

ministry seemed to mix together economic and religious goals in its charter, its incorporation would be "inconsistent with the Buddhism Chapter."[91] In the third case (relating to the incorporation of an order of Catholic nuns), the Supreme Court went further, opining that not only was such mixing "inconsistent" with the Buddhism Chapter, a Christian organization that engaged in such mixing might "impair the very existence of Buddhism or the Buddha Sasana."[92] No further explanation was given in this case either.

In these cases – all of which gained widespread attention in the national media as well as in the reports of human rights and advocacy groups abroad – litigants used the Buddhism Chapter to compel the state to protect Sri Lanka from global forces, religion from non-religion, Buddhism from the profane. In Ven. Kusaladhamma's petitions against Buddha images, the division between the two corresponded to the contexts of producing, displaying and using religious images. In the Buddhist petitioners' objections to incorporating Christian groups, litigants and judges divided religion from non-religion (or, rather, religious from non-religious activity) according to persons' motivations for acting: religion was motivated by spiritual considerations as opposed to material ones. In both cases, litigants identified as threats not only individual merchandizers or retailers, or specific Christian social work organizations, but larger global forces: Western capitalists, international industrialists and Christianity writ large.

Expanding and Consolidating Conclusions

Invoking the Buddhism Chapter in court has provided a powerful mechanism for expanding the visibility and political importance of protecting Buddhism in Sri Lankan life. While Sri Lanka's courts have not always affirmed litigants' claims about Buddhism, the very act of legal contestation has elevated into matters of public concern questions about the nature of Buddhism, who is authorized to speak for it and how it ought to be protected. In pursuing these questions, courts and litigants have endorsed and publicized certain types of religious divisions: between Buddhists and anti-Buddhist governments, between Buddhist monks and laypersons, between orthodox monks and heterodox monks,

---

[91] SC (SD) 19/2003 *Regarding Provincial of the Teaching Sisters of the Holy Cross of the Third Order of Saint Francis in Menzingen of Sri Lanka (Incorporation) Bill.*
[92] Ibid.

184 LEGAL BATTLES FOR BUDDHISM

between Buddhists and non-Buddhists (Hindus, Christians, Muslims and Tamil separatists), and between Buddhism and the corrupting effects of global industry, transnational Christianity and the West. Litigants and judges have also validated the need to protect a variety of objects (temples, educational institutions, practices, monks, texts, archaeological sites, villages, images and consciences) *from* a variety of threats (government agents, heterodox monks, LTTE militants, Muslim interlopers, international corporations, foreign governments and Christian proselytizers).

Since its introduction in 1972, the range of interpretations of the Buddhism Chapter has expanded, keeping pace with and reflecting a growing number of political and social concerns. The very mechanisms designed to expand the availability of public law remedies – protocols of judicial review and fundamental rights jurisdiction inspired by traditions of liberal constitutionalism – have opened channels for making public, constitutional claims about Buddhism. In fact, today one even finds a consistent, almost routinized, format for Buddhist-interest litigation. In most cases, litigants use judicial review or fundamental rights petitions to advance specific arguments about how to protect Buddhism: they claim that a certain bill or government initiative contravenes or is likely to contravene the state's duties to Buddhism and/or certain fundamental rights;[93] once the case has been granted leave by the Supreme Court they then use the hearing to publicize and validate particular visions of Buddhism, threats to it and the ideal nature of the state's relationship with it. This format has been employed frequently. As a result, Sri Lanka has seen a gradually expanding climate of Buddhist-interest litigation.[94] Among the key actors are Colombo's lay Buddhist organizations, such as the ACBC and SUCCESS. In all of the cases

---

[93] The "other things" referred to frequently include infringements of fundamental religious rights outlined in Articles 10, 12 and 14(1)(e).

[94] One might even point to a broader culture of Buddhist legal activism beyond Buddhist-interest litigation. This relates to the introduction or reformation of laws directly or indirectly relating to Buddhism. One prominent example of this was an attempt by the JHU in 2004 to amend the constitution to make Buddhism "the Official Religion of the Republic." *Nineteenth Amendment to the Constitution (Private Member's Bill)* (October 29, 2004) *Gazette of Democratic Socialist Republic of Sri Lanka*, P. II. Earlier in 2004, the JHU had attempted to introduce another Private Member's Bill, which, capitalizing on the momentum gained in the incorporation cases described earlier, aimed to criminalize "unethical conversion" throughout the country. Stephen C Berkwitz, "Religious Conflict and the Politics of Conversion in Sri Lanka," in *Proselytization Revisited: Rights Talk, Free Markets and Culture Wars*, ed. Rosalind I J Hackett (London: Equinox, 2008).

examined earlier except one (the Ven. Kusaladhamma case involving the profanation of Buddhist images), petitioners represented and/or had membership in prominent lay Buddhist organizations based in the island's capital. In certain cases, most visibly in the Dīghavāpi case, Colombo-based Buddhist monks and monastic organizations also served as interveners or primary petitioners. Moreover, a growing number of Buddhist groups – including the recently ascendant *Bodu Bala Sēnā* (or Army of Buddhist Power) – have developed their own legal advocacy departments.[95]

At the same time that Buddhist-interest litigation expands the visibility, salience and perceived pertinence of Buddhism in public life in Sri Lanka, it also consolidates diverse types of disputes and issues through a particular format and language. In one sense, making legal claims about Buddhism remains an activity whose main participants, including the Supreme Court itself, are based in the country's largest city and capital. In another sense, legal interpretations of the state's constitutional duties to protect Buddhism are projected onto events, politics and histories that occur in the areas farthest from Colombo: fighting between the Sri Lankan army and the LTTE in the North, the planting of Christian churches in the Dry Zone, the building of Muslim houses in the Eastern Province, and the merchandizing of Buddha images in the UK and United States. Buddhist-interest litigation has, therefore, an expanding ambit but a consolidating logic. It brings together and reframes a wide variety of issues and disputes from around the island through the legal claims of a relatively small number of actors in Colombo. In this process, lawyers, litigants and judges focus – and recode – complex, situational disputes according to the rigid dialects of rights and obligations, and the adversarial structure of courtroom litigation.

Undoubtedly, Buddhist-interest litigation has succeeded in generating public visibility and legitimacy for particular, often partisan, visions of Buddhism and the potential harms to it. Petitions against Ven. Sumana's application to the bar represent one instance in which invoking the Buddhism Chapter in court generated so much public opposition that, despite the Supreme Court's initial judgment, Ven. Sumana was ultimately unable to become a lawyer. Media coverage of the Dīghavāpi and the incorporation cases also represent instances in which legal action successfully raised public awareness about the alleged harms to

---

[95] Schonthal, "Environments of Law."

186   LEGAL BATTLES FOR BUDDHISM

Buddhism posed by Muslims and Christians. The publicity-generating quality of Buddhist-interest litigation was especially pronounced in the case of Ven. Kusaladhamma's petition against profaning Buddha images. What began as one monk's attempt to influence the practices of local retailers and importers eventually fed into a coordinated government initiative to introduce a UNESCO resolution (which was eventually passed) on the "Misuse of Religious Symbols and Expressions," which aimed to curb the "increasing trend in the use of religious images in commercial items and other non-religious contexts."[96]

In a self-perpetuating way, then, Buddhist-interest litigation not only publicizes litigants' claims, it also gives greater publicity to the Buddhism Chapter of the constitution itself. This leads to further legal and extra-legal attempts to actualize or defend Buddhism's "foremost place." Two interesting examples of this took place in March 2010, six months after the Dīghavāpi case (involving Muslim settlements near a Buddhist temple). In one case, a Sri Lankan-born Bahraini resident, Sara Malani Perera, was detained at the airport and held for one month at the Mirihana Police Station following complaints made to the Department of Buddhist Affairs that she had published books that were insulting to Buddhism.[97] In a roughly contemporaneous instance, the Sri Lankan government denied American rap-musician Akon a visa to enter the country on account of the fact that one of his music videos had insulted Buddhism by showing girls dancing poolside near a Buddha statute.[98] In a more recent case from 2014, a British woman was detained and deported when two taxi drivers and a plain-clothes police officer registered their offense at the tattoo of the Buddha on her arm.[99] In all three instances, the government's constitutional duties to Buddhism appeared prominently in public and media discourse, even though these cases were dealt with as matters of criminal law, rather than constitutional law.[100] Similar dynamics also apply to national politics where government and

---

[96] Interview with Kusaladhamma's lawyer April 4, 2009. "The misuse of religious symbols and expressions" (August 27, 2004), *Agenda Item 170 EX/36, UNESCO*: http://unesdoc .unesco.org/images/0013/001362/136204e.pdf (Accessed August 22, 2015).

[97] Interview with Perera's lawyer, August 18, 2010.

[98] N.a. (March 24, 2010), "Akon Refused Visa After Protests," *BBC World News*: http:// news.bbc.co.uk/2/hi/8584546.stm (Accessed July 5, 2012).

[99] N.a. (April 22, 2014), "Sri Lanka to deport Buddha tattoo British woman," *BBC World News*: www.bbc.com/news/world-asia-27107857 (Accessed August 22, 2015).

[100] Perera and the British tourist were charged under the Chapter XV of the Sri Lankan Penal Code, "Offenses Relating to Religion."

EXPANDING AND CONSOLIDATING CONCLUSIONS   187

opposition politicians have reacted to Buddhist-interest litigation by calling for the creation of subsidiary legislation to secure the well-being of the Sasana.[101] Although Buddhist-interest litigation tends to be centred in Colombo, one also finds constitutional discourse being used to justify and encourage religious and political activism in places far away from the capital. To take one dramatic example: In April 2012, two senior Buddhist monks used the language of the Buddhism Chapter to help rally the sentiments of large crowds of Buddhist demonstrators who had gathered outside of a Dambulla mosque demanding that it, and a nearby Hindu temple, be demolished because they had been built on Buddhist sacred ground.[102]

Giving constitutional privileges to Buddhism has made it an object of elite legal attention. It has given judges and constitutional courts formal authority to pronounce on matters of Buddhism. In practice, the judges of apical courts have tended to be reluctant in exercising that authority fully, for fear of violating the courts' claims to secularity, or encroaching on ecclesiastical authority of monks, or engaging in conspicuous acts of Buddhist partisanship.[103] Yet, while judicial elites remain cautious, citizens and lawyers appear less reserved in using the authorized language and public forums of constitutional law to make claims about Buddhism. In this respect, then, constitutional protections for Buddhism in Sri Lanka have served less as "shields against the spread of religiosity," as Ran Hirschl might have it, than as powerful vehicles for making religiosity public.

---

[101] For example, in the weeks following the Perera and Akon affairs, parliamentarians called for new statutory protections for the Buddha Sasana. Somarathna, Rasika (May 31, 2010) "Acts to Protect Buddhism," *Daily News*: http://archives.dailynews.lk/2010/05/31/news01.asp (Accessed August 22, 2015).

[102] Groundviews (April 23, 2012), "Bigoted Monks and Militant Mobs: Is this Buddhism in Sri Lanka Today?" *Groundviews: Journal for Citizens*. http://groundviews.org/2012/04/23/bigoted-monks-and-militant-mobs-is-this-buddhism-in-sri-lanka-today/ (Accessed April 26, 2012); Luke A Heslop, "On Sacred Ground: The Political Performance of Religious Responsibility," *Contemporary South Asia* 22, no. 1 (2014): 21–36. For another evocative example see W N Oshan Fernando, *The Effects of Evangelical Christianity on State Formation in Sri Lanka*, Ph.D. Dissertation, Department of Anthropology, University of California at Santa Barbara, September 2011, p. 305.

[103] The Supreme Court's decision in the Menzingen incorporation case might be considered an exception. Yet, even in that case, the court refused to pronounce specifically on what protecting Buddhism entailed. The most extensive interpretations of Buddhism's foremost place remain the majority and dissenting opinions of the Ven. Sumana Case in 1977.

6

Battles within Buddhism

From the time it was first suggested, the idea of giving Buddhism special constitutional status in Sri Lanka had descriptive as well as prescriptive dimensions. On the one hand, those who advocated for Buddhism's privileged status claimed to be describing in law an observable fact: Buddhism, by virtue of its demographic preponderance and long history on the island, had a *de facto* preeminence over other religions. On the other hand, the most ardent proponents of the Buddhism Chapter aimed not just to describe reality but to transform it. They viewed constitutional obligations to support Buddhism and to give it the "foremost place" as weighty prescriptions, instructions for bureaucrats, politicians, judges and others to create a new Buddhist era on the island. Many supporters of the Buddhism Chapter imagined this new era as a restoration of a glorious past. Constitutional law would help remake modern Sri Lanka along the lines of the island's ancient kingdoms. In those kingdoms, supporters argued, Buddhist kings ruled benevolently over pious monks and fertile paddy lands. Supporters of special prerogatives for Buddhism hoped to use law to "make [Sri] Lanka's Buddhist people into a strong and unified body (*eksat prabala āyatanayak*) once again."[1]

Sri Lanka's Buddhism Chapter has changed the lives of Buddhists on the island. However, the nature of these changes has not been what drafters and campaigners had hoped for or expected. As seen in Chapter 5, when it comes to Buddhist-interest litigation, constitutional prerogatives for Buddhism have not simply empowered state officials to act on behalf of Buddhism in a concerted and custodial manner. Instead they have given citizens new opportunities to express their own particularistic understandings of Buddhism in highly public

---

[1] All-Ceylon Buddhist Congress, *Bauddha Toraturu Parīkṣaka Sabhāvē Vārtāva* (Colombo: Visidunu Prakāśakaya, 2006), 367.

and consequential ways. They have enabled politicians, monks, lay Buddhist organizations and others to use law as a way to make their claims about Buddhism politically salient and to make their political agendas religiously salient. They have multiplied rather than redressed public anxieties over Buddhism.

Yet, there have been other unintended consequences as well. Litigating the Buddhism Chapter has, in certain cases, directly undermined the solidarity of Buddhists on the island and contributed to the fracturing of Sri Lankan Buddhism. Rather than solidifying a "strong and united body" of Buddhists as lobbyists hoped,[2] enforcing constitutional protections for Buddhism has deepened divisions among Buddhist monks and lay persons, pitting one Buddhist organization against another and one monastic fraternity (*nikāya*) against another, even dividing trustees and incumbent monks within a single Buddhist temple.

We have already encountered one such division in Chapter 5. In the Supreme Court case involving Ven. Sumana's application to the bar, petitioners and respondents used the language of protecting and fostering Buddhism to legitimate opposing views of Buddhist orthodoxy. As this chapter will show, the case of Ven. Sumana is neither isolated nor unique. By including special prerogatives for Buddhism in the constitution, constitutional designers have invited disagreements among those who identify as Buddhists over what Buddhism is and who has the authority to speak on its behalf. Like religious groups in many countries, Sri Lankan Buddhists have never fully agreed on all aspects of their tradition. In fact, as seen in previous chapters, disagreements over Buddhism split religious leaders, civil society groups and politicians throughout the twentieth century. Accordingly, strong differences of opinion exist as to what it means to protect and foster Buddhism. Invoking the Buddhism Chapter in court has shifted those disagreements into new forums and raised the stakes of those conflicts. In Sri Lanka today, disputes over how to protect Buddhism are not just matters for political and doctrinal debate among Buddhists; they are matters that involve legal sanctions and state power. Through the force of constitutional law, localized, intrareligious disagreements over Buddhist doctrine have become matters to be dealt with by judges, lawyers and state officials.

---

[2] Ibid., 367.

Constitutional Microhistory and the Case of Ven. Wimalawansa

In this chapter, and the one to follow, I use the techniques of constitutional microhistory at the level of individual court cases. To see fully the ways in which constitutional law deepens existing lines of religious tension one must also look closely at how constitutional categories and legal action come to impact and alter existing disputes as they oscillate between societal conflicts and legal ones. The court case considered in this chapter involves the seemingly unremarkable matter of a Buddhist monk trying to obtain a driving license. By studying this case in the mode of constitutional microhistory, one sees how the logic and protocols of constitutional litigation came to transform a single, isolated affair into a highly acrimonious and highly public dispute over the standards of monastic orthopraxy and the nature of Buddhism itself. Following this case also reveals how constitutional provisions designed explicitly to solidify the status and well-being of Buddhism, when invoked in litigation, exposed and deepened existing lines of division and called into question the unity of the tradition itself.

During its 10-year span, from 2004 to 2014, the case involved multiple petitioners and respondents, along with numerous cycles of appeal and reversion between the Court of Appeals and the Supreme Court. The precipitating events were, however, quite straightforward. In May 2004, a Buddhist monk, Ven. Paragoda Wimalawansa Thero, chief incumbent of two Colombo-area temples,[3] applied for a Driving License at the Verahara office of the Commissioner of Motor Traffic (CMT). In an interview, as well in his legal submissions, Ven. Wimalawansa explained that he required a license so that he could carry out his ecclesiastical duties more efficiently. These duties, similar to those of many monks in Sri Lanka, included preaching (*bana*) and receiving alms (*dāna*) as well as a variety of ritual obligations. In addition to this, Wimalawansa served as an assistant principal and lecturer at a college 15 kilometers away,[4] a

---

[3] The chief incumbent monk of a temple, or *vihāradhipati*, acts as both the highest ecclesiastical authority of that temple as well as the controller of that temple's assets and property. Wimalawansa declared his status as *vihāradhipati* for two temples, Sri Sakyamuni Vihāraya in Waskaduwa and Sri Jayawardhanaramaya, Wadugoda.

[4] Interview with Ven. Wimalawansa Thero, December 14, 2014. He was Assistant Principal and Lecturer in Buddhist Civilization and Computer Studies at the Moratuwa Maha Vidyalaya, having acquired a number of advanced degrees, including a Ph.D., in order to do this.

deputy secretary of a regional Buddhist organization,[5] and a teacher at several Buddhist Sunday schools (*daham pasal*).

Wimalawansa explained that, while he used public transportation regularly, he found it extremely difficult. Particularly frustrating was the fact that, as a monk, he was required to be at the temple for his only meal of the day, which, according to monastic law, had to be consumed before midday. This time-sensitive practice clashed frequently with late-running and erratic bus schedules. Taking matters into his own hands, Ven. Wimalawansa took steps to start driving himself. He attended driving classes and tried to acquire a car.[6] He even participated in a small, Colombo-area monastic group called *Apē Urumaya* (Our Heritage), which was dedicated to addressing difficulties among monks including helping them get driving licenses.[7] In June 2004, he met with an officer of the CMT to file his application for a driving license, but was rebuffed. The officer explained that Buddhist monks could not be issued with driving licenses.

Ven. Wimalawansa's legal submissions describe how, upset by the officer's decision, he returned to his temple and drafted several letters to the CMT officer protesting the refusal. When the officer failed to reply, Ven. Wimalawansa returned to the CMT office and requested to meet with the acting Commissioner. Court records show that, after speaking with Ven. Wimalawansa, the acting Commissioner agreed to receive the monk's application on one condition: the Commissioner would first seek advice from the Ministry of Buddhist Affairs,[8] the government office charged with assisting temples and supporting Buddhism on the island. Consenting to this arrangement, Ven. Wimalawansa wrote three letters to the Ministry arguing passionately that obtaining a driving license did

---

[5] The *śāsanarakshaka balamaṇḍalaya* (The Buddhism Protection Council) in Kalutara.

[6] In his petition, he explained that he had told the then-Principal of the Moratuwa Vidyalaya about his plans; and the principal approached two separate deputy Commissioners of Motor Traffic on his behalf. One indicated that Buddhist monks were not eligible for drivers' licenses. The other indicated that obtaining a license would be possible provided that he received a letter from the Buddha Sasana Ministry. On hearing this news, the monk wrote a letter to the Ministry and met with its secretary. However, the secretary explained that he had no power in this matter.

[7] Interview with member of *Apē Urumaya*, Ven. Bodagama Seelawimala Thero, Malabe, December 14, 2014.

[8] Since that time (2004), and during the course of the case, the Ministry of Buddhist Affairs was replaced by a Department of Buddhist Affairs under a Ministry of Buddha Sasana and Religious Affairs. On Sri Lanka's bureaucratic infrastructure for regulating religions see: Schonthal, "Environments of Law."

192 BATTLES WITHIN BUDDHISM

not violate Buddhist teachings (more on this later). Yet the letters failed to convince the Commissioner of Buddhist Affairs, who instead asked for an opinion from an island-wide monastic council consisting of senior Buddhist monks.[9] That council concluded that it was inappropriate for a monk to obtain a driving license. The Commissioner of Buddhist Affairs relayed the decision to the CMT, who relayed it to Ven. Wimalawansa. The monk's application would be refused. Buddhist monks, he was told, were not supposed to drive because doing so would violate Buddhist monastic law. Therefore, by granting him a license, the office would contravene the state's constitutional obligation to protect Buddhism.

Ten Years in Court: Further Particulars of the Case

At this point, the matter went to the courts. Shortly after receiving the letter, Ven. Wimalawansa petitioned the Court of Appeals for a writ overturning the acting CMT's decision and requiring him to issue a license. The CMT, named as the respondent, filed his objections almost a year later, in June 2005. Oral arguments were scheduled to take place the following September.[10] However, in July, an application for intervention was filed with the Court of Appeals. This came from four members of the Dāyaka Sabhāva (board of lay trustees) of one of Ven. Wimalawansa's temples.[11] The petition requested that the Dāyakas be allowed to intervene on behalf of the CMT, to oppose the license.[12] The court refused the intervention, dismissing the Dāyakas' petition without a hearing.

The Dāyakas refused to acquiesce. Late in 2005, they filed a petition for special leave to appeal to the Supreme Court to challenge what they saw as the Court of Appeals' unfair dismissal of their request for intervention.[13] Ven. Wimalawansa opposed this new petition with a counter-petition himself, claiming that the petitioners had no legitimate interest in the case as they were not in fact members of the Sakyamuni Vihara Dāyaka Sabhāva. That temple, Ven. Wimalawansa argued, had no Dāyaka Sabhāva.

By the middle of 2007, the Dāyakas received a favorable verdict from the apical court requiring that they be given a hearing by the Court of

---

[9] *Samasta Lanka Sāsanārakṣaka Maṇḍalaya (the All-Lanka Buddhism Protection Council).*
[10] Weerasooria, *Buddhist Ecclesiastical Law*, 738.   [11] *Sri Sakyamuni Vihāraya.*
[12] According to the Dāyaka Sabhāva, it was the CMT that had, in fact, first suggested that they intervene. Interview with Dāyaka Sabhāva, Waskuduwa, December 14, 2014.
[13] The Court of Appeals had rejected their petition unfairly as the petition had been considered by only one judge, not the complete court.

TEN YEARS IN COURT 193

Appeals. Proceedings then recommenced in the Court of Appeals with an important question: who were proper parties to the case? Answers to this already contentious question were complicated by the fact that two other Buddhist monks who also wanted driving licenses became petitioners alongside Ven. Wimalawansa, also filing separate writ petitions against the CMT. Moreover, the CMT had requested that the Court of Appeals require the Commissioner of Buddhist Affairs to be a party to the case, insofar as the case involved matters of Buddhism and potential violations of the Buddhism provisions of the constitution.

From here, the legal records reveal another trail of procedural disputes and appeals. Having yet to consider the issue of the Dāyaka Sabhāva's intervention, the Court of Appeals made an initial order against the intervention by the Commissioner of Buddhist Affairs (CBA). This led to another special appeal to the Supreme Court. This time, it was the CMT who filed a petition, requesting that the island's highest court require the appellate court to include the CBA as a "necessary party" insofar as the case had important implications for the state's constitutional obligations to Buddhism.

Delays continued to mount. It would be two years before this second special appeal was argued in the Supreme Court (July 2009) and another two years before the court issued its judgment (October 14, 2011). When the judgment finally came, Justice Amaratunga, writing for the unanimous three-justice bench, ruled that the role of the CBA was not as broad as the CMT suggested. The CBA, Amaratunga clarified, was not a general advisor on Buddhist affairs, but an officer charged with helping to manage Buddhist temple properties. Therefore, the CBA was not a *necessary* party to the case. However, the court insisted, if the CBA *wanted* to intervene, he could file his own application as an *interested* party.[14]

In 2012, the case returned – yet again – to the Court of Appeals. This time, all parties were heard. The CBA intervened as an interested party, representing the views of two important groups of senior monks (discussed later) who had written letters opposing the granting of a driving license.[15] The members of the Dāyaka Sabhāva were also included. In

---

[14] SC Appeal No. 84/2007 *B. Wijeratne (Commissioner of Motor Traffic) v. Venerable Dr. Paragoda Wimalawansa Thero.*

[15] According to one lawyer involved with the case, the two bhikkhus who petitioned subsequent to Ven. Wimalawansa also named the CBA as a respondent to their petitions.

194 BATTLES WITHIN BUDDHISM

addition, the initial petition made by Ven. Wimalawansa was now one of a series of three linked petitions in which Buddhist monks sought orders requiring the CMT to issue them with driving licenses. The stage was set for drama.

Whose Rules? Which Buddhism?

In general terms, the events of the Ven. Wimalawansa case mirror those of many legal contests: it began with a particular grievance, which was then channeled through the courts, where lawyers, judges and litigants construed arguments for and against that grievance in terms of broader abstract, legal principles. Of note in Ven. Wimalawansa's case is the array of parties and issues that became involved. On the one side was a Buddhist monk supported by roughly 15 other Buddhist monks citing, among other things, the state's constitutional obligations to Buddhism to argue that he should be granted a driving license. On the other side were government administrators and other Buddhist monks invoking the same constitutional obligations to argue that Ven. Wimalawansa should not be issued with a driving license.

That monks would argue with each other over the standards of Buddhism and monastic comportment is not surprising. Debates about what monks should and should not do have a long history on the island, as well as in other parts of the Buddhist world. A variety of Pali and Sinhala sources provide accounts of historical controversies (*vādaya*) over how the community of monks, the *sangha*, ought to act, dress, eat, preach, chant and engage with texts.[16] In the nineteenth and twentieth centuries, Sri Lankan monks and lay Buddhists argued regularly about the appropriateness of monks engaging in "worldly" (*laukika*) practices, such as propitiating deities, teaching in public schools, practicing Ayurvedic medicine and doing astrology. Sri Lanka's colonial and, later, independent governments enacted a series of ordinances to regulate monks' abilities to acquire and alienate property. By issuing these ordinances they aimed to prevent monks from treating monastic property as a source of wealth, while encouraging them to focus their energies on contemplation, preaching and "other worldly" (*lōkōttara*) affairs – those things associated with gaining a better rebirth

---

[16] Malalgoda, *Buddhism in Sinhalese Society, 1750–1900*, 131, 169. Blackburn, *Buddhist Learning and Textual Practice in Eighteenth-Century Lankan Monastic Culture.*

and, ultimately, enlightenment.[17] Major reports on Buddhism produced in the 1950s by government and civil society groups eulogized this *lōkōttara* monastic ideal and devoted entire sections to outlining legal and institutional devices for preventing monks from participating in employment, politics and other *laukika* matters. Since 1931, in fact, the state has enforced the barrier between monastic and secular vocations both ways: Sri Lankan law makes it a criminal offense for any person who has not been ritually ordained as a monk to wear orange monastic robes.[18]

This ideal of the serene, cloistered, otherworldly monk striving quietly for enlightenment did not go unchallenged. Throughout the twentieth century influential and vocal groups of monks spoke out against what they saw as attempts to limit the influence of monks on society. In one important episode in the 1940s, monks from one of the island's most important monastic colleges publicly challenged the most powerful politician at the time, D S Senanayake, in demanding recognition of monks' rights to participate in politics as lobbyists, campaign volunteers and even (in some cases) political candidates.[19] Since that time, Sri Lanka's monks have asserted their rights to participate in almost all spheres of society: from education, to social work, to politics. Since 2004, a number of robed monks have even served as members of Sri Lanka's parliament.

Debates over proper monastic conduct persist in Sri Lanka, in large part, because there is no island-wide ecclesiastical body with the power to determine or enforce monastic discipline for all monks. Sri Lanka has no single, unanimously accepted monastic hierarchy, a national *sangha*, which

---

[17] "Enlightenment" is the common translation for the Pali word, *nibbāna*, the more precise meaning of which is blowing out or extinguishing.

[18] The exact term is to "hold himself out to be" a monk. Article 42 of the Buddhist Temporalities Ordinance No. 19 of 1931. There have been legal debates on precisely who is a monk. E.g., *Saranajothi Thero v. Dharmarama* (1959) 61 *New Law Reports* 76.

[19] On February 2, 1946, this group, from Vidyalankara Pirivena, drafted a public declaration, called the "Declaration of the Vidyalankara Pirivena," which blamed "invaders from the West, who belonged to an alien faith" for popularizing the idea that the affairs of the *sangha* and the affairs of the nation should be kept separate. Rejecting the idea that monks should stay aloof from politics, the document declared that "it is nothing but fitting for bhikkhus to identify themselves with activities conducive to the welfare of our people – whether these activities be labeled politics or not – as long as they do not constitute an impediment to the religious life of a bhikkhu." Walpola Rahula, "Appendix II: The Vidyalankara Declaration," in *The Heritage of the Bhikkhu* (New York: Grove Press, 1974).

might act as the final arbiter for Buddhist orthodoxy. Sri Lanka is not unusual in this respect. For most of Buddhist history, the ideal of a stable and centralized ecclesiastical hierarchy was achieved only incompletely and only through the heavy-handed efforts of powerful kings who, through a mixture of patronage and coercive power, worked to support one "pure" group while branding others as heterodox. Even in those cases, however, reform movements and other challengers continued to exist. The few national monastic hierarchies that one sees in the contemporary Buddhist world – for example, the lama system for monks of the Geluk school in Tibet or the council of great monks (*mahatherasamkhom*) in Thailand – are of relatively recent origins. These hierarchies also emerged from (and continue to depend upon) acts of coercion and control by the state designed to prevent schism and deny legitimacy to other monastic groups who claim their own forms of autonomy and authority.[20]

In the Buddhist-majority countries of Southern Asia today, Sri Lanka's sangha remains more decentralized than most, containing many different claimants to Buddhist authority. Unlike the government of Thailand (and, to a lesser extent, the governments of Myanmar, Cambodia and Laos), the Sri Lankan government has failed in its efforts to create, even nominally, a single, national council of monks representing all sects. Nor has it standardized or codified any of the many written and oral codes of conduct (*katikāvata*) to which the island's monks adhere.[21] A variety of monastic and lay groups in Sri Lanka claim the right to interpret and act on behalf of Buddhism. Among those with the broadest credibility are the two chief monks of the island's oldest monastic fraternities (the Malvatu and Asgiri branches of the Siyam Nikāya), located in Kandy, the site of the island's last Buddhist kingdom. These two *mahānāyaka*-s, or great leaders, have some control over a disproportionately large number of the island's temples and temple-lands.[22]

---

[20] Stanley Jeyaraja Tambiah, *World Conqueror and World Renouncer: A Study of Buddhism and Polity in Thailand Against a Historical Background* (New York: Cambridge University Press, 1976). Justin McDaniel, *The Lovelorn Ghost and the Magical Monk: Practicing Buddhism in Modern Thailand* (New York: Columbia University Press, 2013). Rachel M McCleary and Leonard WJ van der Kuijp, "The Market Approach to the Rise of the Geluk School, 1419–1642," *The Journal of Asian Studies* 69, no. 1 (2010): 149–180.

[21] There have been attempts in the past. Even now, at the time of writing, there exist attempts to standardize and give official legal status to the codes of conduct for each of the major monastic fraternities by way of a Katikavata Act.

[22] Pamphlet: "*Vihārasthāna hā bhikṣūn vahansē saṅgaṇanaya* (Census of bhikkhus and temples)," 2012. Obtained by the author from the Department of Buddhist Affairs in January 2014. Formal registers, such as the records of monastic landholdings held by the

They also appear regularly in the newspaper consulting with politicians, civil society leaders and other monks about matters of Buddhism. Their authority, however, is not unchallenged. In the last 200 years, dissatisfied monks have developed new semiautonomous chapters (*pārśava*-s) within the Asgiri and Malvatu branches of the Siyam Nikāya. Others have broken away from the Siyam Nikāya entirely to form new monastic fraternities.[23]

A variety of competing interests and interpretations of Buddhism define this decentralized monastic constellation. Principles of division include strong allegiances to particular senior monks, regional affiliations and even caste identities.[24] Also in competition for authority over Buddhism are lay Buddhist organizations who claim for themselves the right to interpret the texts of Buddhism directly.[25] Finally, there are government representatives – the president, the Commissioner of Buddhist Affairs and others – who also at times speak and act on behalf of Buddhism.

In drafting the Buddhism Chapter, Sri Lanka's constitutional designers tried to accommodate the non-centralized nature of Buddhist authority by giving Buddhism the "foremost place" rather than calling it the "state religion." Where "state religion" (S: *rajyāgama*) seemed to imply substantial government power over Buddhism, the phrase "foremost place" eschewed any indication of where the proper sources of Buddhist authority lay.[26] Drafters agreed to the phrase largely as a way to sidestep contentious disputes among lawmakers and lobbyists over how much authority, if any, the state ought to have over Buddhism and Buddhist monks (see Chapter 4).

Commissioner of Buddhist Affairs, cited here, suggest significant hierarchical control over temple lands. However, in reality, the direct influence of the *mahānāyaka-s* is limited and tends to be felt primarily through the grant of higher ordination rather than through the control of property and monastic landholdings. I am grateful to H L Seneviratne for highlighting this for me.

[23] On the development of these alternative monastic fraternities generally see: Malalgoda, *Buddhism in Sinhalese Society, 1750–1900*. On challengers within the Asgiri branch of the Siyam Nikāya, see: Abeysekara, *Colors of the Robe*, 174–194.

[24] Ananda Abeysekara, "Politics of Higher Ordination, Buddhist Monastic Identitiy, and Leadership at the Dambulla Temple in Sri Lanka," *Journal of the International Association of Buddhist Studies* 22, no. 2 (1999): 255–280.

[25] For example: Steven Kemper, "Buddhism Without Bhikkhus: The Sri Lanka Vinaya Vardana Society," in *Religion and Legitimation of Power in Sri Lanka*, ed. Bardwell L Smith (Chambersberg, PA: Anima, 1978), 212–235.

[26] De Silva, *Safeguards for the Minorities in the 1972 Constitution*.

198 BATTLES WITHIN BUDDHISM

Buddhism #1: Ven. Wimalawansa's Pragmatic Buddhism

In making his petition, Ven. Wimalawansa was challenging certain conventions. Buddhist monks did not normally drive cars in Sri Lanka;[27] and Buddhist texts said nothing about driving licenses. Neither fact deterred him. In interviews and legal submissions, Ven. Wimalawansa argued for the necessity of adjustment and change within the Buddhist tradition. Buddhism, he argued, was not a static entity, but a dynamic one designed to develop and accommodate new situations. Defending this position in a written submission filed in 2008, Ven. Wimalawansa highlighted a well-known passage in the Pali story of the Buddha's death, the Mahaparinibbana Sutta. In that story, the Buddha, on his deathbed, instructs his chief disciple, Ananda as follows: after his passing, the monks should *hold onto the major principles* of monastic life but "abolish the lesser and *minor* precepts."[28] The Buddha does not, however, explain which principles are which. According to Ven. Wimalawansa, the open-endedness of the Buddha's words is instructive because it shows that the Buddha never intended monastic life to progress unchanged, in frozen form, oblivious to or segregated from technological and cultural changes in society. Rather, Ven. Wimalawansa argued, the Buddha intended that monastic life should move *with* society, developing and adapting accordingly. Monks' driving, he suggested, was just the sort of adaptation that the Buddha had in mind.

Among the documents submitted with his petitions, Ven. Wimalawansa included a personal letter that he had written to the CMT in 2004. In this document, now a matter of public record, one sees very clearly this progressive view of Buddhism. In the letter Ven. Wimalawansa insists that "there are some people who do not want monks progressing forward (*idiriyaṭa yanavā*) with society. What they want is to hold monks back in the 6th century while they go into the 21st century."[29] These people, Ven. Wimalawansa argues, do so in the name of defending a culture (*saṅskṛtiyak*) and custom (*sampradāyak*). Yet he describes

---

[27] Although Ven. Wimalawansa adduced some evidence (a newspaper article) of another driving monk, the fact remained that to date this was an anomaly in Sri Lanka. Evidence was submitted that Buddhist monks drive cars in Malayasia, Singapore, the United States and elsewhere.

[28] Emphasis mine. Written Submission from Petitioner-Respondent Ven. Dr. Paragoda Wimalawansa Thero *in SC 84/2007 (SC/Sp.LA/ 240/2007, CA Writ. App. 1978/2004).* Submitted January 23, 2008, p. 2.

[29] Letter Submitted as Evidence (P4) from Ven. Dr. Paragoda Wimalawansa Thero to Commissioner for Motor Vehicles, dated December 1, 2004.

culture and custom as worldly (*laukika*) in nature and therefore disconnected from, rather than binding on, the *lōkōttara* vocation of monks.[30] Monks, Ven. Wimalawansa urges, must remain above culture and custom in order to help guide society toward what is good and virtuous (*yahapat*). Ven. Wimalawansa reports that true monks eschew custom and culture for broader concerns with good and bad (*honda naraka*), virtue and vice (*yahapata ayahapata*), and what is to be done and not to be done (*kaḷa yutta nokaḷa yutta*). Ven. Wimalawansa expressed an understanding of Buddhism in which monks helped to transform society and culture; in this project, minor monastic rules and customs could be subordinated to the heroic pursuit of larger, otherworldly (*lōkōttara*) goals.

In Ven. Wimalawansa's vision of Buddhism, clinging to static conventions not only undermined the project of virtuous leadership, it transgressed the basic principles of the Buddha's teaching itself, the *dhamma*. In his original letter to the Commissioner of Motor Vehicles written in 2004, he asserts,

> In the present era, a monk driving a vehicle is not contrary to the dhamma (*dharma virōḍha*). Nor is it against the code of monastic discipline (*Vinaya*). In fact, [not permitting it] would contravene dhamma and Vinaya. The teaching of the Buddha is based on the principles of the *trilakṣana* [the three characteristics of existence]. Buddhism teaches primarily that everything is impermanent and changing and that nothing in this world (*melova*) is permanent (*nitya*). [It teaches] that with every moment all things are changing. [It teaches] that the essence (*svabhāva*) of all things is becoming, existing and perishing ... A monk will not lose [his] monkliness (*bhikṣutvaya*) for driving a vehicle. No evil (*pāpā*) would accrue. There [would be] no violation of the Vinaya rules.[31]

In his letter, Ven. Wimalawansa points out that the Buddha himself emphasized the inevitability of change. Like all things in the world, the monk reasoned, monastic discipline (Vinaya) was also subject to change. Drawing upon Vinaya texts, Ven. Wimalawansa argued that the Buddha had asked monks to reject only four particular types of activities: the major *pārājīka* offences of the Vinaya, which normally lead to a monk's

---

[30] On the significance of the terms *laukika* and *lōkōttara* see John Holt, *Buddha in the Crown: Avalokitesvara in the Buddhist Traditions of Sri Lanka* (New York: Oxford University Press, 1991), 3–26.

[31] Letter Submitted as Evidence (P4) from Ven. Dr. Paragoda Wimalawansa Thero to Commissioner for Motor Vehicles, dated December 1, 2004.

200   BATTLES WITHIN BUDDHISM

expulsion from the order. These serious offenses are sexual impropriety, killing a person, stealing, and improperly claiming spiritual attainments. Other guidelines for monastic conduct, the letter implied, could be changed and reevaluated with changing times.

Ven. Wimalawansa's written submissions presented Buddhism as a pragmatic tradition, a realistic worldview (*yathārtha darśanaya*) that recognized the need to be flexible in light of changing realities. This pragmatic understanding of Buddhism appeared prominently in another letter that Ven. Wimalawansa wrote to the Commissioner of Buddhist Affairs, which he submitted as evidence. Here Ven. Wimalawansa argued that changing technological conditions necessitated changing approaches to thinking about Buddhist orthopraxy. For monks to survive in the contemporary age, they had to adopt modern ways of life. In the past, Ven. Wimalawansa insisted, monks were supported completely by the laity. Today this support had diminished, requiring monks to earn income, perform maintenance around the temple and, in some cases, even cook their own food.[32] Ven. Wimalawansa argued that it was these modern-day burdens that required his being able to drive. Monks like him were no longer simply full-time specialists in *dhamma*, ritual and self-cultivation; to sustain themselves, they had to work as teachers, administrators, even cooks. They reluctantly took on *laukika* commitments and those commitments were necessary to sustaining their *lōkōttara* pursuits. According to Ven. Wimalawansa, for ordinary monks living in ordinary Buddhist temples – temples without the wealth and resources of the island's *mahānāyaka*-s – driving a car was not a luxury but a practicality.

Ven. Wimalawansa's petition gained backing from a variety of monks and Buddhist lay persons from around the island. He submitted letters from these supporters to the court as evidence. In one letter, the head monk of one Buddhist "protection" association argued that monks' driving constituted a logical next step in a series of historical progressions through which monks adjusted their lives to modern technology. When motor cars were first imported, he recalled, people at the time debated whether or not monks should be allowed to ride inside of them; today monks frequently do so. He also pointed out that similar debates had taken place decades ago over the question

---

[32] The idea of monks cooking their own food is a particularly provocative one insofar as the defining act of Buddhist monastic life is begging for food. The Pali term for a monk, *bhikkhu*, literally means one who "desires a share," meaning one who begs.

of whether televisions should be permitted at Buddhist monasteries. In both cases, new technologies changed monastic life and had become regular features of modern temple life. Those features helped modern-day monks manage their busier modern-day schedules.[33] Along with other supporting letters from monks, the head monk's letter implored the court to look outside the customs of Sri Lanka: monks in other modern countries – Malaysia, Singapore and the United States – regularly operated automobiles.

Many of Ven. Wimalawansa's supporters defended monks' driving on economic grounds. One letter from Ven. E. Sumanasiri Thero, the senior monk and principal of a monastic training center (*pirivena*) near Kurunegala, argued that, by denying monks the ability to drive cars, the Sri Lankan state was, in fact, placing a greater financial burden on local Buddhist communities. Lay Buddhists were forced to pay costly car-hire fees in order to transport monks to their residences for rituals.[34] Ven. Sumanasiri argued that, even when the temples owned cars as part of their monastic property, the cost of employing a driver was often prohibitively expensive, meaning that some of those vehicles were not used.[35] The supporting letters and legal submissions indicate that these economic reasons weighed heavily on the minds of those who supported Wimalawansa. Interviews with the Buddhist monks who joined Wimalawansa's case as co-petitioners confirmed this further: in their eyes, driving licenses might be unnecessary for monks living in wealthy monasteries, but they were essential for monks at less prosperous temples.[36]

Buddhism #2: Opponents' Traditionalist Buddhism

Ven. Wimalawansa's submissions evoked a vision of Buddhism as an adaptive religion, which, while oriented around certain core principles, accommodated and responded to the changing conditions of modern society. Ven. Wimalawansa's opponents, however, cast Buddhism in

---

[33] Letter Submitted as Evidence (P22) from the Mahiyangana Śāsanārakṣaka Bala Maṇḍalaya (Mahiyangana Board of Authority for the Protection of Buddhism) to Ven. Wimalawansa Thero, July 27, 2005.

[34] Letter Submitted as Evidence (P25) from Ven. E, Sumanasiri Thero, November 23, 2004.

[35] Letter Submitted as Evidence (P20) from Ven. Mahakumbukgollawe Rathanapala Thera, October 14, 2004.

[36] Interview with Ven. Diyagama Somaratana Thero, December 14, 2014, Hokkandara; Ven. Bodagama Seelawimala Thero, Malabe, December 14, 2014.

other terms. Their submissions portrayed Buddhism as a more structured tradition, which was defined by an opposition between worldliness and otherworldliness (*laukika* and *lōkōttara*) and a strong contrast between lay and monastic life. These ideas appeared clearly in the legal briefs filed by the multiple parties who served as respondents to Ven. Wimalawansa's petition. These parties included the Commissioner of Motor Traffic and the Commissioner of Buddhist Affairs (represented by the Deputy Solicitor General) as well as two important groups of senior monks and the council of lay trustees, or Dāyaka Sabhāva,[37] of one of Ven. Wimalawansa's own temples.[38]

For those who opposed Ven. Wimalawansa, driving monks posed a serious threat to the purity and continuity of Buddhism in Sri Lanka. In a letter submitted from the Dāyaka Sabhāva to the Minister of Buddhist Affairs submitted as evidence, the lay trustees of Ven. Wimalawansa's temple implore:

> Honorable Minister, the only place in the entire world where Buddhism exists in its uncorrupted (*nirmala*) form is here on this tiny island; [therefore] care has to be taken by Buddhists [here] to keep this uncorrupted form of Buddhism for a very long time. It is mainly because of their restrained and calm demeanor (*saṅsun iriyav*) and their attractive behavior (*ākarṣanīya aevatum paevatum*) that Buddhist monks gain the faith (*bhaktiya*), loving respect (*gauravādaraya*), faith and admiration (*pahan sita*[39]) of the Buddhist people. If this ultimate bond (*uttarītara baendīma*) between the mahasangha (great community of monks) and lay people is strained, then without a doubt the supreme status of Buddhism would topple in no time. If the mahasangha begin to drive vehicles, then there is a risk of the lay people loosing the confidence (*pahan bava*) they had for them.[40]

The letter presents the state's constitutional duties to protect Buddhism as duties to maintain a pure tradition – a tradition that was "uncorrupted" (*nirmala*) in Sri Lanka alone. In purposeful contrast to Ven. Wimalawansa, the trustees asserted that the key to Buddhism's survival

---

[37] Petition of D P De Silva, F T de Silva, A W de Silva, and W P de Silva in CA Writ 1978/ 2004, July 19, 2005.

[38] Although, as stated previously, Ven. Wimalawansa denied that they were indeed trustees.

[39] This phrase comes from the Pali word *pasāda*, an important term with definitions ranging from happiness, to faith, to confidence, to emotional attachment, to joy. Thank you to Asanga Tilakaratne for pointing this out to me.

[40] Letter Submitted as Evidence (R6) from D P De Silva, F T de Silva, A W de Silva, and W P de Silva to Minister of Buddhist Affairs, October 18, 2004.

BUDDHISM #2: OPPONENTS' TRADITIONALIST BUDDHISM   203

on the island was not its adaptability but the continuity of enduring bonds between monks and laity. These bonds were, in turn, based on fragile relationships of exchange: monks earned the respect and admiration of laypeople by virtue of their ability to exude calmness, equanimity and disciplined detachment from the world;[41] the laity gained merit and wisdom by supporting monks. In this vision of Buddhism, otherworldly (*lōkōttara*) and worldly (*laukika*) concerns existed in a relationship of tension. Worldliness threatened the *sangha*, and this in turn imperiled the reciprocity between the sangha and the laity, which was the basis of Buddhism. Rather than Buddhism guiding and responding to changes in society, Buddhism – particularly the pristine Buddhism of Sri Lanka – was something to be preserved in a pure form in the face of a changing society.

This understanding of Buddhism gained support from an influential group of six senior scholar-monks who had written to the Commissioner of Buddhist Affairs condemning Wimalawansa's petition (which had, by this time, gained widespread public notoriety). All of the monks were chief prelates or deputy-chief prelates, *mahānāyaka*-s and *anunāyaka*-s, of particular monastic fraternities. They were also board members of one of the most important and prestigious Buddhist projects on the island: the publishing and critical editing of the Pali Tipiṭaka, the "three baskets" of wisdom that form the core of Theravada Buddhism's textual tradition. The board members wrote both as senior monastic figures and as recognized authorities on monastic comportment, or Vinaya (which formed one of the three baskets of wisdom). In their letter,[42] the board members acknowledged Ven. Wimalawansa's argument that there was no specific rule against driving motorcars. However, they countered, the absence of this particular prohibition did not mean that monastic life should take up all of the conveniences of modern technology. Rather, they argued, one ought to consider the matter of driving licenses in light of another broad principle that ran centrally through the entire Vinaya corpus: the concern with eliminating any negative public image of monks in society. Thus, they argued:

---

[41] One of the senior monks (*mahānāyaka-s*) who opposed Ven. Wimalawansa explained to me in an interview that monks behavior ought to be *hikmīma*, meaning disciplined, tamed, restrained. Interview December 20, 2014, Colombo.

[42] Letter Submitted as Evidence (R12) from Tipiṭaka Compilation Board to Commissioner of Buddhist Affairs, November 16, 2006.

204   BATTLES WITHIN BUDDHISM

> [*Vinaya* rules] were assigned as a result of popular displeasure over the unsuitable conduct (*nogaelaepena kriyā*) of monks in society. Public displeasure created by these actions can be seen in many of the background stories in the Vinaya precepts. For example, in [phrases such as the Pali] "*Manussa ujjhayanti*" [the people were angry], "*Kheeyanti*" [they were frustrated], "*Vipachenti*" [they were irritated]. These days, as well, a Buddhist who is devoted to the Sasana wouldn't approve Buddhist monks' driving. In elaborating the precepts for monks, Lord Buddha took into consideration several societal criteria (*samāja nirṇāyaka*). Among these, there are ten reasons highlighted within the Vinaya Pitaka. Included among these are the following two: pleasing[43] (*paehaedīma*) those [laity] who are not pleased and [pleasing] further those who are already pleased ("[Pali] *appasannānaṃ vā pasādāya, pasannānaṃ vā bhīyobhāvāya*").[44]

The Tipiṭaka Board argued that, not only was it important to conserve long-standing conventions of monastic conduct, it was essential that monks act in ways that please and impress the laity. If the Dāyaka Sabhāva warned that driving monks threatened the fragile reciprocity between laity and sangha, the Tipiṭaka Board made an even stronger claim: keeping and maintaining the respect of the laity was a fundamental goal of the Vinaya Pitaka itself. Therefore, driving monks transgressed not only individual rules, but the entire spirit and purpose of monastic law. Allowing monks to drive would not just damage the status of monks in society, it would tear the fabric of Buddhist life entirely and, in so doing, create the conditions for "various forces" (*vividha balavēga*) to rise up against Buddhist society.[45]

---

[43] The term can also mean to gladden, render happy, to induce trust and affection in someone or something.

[44] Letter Submitted as Evidence (R12) from Tipiṭaka Compilation Board to Commissioner of Buddhist Affairs, November 2006. This paragraph translates a Sinhalese original that contains Pali words. All bracketed translations and annotations are added by me to gloss and clarify the Pali and to refer to the original Sinhala terms.

[45] The logical links between monks' reputation and their driving are somewhat obscure in the petition itself. However, in an interview from December 2014, one member of the Tipiṭaka Board explained the link in terms of the requirements for bodily comportment for monks. In his explanation, a defining feature of monastic life is its emphasis on decorum and its forbidding of behaviors such as running, dancing, gobbling food, touching women, etc. He saw driving in this light: "Let it be anywhere in the world, monks driving is unacceptable and wrong. Monks should have discipline (*hikmīma*). When a monk gets a license and starts to drive, his disciplines would all be gone. If any damage happened to the tire for instance, the monk has to fix that which in turn is a mark of no discipline ... Acceleration, breaking, changing a tire are occasions where monks [are] losing their disciplines. In Sri Lanka monks are highly respected and once you sit on a driving seat that is very inappropriate." Interview December 20, 2014.

Citizen or Bhikkhu?

Ven. Wimalawansa's case was not just a matter of Buddhist law. Had this been the case, it might have been addressed by one of the island's monastic tribunals (*adhikaraṇa sabhā*) or executive committees (*karaka sabhā*) that normally hear plaints and make rulings about monastic behavior for individual fraternities. These intra-fraternity rulings are not normally enforceable by the government unless they involve the control of temple property,[46] in which case the initial monastic decision may be appealed or reheard by civil courts. Civil courts then adjudicate those cases in accordance with a specially designed statute (called the Buddhist Temporalities Act) and a special strand of Sri Lankan case law called Buddhist Ecclesiastical Law.[47]

Ven. Wimalawansa's case was different. It involved not only questions concerning the interpretation of Buddhism, but questions concerning the links between Buddhist law and constitutional law. If Buddhist authority resided with monks – a point on which both sides appeared to agree – what role did state agents (in this case, non-monks) have in enforcing Buddhist norms? Buddhist monastic life employs elaborate rituals, habits of dress and codes of conduct to distinguish monks from laity. Sri Lankan statue law even makes it a legal offense to "pass oneself off as a monk." How did the monk-lay distinction fit with a constitutional framework that *also* espoused equality under the law?

The question of whether monks are considered citizens for the purposes of state law has occupied Buddhists throughout the world. The question arises in reference to a variety of issues. In Theravada-majority countries,[48] all of which give special constitutional status to Buddhism, special laws often apply to the education, finances and registration of Buddhist monks. In Sri Lanka, for example, monks who are found guilty of serious criminal offenses must disrobe before going to prison. That is, they must become normal citizens again before undergoing penal sanctions. From the 1940s to the early 1970s, throughout most of the Buddhist world (although not in Sri Lanka), Buddhist monks (and in some cases nuns) were banned from

---

[46] Benjamin Schonthal, "The Legal Regulation of Buddhism in Contemporary Sri Lanka," in *Buddhism and Law: An Introduction*, ed. Rebecca R French and Mark A Nathan (New York: Cambridge University Press, 2014).

[47] For a very helpful collection of these cases see W S Weerasooria, *Buddhist Ecclesiastical Law* (Colombo: Postgraduate Institute of Management, 2011).

[48] This list includes Myanmar, Thailand, Laos, Cambodia and Sri Lanka.

206   BATTLES WITHIN BUDDHISM

voting.[49] Two countries – Thailand and Myanmar – still enforce this rule today. In designing these laws, political elites posited a necessary opposition between the legal status of monks and that of normal citizens. As U Nu, the former prime minister of Burma, succinctly put it, "a [monk] is not like a man"; his concerns ought not to be with exercising his rights as a citizen but with "self-purification ... discipline and penance," activities which do not sit easily alongside the world of political engagement.[50]

Was Ven. Wimalawansa a monk or a citizen? Ven. Wimalawansa's case generated opposing answers to that question. In his submissions, Ven. Wimalawansa made clear that his status as a monk was distinct from, but did not nullify, his status as a citizen. He argued that monks were both clerics *and* citizens; therefore, they ought not to be burdened more than other citizens, nor deprived of rights enjoyed by other citizens:

> I state that I applied to the Commissioner of Motor Traffic in the capacity of a Sri Lankan citizen for a driving license and not as a Buddhist Monk. I state that if the Petitioners were concerned about Damma [*sic*] and Vinaya being violated by me by obtaining a license then they should take steps regarding me continuing to be a monk urging the same before appropriate [monastic] authorities. ... I respectfully state that just because I am monk [*sic*] I cannot be prevented from enjoying my rights guaranteed to me by the legislature of this country ... by way of the Motor Traffic Act. I further state that the Petitioners or any other authority has no right whatsoever to deprive me of my rights that has been granted to me by the legislature of this country .... I state there is no law in Sri Lanka to cancel a driving license obtained by a Buddhist Monk [either] before becoming a monk [or] consequent [*sic*] to him becoming a monk. Therefore I reiterate that I have been deprived of my rights.[51]

In Ven. Wimalawansa's view, monks interacted with state services and state laws such as the CMT not as representatives of Buddhism but as citizens like anyone else. In Ven. Wimalawansa's estimation, to be treated only as a representative of the island's protected, "foremost" religion was to be held to an unfair (and extra) standard of scrutiny.

---

[49] These policies remain in place in Myanmar and Thailand today, with reversals having occurred following periods of Communist rule in Laos and Cambodia. Tomas Larsson, "Monkish Politics in Southeast Asia: Religious Disenfranchisement in Comparative and Theoretical Perspective," *Modern Asian Studies* 49, no. 1 (2015): 1–43.

[50] U Nu, *Burma Under the Japanese, Pictures and Portraits,* (New York: St. Martin's Press, 1954), 91–92. This quote was suggested to me by Larsson, above.

[51] Submission filed (in English) by Ven. Dr. Paragoda Wimalawansa Thero in CA 1978/ 2004, February 27, 2006, Par. 10.

CITIZEN OR BHIKKHU? 207

This argument about the legal status and identity of Buddhist monks appeared clearly in the submissions made by Ven. Wimalawansa's monastic and lay supporters. A letter from Ven. Dankande Bodhiwansa Thero, director of a social work organization and chief incumbent of a temple near Colombo accused the CMT of violating Ven. Wimalawansa's "human rights"[52] and pointed out that there is no separate category of persons in law for Buddhist monks. The letter also called attention to the fact that since 2004 Sri Lankan monks had served as members of parliament. A letter from another senior monk argued that "a monk too is a citizen of this country and he is subjected to all the laws of this land," including those requiring him to pay taxes on income.[53] A supporting letter from a police sergeant from Kandy further made the point: as a law enforcement officer, he assured the court that no special legal limitations applied to monks or other religious leaders when it came to the operation of motor vehicles.[54]

According to the submissions of Ven. Wimalawansa and his support-ers, monastic norms and state law were distinct; monks, by virtue of their simultaneous status as clerics and citizens, were subjects of both.[55] Yet, these submissions suggested, the structures of law were separate, not overlapping. State officials – who were lay people – had no authority to defend or enforce monastic law. They also had no right to deny monks' rights as citizens and subjects within state law. When monks approached state authorities (such as the CMT), they did so as unmarked citizens, not as subjects of a special type. Those agents were, therefore, required to treat them as they would any other citizen and not apply extra burdens to them.[56] Ven. Wimalawansa and his supporters argued that monastic law

---

[52] Letter Submitted as Evidence (P23) from Ven. Dankande Bodhiwansa Thero to Ven. Wimalawansa Thero, July 1, 2005.

[53] Letter Submitted as Evidence (P25) from Ven. E Sumanasiri Thero to Ven. Wimalawansa Thero, November 23, 2004.

[54] Letter Submitted as Evidence (P26) from N W A R M U E L Weerasanghe to Ven. Wimalawansa Thero, October 29, 2004.

[55] As one of Ven. Wimalawansa's co-petitioners put it in an interview: lay people only register once with the government (as citizens), but monks register twice – once at birth (as citizens) and once when they are ordained (as monks). Interview with Ven. Diyagama Somarathana Thero, December 14, 2014, Hokkandara.

[56] "It is respectfully submitted that the Petitioner maintains that it is not the task of the courts to decide the matters pertaining to Vinaya as it is outside the domain of Court. The Motor Traffic Act should not be interpreted in light of Vinaya Pitakaya, which would be a very dangerous approach." Written Submission of Ven. Paragoda Wimalawansa Thero, *CA 1978/2004*, dated February 24, 2014, p. 25.

208 BATTLES WITHIN BUDDHISM

and Buddhist norms were therefore doubly out-of-bounds to state agents: not only were the powers of state officials limited to upholding state laws, state officials (as laypersons) had no authority to pronounce on the activities of Buddhist monks or the principles of Buddhist doctrine. In this way, Ven. Wimalawansa's position touched on a variety of hallowed principles for jurists and monks: for jurists, it spoke of non-discrimination, equal enforcement of law, and the rights of citizens; for monks it spoke of clerical autonomy and the idea that Buddhist law ought to be the province of monks rather than bureaucrats.

Ven. Wimalawansa's opponents concurred that state laws and Vinaya laws ought to remain separate. Yet they refused the idea that one could choose which one applied. Monks, they insisted, were always *primarily* subjects of Vinaya because Vinaya and state laws were not parallel systems of law but overlapping ones. When it came to the conduct of monks, Vinaya laws were the primary structures of regulation; fundamental rights guarantees did not nullify Vinaya obligations. A letter from the four head monks (*mahānāyaka*-s) of the island's four largest monastic fraternities explained this position through analogy to the work of judges and lawyers: just as judges and lawyers were bound by particular stringent professional codes of conduct that did not apply to ordinary citizens, so too were monks subject to Vinaya rules.[57] The senior monks of the Tipiṭaka Compilation Board took a similar approach, arguing that the matter of monks driving cars fell firmly within the jurisdiction of monastic law, not national or international human rights. "The *laukika* path [of human rights law] is one thing," they wrote, "the *lōkōttara* path [of Buddhist monks] is another."[58] There was no conflict of laws. Vinaya rules, alone, applied to matters of monastic comportment.

Where state law did come into play, in the senior monks' estimation, was in the obligation under the Buddhism Chapter of the constitution to protect Buddhism. The four senior monks contended that the state had a clear constitutional obligation to countervail what were obviously the "anti-Buddhist activities (*śāsana virōdha kriyā*)" of Ven. Wimalawansa.

---

[57] Letter Submitted as Evidence (R11) Letter to Commissioner of Buddhist Affairs from the following four *mahānāyaka-s: Thibbaṭuvavē Śrī Siddhartha Sumaṅgalābhidhāna Mahānāyaka Sthavira of the Malvatu Mahā Vihāraya; Udugama Ratanapāla Buddharakkhitābhidhāna Mahānāyaka Sthavira of the Asgiri Mahā Vihāraya; Davuldena Ñāṇissarabhidhāna Uttarītara Mahānāyaka Sthavira of the Amarapura Mahā Nikāya; Vevaeldeṇiyē Medhalaṅkārābhidhāna Mahānāyaka Sthavira of the Rāmañña Mahā Nikāya.*

[58] Letter Submitted as Evidence (R12) from the Tipiṭaka Compilation Board to the Commissioner of Buddhist Affairs, November 16, 2006.

The Tipiṭaka Board argued that, if the CMT ignored Buddhist monastic law and treated Ven. Wimalawansa as it did all citizens, he would be undermining his constitutional obligation, as an officer of the state, to protect Buddhism because he would be "making un-Buddhist and un-monastic conduct into [something] approved by law itself" (*asāsanika aśrāmaṇika kriyāva sammata karīma nītiyen ma*)![59]

The Court's Decision

The final judgment in Wimalawansa's case came in March 2014. The verdict was handed down by a unanimous two-judge bench of the Court of Appeals. In the judgment, written by Justice Anil Gooneratne, the court rejected Ven. Wimalawansa's application in strong and resolute terms. The logic of the judgment reflected the arguments of Ven. Wimalawansa's opponents: the court agreed that the state had a constitutional obligation to protect the uncorrupted (*nirmala*) Buddhism of Sri Lanka, and it affirmed the *dicta* of the *mahānāyaka*-s (senior monks) and the Tipiṭaka Board. It also upheld the idea that the state ought to enforce Vinaya prohibitions. As it related to the question of monks' identities as citizens versus as representatives of Buddhism, the court clearly indicated that a monk's civil and legal status was different to that of a layman.

The court's decision aligned with the asymmetries of power that formed the backdrop of the case. Although a variety of monastic and lay supporters backed Wimalawansa's petition, the idea of driving monks was opposed by government officials (represented by the Attorney General) and by some of the island's most influential monastic leaders. Moreover, Ven. Wimalawansa was a single monk of limited means (his attorney took the case *pro bono*) challenging a long-standing *status quo*. In its opinion, the court validated the arguments of Ven. Wimalawansa's opponents in decisive language, even insisting, in one particularly strong flourish, that "a Buddhist Monk [capitalized in the original] cannot do and should be prohibited from doing any and every act, done by a layman, in his daily routine life."[60] The opinion portrayed monastic life

---

[59] Ibid. This was, of course, the starting point of the conflict to begin with: the officer at the CMT deferred the decision about Ven. Wimalawansa's license application to the CBA because of concerns over his constitutional obligations, stated in the Buddhism Chapter, to protect Buddhism; this posture recognizes both the distinctiveness of Buddhist and state law and the need for the second to buttress the first (see later).

[60] *Venerable Paragoda Wimalawansa Thero and Others v. Commissioner of Motor Traffic* (2014) unreported judgment with author, 27. This inconsistency was glossed further by

210 BATTLES WITHIN BUDDHISM

as not just different from lay life but "inconsistent to [sic] that of a lay person."[61] For the court, perhaps even more than for the Tipiṭaka Board or the *mahānāyaka*-s involved in the case, "the life of a Buddhist Monk in its pure form, is incompatible with lay life."[62] If Ven. Wimalawansa was not prepared to live in that way, the court insisted, "it is better [for him] to give up robes."[63]

The court's judgment provided a temporal endpoint to legal dispute; but it also generated new lines of tension. One reason for this is that, in deciding the matter, the court exercised its own authority to speak for Buddhism. In legitimating his judgment, Justice Gooneratne (writing for the court) referred partially to the letters written by the senior monks against Ven. Wimalawansa's petition, but he also relied heavily on two other types of sources: scholarship and case law from former Sri Lankan Supreme Court justices and his own interpretations of Buddhist texts. Gooneratne's opinion discussed Buddhist philosophy and offered exegeses of the doctrine of the "middle way."[64] Drawing upon a book by a former Sri Lankan justice, C G Weeramantry, called *Tread Lightly on the Earth,* Justice Gooneratne wrote about the importance of morality, wisdom and mental cultivation. Analyzing nearly 20 lines from the Digha Nikāya as well as three long sets of verses from the Dhammapada, the judgment considered the meaning of the Buddha's eightfold path.[65] The result was that, in the end, the court's decision (its form, content and authorial voice) seemed to contradict certain core convictions of all the parties involved in the matter: it placed a lay person in the position of explaining Buddhist doctrine to monks; it positioned a *laukika* institution as an authority on the requirements of a *lōkōttara* life.

---

quoting the dissenting opinion in the *Sumana* case referred to earlier: "The life of a Monk, as laid down by the Buddha, is thus at complete variance with that of lay life. The spirit and flavour of the Dhamma is one of renunciation of giving up worldly affairs, and strenuous exertion for the development of virtue and mental developments. And it is in the secluded and monastic life as a monk that the Dhamma can be practiced to the full . . . The institution of the Sangha was established by the Buddha as have [sic] for those who wish to get away from lay life and who need the optimum conditions for pursuing the arduous life of virtue, meditation and wisdom demanded by the Teaching. A person who enters the Order should be mindful of this change of status and recall this difference as often as possible." Ibid., 19, 20: per Wanasundera J vide Rev. Sumana Thero's case 2005 (3) SLR at 390.

[61] Ibid., 27.   [62] Ibid., 27.   [63] Ibid., 27–28.   [64] Ibid., 21.   [65] Ibid., 22.

THE COURT'S DECISION   211

The fault was not Gooneratne's. Almost all of the legal experts with whom I spoke described Justice Gooneratne as a respected and serious judge and a pious Buddhist.[66] While his judgment indulges in certain flourishes of Buddhist scholarship, it also reflects the predicament in which the court found itself: constitutional litigation placed Gooneratne, writing for the court, in the position of acting as a Buddhist expert. Buddhism Chapter litigation forced the court to arbitrate a dispute between two groups of monks with distinct interpretations of the tradition. This fact was not lost on those who won the case. Even the most outspoken critics of Ven. Wimalawansa, the lay trustees associated with one of his temples, felt considerable discomfort with the outcome. The following is an excerpt from a group interview I conducted nine months after the verdict:

> Q: Do you see any problem with the court [in its decision] telling a monk [Ven. Wimalawansa] what to do?
>
> A: We are terribly hurt by this. We don't like any member of the laity, the court or even the king telling monks what to do. In this regard monks should behave in such a way that avoids such circumstances. It is a mark of disgrace for monks. Within the social hierarchy monks occupy the highest position, even above the king. There is even a story of a Samanera (novice monk) who sat on the king's throne ... [Monks] are not given this type of respect at the courts; they are treated as lay people.
>
> Q: You went to court to protect Buddhism. But going to court is also a threat to Buddhism because it allows the judge to act as an authority over Buddhism?
>
> A: Yes, we agree with you. That's what we said. But we had to go to court because of this monk's misconduct. Monks should behave in such a way that prevents them from going to court. [However] Ven. Wimalawansa should have at least sat in the front row. He did not even do that. We were the ones who sat in the front row of the court and he sat behind us. We didn't like this . ... At the same time we needed to protect the Sasana as well.[67]

---

[66] Ven. Wimalawansa was not as confident. He voiced distinct concerns about the politicization of the courts under the Rajapaksa regime and felt that the court had already made up its mind before hearing the evidence. As evidence, he pointed to the unusually short timeframe from the final hearings to the eventual judgment. Letter from Wimalawansa to Author, August 14, 2015.

[67] Group interview with Dāyaka Sabhāva, Waskuduwa, December 14, 2014. Mr. D P de Silva speaking.

The interview excerpt reveals something about the felt experience of pyrrhic constitutionalism. It shows the exasperation felt by participants on account of deep incongruities among the goals and effects of litigation. Successful litigation unwittingly produced undesirable outcomes. Pursuing constitutional protections for Buddhism generated disconcerting dilemmas of authority and orthodoxy for the Buddhists involved in the case. By using law to protect certain features of Buddhism, participants ended up violating other features of Buddhism. In this sense, it did not matter who won the case: both sides would have faced inevitably the same double-bind.

Conclusion: Pyrrhic Constitutionalism and the Impossibility of Protecting Buddhism

Jacques Maritain, one of the architects of the United Nations' Universal Declaration of Human Rights, reportedly quipped that the drafters of the Declaration agreed on its contents only on the condition that no one asked them about why they agreed.[68] That is, they could agree on particular principles but not on the meaning of or rationale behind those principles. The same could be said about drafters of the Buddhism Chapter: those who incorporated special protections for Buddhism into the constitution saw this as a good thing, even if they did not agree on precisely what they were protecting.

The problem is that vague consensus around multivalent principles works only as long as those principles remain multivalent. Once they are defined in courtrooms, the very same words that serve as signs of agreement become sources of interpretive competition. From one perspective this is nothing new. Law generates these conundrums all the time: people disagree about the meanings of freedom, equality, neutrality and a variety of other constitutional principles. Judges and legislatures interpret the meaning of those principles over time, to suit the times. The inevitable ambiguity of language is managed or mitigated through the interpretive discipline of *stare decisis* and, in some cases, statutory definitions.

Yet, religion, or Buddhism, is not quite the same as abstract ideas like equality or freedom. Religion and Buddhism suggest not simply aspirational social conditions, but a shifting amalgam of institutions, ideas,

---

[68] As cited in Glendon, *A World Made New*, 77.

CONCLUSION   213

persons, texts, properties, practices and customs. In short, they imply things both abstract and concrete. Unlike freedom or equality, legal, religious and popular discourses treat Buddhism (and, often, religion) as an agent: an observable thing-in-the-world that, like a citizen, can be acted upon, harmed or protected. As used by parties in the Ven. Wimalawansa case, Buddhism has a distinct solidity to it, a flavor of personhood – with all the complexities that implies.[69]

When it comes to special constitutional protections for religion, the problem is not simply one of semantic ambiguity and competing interpretations. A more general dilemma stands at the heart of special constitutional protections for Buddhism or other religions. On the one hand, these clauses claim to secure the protection or primacy of one set of (religious) institutions. On the other hand, they do so using mechanisms that perform the supremacy of another set of (state) institutions. Religiously preferential constitutions purport to create an arrangement of mutual support between presumptively separable elements. However, this support can never be perfectly achieved because, in constitutional regimes, state-legal authority constitutes itself not only as that which protects religious authority, but as that which defines it: if constitutions announce the state as protector of religion, constitutional courts require the state to define the nature of the religion to be protected. In mirror fashion, claimants to religious authority justify their status within and autonomy from these state-legal regimes by asserting a privileged access to alternative sources of religious knowledge and power – sources that, by their reckoning, exist outside of the nation-state. Therefore, in the absence of pure and uncontested theocracy – a very rare feat! – constitutional protections for religion cannot but transgress certain features of religious membership, authority or practice. In other words, in enforcing constitutional protections for religion, states can never hand off responsibility for religion to religion: in protecting and empowering (what they determine to be) legitimate representatives of religion, state agents

---

[69] The idea that Buddhism is an agent that has its own life is not entirely an artifact of law. This idea can be found within Theravada Buddhist textual traditions. The most common equivalent for Buddhism in Pali and vernacular Theravada texts is *sāsana*, a term that, as we saw in Chapter 5, refers to the entire dispensation of the Buddha. Buddhist texts describe that dispensation as having its own finite lifespan in the world. Over great spans of cosmic time, the *sāsana* of the Buddha comes into and out of existence much like a human life. Sources differ on how long the lifespan is, but five thousand years is one common figure. Alicia Turner, *Saving Buddhism: The Impermanence of Religion in Colonial Burma* (Honolulu: University of Hawai'i Press, 2014).

necessarily transgress the very claims of autonomy and authority on which those representatives depend.[70]

This conundrum both initiated and concluded the Ven. Wimalawansa case. Ven. Wimalawansa treated the idea of a government official (a lay person) pronouncing on the orthodoxy of his (a monk's) actions as an attack on Buddhist authority and autonomy. Similarly, those monks who opposed Wimalawansa may have received a favorable ruling from the Court of Appeals, but the very logic and interpretive license shown in that ruling ultimately undermined their claims of independence and authority over Buddhism. Lay trustees felt the same way, as the above interview excerpt shows. Thus, the very parties who "won" the case felt harmed by the logic and assumptions that undergirded the decision.

In this way, religiously preferential constitutions are no different than secular ones. What Hussein Agrama says of "secular power" one could say analogously for religiously preferential legal regimes.[71] Just as secular power continuously provokes and entangles states and citizens with the very questions of definition it claims to resolve (namely, questions concerning the line between religion and politics), so too do religiously preferential constitutional orders provoke and entangle states and citizens with the questions *they* claim to resolve (questions about the conditions of – and possibilities for – the state protection of Buddhism or other religions). Put differently, when looked at microhistorically one sees how the very constitutional clauses used to secure the integrity of Buddhism provide the conditions under which that integrity is constantly rendered under threat. Protecting Buddhism in constitutional law, while it may announce a particular hierarchy among religions, also generates conditions for sharp contests over the boundaries of membership, orthodoxy and authority.

Let me be clear: the particular contours of the Ven. Wimalawansa debate were not generated because of law. As stated earlier, Buddhist monks and laypersons have disputed the principles of Buddhism for centuries. Debates over Buddhism pre-exist legal action. However, the frameworks and forums of legal action are not simply a rehashing of long-standing debates. The format of litigation – in which petitioners face off against respondents in an agonistic struggle over remedies – amplifies

---

[70] Even in cases where, e.g., Shariah is recognized as "a" or "the" source of law, it is on the authority of the constitution, itself, that such an assertion rests!

[71] Hussein Ali Agrama, *Questioning Secularism: Islam, Sovereignty, and the Rule of Law in Modern Egypt* (Chicago: University of Chicago Press, 2012).

CONCLUSION

the rigidity of disputes and firms up lines of opposition. Participants in the Ven. Wimalawansa case lined up, by necessity, for Ven. Wimalawansa's vision of Buddhism or against it. Once the motors of legal action began revving, each side gripped more tightly to their vision and engaged in a point-counterpoint methodical rejection of the other's position. This process *obscured* previously existing principles of compromise or coordination, such as litigants' shared commitment to protecting the autonomy and authority of Buddhist monks to pronounce on ecclesiastical matters.

Litigants also produced a range of new and ramified arguments as the case progressed. This self-multiplying quality of legal argumentation can be seen in the fact that, by the end of the affair, Ven. Wimalawansa offered a number of rationales for why he should be granted a driving license, some of which came to conflict logically. For example, at the beginning of the case, Ven. Wimalawansa insisted that he needed to drive in order to fulfill his religious obligations to minister, teach and conduct Buddhist rituals; to refuse him a license was therefore to limit Buddhism through limiting the Buddhist work of a pious monk. Yet, as the case progressed, Ven. Wimalawansa seemed to undermine this argument in stressing a differing claim: he insisted that his application to the CMT was not made as a monk but as a generic citizen; the refusal, therefore, violated his individual fundamental rights.[72] Inconsistencies such as these are not faults of constitutional (and legal) argument, but regular features of them. To win a case, litigating lawyers routinely offer as many arguments as possible related to as many legal principles as possible, in a buckshot attempt to influence judges and juries. Through this process, legal arguments not only deepen and sharpen debates, they also project debates into ever-broadening terrains of disagreement, locking litigants in conflict on multiple fronts.

As it relates to Buddhism in particular, the context of legal action (particularly constitutional litigation) seems especially poorly suited for acknowledging the social and political dimensions of Buddhist monasticism – much more so than debates that take place in newspapers or parliament. Take for example debates about the participation of monks in politics in the 1940s referred to earlier. Those who participated in those debates were explicit about the links between monks' political affiliations and their understandings of Buddhism. However, when debates about monastic conduct enter the legal arena, these critical

---

[72] Thanks to Jolyon Thomas for pointing out this particular inconsistency.

dimensions are often deliberately ignored or obscured in the sanitizing vocabulary of law. One important reason is that courts are, by definition, supposed to be venues different from and countervailing to politics. Undisguised polemics against particular political groups make for poor legal arguments. Where there are axes to grind, the language used is artificially objective and impersonal in nature. Rather than take the sting out of polemics, though, legal vocabularies appear to legitimate and naturalize them. At the same time that legal reasoning spreads disagreements into a broad range of argumentative terrains, they also narrow them and bleach them of content and claims which, although essential to the matter, are deemed irrelevant to the points of law under dispute. Ven. Wimalawansa's feelings of frustration, his desires and personal history are transmuted into broad, general claims about what Buddhism is and how the state ought to protect it. Sifted out, as the case progressed, was a consideration of the defining conditions of Ven. Wimalawansa's situation: his location in the outskirts of Colombo and his struggles to meet the rising costs of living, his sense of alienation from elite monastic establishments, and, importantly, the very serious financial struggles faced by both him and his temple.

When it comes to protecting Buddhism in Sri Lanka, constitutional practice has achieved only a pyrrhic victory. Legally successful attempts to use the Buddhism Chapter to protect Buddhism have also produced undesirable consequences for winning and losing parties: they have contributed to the fracturing of solidarity among Buddhist groups and to the undermining of monastic authority. In the process of fostering Buddhism, constitutional agents have transformed long-standing, low-intensity, ambient differences of opinions among monks into public, high-stakes, agonistic conflicts over Buddhist orthodoxy and orthopraxy. Favoring Buddhism in law has provoked and intensified many of the problems it was meant to resolve. Rather than "mak[ing] [Sri] Lanka's Buddhist people into a strong and unified body (*eksat prabala āyatanayak*) once again" constitutional practice has confirmed the impossibility of so doing.

7

Constitutional Conversions

Of the various conflicts involving religion in Sri Lanka, some of the most incendiary have been conflicts over religious conversions, in particular conversions to Christianity. Although Christians comprise less than 8 percent of the population, the perceived threat of Christian conversions draws upon concerns about Christians' superior wealth, influence and international support – and therefore their superior abilities to attract or (as critics would have it) inveigle new congregants. These concerns are framed by colonial history. Contemporary critics of conversion in Sri Lanka characterize Christian proselytism as a neocolonial project, a coercive act through which powerful, foreign or foreign-funded organizations impose their theologies on weaker locals. This vision of proselytism has been used to justify violent attacks against churches and congregations; and this violence has become a depressingly regular feature of Sri Lankan life over the last two decades.

Anxieties over conversion are by no means unique to Sri Lanka. Religious conversion, in the words of one scholar, "ranks among the most destabilizing activities in modern society" and remains a key object of strife throughout the world.[1] Conflicts over conversion abound not only in the global South, but throughout Europe and North America. Although not always acknowledged, the act of proselytizing (or perceived proselytizing) has been important in numerous First Amendment cases in the United States[2] and in a multitude of legal commissions and religious rights cases in Canada and Europe.[3]

---

[1] Gauri Viswanathan, *Outside the Fold: Conversion, Modernity, Belief* (Princeton, NJ: Princeton University Press, 1988), xvi.

[2] E.g., *Cantwell v. Connecticut*, 310 U.S. 296 (1940), *Good News Club v. Milford Central School*, 533 U.S. 98 (2001), and school prayer cases.

[3] E.g., Bouchard and Taylor, *Building the Future*. Robert O'Brien and Bernard Stasi, *The Stasi Report: The Report of the Committee of Reflection on the Application of the Principle of Secularity in the Republic* (Buffalo, NY: William S Hein & Co, 2005). *Lautsi v. Italy*,

218   CONSTITUTIONAL CONVERSIONS

If religious conversion remains a common topic of controversy, it is also a matter for which constitutional law is frequently prescribed as a solution. People look to constitutions for two reasons. On the one hand, the superior status of constitutions *vis-à-vis* other forms of law suggests that constitutional solutions might be more consequential or authoritative and, therefore, more capable of generating definitive resolution. On the other hand, constitutions almost always contain explicit protections for religion, often in the form of religious rights; and religious rights, people frequently insist, remain a natural framework for interpreting and mediating conflicts over proselytism. Advocates of constitutional solutions hope that, through the correct interpreting and balancing of religious (and sometimes other) rights, lawyers and courts might mitigate the intensity of conflicts over conversion and, ultimately, transform the chaos of clashing bodies into an ordered regime of competing (legal) claims.

Trust in the powers of constitutions to manage or ameliorate conflicts over conversion draws upon a particular understanding of how courts work. It assumes that courts take dyadic conflicts from life (a fight between opposing parties) and resolve them through the triadic structure of litigation in which a third party (usually the judge) mediates the dyadic struggle according to existing legal norms.[4] This triadic prototype explains and justifies what occurs in many public law settings, including contexts of constitutional review and religious rights litigation. The triadic prototype is also embodied in the rigid requirements of courtroom adjudication. For admission to the judicial process, social issues, such as that of religious conversion, must be presented as a two-sided conflict between competing (groups of) litigants. This binary is then extended through the polemical interventions of other parties, including intervening petitioners, witnesses or experts. The prototype is further called into being through the mise-en-scène of litigation: in most cases, lawyers for the parties sit on opposing sides of a courtroom, and below the mediating "third" of the judges.

This triadic view of courts is both true and false. It is true in that it captures the self-presentation of the legal process in many religious-rights

---

App. No. 30814/06, 2011 Eur. Ct. H.R. (G.C.). *Larissis and Others v. Greece*, App. No. 23372/94, 26377, 94 and 26378, 94 Eur. Ct. H.R.

[4] Martin M Shapiro, *Courts: A Comparative and Political Analysis* (Chicago: University of Chicago Press, 1986), 1–7.

cases throughout the world. It is the prototype through which litigation frequently plays out in Sri Lanka.[5] However, it is false in that it misrepresents the relationships between life and law and the nature of conflicts outside and inside of courts, particularly as it relates to complex matters such as religious conversion. Outside of courtrooms, disputes over religious conversion remain multifaceted and inflected by considerations of history, politics, language, economics, and local relationships. Ideas of heaven, hell, salvation, and faith play a role, as do ideas about inequality, globalization and colonialism. Inside of courtrooms, the complexity of real-world conflicts chafes against clean analysis according to the abstract language of religious rights. Moreover, as they emerge in Sri Lankan society, conflicts over conversion do not always appear as a two-sided fight between unequivocal defenders and opponents of proselytizing. Yet, this is precisely what religious rights litigation in Sri Lanka presumes and unwittingly encourages.

To give a litigation-ready structure to conflict, diverse and overlapping interests must be expressed in terms of adversarial binaries. To make grievances legally legible and efficacious, complex social issues must be expressed in terms of formal legal norms. These requirements obscure the significant local, circumstantial and particularistic facets that characterize conflicts over conversion in their extrajudicial condition. Constitutional law in Sri Lanka has not sublimated societal disputes into legal argumentation; it has created for legal adjudication the types of disputes that law can handle: adversarial, dyadic disputes over abstract legal norms.

This chapter demonstrates the effects of pyrrhic constitutionalism on disputes over conversion in Sri Lanka. It argues that the constitutional mediation of these disputes has further polarized them and rendered them more intractable. In what follows, I demonstrate how the turn to constitutional law as a way to express, understand and manage religious conversion has transformed a complex and many-sided social issue into a stark clash between purportedly bounded religious traditions, fixed religious communities, absolute religious norms, and universal legal rights. Moreover, it has done so in such a totalizing and thorough way so as to render legal contests unresolvable by the very judges for whom the dyadic dispute was produced.

---

[5] Moustafa, "Liberal Rights Versus Islamic Law?" Scheingold, *The Politics of Rights.*

220 CONSTITUTIONAL CONVERSIONS

These polarizing effects of constitutional law do not appear only in litigation. This chapter also demonstrates how Sri Lanka's constitutional paradigms for managing religion have spread more generally into the domains of politics and public debate. Constitutional language has become an important popular lexicon for conceiving and expressing grievances about religion outside of courtrooms. Apart from its legal life in courtrooms and legislatures, constitutional law has a life in society: the language of Buddhist protections and religious rights inflects political discourse about religion, structures religious alignments in politics and determines the ways that people conceptualize, express and (attempt to) resolve conflicts over religion. These two lives of law – its legal life and its societal life – appear to exist in a mutually reinforcing circuit: on the one hand, the more people approach conversion legalistically, the more likely they are to call for legislative and judicial action to deal with conversion; on the other hand, the more legal action takes place, the greater the tendency for people to approach conversion legalistically.

As in the previous chapter, I advance these arguments using methods of constitutional microhistory, focusing on the life of one important court case, involving (in this instance) the constitutional review of legislation designed to criminalize certain forms of proselytizing. As before, I dig beneath the official legal archive of published court determinations and gazetted parliamentary bills. I attempt to move beyond the dominant narratives of constitutional law by going outside the narrow archive of published official documents.[6] In so doing, I draw upon a variety of sources from law's extended archive, including: unpublished submissions, affidavits and petitions; draft laws that were not debated; and interviews with parties inside and outside of the legal process.

The chapter unfolds in two sections. In Section I, I examine the history of anxieties over Christian conversion on the island and consider recent public debates over whether (and how) the state ought to manage them. I then discuss the drafting of two bills that aimed at criminalizing "unethical" techniques of religious conversion with reference to differing paradigms of managing religion contained in Sri Lanka's constitution. Only one of these bills gained a hearing in

---

[6] Redding, "Invisible Constitutions," 346.

parliament, and in Section II of the chapter I look at legal challenges to the bill, challenges that were heard in an important court case in 2004. Through detailed analysis of unpublished (and as-yet unexamined) documents by litigants for and against the bill, I show how opponents and supporters of conversion legislation used similar terminology and cited identical legal provisions to authorize deeply opposing visions of Buddhism's "foremost place," freedom of conscience, religious conversion, and religious diversity.

Through exploring in detail the constitutional management of conversion in modern Sri Lanka, one gains a sense for how pyrrhic constitutionalism works on the ground as well as a sense for the ways in which the process of mediating conflicts through constitutional law has, ultimately, worked to weaken the potential for concord and compromise.

SECTION I: HISTORICIZING "OFFENSIVE" CONVERSIONS

The Legal and Societal Lives of Law: A Technical Prologue

The history of constitutionalizing debates over religious conversions in contemporary Sri Lanka is a two-level story. On one level, it is a story about how popular concerns over Christian evangelism became legislative and legal concerns. On another level, it is a story about how constitutional rubrics came to structure politics and society. To view precisely the contours of this story, one has to understand certain intricacies of parliamentary procedure and Supreme Court jurisdiction in Sri Lanka.

The relative ease with which issues migrate between popular and legal discourse owes much to the design of Sri Lanka's constitutions, which, like many others, treats these migrations as a good thing. A permeable membrane between law and society is thought to make legal remedies more accessible to citizens and to make legal instruments more responsive to the concerns of society. In Sri Lanka, these migrations are abetted by two features of the legislative and legal systems – features that are not unique to Sri Lanka but are shared by many parliamentary and semi-parliamentary democracies around the world. The first such feature is the Private Member's Bill, a legislative device that allows any member of parliament to introduce a bill in his/her own name, without necessarily gaining the consent of the government or his/her political party. The second feature is citizen-initiated constitutional review of legislation. As discussed in previous chapters, Sri Lanka's constitution gives to any citizen or group (provided three-fourths of the group's members are citizens) the right to challenge the constitutionality of a bill that has been introduced to parliament.[7] While these rights may seem circumscribed when examined alongside procedures of post-enactment judicial review in other countries, they are used regularly and give citizens considerable leeway to contest proposed legislation by making a petition to the Supreme Court within one week of the bill being placed on the Order Paper of parliament.[8] In the event that the Supreme Court determines a bill to be unconstitutional, there are significant ramifications for the future of the legislation. The parliament must ratify such a bill through one of two special, intentionally difficult procedures:[9] bills deemed to violate "ordinary" articles of the constitution require a two-thirds majority vote in parliament, while bills deemed to violate important, "entrenched" sections of the constitution require a two-thirds majority vote *plus* a general referendum of the people.[10] Either procedure, but especially the second, presents a tremendously difficult hurdle for enactment, essentially making the bill's passage unfeasible in all but a very few instances.[11] Beyond the legal and legislative consequences of a successful judicial review petition, the very fact of challenging a bill in the Supreme Court produces further public engagement with lawmaking because of the significant media coverage and public visibility that

---

[7] Article 121(1). See also *Standing Orders of Parliament*, Numbers 47, 48. In Chapter 6 I referred to another feature of Sri Lanka's constitution that increases the likelihood of Supreme Court intervention in religious issues: the fact that the Supreme Court has original jurisdiction over the "protection of fundamental rights" (Art. 118), and any citizen has the right to petition the Supreme Court directly in cases in which they allege the state has violated (or, is likely to violate) their fundamental rights (Arts. 17, 126).

[8] In practice, there are instances when this right is limited by the fact that tabled parliamentary bills can sometimes be difficult to access publically.

[9] This is not to say that these are the only methods of procedural entrenchment in the constitution. Two others relate to measures pertaining to devolution in the Thirteenth Amendment: 154(G)(2)(a) and 154(G)(2)(b).

[10] Art. 83. Entrenched articles relate to: the nature of the state, its unitary character, the sovereignty of the people, the duration of Parliament (Arts. 1–3), the flag of Sri Lanka, the national anthem, the date of the National Day (Arts. 6–8), the status of Buddhism (Art. 9), freedom of "thought conscience and religion" (Art. 10), freedom from torture (Art. 11) and the terms of office for the President and Parliament (Art. 30(2), 62(2)).

[11] One these very rare instances happened in 2010 when then-President Mahinda Rajapaksa, riding a tide of popular support after the war and enjoying a rare three-quarters majority for his coalition in parliament, pushed through a constitutional amendment eliminating presidential term limits and expanding executive powers. The changes introduced by the amendment have since been rolled back via another major amendment in 2015.

THE LEGAL AND SOCIETAL LIVES OF LAW 223

accompany such cases and because these cases often become some of the island's most hard-fought and most high-profile legal struggles.[12]

One further aspect of Sri Lanka's legal system enhances the probability that, if citizens challenge a bill even remotely linked to religion, courtroom arguments will drift toward in-depth debates over the meaning and applicability of Sri Lanka's two constitutional duties with respect to religion, the duties to promote Buddhism (Article 9) and to protect the fundamental rights of every individual to "freedom of thought, conscience and religion, including the freedom to have or adopt a religion or belief of his choice" (Article 10). This aspect is that both Article 9 and Article 10 of the constitution are "entrenched" constitutional sections, constituting two (of the thirteen) parts of the constitution deemed important enough to require special amendment procedures. Also important is the fact that neither Article 9 nor Article 10 may be limited in order to protect other interests – such as national security or public order – as can other rights listed in the constitution.[13] Thus, litigants who oppose or support proposed legislation, including Private Member's Bills, often focus their arguments on the ways in which the bills do or do not conform with Buddhist prerogatives and/or freedom of thought, conscience and religion – strategies that routinely push these dimensions of managing religion into the foreground of legal debate.

The devices and procedures described here are not peculiar to Sri Lanka, nor are they problematic as elements of constitutional law. Modeled on laws in other Commonwealth countries, they were included in Sri Lanka's constitution to permit greater popular influence in the processes of making and reviewing the island's laws, as well as to make sure that important constitutional principles were not compromised or violated. The technique of the Private Member's Bills permitted politicians to debate issues of public concern (or issues important to only one small

---

[12] Some of the most important court cases in contemporary Sri Lanka have been of this type. One of the largest cases was the Thirteenth Amendment to the Constitution case described in Chapter 6. *Regarding the Thirteenth Amendment to the Constitution and Provincial Councils Bill* (1987) 2 SLR 333.

[13] These limits apply to all fundamental rights with the exception of Article 10. See Article 15(7) of Sri Lanka's Constitution: "The exercise and operation of all the fundamental rights declared and recognized by Articles 12, 13(1), 13(2) and 14 shall be subject to such restrictions as may be prescribed by law in the interests of national security, public order and the protection of public health or morality, or for the purpose of securing due recognition and respect for the rights and freedoms of others, or of meeting the just requirements of the general welfare of a democratic society."

224 CONSTITUTIONAL CONVERSIONS

group) within the country's highest legislative body, even if those issues were not part of the ruling coalition's political agenda. Procedures of judicial review were included so that all of Sri Lanka's citizens could challenge prospective legislation that might adversely affect their constitutional rights. Pre-enactment, rather than post-enactment, review was chosen to hasten the process and render it more efficient – to encourage close scrutiny of legislation before it affected society in ways that were difficult to undo. By entrenching Articles 9 and 10, Sri Lankans ensured that cornerstone principles pertaining to the constitutional management of religion would be protected. These elements of constitutional law have made the island's supreme law more responsive to and reflective of the demands of its citizens.

The Problem with Conversion: Old and New

Anxieties over religious conversion in Sri Lanka have very deep roots, which tap into the island's long history of colonial occupation. Winning souls for the Roman Catholic Church motivated Portuguese officials and soldiers, who, from 1505 to 1656, actively converted local inhabitants while also destroying Buddhist and Hindu temples and confiscating temple lands. Dutch colonizers (1656–1796) also hoped to introduce Christianity to the island. While Dutch proselytizing campaigns were less aggressive than their Catholic predecessors, they nevertheless made use of powerful social and economic inducements, such as the requirement that only converts to Dutch Reformed Christianity could gain lucrative employment in the colonial government or attend prestigious Christian schools.[14] British governors (1796–1948), as described in Chapter 2, tried to avoid direct complicity in Christian conversions. Yet, colonial officers in London and Ceylon steered British policy in a direction friendly to Christian sects, especially Protestant ones, and created a legal and administrative environment conducive to the spread of churches, ministries and Christian schools.[15]

Alarm at colonial support for Christianity fueled religious and political activism in the late colonial and early postcolonial periods. In the late-nineteenth century, Buddhist and Hindu leaders attempted to revitalize local religious traditions as a way to resist missionaries' enticements of heaven, employment and better education. Figures such as the Buddhist

---

[14] Berkwitz, "Religious Conflict and the Politics of Conversion in Sri Lanka," 202.
[15] De Silva, *Social Policy and Missionary Organizations in Ceylon: 1840–1855.*

THE PROBLEM WITH CONVERSION: OLD AND NEW 225

lay preacher Anagarika Dharmapala and the Saiva scholar Arumuka Navalar offered their own programs of moral, ethical and ritual reform designed to compete with those of Christian groups.[16] Later, in the otherwise politically divisive years surrounding independence, opposition to Christian conversions formed an important topic about which Sinhalese Buddhist and Tamil Hindu political leaders could agree. According to one scholar, Hindu leaders in 1948 worried more about spiritual conquest by priests than political domination by Sinhalese voters, paraphrasing the sentiments of the largest Hindu organization as follows: "Our enemies are the Christians, not our temporary abduction by the Sinhalese."[17]

In the early decades of independence, criticisms of Christian conversion appeared frequently in the speeches and pamphlets of Buddhist politicians and activist groups, while criticisms of Christian *and* Buddhist conversions appeared in the political demands made by some Hindus from the island's Tamil-majority regions. In the 1950s, the All-Ceylon Buddhist Congress proposed making the conversion of non-Christian children in Christian schools a penal offense.[18] In the 1960s, the Buddhist National Force (BJB, or *Bauddha Jātika Balavēgaya*) prevailed upon the government to investigate Catholic conversions that were taking place, among other places, in the country's prisons.[19] At the same time, Hindu political leaders in Jaffna were joining Buddhist groups in railing against the alleged conversion campaigns of "Catholic Action" groups.[20] From the 1940s through the 1970s, the topic of conversions to Christianity was a hugely salient and sensitive issue for Buddhists and Hindus alike, one linked with concerns not only about religious autonomy and demography but also about colonial influence, territorial control and inequalities of power.

[16] Seneviratne, *Work of Kings*. Gananath Obeyesekere, "Religious Symbolism and Political Change in Sri Lanka," in *The Two Wheels of Dhamma: Essays on the Theravada Tradition in India and Ceylon*, ed. Bardwell L Smith (Boston, MA: American Academy of Religion, 1972). Young and Jebanesan, *The Bible Trembled*.

[17] Bruce Matthews, "Christian Evangelical Conversions and the Politics of Sri Lanka," *Pacific Affairs* 80, no. 3 (2007): 455–472.

[18] G P Malalasekera, "Buddhism and the State" *The Buddhist*, February 1956, 176; Buddhist Committee of Enquiry, *The Betrayal of Buddhism*, 83–90.

[19] "Catholic Action Movement in Ceylon" *World Buddhism*, August, 1962, p. 7; see also Bauddha Jathika Balavegaya, *Catholic Action – A Menace to Peace and Goodwill* (Colombo: The Bauddha Pracharaka Press, March, 1963).

[20] K Vaithianathan and All-Ceylon-Hindu Congress, *Catholic Action and Thiruketheeswaram (Pamphlet)* (n.p., n.d.).

226 CONSTITUTIONAL CONVERSIONS

Since 1990, a variety of Buddhist and Hindu groups have expressed new anxieties over Christian conversions, reflecting a new set of global and local influences. These influences include an upsurge in evangelical and charismatic Christian missionary work that has been taking place throughout Africa and Asia over the last three decades.[21] Although Christian evangelicals (e.g., Baptists) and charismatics (e.g., Pentecostals) have been present in Sri Lanka for some time,[22] greater numbers of missionaries and new churches started coming to the island in the 1980s. These new groups arrived at a time of immense change and instability linked to an intensifying civil war violence and the rapid opening of Sri Lanka's economy to private enterprise, foreign investment and international aid (see Chapter 5). Christians' presence as charity and development workers in war-affected areas attracted the attention of critics, who suspected them of using humanitarian aid as a pretext for proselytizing.

These recent criticisms of Christian conversions in Sri Lanka differ in important ways from those visible in the first three decades after independence. In the 1940s–1960s, critics focused mainly on the links between Christianity, political power and the island's urban elite. In particular, they voiced concern over the numbers of (primarily Catholic) Christians in influential positions in government, law, education and business. By contrast, recent criticisms focus on the influence of Christian missionaries on the island's poor, disadvantaged, rural populations. They also focus less on the island's large, established Christian bodies – Catholics, Methodists, Presbyterians, Anglicans, and members of the Dutch Reformed Church (collectively referred to as "mainline" Protestant groups) – than on smaller, independent, evangelical and Pentecostal churches, such as the Assemblies of God, which make up less than 1 percent of the population.[23] This new genre of criticism attributes Christians' power and authority not to links with international churches (e.g., the Vatican), but to links with international development organizations (such as the World Bank), Western governments (particularly the United States of America) and multinational treaty organizations (such as the United Nations).

---

[21] Joel Robbins, "The Globalization of Pentecostal and Charismatic Christianity," *Annual Review of Anthropology* 33, no. 1 (2004): 117–143.

[22] Baptists have been in Sri Lanka since the early 1800s and the first Pentecostals came around 1920.

[23] Fernando, *The Effects of Evangelical Christianity on State Formation in Sri Lanka.*

THE PROBLEM WITH CONVERSION: OLD AND NEW   227

Like older criticisms of conversion, recent condemnations have come from both Hindu and Buddhist groups, each of which voice similar sets of concerns about the abilities of wealthy, foreign-funded Christians to weaken and discredit the religious traditions of comparatively poorer Sri Lankans. As one especially vocal Sinhala Buddhist political body described it:

> Today we have another group of Christians calling themselves Fundamentalists or Evangelists who have adopted another method of conversion. That is using their wealth which they seem to have in abundance to buy Christian converts from among the poorest which to say the least is most unethical and unchristian ... Evangelists come here not to bring the light of Heaven to benighted Asians but to undermine and destroy our traditions, culture and heritage.[24]

Similar images were conjured by the Hindu author of one Tamil-language editorial from 2000 (celebrated and reprinted in the *Hindu Organ*) who urged Hindus to recognize the threat posed by new, foreign, extremist (T: *tīviramaṭaintuvarum*) Christian groups, supported by foreign powers who "exploit the situation of poverty and war" to undertake a project similar to colonial-era Christians: to inculcate Christianity and destroy local cultural values.[25]

However, unlike these older anxieties, recent criticisms regarding conversion have come also from the island's mainline Christian groups, who worry about losing adherents to Christian "fundamentalists" (S: *kristiyāni mūladharmavādayo*). In a study on recent evangelical movements in South Asia, sociologist Sasanka Perera describes the profound anxiety felt by mainstream Catholic and Protestant churches in Sri Lanka concerning the threat of evangelical conversions. Drawing from a series of interviews conducted in 1998, Perera describes the frustration of Anglican and Catholic clerics (in urban and rural areas) regarding the success of "fundamentalist" Christians in winning converts from their flocks. Perera even narrates the story of one Catholic priest who

---

[24] Sinhala Commission, *Report of the Sinhala Commission (Part II)* (Colombo: Samaya-wardhana Press, 2001), 7–10.

[25] "*Matamārrattil īṭupaṭuvōr Maṇitanēyamarravarkaḷ*" (Those who engage in Conversion Have no Compassion for Humanity). Reprinted in *intucātanam*, November 12, 2000, p. 26. See also: "Public Appeal: The Wholehearted Support of the Hindu Organizations For the Proposed Legislation to Prevent Unethical and Fraudulent Religious Conversions," issued February 12, 2003. All-Ceylon Hindu Congress, *Inthu Oli: All-Ceylon Hindu Congress Golden Jubilee Commemoration* (Colombo: All-Ceylon Hindu Congress, n.d.), 149.

228 CONSTITUTIONAL CONVERSIONS

admonished his parishioners to "beat those fundamentalists out of the village if they come back."[26] Newspaper reports reveal the commonness of sentiments such as these in the late 1990s and early 2000s. For example, in an interview with *The Island* newspaper in August 2003, the Bishop of Kurunegela accused "fundamentalists" of "stealing sheep from our flock," and stressed that Sri Lanka's Catholics "are dead against unethical conversion."[27]

The organizing trope of devotee-stealing fundamentalists illustrates nicely the nature of recent worries over conversion. Although political and religious groups tend to direct these allegations toward particular evangelical or charismatic sects (Assemblies of God, in particular), their discourse also contains a generic image of zealous, foreign-funded, Christian leaders who aggressively push their theology on polite and defenseless locals. In fact, in this regard, concerns over conversion were even shared among some of the very evangelical Christians that were often implicated as agents of "unethical conversion" (unethical, S: *sadācāra virōdhī*). In an interview from 2009, one evangelical Christian leader explained to me his frustration at the "unwise" evangelizing of some American Christian groups who engaged in humanitarian aid following the December 2004 Tsunami. He also took care to distance "mainstream" evangelical churches from the many "non-trinitarian" groups that were operating in Sri Lanka and who were often mistakenly taken as representative of all evangelicals:

> [There are] quite a number of groups like this, which would function very separately, very individualistic; and they're the ones who go house to house visiting. That's actually the Jehovah's Witnesses, you know. Again, they have very different ways of doing [things]. But, again, they are very foreign-based. You find two Mormons, black trousers, white shirt, close cropped hair, with a tie and then sometimes they will take a local guide. So, you know, that's a different group and a lot of foreigners are involved in it [conversions], a lot of Americans are involved in it. ... But that wouldn't come under mainstream evangelical groups at all.[28]

Although this interview occurred years after the court case described next, it indicates the varied nature of social anxieties over conversion,

---

[26] Ibid.

[27] "Reply [by Buddhist/Hindu Alliance] to Christian Council's Appeal to Ease Tensions Amicably" *The Island*, October 15, 2003. Namini Wijedasa, "Well-intentioned social work or unethical conversion?" *The Island*, August 24, 2003.

[28] Interview, February 5, 2009.

THE PROBLEM WITH CONVERSION: OLD AND NEW 229

and the ways in which those anxieties cut across religious communities in broad and complex ways. It also indicates the multifaceted nature of such anxieties. More than just fears about demography or violations of religious freedom, anxieties over conversion implicated and continue to implicate a raft of concerns about which Sri Lankans feel strongly: concerns about foreign influence and power, about economic change and capitalism, about social inequality and the vulnerabilities of the island's rural agricultural communities, about the ravaging effects of civil war, and about the changing nature Sri Lankan society.

This brief social history of conversion highlights just how complex and many-sided the issue has always been, and never more so than in the late 1990s and 2000s, when concern over religious conversions involved not a simple conflict between Christians and Buddhists (or Christians and non-Christians) but a more widespread panic, stoked by a variety of different groups, that crossed ethnic, linguistic and religious boundaries. Concerns over conversion were expressed by Buddhists, Hindus, Protestants and Catholics; by evangelicals and non-evangelicals; by urbanites and villagers; by Sinhalese and Tamils. More-over, anxieties over conversion – often predicated on caricatured images of Christian fundamentalists – interlinked with broader feelings about history, globalization, civil war and economic inequality. This is not to say that all of Sri Lankan society remained obsessed with the specter of "unethical conversions." Indeed, for some Sri Lankans, it was not an issue of particular importance; for others, it seemed to be a fictitious or trumped-up problem, one invented by political and religious entrepreneurs who sought to gain from scapegoating evangelical groups.[29] Nevertheless, as a topic of public debate and an object of private alarm, anxiety over fundamentalists and conversion implicated a remarkably wide swath of peoples and concerns.

During this period, a number of religious and non-religious groups proposed creative solutions to address some of these concerns over conversion. One example was the creation by certain mainline Christian groups of a "Code of Ethics," which priests were asked to use in deciding how and when to proselytize. Among other things, the Code committed

---

[29] One particularly important Buddhist voice that opposed conversion was the monk, Ven. Soma Thero. Stephen C Berkwitz, "Resisting the Global in Buddhist Nationalism: Venerable Soma's Discourse of Decline and Reform," *Journal of Asian Studies* 67, no. 1 (2008): 73–106.

230 CONSTITUTIONAL CONVERSIONS

missionaries to "ensure that [their] methods of mission ... [and] public worship are sensitive to the immediate cultural and human environment."[30] Another example was the proposal of an independent interreligious committee that would investigate allegations of unethical conversion. This idea, which was supported by a variety of religious groups, was oriented around the creation of a pan-island multi-religious body that could deal with matters of religious conflict using local, regional and national-level religious clerics.[31]

A final, particularly surprising example was the formation in 2002 of a Buddhist-Hindu "solidarity group," consisting of a number of educated professionals from the Colombo area, representing more than a dozen lay Buddhist organizations and two major Hindu organizations.[32] In other contexts, many of these groups had been political rivals: Hindu participants had formerly protested against the state's promotion of Buddhism and the gradual "colonization" of Tamil-majority areas of the island by Sinhalese Buddhists; several Buddhist participants had formerly supported military action to defend Buddhist temples in the North and East.[33] The "shared" problem[34] of conversion united them. Consisting disproportionately of lawyers, they soon formed a "Buddhist-Hindu Committee" and set out to design legislation which, drawing on the religious guarantees in Sri Lanka's constitution, would limit missionary techniques that might "take advantage of people in distress, or in need" or of "low intellect."[35]

---

[30] Draft – "Code of Ethics for Mission," National Christian Council of Sri Lanka. In possession of author, n.d.

[31] Interview with senior member of Methodist Church, May 6, 2009.

[32] Buddhist organizations included: the All-Ceylon Buddhist Congress, the All-Ceylon Women's Buddhist Congress, the Bauddha Sanrakshana Sabha, the Buddhist Theosophical Society, the Buddhist News, the Young Men's Buddhist Association, SUCCESS and others. Hindu organizations included: All-Ceylon Hindu Congress and Hindu Council of Sri Lanka.

[33] All-Ceylon Hindu Congress, *Inthu Oli: All-Ceylon Hindu Congress Golden Jubilee Commemoration*, 168.

[34] Press Release Draft: "Buddhist and Hindu Committee" Releases Draft Bill to Protect Freedom of Conscience. Copy in possession of author.

[35] Interview with organizer of the group, May 15, 2009. As another participant described it: "We [Buddhists] got together with the Hindus, because the Hindus are also very badly affected by this conversion thing, these unethical conversions ... because all the estate Tamils they were Hindus and the estate was an ideal place for these fellows [Christian NGOs and missionary groups] to go and pour in all their aid and things like that and convert those estate people who were virtually illiterates also. Then even in the North they were doing this. And the Hindus were not so well organized – not that we [the Buddhists]

Constitutionalizing Conversion

The Buddhist-Hindu Committee's turn to law follows a trend toward constitutionalizing the issue of conversion, which had begun in 2000, with the first of the three "incorporation cases" (discussed in Chapter 5). In those cases (from 2000, 2001 and 2003) Buddhist petitioners successfully challenged the constitutionality of three parliamentary bills designed to give legal incorporation to proselytizing Christian groups. Buddhist petitioners claimed that the groups' legal charters revealed an intent to engage in unethical proselytizing. They therefore posed a threat to non-Christians' constitutional rights to freedom of conscience and might plausibly "impair the very existence of Buddhism or the *Buddha Sasana*."[36] Taking inspiration from these cases, the Buddhist-Hindu Committee drafted a bill designed to limit conversion by way of a thorough-going appeal to the importance of Article 10 of Sri Lanka's Constitution, which protected citizens' rights to freedom of "thought, conscience and religion." In fact, the Committee named its bill "The Protection of the Freedom of Thought, Conscience and Religion Bill" and used constitutional language to describe its aim: it would protect against "coercion or allurement that *would impair or influence such other person's freedom to have or adopt a religion or belief of his choice*."[37] In January 2004, the Committee sent the bill to the President, hoping it would be introduced into parliament by the government.

By late 2003, the trend toward constitutionalizing conversion was gaining momentum elsewhere as well. Along with the incorporation cases, a climate of legal enthusiasm was being stoked by events in India, where a number of states had recently introduced statutes to limit Christian evangelism.[38] Calls to "outlaw" conversion also appeared with increasing regularity in Sri Lankan newspapers.[39] In April 2004, promises to introduce new laws against conversion featured

---

are organized – but they were less organized then the Buddhists also. And the Hindus said let's get together and put up a bill. So, we sat." Interview with Buddhist member of Buddhist-Hindu Committee, May 17, 2009.

[36] SC Special Determination 19/2003 *Regarding Provincial of the Teaching Sisters of the Holy Cross of the Third Order of Saint Francis in Menzingen of Sri Lanka (Incorporation) Bill.*

[37] Draft Copy, Sixth Version, *The Protection of the Freedom of Thought, Conscience and Religion Bill,* October 10, 2003, Section 2. Copy in possession of author. Italics mine. (Herein referred to as Buddhist-Hindu Bill.)

[38] Laura D Jenkins, "Legal Limits on Religious Conversion in India," *Law & Contemporary Problems* 71 (2008): 109. Sen, *Articles of Faith.*

[39] See, e.g., Aryadasa Ratnasinghe, "Point of View: Anti-conversion Legislation," *The Island,* October 15, 2003.

232 CONSTITUTIONAL CONVERSIONS

prominently in the island's general elections in the campaign speeches of a new political party, consisting almost entirely of Buddhist monks, called the *Jātika Heḷa Urumaya* (National [Sinhalese] Heritage Party), or JHU. The JHU's campaign manifesto declared the party's intent to create a righteous state (*dharmarājya*) that honored its constitutional obligations to protect Buddhism and, accordingly, would place strict legal limitations on proselytism.[40] The declarations won support from voters and helped the JHU win nine seats in the island's 225-person legislature. Only weeks after entering parliament, in May 2004, members of the JHU produced their own conversion bill. They took as their template an ordinance that had been ratified (and later repealed) in the state legislature of Tamil Nadu.[41] Revising it only slightly, the head of the JHU introduced the "Prohibition of Forcible Conversion of Religion Bill" to Sri Lanka's parliament.

The JHU's bill cast conversion in terms of its pro-Buddhist politics. In a long preamble, which was prepended to the technical part of the bill and which constituted almost 20 percent of the total text, drafters linked the need for limits on Christian proselytism to constitutional (and historical) obligations (first) to protect Buddhism and (second) to protect other religions:

> WHEREAS, Buddhism being the foremost religion professed and prac-ticed by the majority of people of Sri Lanka due to the introduction by the great Tathagatha, the Sambuddha in the 8th Month after he had attained Buddhahood on his visit to Mahiyangana in Sri Lanka and due to the complete realisation after the arrival of Arahat Mahinda Thero in the 3rd Century B.E. [*sic*]
>
> AND WHEREAS, the State has a duty to protect and foster the Buddha Sasana while assuring to all religions the rights granted by Article 10 and 14(1)(e) of the Constitution of the Republic of Sri Lanka

---

[40] M Deegalle, "Politics of the Jathika Hela Urumaya Monks: Buddhism and Ethnicity in Contemporary Sri Lanka," *Contemporary Buddhism* 5, no. 2 (2004): 83–103. Berkwitz, "Religious Conflict and the Politics of Conversion in Sri Lanka." N DeVotta and J Stone, "Jathika Hela Urumaya and Ethno-religious Politics in Sri Lanka," *Pacific Affairs* 81, no. 1 (2008): 31–51.

[41] Tamil Nadu Prohibition of Forcible Conversion of Religion Act, No. 56 of 2002. The repeal of the act was effected, officially, with a *Repeal Act* in 2006 (No. 10 /2006). However, by that time it had long been defunct: In May 2004, the Forcible Conversion *Ordinance* was repealed, ending the legal enforcement of conversion limits. See also: "Minister of Hindu Affairs Deserves Plaudits" Opinion, *The Island*, May 10, 2003. www.island.lk/2003/05/10/opinio03.html. "Lanka to Follow Jayalalitha on Forced Con-version Law," *The Island*, December 29, 2003.

> AND WHEREAS, the Buddhist and non Buddhist [*sic*] are now under serious threat of forcible conversions and proselytizing by coercion or by allurement or by fraudulent means
>
> AND WHEREAS, the [Buddhist monks] and other religious leaders realising the need to protect and promote religious harmony among all religions, historically enjoyed by the people of Sri Lanka . . .[42]

In the rhetorical architecture of the preamble of the JHU bill, "forcible conversion" threatened first Buddhism in Sri Lanka and second other religious traditions; it violated first the state's duties to protect and foster the Buddha Sasana and second the rights assured to other religions; it constituted first a menace for Buddhist persons and second a menace for non-Buddhists; it concerned first the island's Buddhist monks and second other religious leaders.

In a manner similar to the Buddhist-Hindu Committee, the JHU interpreted conversion as something done to someone else: to convert was to *cause someone else* to adopt a different religion. What made conversion illegal were the conditions under which conversion occurred. In the words of the JHU bill, "No person shall convert or attempt to convert, either directly or otherwise . . . by the use of force or by allurement or by any fraudulent means nor shall any person aid or abet any such conversion."[43] The meaning of allurement, force and fraudulent means was further specified in an "Interpretations" section of the bill:[44]

> (a) "allurement" means any offer of any temptation in the form of –
>   (i) any gift or gratification whether in cash or kind; (ii) grant of any material benefit, whether monetary or otherwise; (iii) grant of employment or grant of promotion of employment.
>
>   . . .
>
> (b) "force" shall include a show of force including a threat or harm or injury of any kind or threat of religious displeasure or condemnation of any religion or religious faith;
> (c) "fraudulent" means [*sic*] includes misinterpretation or any other fraudulent contrivance;

The JHU bill also required that anyone who knew about a conversion or was involved in it must report them to local government officials. Special

---

[42] *Prohibition of Forcible Conversion of Religion Bill*, presented by Ven. Dr. Omalpe Sobhitha Thero. *Gazette of the Democratic Socialist Republic of Sri Lanka*, May 28, 2004, Pt. II. Italics added. (Herein referred to as *JHU bill*.)
[43] Ibid., Section 2, italics mine.   [44] Ibid., Section 8.

234 CONSTITUTIONAL CONVERSIONS

penalties applied to any participant in a conversion ceremony (including converts themselves) who failed to inform state authorities about the event.[45] Punishments included prison terms (for up to five years) and fines (of up to SLR 150,000 [USD 1,500]), with increases possible if converts were women or children or among one of 11 types of vulnerable populations, including welfare beneficiaries, prisoners, disabled persons, members of the army or police, students, and refugees.[46]

Thus, in the first half of 2004, two conversion bills – both of which framed conversion in terms of constitutional rubrics for managing religion – looked to gain a hearing in Sri Lanka's parliament. Ultimately, the JHU bill was the first and only bill to be considered by legislators: the head of the JHU, Ven. Omalpe Sobhita, introduced the JHU draft as a Private Member's Bill while the Committee bill was under consideration with the government.[47] On July 21, 2004, the JHU bill appeared on the Order Paper of Parliament. On July 22, 2004, more than 20 citizens and groups petitioned the island's Supreme Court to review the bill's constitutionality. The case would be one of the largest and most publicized court cases concerning religion in the island's history.

SECTION II: LITIGATING CONVERSION

Consolidating a Conflict

The JHU-bill case polarized the issue of conversion in new and profound ways. As described earlier, concerns over conversion had cut across religious boundaries and implicated complex political, historical and

---

[45] Ibid., 2b.   [46] Ibid., Section 4, read with Schedule 1.

[47] Weeks before the JHU joined together as a political party, on January 29, 2004, the Buddhist-Hindu Committee conveyed a copy of its proposed legislation to the president with a letter urging her to place the bill before parliament as an "urgent bill" (Letter from "The Buddhist-Hindu" Committee to Her Excellency Chandrika Kumaratunge; in author's possession). The government did not introduce the Committee bill as requested; yet certain prominent ministers, including the prime minister and Minister of Buddha Sasana, Ratnasiri Wickremanayake, used the provisions of the bill as the basis for a government-authored conversion bill, entitled "Protection of Freedom of Religion Bill," which was composed between January and June 2004. That bill did not secure cabinet approval until June 2004. Even after approval, however, the proposed law languished 12 more months before being published in the Gazette and placed on the order paper of parliament. No debate was ever held.

social concerns. Nevertheless, the format and imperatives of constitutional litigation effectively transformed the issue of conversion into a blunt contest between non-Buddhists (along with liberals and secularists) and Buddhist groups, including many Buddhist groups that had not previously seen eye-to-eye. With the arrival of a litigious framework, moderate parties – Buddhists, Hindus, Christians and non-religious persons who had previously voiced sympathetic concern over the possibility of insensitive conversion practices but sought creative, middle-ground solutions – found themselves pulled toward the inflexible position of supporting one side (that of the nationalist Buddhist JHU and its bill) or the other side (that of opponents calling for pre-enactment judicial review to prevent legal limitations on conversion) in response to an issue that, for them, was much more multifaceted. Those who opposed legal limits on conversion, even if they were concerned about conversion activities, felt compelled to oppose such a harsh and inflexible law. At the same time, those who favored a legal solution felt that, even if they did not approve of the terms of the JHU bill, they should at least intervene on its behalf to ensure that the court would not rule unconstitutional the very idea of a legal limitation on religious conversion. A dyadic dispute was produced: Hindus and Christians who had pursued other creative solutions for their concerns over conversion now petitioned against the bill; Buddhist groups that had previously worked alongside Hindu organizations to draft their own bill now joined the JHU in its legal defense.

Members of the Buddhist-Hindu Committee underwent a particularly dramatic division. In the legal challenges to the JHU bill, the Hindu members of the Committee split from the Buddhist members. Hindu members clearly objected to the JHU's efforts to frame the issue of conversion as an offense against constitutional obligations to protect Buddhism. Notably, the same lawyer from the All-Ceylon Hindu Congress who had been one of the key architects of the Buddhist-Hindu bill petitioned the court as an opponent of the JHU bill. Even more surprising was the fact that Buddhist members of the Committee rushed to support the bill because Buddhist members had initially rejected the JHU and its conversion bill. As one member of the Committee recollected:

> Then [after the Hindu-Buddhist Committee had submitted our bill to the Government] these JHU people came on the scene. And they thought this is a good political ploy to get some of the Buddhists [to support them]. So, they, without any reference to us, they put away our bill. We made it

236 CONSTITUTIONAL CONVERSIONS

> available to them. We said, here's the bill, if you want to do the right thing let them do it. But they didn't take that. They brought some Indian bill! And on the basis of that Indian bill they put forward something. Sabotage! They undercut our bill and put their own bill in the name of the JHU.[48]

The JHU's sabotage was double for members of the Committee who represented Colombo lay Buddhist organizations. On the one hand, members felt that the JHU had undercut their long-standing and methodical efforts to produce a legally sound conversion bill, hastily hijacking an issue on which they had been working for many months. On the other hand, Buddhist members of the Committee viewed the formation of an all-monastic political party itself as an assault on Buddhism because, as in the case of driving monks in Chapter 6, it improperly immersed monks in worldly affairs. "Religion has to be different from politics," argued one member, "monks can be king makers, but should never become kings."[49] The significance of these objections should not be overlooked: Buddhist members whom I interviewed saw the JHU's actions as politically and religiously offensive. Nevertheless, the Buddhist members of the Committee ultimately supported the JHU bill: "[S]ome people felt, what is the point in this [JHU Conversion] bill, it is bloody useless; we will not have this bill. But most of the people felt [that] well half a loaf is better then none, let us at least have this."[50]

The kind of religious polarizations that occurred among members of the Buddhist-Hindu Committee also occurred among Buddhists and Christians, more generally. A number of Sri Lanka's Christian organizations had initially joined Buddhist groups in encouraging clergy to look more closely at the techniques they used to proselytize. However, by the middle of 2004, virtually all Christian groups united in public objection to the JHU bill.[51] One senior clergyman in the Methodist Church explained: "if you look, between 2002 and 2004, there were lots of deliberations [among Christians and between Christians and Buddhists].

---

[48] Interview with member of committee, May 15, 2009.
[49] Interview with member of committee, May 11, 2009.
[50] Interview with member of committee, May 17, 2009.
[51] "No links with fundamentalist sects, say Catholic Bishops," *Daily News*, December 19, 2003. Prior to the JHU bill being published, even the National Christian Evangelical Alliance of Sri Lanka, the coordinating body for many evangelical churches on the island, issued a press release expressing a "clear and strong objection to any form of unlawful or unethical conversion." "Evangelical Christians condemn unethical conversion," *Sunday Island*, January 18, 2004.

CONSOLIDATING A CONFLICT 237

Then once the bill went onto the table, everything came to a standstill ... that is where, I think, we got worried."[52]

These polarizations along religious lines were reflected particularly strongly in the composition of the parties to the JHU-bill case. For the most part, litigants' affidavits suggested a story of non-Buddhists versus Buddhists: Almost all of those who contested the bill declared their affiliations to Christian or Hindu groups or to secular non-governmental organizations. Even the petitioners who identified themselves (in affidavits) as Buddhists claimed, as their primary identity for purposes of establishing legal standing, association with public-interest and human rights organizations.[53] By contrast, all of those who supported the bill, including members of the JHU and Buddhist organizations, signed affidavits affirming in clear and strident terms that they were Buddhists who were concerned about the well-being of Buddhism.

In total, 21 petitioners challenged the bill.[54] Petitions against the bill were submitted by the National Christian Evangelical Alliance of Sri Lanka (the largest coordinating body of Evangelical Christians on the island), the National Christian Fellowship of Sri Lanka, the Salvation Army, the Hela Kithunu Urumaya (which described itself in its affidavit as "the religious liberties arm of the Catholic Church"), the Methodist Church, the Anglican Church, the Catholic Church, and the Dutch Reformed Church. The last five Christian groups – "mainline" Christian churches – submitted virtually identical petitions and were represented by many of the same lawyers. The largest Hindu organization on the island, the All-Ceylon Hindu Congress, filed a petition drafted by a former member of the Buddhist-Hindu Committee. Non-governmental organizations, individuals and political parties also opposed the bill, including a former senior civil servant and "convener" of the group "Solidarity for Religious Freedom" (who identified himself as a Buddhist in his affidavit), a well-known legal scholar and author (who also identified himself as a Buddhist), a professor of constitutional law at the

---

[52] Interview with Rev. Ebenezer Joseph, May 6, 2009.

[53] One interesting exception is SC (SD) 2/2004 (Ruwan Sampath Jayasuriya). His petition diverges from the rest in that, in his affidavit, he describes himself simply as "a Buddhist" who "affirms" the main provisions regarding forcible conversion, and contests only certain technical parts of the bill, particularly the requirement that converts and others report conversions to government officials, in Clause 3. Media reporting on the case as well as the judgment itself make no mention of his petition.

[54] The names of the organizations are reproduced as they appear in the petitions, including the transliterated Sinhala names.

238 CONSTITUTIONAL CONVERSIONS

University of Colombo, a long-standing human rights NGO in Colombo, the largest public litigation NGO on the island, and a very small political party whose members had been actively involved in constitutional reform.[55]

A similar number of "intervenient petitioners" opposed those petitioners and offered their own submissions *supporting* the JHU bill in the Supreme Court. They included Buddhist monks affiliated with the JHU (many of them parliamentarians recently elected in the April 2, 2004 general elections), lay members of the JHU, prominent university academics (one of whom had been a member of the Buddhist-Hindu drafting committee) and a variety of other Buddhist professionals with government, media and other backgrounds. Monastic and lay representatives from several Buddhist activist organizations also submitted intervenient petitions in favor of the bill. Petitions were filed by SUCCESS (members of which participated in the Buddhist-Hindu Committee), the Sinhala Jathika Sangamaya (Sinhala National Association) and the National Sangha Conference. While upwards of 30 different lawyers appeared on behalf of the intervenient petitioners, almost all of the documents put before the court in support of the JHU bill – with the exception of those put forward by two intervenient petitioners (SUCCESS and the Society for the Conservation of Buddhism) – looked similar in their content and arguments. This included the affidavits, all of which described the standing of the petitioner as a Buddhist who engaged in religious worship and teaching and who "strive[d] to protect and foster the Buddha Sasana."[56] Remarkably, the same lawyer who acted as lead draftsman of the Buddhist-Hindu Committee bill acted as lead counsel supporting the JHU bill in court.

Debating Religion

It was not just the opposed sets of petitioners[57] that polarized the issue of conversion when it went to court. Even more significant were the linguistic requirements of legal argumentation, which had a profound

---

[55] SC (SD) 10/2004 (R M B Senanayake); SC (SD) 15/2004 (Asanga Welikala); SC (SD) 22/2004 (Veeravagu Thambirajah Thamilmaran); SC (SD) 20/2004 (Civil Rights Movement); SC (SD) 20/2004 (Centre for Policy Alternatives); SC (SD) 11/2004 (The Liberal Party, with Anura Samarajeewa, member of the party). The Liberal Party only garnered .06% of the national vote in the 2000 general elections.

[56] E.g., Affidavit, Ven. Rajawatte Vappa Thero (JHU member) SC (SD) 10/2004.

[57] In some cases the petitioners and intervenient petitioners included multiple persons. By referring to petitioners, then, I am referring to the 21 separate sets of submissions from petitioners and 19 separate sets of submissions from intervenient petitioners.

THE "FOREMOST PLACE" OR "FOREMOST RELIGION"? 239

effect on the way the issue of conversion was interpreted and expressed by petitioners, judges and observers in national and international media. Rather than considering conversion in its historical and contextual complexity, the parameters and incentives of constitutional litigation – in this case constitutional review – meant that litigants framed their arguments primarily in terms of those concepts and categories that were most valuable from a legalistic point of view, namely those enshrined in the constitution's entrenched articles, Articles 9 and 10. (This was, of course, the very reason that the Hindu-Buddhist Committee and the JHU had foregrounded these articles clearly in their respective bills.) These framing conditions of constitutional litigation had the effect of funneling disputes inside the courtroom toward fierce debates over what it meant to protect Buddhism and guarantee freedom of conscience. Yet, by making their arguments in these terms, litigants on both sides were justifying their claims using the most inflexible principles of constitutional management, those concepts and categories construed by the constitution's drafters as core rubrics that ought not to be limited or compromised in any way. Through this process, petitioners on both sides came to express their views in unyielding, zero-sum terms.

The "Foremost Place" or "Foremost Religion"?

Chapters 5 and 6 of this book examined how the language used by Sri Lanka's constitution-designers to address the grievances of Buddhists ultimately created new avenues and incentives for making contentious claims about Buddhism in the island's higher judiciary. These chapters also showed how constitutional provisions designed to encourage solidarity among Buddhists actually aggravated contests over the boundaries of Buddhist orthodoxy and orthopraxy. A close analysis of the JHU-bill case illuminates an analogous dynamic. It shows how the very language used by constitution drafters to avoid contentious questions about the relationship between Buddhism's "foremost place" and fundamental religious rights came to sanction competing arguments regarding these very questions.

Litigants in the JHU-bill case offered, with equal vigor, opposing interpretations of the state's duties to Buddhism described in the constitution's Buddhism Chapter, Article 9.[58] These competing interpretations

---

[58] To remind readers, Article 9 of Sri Lanka's Constitution reads: "The Republic of Sri Lanka shall give to Buddhism the foremost place and accordingly it shall be the duty of the State

240   CONSTITUTIONAL CONVERSIONS

paralleled competing perspectives advanced – and evaded – during the process of drafting Sri Lanka's constitution. Those who opposed the bill argued that the second constitutional prerogative imposed upon the first: fundamental rights to freedom of conscience and manifestation of religion constrained Buddhism's primacy. That is, they argued that state patronage of Buddhism was limited by the government's duties to uphold general religious rights. Of particular concern to the bill's opponents was the fact that the JHU bill's preamble rendered Buddhism as the "foremost *religion*." Moreover, the Sinhala copy of the bill used the phrase "ultimate" or "greatest" (S: *uttarītara*) instead of "foremost" (S: *pramukha*) to describe the status of Buddhism in the constitution. Opponents of the bill argued that these rhetorical sleights-of-hand implanted an unconstitutional majoritarian bias into the bill. Echoing arguments of certain constitution-drafters, the All-Ceylon Hindu Congress insisted that, properly interpreted, the Buddhism Chapter placed all religions "at par with each other [and] on an equal footing."[59] The mainline churches similarly insisted that existing constitutional protections for religion must be seen as confirming the equality and equal importance of all religions:

> the phrase "foremost religion" when conferred on any religion connotes the superiority over other religions, which is a subjective, unempirical perception which may not be foisted upon others. In terms of pluralist democracy, *all religions are equal* and a particular religion would be foremost to those who profess it, as against other religions. Thus, Buddhism is only the foremost to those professing Buddhism. Hence, the said Bill which *falls to recognize in its preamble and protect through its clauses, the fact that Hinduism, Islam, Christianity etc. are* [also] *the respective foremost religions to those in Sri Lanka* who profess such great faiths which also have been historically practiced for centuries.[60]

Buddhism's "foremost" status, in this reading, pertained to its having the largest number of followers, rather than any special, distinct, historical or

---

to protect and foster the Buddha Sasana, while assuring to all religions the rights granted by Articles 10 and 14(1)(e)." Article 10 reads: "Every person is entitled to freedom of thought, conscience and religion, including the freedom to have or to adopt a religion or belief of his choice."

[59] SC 12/2004, Affadavit, Kandiah Neelakandan, All-Ceylon Hindu Congress.

[60] Written Submissions, 7/2004, Rt. Revd. Kumara Illangasinghe, Anglican Bishop of Kurunegala and Duleep de Chickera, Anglican Bishop of Colombo, p. 5. Also repeated *verbatim* in other submissions of mainline churches, the Catholic petitioners and the submission of V Thamilmaran. Italics mine.

THE "FOREMOST PLACE" OR "FOREMOST RELIGION"?   241

qualitative superiority – as the preamble seemed to suggest. The "foremost" status of Buddhism referred not to the differential value of Buddh*ism* as a religion but to the relatively greater numbers of Buddhists who lived in Sri Lanka. A "pluralist democracy," like Sri Lanka's, admitted no difference in the worth of religions. At most, opponents argued, the Buddhism clauses prescribed a kind of "affirmative action," a program of support designed to assist one religious group – but only to the extent that other groups were not disadvantaged.[61] Some even argued, more creatively, that to place Buddhism above other religions would be to transgress against the religion itself by violating Buddhist teachings of tolerance and equality.[62] In the words of one petitioner, a majoritarian interpretation of Article 9 would do "grave and irreparable injustice and injury to the ideals of tolerance, forbearance, co-existence and universal kindness which any true Buddhist could take pride and satisfaction in."[63]

In defending the bill, intervenient petitioners insisted that Buddhism did have a superior status as a religion; however, they also insisted that no tensions existed between Buddhism's special status and general religious rights, because the multireligious milieu that one found in Sri Lanka was made possible by the fact that Buddhism was an especially tolerant dominant religion. In their arguments, which had deep parallels with those offered in 1970–1972, the "foremost place" of Buddhism referred to "an empirically verifiable fact":[64] Buddhism was the "established" religion of Sri Lanka in the same way that the Anglican Church was the "established" religion of England. The fact of this establishment, they insisted, did not encroach upon the liberties or rights of other religious groups. Rather, the constitutional establishment of religion was common in many modern democracies (including the United Kingdom, Greece and Ireland).

---

[61] E.g., Written Submissions, SC (SD) 4/2004, Rev. A Noel P Fernando, President, Methodist Church, p. 4. Also *verbatim* in other submissions of mainline churches and the Catholic petitioners. Several petitioners pointed out that the Supreme Court had ignored this critical fact in the Menzingen case. Six of the petitioners against the bill even made a special application to the court, prior to the proceedings, requesting that the court ignore the Menzingen determination and the two incorporation determinations which proceeded it on account of the fact that, in those cases, Christians had not had adequate opportunity to submit arguments. Even more emphatically, they requested that the court convene a full five-justice bench and that the bench "should include Judges who have not participated in the [incorporation] applications." Application on behalf of petitioners SC (SD) Nos. 5/04, 6/04, 13/04, 14/04, 17/04 , submitted to Court July 30, 2004.
[62] Further Written Submissions, SC (SD) 10/2004, R M B Senanayake, pp. 3–4.
[63] Petition, SC (SD) 15/2004, Asanga Welikala, p. 2.
[64] Written Submissions, SC (SD) 4/2004, Intervenient Petitioner, SUCCESS, p. 4.

242 CONSTITUTIONAL CONVERSIONS

Moreover, Buddhism was an especially accepting religion.[65] Established Buddhism in Sri Lanka, argued one submission, had produced "peaceful religious harmony ... from time immemorial."[66] Only with the emergence of new Christian sects on the island had this harmony been ruptured:

> It is interesting to probe who created the present situation. The fundamentalists through the Non Governmental Organisations funded by foreign countries with the sole objective of destabilizing the strong culture of Sri Lanka which is tolerant and blended with interreligious [sic] and ethnicity, are behind the present crisis. In fact, they have been successful in putting the "cross" against other religions. ... Therefore it is submitted that this Anti Conversion Bill is needed as a foundation for all traditional temples, churches, Kovils [independent Hindu temples] and Mosques together to dispel the fear and to strengthen the religious harmony we have had so far by nipping in the bud of the action of these fundamentalists.[67]

In the intervenient petitioners' arguments, then, the primacy of Buddhism expressed in the JHU bill (and in their reading of the constitution) referred not only to its demographic primacy, but also to its essential role in producing a tolerant, harmonious "strong culture of Sri Lanka."

Conscience and Conversion

Taken in comparative perspective, the debates over the meaning of Buddhism's "foremost place" are, perhaps, not that surprising. After all, litigants and courts throughout the world use similarly multivalent constitutional provisions – provisions that also reflect "incompletely theorized" or "incremental" constitutional bargains.[68] Somewhat more surprising, however, is the fact that litigants engaged in polarizing disputes over issues about which the constitution's framers showed strong agreement, even consensus. There were no debates among Sri Lankan

---

[65] Written Submissions, SC (SD) 4/2004, Intervenient Petitioner, Ven. Omalpe Sobhita Thero, p. 2. (And repeated verbatim by almost all intervenient petitioners. See note above.) Note: The version of the constitution of Ireland used to prove their point was obsolete.

[66] Written Submissions, SC (SD) 12/2004, Intervening Petitioner, Ven. Medagama Dhammananda Thero Society For Conservation Of Buddhism, Asgiri Maha Viharaya, p. 4.

[67] Ibid., pp. 4–5.

[68] Lerner, *Making Constitutions in Deeply Divided Societies.* Sunstein, "Incompletely Theorized Agreements."

FREEDOM OF CONSCIENCE AS A POSITIVE FREEDOM 243

constitution drafters – both in 1970–1972 and in 1977–1978 – over fundamental rights protections for "freedom of thought, conscience and religion" which would be embodied in Article 10 of the 1978 Constitution. This language was taken directly, and without disagreement, from the International Covenant on Civil and Political Rights. Yet, over the course of the conversion bill case, even this core principle of constitutional consensus came to be split. Both groups of petitioners agreed that conscience was a private, internal domain of personal beliefs. Nevertheless, the demands of constitutional litigation pushed litigants toward adopting opposing positions on how conscience functioned. Opponents of the bill treated freedom of conscience as a positive freedom to make decisions about one's own religiosity; defenders of the bill glossed it as a negative freedom from external "fetters" on one's mind. Over the course of the case, freedom of conscience underwent a thorough process of redefinition by opposing groups of lawyers. Litigants and observers used these competing glosses not only to rationalize opposing stances on the constitutionality of the JHU bill, but to confirm and naturalize the existence of a deeper and starker clash of worldviews between Christians and Buddhists and between the West and Asia. Through constitutional litigation, freedom of conscience – a legal rubric whose importance had been widely affirmed – became a rubric that confounded compromise by giving the conflicts over conversion an air of universality and inevitability. Litigation transformed a shared principle of agreement into a principle of polarization.

Freedom of Conscience as a Positive Freedom

For opponents of the bill, affirming the internal, private qualities of conscience made legal sense in two ways: it rendered impracticable the assessment and enforcement of an offense against conversion, and it rendered impossible the idea of an "unethical conversion." In the first instance, opponents argued that because the "content, substance, relative merit and accuracy" of conscience were matters purely "subjective, personal and intangible," judges or state officials could not truly assess or manage conscience.[69] It was, therefore, impossible to do what the JHU

---

[69] SC (SD) 7/2004, p. 3 (and repeated *verbatim* in other mainline church and Catholic submissions, as above). See also: Written Submission, 15/2004, A Welikala, pp. 2–3; Written Submissions, 22/2004, V Tamilmaran, pp. 3–4.

244 CONSTITUTIONAL CONVERSIONS

bill purported to do. One could not police shifts in citizens' beliefs.[70] In attempting to prosecute violations of freedom of conscience, opponents argued, the proposed bill actually undermined that freedom in four ways. First, by limiting the ways in which religious ideas could be spread, it limited the range of beliefs to which citizens were exposed.[71] Second, by labeling certain types of religious choices as the product of "forcible" (and thus illegitimate) conversions, it denied citizens' powers to "make a personal choice as to what religious beliefs they should adopt, retain, discard, affirm, amend, approve, reject or endorse."[72] Third, by requiring that converts (and/or those who conducted conversion ceremonies) report religious conversions to government authorities, it violated citizens' rights to keep their religious beliefs "private" and not subject them to the "coercive machinery of the State."[73] Fourth, by specifying persons who were particularly vulnerable to conversion, the JHU bill denied the universality of freedom of thought, conscience and religion.[74] For petitioners against the bill, then, freedom of conscience was a positive freedom, the society-wide *freedom to* encounter different religious views – to adopt, modify or refuse them – as well as to keep them private.

In the second instance, opponents of the bill argued that if conscience was voluntary, internal and private, then the very idea of "forcible" conversions appeared logically impossible. If "true" religious beliefs were purely internal, beyond the reach of others, then "true" changes in religious conscience had to be internal acts, personal self-realized changes – real conversions had to be "voluntary, internal and enacted

---

[70] Written Submissions, SC (SD) 7/2007, pp. 3–4 (and repeated *verbatim* in other mainline church and Catholic submissions, as above).

[71] See also: Written Submissions, SC (SD)10/2004, R M B Senanayake, p. 2.

[72] SC (SD) 7/2004, p. 11 (and repeated *verbatim* in other mainline church and Catholic submissions, as above). As described in another submission, this amounted to tampering with one's "thought processes" and "autonomy of decision." Written Submissions, SC (SD) 5/2004, Godfrey Yogarajah of NCEASL, p. 8.

[73] SC (SD) 7/2004, p. 11 (and repeated *verbatim*, as above).

[74] "All human beings have an equal right to freely determine their own religions according to their subjective preferences, irrespective of their gender, level of education, social and economic status. To assume that by belonging to any of the classes set out in Schedule 1 of the Bill some adults are less competent than others to decipher what religion they should follow is inconsistent with, contravenes and violates Article 10, 12(1) and 12(2) of the Constitution." SC (SD) 7/2004, p. 5, (and repeated *verbatim*, as above).

FREEDOM OF CONSCIENCE AS A NEGATIVE FREEDOM   245

by the convert not by the proselytizers."[75] Far from a "change of label," *bona fide* religious conversions connoted "a spiritual experience," "an inward experience of faith" that could not be discerned from "external evidence."[76] In this argument, "real" or "authentic" conversions contrasted with "nominal" or "formal" conversions. The first was invisible and impossible for outsiders to assess; the second was observable – "signaling to the world outside a mere nominal identification of one's religious beliefs," – but "a mere illusion ... of no spiritual value or benefit to the evangelist or pastor or to the subject convert who participates in the 'conversion-exercise.'"[77] An "unethical" conversion was therefore a bogus conversion, which "no sensible Christian would tolerate, endorse or encourage."[78] However, assessing whether or not a conversion was unethical remained a practical impossibility.

Freedom of Conscience as a Negative Freedom

Arguing for an internalized conscience served a different purpose for Buddhist supporters of the JHU bill. For them, asserting the private, personal, internal character of conscience meant that conscience was especially precious and fragile, and therefore uniquely vulnerable to violation by outside influences. That is, the intimacy of conscience led *not* to the idea that it was impossible to police but to the idea that it was essential to defend. Supporters of the JHU bill took as

---

[75] Written Submissions, SC (SD) 5/2004 and 6/2004, Godfrey Yogarajah and NCEASL, p. 3.

[76] Ibid., p. 1.

[77] Ibid., pp. 2–3. The submission also stated: "[T]he external and visible evidence of the conversion phenomenon is such that as far as external appearances go, it is not humanly possible in all cases to distinguish with certainty the genuine and authentic conversions to the Christian faith from those which are a sham, especially where the allegation is that they were the result of various allurements held out to those who were converted. In consequence the penal provisions in the Bill and the machinery in the Bill provided for enforcement have such a broad spectrum of effect that they will strike at or hit both the genuine and as well the fraudulent conversions. The enforcement provisions of the Bill will be capable of destroying willy nilly, the most precious freedoms given by Article 10 ..." Ibid., pp. 3–4.

[78] Ibid., p. 3. "It is absurd to suggest that any religious group conscious of its scriptural task and which has at heart the spiritual welfare of its members will resort to force or fraud or bribery to bring others into their fold. That would be a kind of hypocrisy. A forced conversion or a coerced conversion is a meaningless exercise, an unworthy exercise, a meaningless exercise as far as any responsible persons engaged in evangelism are concerned." Ibid., p. 3; See also: Written Submissions, SC (SD) 13/2004, Fr. Ananda Withana (Parish Priest, Saint Joseph's Church, Negambo), p. 2.

246   CONSTITUTIONAL CONVERSIONS

valid the bill's definition of conversion – an action through which proselytizers altered the consciences of others. Somewhat like Christian petitioners who distinguished true from false conversions, Buddhist supporters of the bill distinguished acceptable evangelism from "unethical proselytizing." In acceptable evangelism, evangelists presented ideas to another person's conscience in such a way that potential converts could either accept or reject them. In the case of "unethical" or "forcible" proselytizing (leading to "forcible conversion"), proselytizers imposed new ideas onto another person's conscience in a way that undercut their ability to choose freely. In this binary, freedom of conscience represented a negative freedom, as *freedom from* outside impositions on "sober reflection," "consideration" and "free thinking."[79] According to this argument, "[t]he question is not whether the converted is given a free choice of religions . . . the question is whether conversion by use of force, fraud and allurement . . . would interfere with that freedom of choice of religions."[80]

To persuade the court of the need for conversion legislation, litigants argued that free conscience denoted the total absence of conditions that might bias decision-making. These conditions included especially freedom from those "coercive" factors outlined in the JHU bill: "force," "fraud" or "allurement." Force, the submissions argued, affected conscience through altering it by fear, either fear of physical force or "divine displeasure." Fraud compromised freedom of conscience in that it involved the willful misrepresentation of reality to other persons such that they made ill-informed choices based on false information. Allurement entailed the swaying of conscience through enticing another with promises of material rewards if he/she alters his/her beliefs; this practice (quoting one of the incorporation decisions) placed a "fetter in the path" of one's free choice insofar as it compromised one's ability to assess belief, by contaminating it with worldly calculations of wealth.[81] In the logic of the intervening petitioners' submissions, the JHU bill did not

---

[79] Written Submissions, SC (SD) 4/2004, Intervenient Petitioner, Ven. Omalpe Sobhita Thero, p. 24. The submission makes a distinction between the Indian Constitution which guarantees the "freedom of conscience" and the Sri Lankan Constitution which guarantees the "freedom of thought," insisting thought is much broader than conscience, and glossing it as "the process or power or manner of thinking, faculty of reason, sober reflection, consideration etc."

[80] Written Submissions, SC (SD) 4/2004, Intervenient Petitioner, Ven. Omalpe Sobhita Thero, p. 24. (And repeated *verbatim* by almost all intervenient petitioners.)

[81] Ibid., pp. 10–11.

FREEDOM OF CONSCIENCE AS A NEGATIVE FREEDOM 247

place impediments on the legitimate act of "expressing" or "teaching" one's religion. It blocked certain illegitimate techniques of "improper proselytism"[82] and those blocks defended freedom of conscience.[83] Put differently, freedom of thought, conscience and religion (as embodied in Article 10 of the Constitution) depended upon the "freedom to choose ... [through] *spontaneous* volition, to make an informed decision which is *not encumbered*, subverted or corrupted in any manner whatsoever by *external* stimulus." It was, therefore, the duty of the state to make sure that freedom to choose could be "preserved and maintained in its *purest* and *most pristine* form."[84]

To make this argument about the structure of conscience even more legally persuasive, supporters of the bill portrayed acts of proselytizing by Christians as aggressive "manifestations" of religion designed to manipulate the minds of would-be converts. Buddhist supporters of the bill, in this way, strategically reduced the complex issue of conversion to two basic competing constitutional rights, the right to "manifest" one's religion versus the right to "have" a religion: "Christians engaged in conversion claim their freedom of expression and the freedom to manifest their religion in worship, observance, practice and teaching [Art. 14(1)(e)], whilst Buddhists and the people of other religions who are being subject[ed] to proselytism complain that their freedom of thought, conscience and religion including the freedom to have or to adopt a religion or belief of their choice [Art. 10] is being intruded upon by these Christian groups."[85] Analyzed in this way, Buddhist interveners insisted upon an obvious outcome: Buddhists'

---

[82] Here, the submissions were referring to a term was used in two cases, one argued before the Indian Supreme Court and one argued before the European Court of Human Rights, respectively: *Rev. Stainislaus v. State of Madhya Pradesh and Others* AIR (1977) SC 908 and *Kokkinakis v. Greence* App. No. 14307/88 (Eur. Ct. H.R.) (1993).

[83] This submission quotes from the majority opinion in *Kokkinakis*. Submissions also quoted from the concurrence of Judges Foghel and Loizen: "[There is] a duty imposed on those who are engaged in teaching their religion to respect that of others. Religious tolerance implies respect for the religious beliefs of others. One cannot be deemed to show respect for the right and freedoms of others if one employs means that are intended to entrap someone and dominate his mind in order to convert him. This is impermissible in the civilised societies of the Contracting States. The persistent efforts of some fanatics to convert others to their own beliefs by using unacceptable psychological techniques on people, which amount in effect to coercion."

[84] Written Submissions, Intervenient Petitioner, SC (SD) 4/2004, Dr. J M K Jayaweera, President of SUCCESS, p. 2, italics mine.

[85] Written Submissions, SC (SD) 4/2004, Intervenient Petitioner, Ven. Omalpe Sobhita Thero, p. 29. (And repeated *verbatim* by almost all Intervenient Petitioners.)

248 CONSTITUTIONAL CONVERSIONS

rights to freedom of conscience were absolute; proselytizers' rights to "manifest" their religion were subject to limits. By the legal algebra of Sri Lanka's constitution, the first would always trump the second.

Competing Universals: Religious Conflict, Conflicting Religions

The legal battle over the JHU bill constituted a dispute between discrete groups of petitioners. (The JHU's introduction of a conversion bill was, after all, an act motivated by and contextualized within a distinctive Buddhist politics in the context of Sri Lanka's civil war.[86]) However, as the JHU-bill case progressed, the language of legal argument projected debates over conversion into universalizing terms. When refracted through the court, historically situated and politically contextualized contests were recoded as global conflicts over universal norms and absolute rights and freedoms. While some petitioners commented on the exclusionary politics of the JHU as a political party, most arguments against the bill were framed as protests against the bill's violation of broader abstract principles embodied in Sri Lanka's constitution or liberal rights theory more generally. This included principles of generally: freedom of religion, freedom of conscience, pluralism and democracy. Similarly, those who supported the JHU bill claimed to defend those same principles. Litigants advocated competing versions of liberalism – alternative ways of defining religious freedom, conversion and conscience. The result of this process of upwards-abstraction was the reification of opposing, purportedly irreconcilable normative regimes – Christian vs. Buddhist, Western vs. Asian – that obscured any existing middle ground and rendered compromise or agreement on a single set of principles impossible.

Those who petitioned against the JHU bill argued that freedom of conscience meant something different to Christians than it did to Buddhists. The mainline churches argued that it was not just the conscience of would-be converts that was violated by the JHU bill; the proposed restrictions violated the conscience of *proselytizers* as well. To understand this, they argued, judges needed to recognize a particular religious doctrine: Christians had a divinely ordained

---

[86] Berkwitz, "Religious Conflict and the Politics of Conversion in Sri Lanka." DeVotta and Stone, "Jathika Hela Urumaya and Ethno-religious Politics in Sri Lanka." Deegalle, "Politics of the Jathika Hela Urumaya Monks: Buddhism and Ethnicity in Contemporary Sri Lanka."

duty to "inform others of the biblical divine truths regarding forgiveness by God and deliverance from sin."[87] As such, Christian proselytizing could not be understood simply as a secondary expression of conscience or a "manifestation" of belief. It was, rather, a necessary concomitant of conscience – a spontaneous "witnessing" of one's devotion.[88] Some Christian petitioners insisted that, for Christians, freedom of conscience must extend not only to the internal domain of beliefs, but to the external presentation of those beliefs because, for devout Christians, the two remain indistinguishable. Christians' outward actions were the direct results of inner piety as well as indications of God working through them. Reflecting several years later, one senior evangelical minister explained:

> I think that this whole thing comes out of a clash of worldviews. You see in the basic Buddhist understanding there is no spirit, you know about spirit? . . . It's very sort of materialistic, now when we say that you have been spiritually transformed how can you be spiritually transformed if you have no spirits, so the argument of their religion is in clash with the argument of ours, you see what I mean. So, naturally they cannot understand it when we say that you have been spiritually transformed, you have enjoyed peace and joy that comes from believing in Christ.[89]

Using this trajectory of argument, the minister explained and justified the inevitability of conflict according to the irreconcilability of religious worldviews. Buddhists' views of proselytizing derive from divergent dogmas concerning the separability of religious belief from "manifestation." Thus, he argued, Buddhists fail to grasp the nature of Christian conversion because of their alternative ways of looking at the world and their "materialistic" vision of the universe.

An even more profound conflict of worldviews was expressed by the lawyer who served as lead counsel for many of the parties who supported the JHU bill.[90] In an interview from 2009 (in the context of further public and parliamentary debate about the JHU bill [see later discussion]), he identified two contrasting paradigms of religious conscience and religious freedom in Buddhist Sri Lanka and the Christian West. In the West, he pointed out, religious freedom tended to focus on "public" freedoms of expression and manifestation, rather than "private" freedoms of thought. In this way, he insisted, Western understandings of religious life differed from those of people in Sri Lanka:

---

[87] SC (SD) 7/2004, p. 8 (and repeated *verbatim*, as above).   [88] Ibid., p. 8.
[89] Interview, February 26, 2009.   [90] Interview, February 4, 2009.

250 CONSTITUTIONAL CONVERSIONS

> Now in a Buddhist country, now there is a little different perspective. In a Buddhist country, for us, freedom of thought is utmost important. [In Christianity], thought is not [important], when you compare with Buddhism ... What god says, [Christians] follow. It's just simple as that. If god tells you to do something, you do it.

> But, in Buddhism, the thought process is very important. So, intrusion into thought is something very sensitive in the Eastern culture, both to Hindus and to Buddhists ... I [will] just give you a small example: Now the West looks at this from the point of view of ... See, it's like going to the supermarket and choosing whatever chocolates that you want. You like bitter chocolate, and you [another person] buy sweet chocolate. And you can eat it, and if you don't like, you can throw it away ... [T]his freedom of choice is looked at from a Christian perspective. Because thought is not important, you taste and see. But for Buddhists, this tasting is a problem because you pollute your mind ... it's not like if you don't like the chocolate you can throw it away, rinse your mouth with some water ... but you pollute your mind ... if you don't like it you can't just erase it from your mind. According to our religion, getting wrong thoughts is resulting in bad karma. So, even for a moment, to have wrong thoughts – and belief in god is one wrong thought – it [will] have consequences to you. Now, that is the philosophical conflict.

In the lawyer's argument, legal contests over the meaning of conscience were symptomatic of much larger conflicts between Buddhism and Christianity, "Eastern culture" versus "the West." In his view, the act of Christian proselytizing appears benign through the Western/Christian approach to freedom of thought (which underscores the desirability of having options from which to choose), but dangerous through the Asian/ Buddhist approach (which underscores the importance of an unperturbed mental state, free from temptation): "For the West, it's freedom of choice. [Choices are] just laid out, like a buffet ... But, for us ... if I don't want something creeping into my mind, or impregnating into my mind, I should be able to stop it."[91]

Both arguments mix assertions about (and reifications of) a religious worldview with a careful legal arithmetic: competing claims about religion make possible competing claims about religious conscience. In the first case, by underscoring the tendency for inner devotion to God to burst forth into expressions of evangelism, the speaker is able to claim as the protection of conscience (which, as I've noted, is entrenched and non-limitable in Sri Lanka's constitution) the protection of particular

[91] Ibid.

types of speech acts. In the second case, by insisting on a particular Buddhist (or "Asian") aversion to unwanted thoughts, the speaker is able to rationalize, under the motive of protecting conscience, restrictions on the contexts in which religious ideas may be introduced or disseminated. In both cases, speakers argue that to protect fundamental rights to freedom of conscience fully, one ought to take into account differences among religious notions of conscience. However, in so doing, each renders one religious system as incommensurable with, or even antagonistic toward, the other. That is, through the process of challenging and supporting the JHU bill, not only did litigants align along religious lines, they also hardened their understandings of religion, by portraying it in terms of fixed, separate, opposing essences.

The Supreme Court Determination

From a procedural standpoint, constitutional review of the JHU bill did exactly what it was supposed to do. It followed the standard prototype of courtroom adjudication by presenting a two-sided dispute over the constitutionality of a parliamentary bill to the mediating "third" of the judges. And it did so with reference to formal, preexisting constitutional rubrics over which judges had explicit authority. However, in doing this, it also cast the issue of conversion in stark and divisive ways: as a conflict over the relationship between Buddhist prerogatives and religious rights, as a debate between those who saw freedom of conscience as a negative versus a positive freedom, as a debate between Buddhists and non-Buddhists. This, in turn, left the judges in a very difficult position for mediation. The litigation was so thorough in its polarization (of people and of interpretations of principles) that it eroded the possibility of identifying acceptable, middle-ground solutions regarding the issues of greatest concern: the question of how constitutional rights ought to be interpreted and apportioned in reference to acts of religious proselytizing. Thus, the very conditions that made constitutional litigation possible – as well as the incentives produced by it – generated a context in which judges could not mediate in any real sense.

The highly polarizing effects of legal argument not only gave the court little room to find common ground, it also exacerbated two external predicaments faced by the judges. These predicaments related to the potential impacts of their decisions in the contexts of local and international politics. As it related to local politics, the polarizing process of litigation forced the court to arbitrate between two equally formidable

252 CONSTITUTIONAL CONVERSIONS

ends of the political spectrum: supporters of populist Buddhist national-ism and minority-rights liberalism, both of whom formed important political constituencies. To affirm the bill's constitutionality would be to alienate the latter; to deny it would be to alienate the former.

As it related to international politics, the JHU-bill case presented judges with an equally poisonous decision. Starting in 2004, a number of foreign governments and human rights groups lobbied the Sri Lankan government to prevent the bill from being enacted. The United States warned about the negative possibilities for aid and trade if the bill were to pass.[92] By ruling the bill unconstitutional, the Supreme Court could avert international sanctions and censure, but doing so would also invite allegations of capitulating to foreign pressure. While not generated by litigation itself, these domestic and international political predicaments deepened on account of the stark presentation of the issue of conversion. As construed by litigants, conversion appeared to be a matter pitting Buddhists against non-Buddhists, Asia against the West, Buddhist pre-rogatives against fundamental rights.

In the end, the demands of constitutional litigation, like the demands of constitutional design, pushed the court toward evasion and equivo-cation. Rather than a strong, clarifying judgment, the Supreme Court drafted a determination that meticulously avoided most of the main interpretive conflicts presented by litigants. The court offered neither an interpretation of the Buddhism Chapter, nor of freedom of con-science. It did not assess the state's respective duties to protect Buddhism *vis-à-vis* assuring fundamental rights for all citizens. The court offered no clarification on the question of whether state agents were in a suitable position to assess whether a conversion was "forcible" or not. The single topic on which the court did exercise interpretive authority was one

---

[92] Interview with senior official in the State Department in Colombo, April 16, 2009. The mandate for U.S. intervention came under the U.S. International Religious Freedom Act (IRFA), a statute passed in 1998 which created a special branch of the State Department designed to monitor the state of "religious freedom" worldwide and to use political and economic sanctions to place pressure on "Countries of Particular Concern" that violated religious freedom. At a roundtable conference for members of the Sri Lankan media, in June 2004, the American Ambassador, warned that "the issue of conversions ... must be dealt with very carefully in order to preserve the rights of individuals" when he was asked whether the passage of the JHU bill would "seriously affect" Sri Lanka's proposed Free Trade Agreement and trade quotas with America. "Religious Conversions: An issue already in Sri Lanka-US relations: US Ambassador," *The Island,* June 28, 2004.

about which many of the parties had agreed: the court affirmed that "forcible" conversion threatened one's freedom of "thought, conscience and religion."[93] This point had been acknowledged not only by Buddhists, but by Christian petitioners as well, who had asserted that using coercive or deceitful means to proselytize offended not only potential converts, but Christians as well. (For them, "real" conversion could never be "forcible" conversion.) In addition, the court insisted that the procedures specified for reporting and prosecuting conversions were unconstitutional.[94] In all, the court affirmed the constitutionality of the bill's aims (the prohibition of "forcible" conversion), while denying the constitutionality of the means of enforcement.[95] In so doing, it left unmediated most of the grand narratives and polarized claims produced for the court by the petitioners, while evading most of the key, contentious issues.

Similar evasions did not occur in the media. Newspapers leading up to and following the JHU-bill case were filled with polemical articles and editorials suffused with constitutional language designed to justify one side or the other. Virtually every argument that appeared in court submissions also appeared in popular media. The constitutional framing of conversion – as a contest over freedom of conscience and Buddhism's foremost place – also framed discussions of conversion outside of courts. Unlike courtroom contests, however, no one in the public domain could cut short these agonistic constitutional arguments. Over time, constitutional language, in all its abstractness and inflexibility, became a dominant frame through which public discussions about conversion were held.

Polarizing Conclusions

By constitutionalizing conversion, Sri Lankans took an already-provocative issue and made it even more contentious. By turning to

---

[93] References here from: SC (SD) 2/2004–22/2004, Determination Prohibition of Forcible Conversion of Religion Bill, published in: Government of Sri Lanka, *Hansard Debates*. Colombo: Government Press, August 17, 2004, pp. 1194–1199.

[94] These included: the types of people who can legally accuse another of "forcible conversion," the requirements that all proselytizers and converts (or those who participate in conversion ceremonies) report conversions to the government, and the discretionary powers given to ministers to add new categories of "vulnerable" people and institute new, related rules and regulations.

[95] Schedule 1, no. 11, Clause 6.

constitutional law, lawyers, politicians, civil society groups, journalists and others transformed an issue of broad concern for a variety of groups into an issue that split Buddhists from non-Buddhists and repelled compromises. Prior to 2004, to talk about reforming and critiquing methods of proselytizing was not necessarily to promote the interests of Buddhists, nor was it to take a position on the privileged status of Buddhism on the island. Moreover, anxieties over conversion were not always expressed in such rigid terms. Through litigation, conversion was transformed from a historical threat to a normative threat. The turn to constitutional categories moved analysis away from the particular, local circumstances and toward general, translocal principles. At no one moment was a single, specific case of "unethical conversion" brought forth as an example. No "unethically converted" victim appeared in court, no affidavit from such persons was found among the submissions.[96] Clashing bodies were not sublimated into clashing arguments. Legal argumentation translated and justified social strife in terms that made it appear even more inevitable and irresolvable.

The turn to constitutional law translated popular concerns over conversion into polarized battles of reified worldviews, abstract ideas and hypothetical circumstances: Buddhist primacy versus religious equality, Buddhist worldviews versus Christian worldviews, Asian thought versus Western thought, independence versus (neo)colonialism, the threat of local majoritarianism versus the threat of foreign powers. It even generated conflicts over the meaning and goals of law itself. At certain moments, law was lauded as a neutral instrument through which justice was to be accomplished and religions were to be rendered free. In other moments, law was condemned as a discriminatory instrument, a tool for Buddhists to oppress non-Buddhists (as certain local and international opponents of the bill pointed out); or, as a tool that reflected the influence (and international hegemony) of Western norms or Christianized understandings of religion (as supporters of the JHU bill occasionally pointed out).

It would be easy to dismiss the history constitutionalizing conversion in Sri Lanka as exceptional. After all, the issue itself was highly contentious, the court case was highly public, and the passions aroused were

---

[96] There were newspaper reports presented as evidence, but these reports were not used to identify actual victims.

extraordinarily deep. However, the same features that affect the JHU-bill case are also at play in other constitutional contexts. That is, a study of constitutionalizing conversion in Sri Lanka illuminates features common to many jurisdictions. Throughout the world, people use constitutional policies toward religion to address contentious issues that affect society in complex and crosscutting ways. Religious conversion is one, but there are others: the public display of religious symbols, the ritual use of banned substances, conscientious objection to military service, and many more issues. As with the case of conversion in Sri Lanka, constitutional language and litigation frame and arrange conflicts about these issues in ways that conform to the triadic prototype of the courts.

The problem is not simply that constitutional law misconstrues social life. These dynamics are well documented in critical legal studies,[97] and, in some cases, even celebrated: scholars have credited the evasiveness of judicial opinions (their avoidance of comprehensive, categorical claims) as a one of law's "virtues."[98] The problem is that the process of constitutional litigation – and its incentives, procedures, discursive requirements, choreographies, etc. – progressively polarize and raise the stakes of conflicts by winnowing away the multifaceted world of facts that form the backdrop and (as I would have it) the salient and indispensible context for these conflicts. In their place, they foreground a limited set of fixed, rigid, abstract legal norms. The more thorough-going the attorneys' arguments, the more thorough this process of winnowing away and abstraction. In this way, constitutional litigation, properly done, transforms the terms of dispute in ways that corrode parties' abilities to recuperate or identify contextual solutions or compromises. Moreover, and more worryingly, once the constitutional imagination colonizes popular discourse, these effects extend further – to life-worlds outside the courtrooms.

Evasive Epilogues

Looking at the history of constitutionalizing conversion in Sri Lanka, one is struck by a profound irony built into the structure of constitutional

---

[97] Berger, *Law's Religion.* Bruno Latour, *The Making of Law: An Ethnography of the Conseil D'Etat* (Cambridge: Polity Press, 2010).
[98] Berger, "The Virtues of Law in the Politics of Religious Freedom."

256   CONSTITUTIONAL CONVERSIONS

adjudication (and, perhaps, courts more generally): the more clearly and comprehensively the dyadic dispute is produced and argued – that is to say, the more successful the parties are in their litigation – the more likely or even necessary it becomes for those charged with mediating the dispute to avoid the key terms of the dispute altogether. Equally revealing are the ways in which this dynamic is intuited and acted upon by governments, even if it is not acknowledged publically. Scholars are not the only ones who recognize the polarizing operations of law on social life. Sri Lanka's government also seemed to recognize this fact, judging from the tactics of evasion that it engaged in – tactics that, while not unusual, are decidedly antagonistic to the rule of law.

Efforts to ratify the JHU bill did not end with the JHU-bill case. Following the case, the Supreme Court sent the bill back to Sri Lanka's parliament for further deliberation and revision. However, almost from the moment it left the court, government officials took steps to avoid further legal debate, aware themselves of the deep political, legal and normative clashes that were now involved. In May 2005, the revised bill received its second reading in parliament, whereupon the government immediately referred it to a special Standing Committee.[99] When, after three and a half years, the Standing Committee issued its report suggesting further alterations to the bill, the government almost immediately directed that the bill be reviewed by another committee, this time a Consultative Committee of the Ministry of Religious Affairs.[100] To date, the Consultative Committee has not released a report, and the bill remains in parliamentary purgatory, having neither been officially expunged from the Orders of Business[101] nor considered in parliament further. The equivocation of constitution drafters, and of the Supreme Court, was thus reproduced further in the tactics of the government. Presumably alarmed by the stark framing of the conversion issue in the JHU-bill case, and the poisonous political dilemmas it presented, the government acted in a manner similar to those charged with drafting and interpreting constitutional law: it equivocated. Although it

---

[99] Hansard, May 6, 2005, 600–608.

[100] www.sundaytimes.lk/090208/News/sundaytimesnews_11.html; www.nation.lk/2009/02/15/news6.htm.

[101] The last listing of the bill I could find on the Order Book of Parliament dates to November 3, 2009 (Sixth Parliament-Fourth Session), where it was Order of Business number 46.

EVASIVE EPILOGUES

did so in its own way, which, ironically, had the effect of trumping the rule of law in acts of sovereign exception.

Tactics of evasion succeeded within the court and the legislature. In these spheres – the domains of law's technical, legal life – equivocation and avoidance were used successfully to muffle the now highly polarized terms of the dispute. However, this evasion took place only after the terms of conflict had already been recast in more rigid ways as a result of their translation into constitutional (and therefore litigation-friendly) categories. The delaying tactics of judges and ministers began only *after* litigants had dug in with their arguments.

Outside of these technical spheres, in the societal life of law – law's presence in media, public discourse and everyday discussions among citizens – evasions of this type could not and did not occur. Once the process of constitutionalizing conversion started in legislatures and courts, it could not be easily stalled on street corners and teashops. As a consequence of legal action, popular interpretations of conversion were progressively captured in a constitutional imaginary. In the months and years that followed, the JHU-bill case stimulated the creation of other laws that attempted to deal with the issue of religious conversion. Weeks after the Supreme Court determination, the JHU introduced another Private Member's Bill that would amend the constitution to make Buddhism the "official Religion of the Republic" and explicitly to make it illegal to "convert [a] Buddhist" or "to spread other forms of worship among the Buddhist [*sic*]."[102] That bill was challenged and ruled unconstitutional.[103] Not long after, a commission was formed by the All-Ceylon Buddhist Congress to inquire into the matter of conversion. Among the

---

[102] In the JHU's proposed version, Article 9 would consist of six separate parts: "9.1. The official Religion of the Republic is Buddhism. Other forms of religions and worship may be practiced in peace and harmony with the Buddha Sasana. 9.2. All inhabitants of the Republic shall have the right to free exercise of their worship. The exercise of worship shall not contravene public order or offend morals. 9.3. The State shall foster, protect, patronise [the] Buddha Sasana and promote good understanding and harmony among the followers of other forms of worship as well as encourage the application of religious principles to create virtue and develop quality of life. 9.4. The inhabitants of the Republic professing Buddhism are bound to bring up their children the same. 9.5. To convert Buddhist [*sic*] into other forms of worship or to spread other forms of worship among the Buddhist [*sic*] is prohibited. 9.6 No person may be forced to join a religious community, to conduct a religious act or to participate in religious education."
"Nineteenth Amendment to the Constitution (Private Member's Bill)." *The Gazette of the Democratic Socialist Republic of Sri Lanka, Supplement*, Part Two, June 8, 2012.
[103] SC (SD) No. 32/2004 *Regarding the Nineteenth Amendment to the Constitution (Bill)*.

258 CONSTITUTIONAL CONVERSIONS

commission's key recommendations was the introduction of conversion legislation similar to that of the JHU and the Buddhist-Hindu Committee.

A further push toward constitutionalizing occurred among the lawyers who opposed the bill. Following the JHU-bill case, many of those lawyers drafted their own legislation, which they hoped would be introduced as a Private Member's Bill.[104] Their new bill, entitled "The Thought, Conscience and Religion Act" prohibited conversion by means of force, fraud or allurement (which it defined in detail, through specific illustrations in an "explanations" section),[105] but specified a different mechanism for enforcing those restrictions. Rather than making conversion a police issue, they proposed to establish an "Inter-Religious Council"[106] empowered to assess and suggest penalties for misconduct.

Similar processes have also taken place outside of Colombo and beyond the discussions of Sri Lanka's legal elites. A particularly vivid example is given by Oshan Fernando, an anthropologist who studied the lives of Christian evangelical communities in southeastern Sri Lanka. Describing the evolution of a political rally in southeastern Sri Lanka organized by local political activists to protest conversions, Fernando quotes a regional political leader as declaring to the crowd: "The constitution of this country states that Buddhism is the foremost religion in this country and is to be protected by the state. As the state official in charge of this area I am duty bound to abide by those fundamentals."[107] Fernando's narrative portrays vividly the ways in which public discourse about conversion has been mediated through constitutional terms. These terms direct listeners' attention away from the local, contextual and social and toward the absolute and authoritative language of law.

*

This is pyrrhic constitutionalism in action. Success in drafting constitutional clauses concerning religion and success in invoking and

---

[104] Interview with one lawyer involved, June 29, 2009.

[105] Copy of most recent draft in possession of author.

[106] Section 4; it would consist of seven Buddhist monks, four Hindu gurus, four Muslim Moulavis and four Christian religious leaders (the Archbishop of Colombo or his nominee, the Chairman or a nominee of the Catholic Bishops Conference, the Chairman or a nominee of the National Christian Council, and the Chairman or a nominee of the National Christian Evangelical Alliance of Sri Lanka) and two others who "do not belong to any of the religions."

[107] As quoted in Fernando, *The Effects of Evangelical Christianity on State Formation in Sri Lanka*, 315.

implementing those clauses in courts and public life have led to the further deepening of the very tensions those clauses were meant to address. The solution has become the problem. Evasive turns of phrase designed to bridge disagreements about religion among constitution-drafters have been treated as firm guidelines for ordering and harmonizing society. In so doing, they have reactivated many of the same debates faced by constitution drafters, while also leading to similar tactics of evasion and equivocation. Fluid and multifaceted social problems have been recoded in fixed and inflexible categories. Broad and common concerns have been reduced to binary disputes. Compromises and creative solutions have been ignored or overwritten. Conflict has been entrenched in the entrenched provisions of law. The constitutionalizing of religious tensions has confounded courts and legislatures, leaving evasion as the preferred, and perhaps only, viable option.

The sources of pyrrhic constitutionalism lie not in legal personnel but in the demands and strictures of legal processes. Pyrrhic constitutionalism results from the apparatus of constitutional adjudication itself and the structures, incentives and requirements through which claims must be made, argued and presented. It will not surprise those familiar with socio-legal studies in other places that, in interviews about the JHU-bill case, almost all lawyers acknowledged vast gaps between what they felt obliged to write in petitions and what they felt would best address the social tensions in question. Moreover, when presented with my argument about the polarizing effects of litigation, most legal professionals with whom I spoke seemed unsurprised, and, in some cases, felt it to be a rather a pedestrian observation. Reading constitutional adjudication in this way may be anathema to committed philosophical liberals. However, it is astonishingly banal for many of the legal professionals involved.

At the same time, lawyers, judges and litigants also point out that constitutional claims and litigation remain, nonetheless, one of the few ways for politically disempowered actors, including small groups such as religious minorities, to gain state recognition and redress. For many disadvantaged groups, constitutional claims – warts and all – remain the best of a variety of poor options (and in some cases the only option) for responding to discrimination, assault, vandalism, intimidation and other harms.

Highlighting pyrrhic constitutionalism is not the same thing as calling for an abandoning of constitutional law. It is, rather, to call for greater awareness and honesty about what constitutional law can and cannot do when it comes to dealing with conflicts that appear to center on matters of religion – or, rather, *what it also does* while authorizing and adjudicating religious rights and freedoms. The creation of constitutional protections for religion (or Buddhism) may codify and entrench certain widely held normative commitments (or, at least, feasible rhetorical expressions of them), but it also encourages claims and disputes about religion (or Buddhism) in national courts. This raises the stakes of those disputes while also limiting the language for dealing with them. Constitutional litigation may provide an opportunity for disempowered groups to gain redress, but it also leads to the deepening and sharpening of conflicts among religious groups, and the framing of conflicts in abstract and irreconcilable terms. It may lead to lawfare rather than resolution. To point this out is not to condemn constitutional practice. It is to inject a spirit of pragmatism and sobriety into our understandings of it.

8

Conclusion

The Costs of Constitutional Law

On September 5, 2008, judges and lawyers in Colombo found themselves confronted by the very problem they had worked so hard to avoid, and it happened in the most public setting imaginable. In Sri Lanka's highest court, in front of the island's most senior judicial official, a group of Buddhist monks ignored the usual tactics designed to avoid a standoff between monks and judges:[1] arriving early to a Supreme Court hearing, they sat down in one of the building's many courtrooms and waited purposefully for the Chief Justice to enter.

The monks had come for the case of Ven. Pannala Pannaloka Thero, a Buddhist monk from Colombo, who was charged with violating a Supreme Court order prohibiting the use of loudspeakers after 10 p.m. Ven. Pannaloka's offense was that he conducted, without a permit, an all-night ceremony in which he used electronic speakers to broadcast Buddhist prayers. In the weeks leading up to the case, Ven. Pannaloka had been summoned to the Supreme Court to face charges of contempt of court. Having failed to turn up on the required date, the monk had been remanded into custody. Ven. Pannaloka now faced two weeks in prison and was appearing before a three-justice bench requesting bail.[2]

Having learned about Ven. Pannaloka's case through the national media and local rumors, several Buddhist monastic organizations expressed outrage. They objected not only to Ven. Pannaloka's remanding, but to the fact of his being arrested for engaging in a Buddhist ritual. On the day of the bail hearing, between 50 and 100 Buddhist monks arrived in the courtroom where Ven. Pannaloka's case was being heard. In a scheme coordinated ahead of time, the assembled

---

[1] This is described in the opening section of the Introduction (Chapter 1) of this book.

[2] Judges' Notes, September 1, 2008, pp. 3–4. SC (FR) Application 38/2005. *Alhaj M.T.M, Ashik and others v. R.P.S. Bandula and others.* The Supreme Court's "noise pollution" order was the outcome of a fundamental rights petition brought by the trustees of one mosque in southern Sri Lanka against the trustees of another mosque nearby. For an analysis of this case and the matters that preceded and followed, see: Schonthal, "Environments of Law."

262   CONCLUSION: THE COSTS OF CONSTITUTIONAL LAW

monks sat in defiance as the justices took the bench, conspicuously transgressing the standard protocols of courtroom etiquette. The meaning of their actions was obvious: it was the judges who ought to stand up for them.

The Chief Justice, angered by the display, instructed the monks to follow the script usually employed by monastic litigants. Addressing Ven. Pannaloka's lawyer, he insisted that the assembled monks should leave and reenter the courtroom again. The seated monks refused. When Pannaloka's lawyer introduced a motion for bail, the Chief Justice dismissed it. The proceedings ended abruptly and, shortly thereafter, the saffron crowd walked out to a mass of waiting reporters.[3]

*

For a period of weeks, the Supreme Court drama was headline news in Sri Lanka. Journalists and bloggers commented eagerly on the events. In their writings, critics and sympathizers of the monks' actions offered alternative interpretations of who was right, who was wrong, and why. One set of critics condemned the protesting monks for their symbolic indication that, as clergy, they were above the constitution and the laws of the state. "Law is law," argued many commentators in one particularly active blog: the obligations of Buddhist monks to adhere to civil law were no different from the obligations of any other litigant.[4] A second set of voices condemned the monks' refusal to stand, but based their rationale less on the priority of civil law over religious norms than on the state's constitutional duties to protect all citizens and religions equally. From this perspective, the fault of the monks lay not in their failure to acquiesce to the "un-Buddhist" requirements of civil procedure, but in their failure to make use of the well-known method of evasion offered to protect monastic propriety – in this case, a method demanded explicitly

---

[3] Chitra Weerarathne, "SC Refuses Bail for Monk Noise Pollution Case," *The Island,* September 9, 2008.

[4] "Law is Law – SL chief justice" www.elakiri.com/forum/archive/index.php/t-103446.html (Accessed May 22, 2012). For similar debates, see also www.lankaenews.com/Sinhala/news.php?id=6441 (Accessed June 20, 2012). This opinion was also voiced by the *mahānāyaka*-s, chief prelates, of the Malvatu and Asgiri chapters of the Siyam Nikāya in Kandy, the oldest monastic fraternities in the country. By standing for judges, the Asgiri *mahānāyaka* argued, monks were not showing deference to a member of the laity, but to the institution of the judiciary. Nadia Fazlulhaq, "JHU Sounds Out New Act to Beat Loudspeaker Rule," *The Sunday Times,* September 9, 2008. See also: "Equality Before the Law, Both Monastics and Lay People," *Daily Mirror,* September 8, 2008.

CONCLUSION: THE COSTS OF CONSTITUTIONAL LAW   263

by the Chief Justice himself.[5] A third group of interpreters defended the defiant actions of the monks by denouncing the biased nature of civil law itself. These critics condemned the country's code of civil procedure as "alien" laws imposed on the population since the colonial era. Those laws, they argued, not only violated Buddhist custom (namely, the custom that laypersons should stand to greet monks), they also flew in the face of the island's current constitutional duties to promote Buddhism.[6]

Energetic public debates regarding the monks' protest exposed the endurance of serious disagreements regarding the legal management of religion in Sri Lanka – disagreements that lawyers normally obscured or avoided by delaying monks' entrance into courtrooms. In these debates, one saw the presence of ongoing conflicts concerning the relationship between religious and civil norms, between the state's obligations to Buddhism and to other religions, and between the limits of state sovereignty and monastic autonomy. One even saw criticisms, reminiscent of critiques of the 1948 Constitution, that Sri Lanka's legal institutions contained colonial vestiges and therefore ought to be redesigned in order to better protect Buddhism. When the usual tactics for avoiding the monk-judge standoff failed, the persistence and depth of conflicts over religion became visible. Sri Lanka's constitution was used to justify all sides.

[5] Vimukti Yapa, "A Monk's Arrest That Stumped the JHU," *The Sunday Leader*, September 14, 2008: 1. Shortly after, new, more formal modes of accommodation were proposed. The president suggested building separate "viewing rooms" for clergy from which they could view the proceedings of trials on closed circuit television. A second suggestion, which has yet to be implemented fully, was to create separate courtrooms for monks. Franklin R Satyapalan, "Buddhist Clergy Urges Setting Up Sangha Courts," *The Island*, September 9, 2008. "Separate Rooms for Buddhist Monks in Sri Lanka Courts," *The Colombo Page*, September 9, 2008.

  Interestingly, the technique is seen not only to protect monks, but to protect pious Buddhist judges. According to one monk in Kandy whom I interviewed: "Generally in the court monks are permitted to go in after the judge is seated. The reason is when a monk comes in, lay people have to stand up. Even the president stands up when we go into the president's house and welcomes us by worshipping. That is to show respect. But the tradition in the court is that everyone has to stand up when the judge comes in. That is to show respect to the law. Everyone inside the court has to stand up when the judge arrives. If a monk happens to stand up while inside the court when the judge arrives, it is not suitable. It will be embarrassing to the judge as well." Interview with Ven. S Mangala, Kandy, August 15, 2009.

[6] Vimukti Yapa, "A Monk's Arrest That Stumped the JHU," *The Sunday Leader*, September 14, 2008. Kelum Bandara and Yohan Perera, "Monks Never Stand Up, Even Before Kings: JHU," *Daily Mirror*, September 10, 2008.

264 CONCLUSION: THE COSTS OF CONSTITUTIONAL LAW

The Constitutional Management of Religion in Sri Lanka –
Through the Lens of Constitutional Microhistory

Contemporary societies are filled with diverse and diverging claims about religion. In our constitutional age, we imagine constitutional law to mediate those claims in both senses of the verb: we imagine that constitutions will represent those claims in public life, while also reconciling and arbitrating among them. In Sri Lanka, as in many parts of the world, political leaders have relied on constitutional law to protect, promote and reconcile popular demands made in the name of religion, and they have done so with perseverance and conviction. Those who lobbied for and designed Sri Lanka's current constitutional provisions on religion aimed to better protect the religious rights of all individuals, while also safeguarding the island's most populous religion, Buddhism. At the same time, they attempted to accommodate diverging views: they framed the Buddhism Chapter using rhetoric that avoided contentious questions about the balance between Buddhist prerogatives and fundamental rights and about the relative priority of civil and ecclesiastical authority.

As a legal project, the constitutional management of religion in Sri Lanka has been extensive and has relied closely upon democratic procedures used in many other parts of the world. Constitutional policies for religion underwent years of sustained debate among lawmakers, religious groups and lobbyists from the 1940s to the 1970s. Sri Lanka's eventual constitutional settlement, the Buddhism Chapter, reflects the work of a popularly elected Constituent Assembly along with the considerable input of religious groups, civil society organizations and citizens.[7] That constitutional settlement has been interpreted and applied regularly by Sri Lanka's higher judiciary in a manner that, more often than not, shows independent judgment and restraint.

However, this Sri Lankan project of making and deploying constitutional law has not accomplished what lawmakers, jurists and lobbyists had hoped for or expected. It has neither allayed concerns about religion, nor harmonized them. Constitutional practice has exacerbated the very anxieties and

---

[7] To those who dismiss the Buddhism Chapter for its privileging of the majority religion, it is important to consider not only the commonness of religiously preferential constitutions globally (see Chapter 5 and Chapter 1), but also the fact that in a recent 2,400-person representative poll conducted in all parts of the island, 89% of respondents declared that constitutional protections for Buddhism were either tolerable (3%), acceptable (6%), desirable (23%) or essential (54%). Collin Irwin, *"War and Peace" and the APRC Proposals* (May, 2010).

struggles it was designed to address. Victories in enacting a constitutional settlement on religion have been pyrrhic victories. Instead of bridging diverse claims about the status of Buddhism and the state's role in supporting it, the Buddhism Chapter has created new opportunities and incentives for citizens to make contentious claims about Buddhism and to provoke conflicts over the relationship between Buddhism and the state. Constitutional clauses designed to secure the integrity and well-being of Buddhism have fueled *intra*religious conflicts among Buddhists, raising the stakes of long-standing disputes among Buddhist monks and laypersons over Buddhist orthopraxy and orthodoxy. At the same time, fundamental religious rights, which drafters included, in large part, in order to balance the interests of Buddhists and non-Buddhists, have contributed to sharpening and justifying *inter*religious conflicts. Using constitutional law to represent and reconcile citizens' claims about religion has had a very high cost. It has contributed to the very problems it was intended to resolve.

Of Advocacy and Analysis

Despite the evidence offered in this book, scholars might still be tempted to view the history of Sri Lanka as a story of insufficient constitutionalism, one that reveals considerable, but still inadequate, effort, skill, sincerity or participation in designing and applying constitutional provisions for religion. Or, they might prefer to frame this history as a story of "thin," procedural democracy triumphing over "thick," substantive democracy, of Sri Lankans' superficial commitment to formal processes overwhelming any concern over actual social outcomes.[8] Indeed, like all such systems, Sri Lanka's constitutional democracy is not without flaws. State-sponsored violence, corruption, patronage and other derelictions of justice have accompanied the island's experiences of civil war, violent social uprisings and autocratic presidentialism.[9]

---

[8] Larry Jay Diamond, *Developing Democracy: Toward Consolidation* (Baltimore, MD: Johns Hopkins University Press, 1999). Jean B Elshtain, "Religion and Democracy," *Journal of Democracy* 20, no. 2 (2009): 5–17. This, they would contrast with constitutional democracy in its fully realized, "thick" form, which, as Elshtain puts it, "requires the vote and a genuinely competitive series of election cycles; a pluralistic civil society, meaning a civil society in which religion engages in all aspects of civil life; and the full panoply of human rights, especially negative rights or immunity rights that curb arbitrary state power." Ibid., 15.

[9] Most recently, one might to point to manipulations and excesses of the post-war Rajapaksa regime – including the infamous (and recently reversed) 18th Amendment, in force

266   CONCLUSION: THE COSTS OF CONSTITUTIONAL LAW

However, when it comes to the legal management of religion, dismissing the history of Sri Lanka as a story of insincere or incomplete constitutional practice would be analytically rash. Doing so not only contradicts the evidence contained in the expanded archive of law, but it prematurely judges constitutional practice in Sri Lanka in terms of its ends: it interprets undesirable social phenomena (namely the persistence of violence and conflict over religion) as indices of deficiencies in constitutional law. It approaches the history of constitutional practice through a thick tangle of normative assumptions about what constitutional law, when properly deployed, can and should do. Such an approach holds empirical observation in thrall to normative evaluation. It collapses analysis and activism by conflating constitutional law as a historical project (a project engaged in by human actors constrained and conditioned by society, economics and politics) with constitutional law as a normative project (a project of realizing certain social, legal and moral standards). It leads inquiry away from a patient, scrupulous account of the complex functions and effects of constitutional practice on the ground; and leads scholars toward a preoccupation with measuring the distance between realities and ideals. Conducted in this way, the study of constitutional law risks losing track of the agents of constitutional law – the humans, situated in places and times, designing, reforming and implementing what they take to be the guiding legal charter of the country – and becoming a mode of advocacy.[10]

---

from 2010 to 2015, which gave the president virtually unfettered power – as evidence of failed constitutionalism in Sri Lanka.

[10] This critique draws upon the larger critiques made by Paul Kahn. Kahn, *The Cultural Study of Law*, 7. Kahn, "Comparative Constitutionalism in a New Key."

Steven D Smith voices a similar concern about the "ontological gap" between scholarship *on* law and belief *in* law: "This disjunction – between what we presuppose and what we profess to believe (or not to believe) is reflected in the quirky combination of skeptical sophistication and apparent naivete that lawyers and legal scholars so often exhibit regarding the ontological status of 'the law.' As noted if the issue is raised in a context calling for critical self-consciousness, lawyers and especially legal scholars will scoff at the notion that 'the law' – an entity exhibiting some of the qualities of a 'brooding omnipresence – somehow exists. But then, the conversation changes ('Did the Fifth Circuit get the law right in Smith v. Jones?' or 'Does section five of the Fourteenth Amendment authorize Congress to expand constitutional rights?') and these same worldly wise skeptics will immediately launch into earnest arguments that make no apparent sense except on the presupposition that 'the law' does exist. Or the lawyers will mock 'legal formalism' and recite that 'we are all realists now' but they go on writing briefs and opinions or articles that sound for all the world like the work of formalists; and then if a critic raises antiformalist objections, they will yawn and say, 'We all understand that. Please don't be

Rethinking Faith in Constitutional Law

However, there is more at stake than just the separation of analysis and advocacy. By holding empirical observation in thrall to normative evaluation, scholars prematurely excuse constitutional practice – both as a human institution and as a normative ideal – from any complicity in producing, perpetuating or amplifying social ills. That is, scholars preserve, without critique, the veracity of the ideals against which they judge the history of constitutional law in the first place. Violence, conflict and discord come to be interpreted as evidence for the imperfection of constitutional regimes and as urgent invitations for their remaking. Utopias go unexamined. Analysis gets done in a millenarian mode, waiting for the saving power of a (more) perfect constitutional law to set things right.[11]

This kind of millenarian yearning has driven multiple efforts to rewrite and revise Sri Lanka's constitutional policies toward religion. In previous chapters, I outlined the efforts made between the 1940s and the 1970s. Further efforts would take place in virtually every decade that followed.[12] Today, constitutional law continues to serve as a dominant framework for thinking about and managing religion in modern Sri Lanka. Sri Lanka's current government, like the governments before it, has treated constitutional reform as central to its "most important goal" of generating a "political settlement to the outstanding issues relating to national unity, ethnicity and religion."[13] Many of the island's NGOs place equal faith in law to combat religious intolerance.[14]

---

patronizing.'" Steven D Smith, *Law's Quandary* (Cambridge, MA: Harvard University Press, 2007), 156.

[11] Schonthal et al., "Is the Rule of Law an Antidote for Religious Tension?"

[12] Government of Sri Lanka, *Report From the Select Committee of the National State Assembly Appointed to Consider the Revision of the Constitution (Parliamentary Series No. 14)* (Colombo: Government Publications Office, 1978). All-Parties Representative Committee, Report of Sub-Committee A and Sub-Committee B as contained in: Rohan Edrisinha et al., *Power-sharing in Sri Lanka: Constitutional and Political Documents 1926–2008* (Colombo: Centre for Policy Alternatives and Berghof Foundation for Conflict Studies, 2009), 801, 813.

[13] "Memorial Speech by Prime Minister Ranil Wickremesinghe at the National Diet (Parliament) of Japan," *Official Government News Portal, Sri Lanka* (October 6, 2015).

[14] Sachin Parathalingam and Kavindya Tennakoon, "Disarming the Juggernaut of Religious Intolerance in Sri Lanka," *Groundviews* (September 7, 2013). The National Peace Council, *(Press release) Rule of Law as Antidote to Religious Intolerance* (July 25, 2012).

268 CONCLUSION: THE COSTS OF CONSTITUTIONAL LAW

There are high costs to this faith in constitutional law, to directing our hopes, energies and time toward a more perfect constitutional practice. In turning to constitutional law to mollify conflicts over religion, scholars, activists and political reformers may be investing their resources in techniques that, while perhaps helpful for some goals of governance (e.g., designing electoral systems, creating public service institutions, preventing torture), may be counterproductive for others. This is the case when it comes to addressing and harmonizing competing claims made in the name of religion.

Constitutional law does not simply translate societal conflicts over religion into another (technical, legal) language. It transforms the way people approach those conflicts, while also transforming the parties to them. It authorizes languages and protocols that add rigidity, agonism and absolutism to the ways in which people view and express disputes – inside and outside of assemblies and courtrooms. Anxieties about proselytism become demands for freedom of conscience. Frustrations with the behavior of particular monks become calls for the state to protect Buddhism. Anti-colonial nationalism and party politics become activism for religious rights.

By undertaking a constitutional microhistory of the Buddhism Chapter – by looking closely the expanded archive of law in Sri Lanka, over time – one sees that "religion" and "Buddhism" are not just complex and multivalent terms, they are also strategic categories deployed (often opportunistically and competitively) by constitutional lobbyists, litigants, lawyers and judges in order to group together particular actors, activities and objects and to render them constitutionally salient. By invoking these categories, constitutional agents distill multifaceted societal conflicts into "religious conflicts" or struggles to "protect Buddhism."[15] In this respect, constitutional practice not only frames conflict in less flexible, less tractable terms, it also leads to the multiplication and interpolation of conflicts over religion into many domains of society by creating inducements and pathways for classifying a wide variety of social issues as matters of religion, or Buddhism.[16]

---

[15] For an analysis of similar dynamics as it relates to global religious freedom advocacy see Hurd, *Beyond Religious Freedom*.

[16] Sullivan, *The Impossibility of Religious Freedom*. As seen in the preceding chapters, those who participate in constitutional practice have used the category of religion in various ways: as a subcomponent of "ethnicity," an ascribed communal identity, a chosen

RETHINKING FAITH IN CONSTITUTIONAL LAW 269

The conflicts examined in this book involve, at once, conflicts over things in the world (ideas, persons, artifacts and spaces) as well as over the use of categories. That is, they are also conflicts over the definitional boundaries of "religion" or "Buddhism." The strong effects of pyrrhic constitutionalism on religion derive, in part, from the fact that the agents of constitutional law use the category of religion in differing (and opposing) ways during the process of creating and applying constitutional law: in the process of creating constitutional law, examined in Part I of this book, lawmakers and lobbyists use the category of religion (or Buddhism) to advance and reconcile competing claims about "religious" things (e.g., churches, temples, organizations, morals, rights, freedoms, histories, priests and monks); however, in the process of applying constitutional law, examined in Part II of this book, litigants, lawyers and judges use the category of religion to argue about which things are, in fact, properly "religious" (e.g., monks who drive cars or study to become lawyers, missionaries who engage in humanitarian aid projects, villagers who live near Buddhist temples).

In one way, the constitutional management of religion appears similar to the management of other multivalent constitutional categories. "Culture" may be the paradigm case in this respect. Yet, even in the constitutions most solicitous of rights and freedoms to culture, such as that of South Africa, the constitutional management of religion assumes comparatively greater importance. This importance is visible in the extensiveness of constitutional protections given to religion (*vis-à-vis* culture, and many other categories). It is also visible in the relative absence of limitations placed on those protections, particularly protections for religious belief. These features are not unique to the constitutions of South Africa or Sri Lanka. Most constitutional regimes treat protections for religion (or a single, favored religion) not simply as one protection among many, but as one of the most important protections ensured by constitutional law – a "first freedom" or even a moral precondition for law itself.[17]

---

individual identity, a regime of beliefs, a fabricated, Christocentric category of Western and Westernized imperial powers, a aggregate noun commensurable or incommensurable with Buddhism, and others. These definitional differences have served various purposes: the affirmation of colonial power, the legitimation of anti-colonial nationalism, protests against government action, the expansion of privileges for those things classifiable as part of the Buddha Sasana, etc.

[17] Michael W McConnell, "Why Is Religious Liberty the 'First Freedom,'?" *Cardozo Law Review*. 21 (2000): 1243–1265. Appleby, Cizik and Task Force on Religion and the

270 CONCLUSION: THE COSTS OF CONSTITUTIONAL LAW

Regardless of whether one deems constitutional law in Sri Lanka to be successful, one cannot deny the success of constitutional law as a global form. The languages of constitutional law – and their constitutive and cognate languages of fundamental rights, freedoms, protections and rule of law – serve today as structuring discourses through which people throughout the world conduct politics, pursue justice, articulate grievances and think about the nature of shared society. As with the discourse of human rights, people appeal to constitutional law with a confidence and ease that, to the sympathetic observer, suggests its naturalness and, to the wary critic, its hegemony. The problem is that this strong focus on constitutional law monopolizes our imagination as well as our resources. It holds our gaze, and in so doing, blinds us to other ways of thinking about and harmonizing differences, which entail very different assumptions about the nature of religion, identity, diversity and worship.

Consider, for example, the long-standing practices of conceiving and managing difference at pilgrimage sites. Sri Lanka has a multitude of pilgrimage sites that are sacred to more than one religious tradition. At these sites – which include, among others, the summit of Adam's Peak (Sri Pada), the sacred sites at Kataragama and the temples at Munnesvaram – pilgrims from a variety of backgrounds worship together. Individual pilgrims might describe themselves as Buddhists, Hindus, Muslims or Christians (if interviewed or asked to fill out government forms), yet they engage in shared activities such as climbing stairs, circumambulating sacra, making offerings, visiting shrines and undertaking austerities (like fasting and fire-walking). In many cases, they also travel together, walking or riding as a single group. In doing this, they act less as adherents of a single religion, e.g., Buddhism or Hinduism, than as devotees of a particular deity or shrine. They join together as fulfillers of a sacred vow or as co-pursuers of divine power.[18] (Ironically, as it relates to the context of this book, devotees often

---

Making of US Foreign Policy, *Engaging Religious Communities Abroad: A New Imperative for U.S. Foreign Policy*. Clark B Lombardi, "Islamic Law as a Source of Constitutional Law in Egypt: The Constitutionalization of the Sharia in a Modern Arab State," *Columbia Journal of Transnational Law*. 37 (1998): 81–123.

[18] Rohan Bastin, *The Domain of Constant Excess: Plural Worship at the Munnesvaram Temples in Sri Lanka* (New York: Berghahn Books, 2002), 2–5. Bryan Pfaffenberger, "The Kataragama Pilgrimage: Hindu-Buddhist Interaction and Its Significance in Sri Lanka's Polyethnic Social System," *The Journal of Asian Studies* 38, no. 2 (1979): 253–270.

undertake pilgrimage as a way to improve their chances of winning a favorable verdict in court!)[19]

This is not to paint an overly romantic portrait of these sites. From time to time, pilgrims fight with each other. They recount different myths to explain the site's power: some cite its connection with the Buddha; others refer to the life of a Sufi saint, or the biblical Adam, or a Saivite deity. Yet myths and ritual practices explain and manage the fact of soteriological diversity – and competition – in a manner different from constitutional law. Rather than litigation, they rely on processes of coordination, incorporation and identification. Buddhist myths recast deities such as Vishnu or Kataragama as protectors or subordinates of the Buddha. Hindu myths identify the Virgin Mary as a Goddess with powers over local demons. Ritual protocols, learned and intuited, work to synchronise and even render complementary the activities of Buddhist monks, Hindu sāmis, Sufi sheiks, Catholic priests and other ritual specialists (such as exorcists, mediums and Kapuralas).[20] While these features do not pertain to all devotional and worship practices in Sri Lanka, they do pertain to many of them – as well as to a great many pilgrimage and "everyday" rituals throughout Asia.[21]

---

[19] Ibid., 261–262. Gananath Obeyesekere, "Social Change and the Deities: Rise of the Kataragama Cult in Modern Sri Lanka," *Man* n.s. 12, no. 3/4 (1977): 377–396.

[20] Michael M Ames, "Magical-animism and Buddhism: A Structural Analysis of the Sinhalese Religious System," *The Journal of Asian Studies* 23, no. 1 (1964): 21–52. Gananath Obeyesekere, "The Buddhist Pantheon in Ceylon and Its Extension," in *Anthropological Studies in Theravada Buddhism*, ed. Manning Nash (New Haven, CT: Yale University Press, 1966). Deborah Winslow, "A Political Geography of Deities: Space and the Pantheon in Sinhalese Buddhism," *The Journal of Asian Studies* 43, no. 2 (1984): 273–291. Holt, *Buddha in the Crown*. R L Stirrat, "Demonic Possession in Roman Catholic Sri Lanka," *Journal of Anthropological Research* 33, no. 2 (1977): 133–157. Jason A Carbine, "Yaktovil: The Role of the Buddha and Dhamma," in *The Life of Buddhism*, ed. Frank Reynolds and Jason Carbine (Berkeley: University of California Press, 2000). Bruce Kapferer, *A Celebration of Demons: Exorcism and the Aesthetics of Healing in Sri Lanka* (Bloomington: Indiana University Press, 1983). Victor C de Munck, "Sufi and Reformist Designs: Muslim Identity in Sri Lanka," in *Buddhist Fundamentalism and Minority Identities in Sri Lanka*, ed. Tessa J Bartholomeusz and Chandra R de Silva (Albany, NY: SUNY Press, 1998).

[21] E.g., McDaniel, *The Lovelorn Ghost and the Magical Monk*. Anna Bigelow, *Sharing the Sacred: Practicing Pluralism in Muslim North India* (New York: Oxford University Press, 2010). Peter Gottschalk, *Beyond Hindu and Muslim: Multiple Identity in Narratives from Village India* (Oxford: Oxford University Press, 2000). Pilgrimage is one such form. Others forms in Sri Lanka might include purification and home-building rituals, healing ceremonies (including *tovil* and exorcisms) and annual processions (*perahera-s*).

272 CONCLUSION: THE COSTS OF CONSTITUTIONAL LAW

I offer this brief analysis of Sri Lankan pilgrimage not to suggest a better way of doing things. I do so to decenter, temporarily, constitutional ways of thinking about and managing difference and, by so doing, to gesture toward the existence of other, long-standing systems of imaging and engaging with normative and social heterogeneity on the island. These systems rely on distinctions other than religion and non-religion, orthodoxy and heterodoxy, rights and limitations, Buddhism and non-Buddhism. They reveal alternative ways of thinking about principles of human affinity and estrangement and the structure or permeability of social boundaries. They offer different frameworks for envisioning the common goals of ritual practice and the commensurability of multiple divinities and cosmologies. At the center of those systems are not rights, beliefs and freedoms but power (S:/T: *haskam, āccaryam*), merit (S: *piṅ*) and devotion (S: *bhakti*, T: *pakti*).[22]

The ritual and normative lives of Sri Lankans have more in common than the structures of constitutional law would suggest. They are more blended and accommodating than the claims of constitutional litigation admit. The boundaries presumed and concretized by constitutional law are confounded everyday in the lives of Sri Lanka's citizens. Those practices, beliefs and traditions that constitutional practice imperfectly organizes under the category of religion – and, in so doing, authorizes *as* religion (or as Buddhism, Islam, Hinduism or Christianity) – partake of alternate vocabularies and imaginaries for thinking about difference and social coherence.[23] Yet, it is these very practices of conceiving and approaching heterogeneity, along with others, which are lost or obscured in an insistence on managing religion through constitutional law.

*

Periods of fieldwork for this book coincided, quite unexpectedly, with the end of the war between the Sri Lankan government and the LTTE. From late 2008, in only a few months, Sri Lanka's military accomplished what many had long considered to be impossible: in a violent military offensive, it decimated the guerilla army that had controlled the island's northern areas for three decades. In the heady and

---

[22] Bastin, *The Domain of Constant Excess*. de Munck, "Sufi and Reformist Designs." Pfaffenberger, "The Kataragama Pilgrimage."

[23] Rohan Bastin, "Saints, Sites and Religious Accommodation in Sri Lanka," in *Sharing the Sacra: The Politics and Pragmatics of Intercommunal Relations Around Holy Places*, ed. Glenn Bowman (New York: Berghahn, 2012).

turbulent, days, weeks and months following the declaration of victory in May 2009, politicians, human rights advocates, diplomats and a range of other commentators assessed the past and prognosticated about the future. Amidst the rhetoric – among the many essays penned by various authors, each declaring the steps that Sri Lanka must take in order to avoid the return of civil war – calls for constitutional reform were omnipresent. In the tentative first moments following a 30-year war, many of the world's experts tethered their hopes for a lasting peace to the practice of constitutional law.

This book urges circumspection in our approach to constitutional law. It asks scholars, policymakers and activists to think again about constitutional law's abilities to mitigate conflicts over religion. Constitutional practice may give way to pyrrhic constitutionalism. A religiously harmonious future in post-war Sri Lanka may not be realized through constitutional law, but in spite of it. The sites of reconciliation, recovery and catharsis lie not in law's rule, but in the creativity, compassion and patience of those who live and trust outside of it.

REFERENCES

A note on references: The following list refers only to the published sources, including published pamphlets, used for this research. References to other archival sources – including draft laws, bills, petitions, legal submissions, documents from the case files, interview transcripts, newspaper reports and other unpublished materials – appear in the footnotes of the individual chapters of this book.

Abeysekara, Ananda. *Colors of the Robe: Religion, Identity, and Difference*. Columbia, SC: University of South Carolina Press, 2002.

"Politics of Higher Ordination, Buddhist Monastic Identity, and Leadership at the Dambulla Temple in Sri Lanka." *Journal of the International Association of Buddhist Studies* 22, no. 2 (1999): 255–280.

"The Saffron Army, Violence, Terror(ism): Buddhism, Identity and Difference in Sri Lanka." *Numen* 48, no. 1 (2001): 1–46.

Ackerman, Bruce. "The Rise of World Constitutionalism." *Virginia Law Review* 83, no. 4 (1997): 771–797.

We the People: Foundations. Cambridge, MA: Belknap Press of Harvard University Press, 1991.

Agrama, Hussein Ali. *Questioning Secularism: Islam, Sovereignty, and the Rule of Law in Modern Egypt*. Chicago: University of Chicago Press, 2012.

"Reflections on Secularism, Democracy, and Politics in Egypt." *American Ethnologist* 39, no. 1 (2012): 26–31.

All-Ceylon Buddhist Congress. *33rd Annual Sessions, Kandy December 29, 1951, English Translation of the Presidential Address by Dr. G.P. Malalasekera (Pamphlet)*. Borella, Colombo: The L.V. Press, December 29, 1951.

Bauddha Toraturu Parīkṣaka Sabhāvē Vārtāva. Colombo: Visidunu Prakāśakaya, 2006.

Buddhism and the State: Resolutions and Memorandum of the All Ceylon Buddhist Congress (Pamphlet). Maradana: Oriental Press, 1951.

All-Ceylon Hindu Congress. *Inthu Oli: All-Ceylon Hindu Congress Golden Jubilee Commemoration*. Colombo: All-Ceylon Hindu Congress, n.d.

Amerasinghe, A R B. *The Supreme Court of Sri Lanka: The First 185 Years*. Colombo: Sarvodaya Book Pub. Services, 1986.

REFERENCES 275

Amarasinghe, C F. "The Legal Sovereignty of the Ceylon Parliament." *Public Law*, (1966): 73–81.

Ames, Michael M. "Magical-animism and Buddhism: A Structural Analysis of the Sinhalese Religious System." *The Journal of Asian Studies* 23, no. 1 (1964): 21–52.

Amunugama, Sarath. "Buddhaputra and Bhumiputra?: Dilemmas of modern Sinhala Buddhist monks in relation to ethnic and political conflict." *Religion* 21 (1991): 115–139.

Anderson, M R. "Islamic Law and the Colonial Encounter in British India." In *Institutions and Ideologies: A SOAS South Asia Reader* (London: Curzon Press Ltd., 1993): 165–185.

Appleby, R Scott, Richard Cizik, and Task Force on Religion and the Making of U.S. Foreign Policy. *Engaging Religious Communities Abroad: A New Imperative for U.S. Foreign Policy.* Chicago: Chicago Council on Global Affairs, 2010.

Arasaratnam, S. "The Ceylon Insurrection of April 1971: Some Causes and Consequences." *Pacific Affairs* 45, no. 3 (1972): 356–371.

Asad, Talal. *Genealogies of Religion.* New York: Johns Hopkins University Press, 1993.

Auerbach, Jerold S. *Justice Without Law? Resolving Disputes Without Lawyers.* New York: Oxford University Press, 1986.

Austin, Granville. *The Indian Constitution: Cornerstone of a Nation.* New York: Oxford University Press, 1966.

Bajpai, Rochana. "Constituent Assembly Debates and Minority Rights." *Economic and Political Weekly* 35, no. 21/22 (2000): 1837–1845.

Bali, Ali, and Hanna Lerner (eds.). *Constitution Writing, Religion and Democracy.* Cambridge: Cambridge University Press, 2016.

Bandaranaike, S W R D. "Revision of the Constitution (Speech Made as Prime Minister, 7 Nov 1957)." In *Towards a New Era: Selected Speeches of S.W.R.D. Bandaranaike.* Edited by G E P De S Wickramaratne. Colombo: Government Press, 1961.

Speeches and Writings. Colombo: Government Press Ceylon, 1963.

Towards a New Era: Selected Speeches of S.W.R.D. Bandaranaike, Made in the Legislature of Ceylon 1931–1959. 2nd ed. Colombo: Government Information Department, 1976.

Barron, Thomas J. "The Donoughmore Commission and Ceylon's National Identity." In *Constitutions and National Identity: Proceedings of the Conference on "The Makings of Constitutions and the Development of National Identity" held in Honour of Professor George Shepperson at the University of Edinburgh, 3–6 July 1987.* Edited by Thomas J Barron, Owen D Edwards and Patricia J Storey. Edinburgh: Quadriga Publishers, 1993.

Bastin, Rohan. *The Domain of Constant Excess: Plural Worship at the Munnesvaram Temples in Sri Lanka.* New York: Berghahn Books, 2002.

REFERENCES

"Saints, Sites and Religious Accommodation in Sri Lanka." In *Sharing the Sacra: The Politics and Pragmatics of Intercommunal Relations Around Holy Places.* Edited by Glenn Bowman. New York: Berghahn, 2012.

Bauddha Jathika Balavegaya (Buddhist National Force). *Catholic Action – A Menace to Peace and Goodwill.* Colombo: The Bauddha Pracharaka Press, March 1963.

Berger, Benjamin L. "The Cultural Limits of Legal Tolerance." *Canadian Journal of Law and Jurisprudence* 21, no. 2 (2008): 245–277.

Law's Religion: Religious Difference and the Claims of Constitutionalism. Toronto: University of Toronto, 2016.

"The Virtues of Law in the Politics of Religious Freedom." *Journal of Law and Religion* 29, no. 3 (2014): 378–395.

Berkwitz, Stephen C. "Religious Conflict and the Politics of Conversion in Sri Lanka." In *Proselytization Revisited: Rights Talk, Free Markets and Culture Wars.* Edited by Rosalind I J Hackett. London: Equinox, 2008.

"Resisting the Global in Buddhist Nationalism: Venerable Soma's Discourse of Decline and Reform." *Journal of Asian Studies* 67, no. 1 (2008): 73–106.

Bhagavan, Manu. "A New Hope: India, the United Nations and the Making of the Universal Declaration of Human Rights." *Modern Asian Studies* 44, no. 02 (2010): 311–347.

Bigelow, Anna. *Sharing the Sacred: Practicing Pluralism in Muslim North India.* New York: Oxford University Press, 2010.

Blackburn, Anne M. *Buddhist Learning and Textual Practice in Eighteenth-Century Lankan Monastic Culture.* Princeton, NJ; Oxford, UK: Princeton University Press, 2001.

Locations of Buddhism: Colonialism and Modernity in Sri Lanka. Chicago: University of Chicago Press, 2010.

Blount, Justin, Zachary Elkins, and Tom Ginsburg. "Does the Process of Constitution-Making Matter?" In *Comparative Constitutional Design.* Edited by Tom Ginsburg. Cambridge: Cambridge University Press, 2012.

Bond, George. *The Buddhist Revival in Sri Lanka.* Columbia, SC: University of South Carolina, 1988.

Bouchard, Gerard, and Charles Taylor. *Building the Future: A Time for Reconciliation (Report Prepared for Commission De Consultation Sur Les Practiques D'Accommodement Reliées Aux Différences Culturelles, Province of Quebec).* 2008.

Brown, Nathan J. *Constitutions in a Nonconstitutional World: Arab Basic Laws and the Prospects for Accountable Government.* Albany: State University of New York Press, 2002.

Buddha śāsana janādhipati komiṣan (Presidential Commission on the Buddha Sasana). *Buddha śāsana janādhipati komiṣan vārtāva* (Report of the Presidential Commission on Buddha Sasana). Colombo: Sri Lanka Government Printing Department, 2002.

REFERENCES

Buddhist Committee of Enquiry of the All-Ceylon Buddhist Congress. *The Betrayal of Buddhism*. Balangoda: Dharmavijaya Press, 1956.

Burgers, Jan H. "The Road to San Francisco: The Revival of the Human Rights Idea in the Twentieth Century." *Human Rights Quarterly* 14, no. 4 (1992): 447–477.

Carbine, Jason A. "Yaktovil: The Role of the Buddha and Dhamma." In *The Life of Buddhism*. Edited by Frank Reynolds and Jason Carbine. Berkeley: University of California Press, 2000.

Carter, John Ross. "A History of Early Buddhism." *Religious Studies* 13, no. 3 (1977): 263–287.

Catholic Union of Ceylon. *Companion to the Buddhist Commission Report: A Commentary on the Report*. Colombo: Catholic Union Press, 1957.

Centre for Policy Alternatives. *Attacks on Places of Religious Worship in Post-War Sri Lanka*. Colombo: CPA Publications, 2013.

Ceylon Board of Ministers. "Reform of the Constitution (Memorandum From Ministers to HMG From 11 Sept 1944)." In *Sessional Paper 14 of 1944*. Colombo: Ceylon Government Press, September 1944.

"Statement by the Ministers on the Reforms Declaration by His Majesty's Government." In *Sessional Paper 19*. Colombo: Ceylon Government Press, June 1943.

Ceylon Daily News. *The Ceylon Daily News Parliament of Ceylon 1960*. Colombo: Lake House, 1960.

The Ceylon Daily News Parliament of Ceylon 1965. Colombo: Lake House, 1965.

The Ceylon Daily News Parliament of Ceylon 1970. Colombo: Lake House, 1970.

Ceylon Daily News' Parliament of Sri Lanka, 1977. Colombo: Associated Newspapers of Ceylon, 1978.

Ceylon National Congress. *25 Years – but Yet! (Pamphlet)*. Colombo: n.p., 1946.

Chandoke, Neera. "Individual and Group Rights a View From India." In *India's Living Constitution: Ideas, Practices, Controversies*. Edited by Zoya Hasan, E Sridharan and R Sudharshan. London: Anthem, 2005.

Chatterjee, Nandini. "English Law, Brahmo Marriage, and the Problem of Religious Difference: Civil Marriage Laws in Britain and India." *Comparative Studies in Society and History* 52, no. 3 (2010): 524–552.

Choudhry, Sujit. "Bridging Comparative Politics and Comparative Constitutional Law: Constitutional Design in Divided Societies." In *Constitutional Design for Divided Societies: Integration or Accommodation?* (2008): 3–40.

Constitutional Design for Divided Societies: Integration or Accommodation? New York: Oxford University Press, 2008.

Cohn, Bernard S. *Colonialism and Its Forms of Knowledge: The British in India*. Princeton, NJ: Princeton University Press, 1996.

Colebrooke, W M G. *The Colebrooke-Cameron Papers: Documents on British Colonial Policy in Ceylon, 1796–1833*. Edited by G C Mendis. London: Oxford University Press, 1956.

REFERENCES

Colonial Government of Ceylon. "1801 Charter of Justice." In *A Collection of the Legislative Acts of His Majesty's Government of Ceylon.* Colombo: Printed at the Government Press by N Berbman, 1821.

A Collection of the Legislative Acts of His Majesty's Government of Ceylon. Colombo: Printed at the Govt. Press by N. Berbman, 1821.

"Reform of the Constitution." In *Ceylon Sessional Paper XVII.* Colombo: Ceylon Government Press, 1943.

Comaroff, John L. "Reflections on the Rise of Legal Theology: Law and Religion in the Twenty-First Century." *Social Analysis* 53, no. 1 (2009): 193–216.

Comaroff, Jean, and John L Comaroff. "Reflections on Liberalism, Policulturalism, and ID-ology: Citizenship and Difference in South Africa." *Social Identities* 9, no. 4 (2003): 445–473.

Theory From the South: Or, How Euro-America Is Evolving Toward Africa. Boulder, CO: Paradigm Publishers, 2012.

Constituent Assembly. *Constituent Assembly Committee Reports.* Colombo: Ceylon Government Press, 1971.

Constituent Assembly Debates. Colombo: Ceylon Government Press, 1971.

Reports of the Committees of the Constituent Assembly to Consider the Draft Constitution. Colombo: Department of Government Printing, 1972.

Cooray, Joseph A L. *Constitutional and Administrative Law of Sri Lanka (Ceylon).* Colombo: Hansa Publishers Ltd., 1973.

"Human Rights and Their Protection in Ceylon." In *Constitutional Government and Human Rights in a Developing Society.* Colombo: Colombo Apothecaries Publishers, 1969.

"The Revision of the Constitution." In *Constitutional Government and Human Rights in a Developing Society.* Colombo: Colombo Apothecaries Publishers, 1969.

Cooray, L J M. *Constitutional Government in Sri Lanka 1796–1977.* Colombo: Stamford Lake Publishers, 2005.

Cossman, Brenda, and Ratna Kapur. "Secularism: Bench-Marked by Hindu Right." *Economic and Political Weekly* 31, no. 38 (1996): 2613–2617, 2619–2627, 2629–2630.

Crouch, Melissa. "Personal Law and Colonial Legacy: State-Religion Relations and Islamic Law in Myanmar." In *Islam and the State in Myanmar: Muslim-Buddhist Relations and the Politics of Belonging.* Delhi: Oxford University Press, 2016.

De, Rohit. "Rebellion, Dacoity, and Equality: The Emergence of the Constitutional Field in Postcolonial India." *Comparative Studies of South Asia, Africa and the Middle East* 34, no. 2 (2014): 260–278.

Deegalle, Mahinda. *Buddhism, Conflict, and Violence in Modern Sri Lanka.* New York: Routledge, 2006.

"Politics of the Jathika Hela Urumaya Monks: Buddhism and Ethnicity in Contemporary Sri Lanka." *Contemporary Buddhism* 5, no. 2 (2004): 83–103.

REFERENCES

De Silva, Colvin R. *Ceylon Under the British Occupation, 1795–1833 (2 Vols)*. Colombo: Colombo Apothecaries, 1953.

Safeguards for the Minorities in the 1972 Constitution. Colombo: Young Socialist Publication, 1987.

De Silva, K M. *British Documents on the End of Empire: Sri Lanka*. London: Institute of Commonwealth Studies, University of London, 1997. Vol. I, lxii.

A History of Sri Lanka. Colombo: Vijitha Yapa Publications, 2005.

"Ivor Jennings and Sri Lanka's Passage to Independence." *Asia Pacific Law Review* 13, no. 1 (2005): 1–18.

Social Policy and Missionary Organizations in Ceylon: 1840–1855. London: Longmans, 1965.

De Silva, K M, and W Howard Wriggins. *J.R. Jayewardene of Sri Lanka: A Political Biography*. 2 Vols. London: Anthony Blond Quartet, 1988.

De Silva, Rangita. "JAL Cooray: A Pioneer Lankan Constitutional Lawyer and Human Rights Jurist." *Sri Lanka Journal of International Law* 6 (1994): 1–16.

De Silva, Viveka S. *An Assessment of the Contribution of the Judiciary Towards Good Governance*. Colombo: Sri Lanka Foundation and Friedrich Ebert Stiftung, 2005.

De Smith, S A. *The New Commonwealth and Its Constitutions*. London: Stevens and Sons, 1964.

DeVotta, Neil. *Blowback: Linguistic Nationalism, Institutional Decay and Ethnic Conflict in Sri Lanka*. Palo Alto, CA: Stanford University Press, 2004.

DeVotta, N, and J Stone. "Jathika Hela Urumaya and Ethno-religious Politics in Sri Lanka." *Pacific Affairs* 81, no. 1 (2008): 31–51.

Dharmadasa, K N O. "Buddhism and Politics in Modern Sri Lanka." In *Bhikshuva Saha Lankā Samājeya*. Edited by Maduluvave Sobhita et al. Colombo: Dharmadhutasrama Pirivena, 1997.

"Buddhist Interests, Activists and Pressure Groups." In *History and Politics, Millennial Perspectives: Essays in Honour of K.M. De Silva*. Edited by Gerald Peiris and S W R de A Samarasinghe. Kandy: International Centre for Ethnic Studies, 1999.

Diamond, Larry Jay. *Developing Democracy: Toward Consolidation*. Baltimore, MD: Johns Hopkins University Press, 1999.

Dias, Reginald F. *A Commentary on the Ceylon Criminal Procedure Code*. Ceylon: Colombo Apothecaries Publishers, 1935.

Donoughmore Commission. *Report of the Special Commission on the Ceylon Constitution*. Colombo: Ceylon Government Press, 1929.

Edrisinha, Rohan, Mario Gomez, V T Thamilmaran, and Asanga Welikala. *Power-sharing in Sri Lanka: Constitutional and Political Documents 1926–2008*. Colombo: Centre for Policy Alternatives and Berghof Foundation for Conflict Studies, 2009.

REFERENCES

Elkins, Zachary, Tom Ginsburg, and James Melton. *The Endurance of National Constitutions.* New York: Cambridge University Press, 2009.

Elshtain, Jean B. "Religion and Democracy." *Journal of Democracy* 20, no. 2 (2009): 5–17.

Ewing, K D. "Law and the Constitution: Manifesto of the Progressive Party." *Modern Law Review* 67 (2004): 734–752.

Feldman, Noah. "Review of Hamoudi, *Negotiating in Civil Conflict.*" *International Journal of Middle East Studies* 47, no. 1 (2015): 177–178.

Feldman, Noah, and Roman Martinez. "Constitutional Politics and Text in the New Iraq: An Experiment in Islamic Democracy." *Fordham Law Review* 75, no. 2 (2006): 883–920.

Fernando, W N Oshan. The Effects of Evangelical Christianity on State Formation in Sri Lanka. Ph.D. Dissertation, Department of Anthropology, University of California at Santa Barbara, September 2011.

Foley, Michael. *The Silence of Constitutions: Gaps, "abeyances," and Political Temperament in the Maintenance of Government.* New York: Routledge, 1991.

Gair, James W, and W S Karunatillake. *Literary Sinhala Inflected Forms with a Transliteration Guide.* Ithaca, NY: Cornell University, 1976.

Ginsburg, Tom, and Rosalind Dixon. "Deciding Not to Decide: Deferral in Constitutional Design." *International Journal of Constitutional Law* 9, no. 3–4 (2011): 636–672.

Ginzburg, Carlo. *The Cheese and the Worms: The Cosmos of a Sixteenth-Century Miller.* Baltimore, MD: Johns Hopkins University Press, 1980.

Glendon, Mary Ann. *Rights Talk: The Impoverishment of Political Discourse.* New York: Simon and Schuster, 1993.

A World Made New: Eleanor Roosevelt and the Universal Declaration of Human Rights. New York: Random House, 2001.

Go, Julian. "Modeling States and Sovereignty: Postcolonial States in Africa and Asia." In *Making a World After Empire: The Bandung Moment and Its Political Afterlives.* Edited by Christopher Lee. Athens: Ohio University Press, 2010.

Godden, Lee, and Niranjan Casinader. "The Kandyan Convention 1815: Consolidating the British Empire in Colonial Ceylon." *Comparative Legal History* 1, no. 2 (2013): 211–242.

Goonesekere, R K W. *Fundamental Rights and the Constitution: A Case Book.* Colombo, Sri Lanka: Law & Society Trust, 2003.

Goonetileke, H A I, and Ivor Jennings. *The Road to Peradeniya: An Autobiography.* Colombo: Lake House, 2005.

Gordon, Sarah Barringer. "'Free' Religion and 'Captive' Schools: Protestants, Catholics, and Education, 1945–1965." *DePaul Law Review* 56 (2006): 1177–1220.

Gottschalk, Peter. *Beyond Hindu and Muslim: Multiple Identity in Narratives From Village India.* Oxford: Oxford University Press, 2000.

Government of Ceylon. *Buddha Śāsana Komiṣan Vārtāva (Buddha Sasana Commission Report).* Colombo: Government Press, 1959.

REFERENCES

Ceylon Legislative Council Debates. Colombo: Government Printers, 1928.

Ceylon Legislative Enactments. Colombo: Ceylon Government Press, 1956.

"Decision of the Constitutional Court on Pirivena Education Bill." In *Decisions of the Constitutional Court of Sri Lanka (Vol. IV).* Colombo: Registry of the Constitutional Court, 1976.

"Decision of the Constitutional Court on Places and Objects of Worship Bill." In *Decisions of the Constitutional Court of Sri Lanka.* Colombo: Registry of the Constitutional Court, 1973.

Interim Report of the Buddha Sasana Commission (Sessional Paper XXV of 1957). Colombo: Government Press, November 1957.

The Joint Select Committee of the Senate and the House of Representatives Appointed to Consider the Revision of the Constitution (Parliamentary Series No. 30, 3rd Session of 6th Parliament). Colombo: Government Press, June 6, 1968.

Report from the Joint Select Committee of the Senate and the House of Representatives Appointed to Consider the Revision of the Constitution Together with Minutes of Proceedings (Parliamentary Series No. 12). Colombo: Government Press, April 4, 1958.

Government of Sri Lanka. *Constitution of the Democratic Socialist Republic of Sri Lanka.* 1978.

Hansard Debates, House of Representatives. Colombo: Government Press.

"Report of the Presidential Commission of Inquiry into the incidents which took place between 13 August and 15 September, 1977," *Sessional Paper no. VII.* Colombo: Government Publications Bureau, 1980.

Report from the Select Committee of the National State Assembly Appointed to Consider the Revision of the Constitution (Parliamentary Series No. 14). Colombo: Government Publications Office, 1978.

Gunatilleke, Gehan. *The Chronic and the Acute: Post-war Religious Violence in Sri Lanka.* Colombo: International Centre for Ethnic Studies and Equitas, 2015.

Habermas, Jurgen. "Why Europe Needs a Constitution." *New Left Review* 11 (2001): 5–26.

Hamburger, Philip. *Separation of Church and State.* Cambridge, MA: Harvard University Press, 2002.

Hamoudi, Haider. *Negotiating in Civil Conflict: Constitutional Construction and Imperfect Bargaining in Iraq.* Chicago: University of Chicago Press, 2013.

Hertzke, Allen D, and Pew Forum on Religion & Public Life. *Lobbying for the Faithful: Religious Advocacy Groups in Washington, D.C.* Pew Forum, May 2012.

Heslop, Luke A. "On Sacred Ground: The Political Performance of Religious Responsibility." *Contemporary South Asia* 22 no. 1 (2014): 21–36.

Hirschl, Ran. *Comparative Matters: The Renaissance of Comparative Constitutional Law.* New York: Oxford University Press, 2014.

282   REFERENCES

Constitutional Theocracy. Cambridge, MA: Harvard University Press, 2010.

Towards Juristocracy: The Origins and Consequences of the New Constitutional-ism. Cambridge, MA: Harvard University Press, 2004.

Holt, John. *Buddha in the Crown: Avalokitesvara in the Buddhist Traditions of Sri Lanka*. New York: Oxford University Press, 1991.

The Buddhist Vishnu. New York: Columbia University Press, 2004.

The Religious World of Kīrti Śrī: Buddhism, Art, and Politics in Late Medieval Sri Lanka. New York: Oxford University Press, 1996.

Horowitz, Donald L. *A Democratic South Africa?: Constitutional Engineering in a Divided Society*. Los Angeles: University of California Press, 1991.

Hurd, Elizabeth Shakman. *Beyond Religious Freedom: The New Global Politics of Religion*. Princeton, NJ: Princeton University Press. 2015.

Irwin, Collin. 'War and Peace' and the APRC Proposals. Colombo: Centre for Policy Alternatives and Peace Polls, May 2010. www.peacepolls.org/peace polls/documents/001173.pdf (Accessed October 15, 2014).

Ismail, Qadri. "Unmooring Identity: The Antinomies of Muslim Elite Self-Formation in Sri Lanka." In *Unmaking the Nation: The Politics of Identity and History in Modern Sri Lanka*. Edited by Pradeep Jeganathan. Colombo: Social Scientists Association, 1995.

Jacobsohn, Gary J. *Constitutional Identity*. Cambridge, MA: Harvard University Press, 2010.

Jayawickrama, Nihal. Human Rights: The Sri Lankan Experience 1947–1981. Unpublished Ph.D. Thesis. University of London, SOAS, September 1983.

"Reflections on the Making and Content of the 1972 Constitution: An Insider's Perspective." In *The Sri Lankan Republic at 40: Reflections on Constitutional History, Theory, Practice*. Edited by Asanga Welikala. Colombo: Centre for Policy Alternatives, 2012.

Jeffries, Charles J. *Ceylon: The Path to Independence*. London: Pall Mall Press, 1962.

Jenkins, Laura D. "Legal Limits on Religious Conversion in India." *Law & Contemporary Problems* 71 (2008): 109.

Jennings, W Ivor. *The Approach to Self-Government*. Cambridge: Cambridge University Press, 1956.

The Constitution of Ceylon. Bombay: Oxford University Press, 1949.

"D.S. Senanayake and Independence." *Ceylon Historical Journal* 5, no. 1–4 (1955): 16–22.

Law and the Constitution. London: University of London, 1933.

"Limitations on a 'Sovereign' Parliament." *Cambridge Law Journal* 22 (1964): 177–180.

"The Making of a Dominion Constitution." *Law Quarterly Review* 65 (1949): 456–479.

Nationalism and Political Development in Ceylon (Institute of Pacific Studies Secretariat Paper, Series 9, Number 10). New York: Institute of Pacific Relations, 1950.

REFERENCES

"Politics in Ceylon Since 1954." *Pacific Affairs* 27, no. 4 (1954): 338–352.

Jennings, W Ivor, and H W Tambiah. *The Dominion of Ceylon: The Development of Its Laws and Constitution*, Westport, CT: Greenwood Press, 1970.

Josephson, Jason A. *The Invention of Religion in Japan.* Chicago: University of Chicago Press, 2012.

Kagan, Robert A. *Adversarial Legalism: The American Way of Law.* Cambridge, MA: Harvard University Press, 2001.

Kahn, Paul W. "Comparative Constitutionalism in a New Key." *Michigan Law Review* (2003): 2677–2705.

The Cultural Study of Law: Reconstructing Legal Scholarship. Chicago: University of Chicago Press, 2000.

Kapferer, Bruce. *A Celebration of Demons: Exorcism and the Aesthetics of Healing in Sri Lanka.* Bloomington: Indiana University Press, 1983.

Legends of People, Myths of State: Violence, Intolerance, and Political Culture in Sri Lanka and Australia. London: Smithsonian Institution Press, 1988.

Kearney, Robert. *Communalism and Language in the Politics of Ceylon.* Durham, NC: Duke University Press, 1967.

Kemper, Steven. "The Buddhist Monkhood, the Law, and the State in Colonial Sri Lanka." *Comparative Studies in Society and History* 26, no. 3 (1984): 401–427.

"Buddhism Without Bhikkhus: The Sri Lanka Vinaya Vardana Society." In *Religion and Legitimation of Power in Sri Lanka.* Edited by Bardwell L Smith. Chambersberg, PA: Anima, 1978, 212–235.

The Presence of the Past: Chronicles, Politics, and Culture in Sinhala Life. Ithaca, NY: Cornell University Press, 1991.

Kissane, Bill. "The Illusion of State Neutrality in a Secularising Ireland." *West European Politics* 26, no. 1 (2003): 73–94.

Kumarasingham, Harshan (ed.). *Constitution-Maker: Selected Writings of Sir Ivor Jennings.* Cambridge: Cambridge University Press, 2014.

The Road to Temple Trees. Colombo: Centre for Policy Alternatives, 2015.

Kuru, Ahmet T. *Muslim Politics Without an "Islamic" State: Can Turkey's Justice and Development Party Be a Model for Arab Islamists? (Policy Briefing).* Washington, D.C.: Brookings Institution, February, 2013.

Lanka Bauddha Mandalaya. *An Event of Dual Significance.* Colombo: Ceylon Ministry of Home Affairs, 1955.

Larson, Gerald (ed.). *Religion and Personal Law in Secular India: A Call to Judgment.* Bloomington, IN: Indiana University Press, 2001.

Larsson, Tomas. "Monkish Politics in Southeast Asia: Religious Disenfranchisement in Comparative and Theoretical Perspective." *Modern Asian Studies* 49, no. 1 (2015): 1–43.

Laski, Harold J. *Liberty in the Modern State.* New York: Harper, 1930.

REFERENCES

The Rise of European Liberalism. New Brunswick, NJ: Transaction Publishers, 1997.

Latour, Bruno. *The Making of Law: An Ethnography of the Conseil D'Etat.* Cambridge: Polity Press, 2010.

Lauren, Paul G. "First Principles of Racial Equality: History and the Politics and Diplomacy of Human Rights Provisions in the United Nations Charter." *Human Rights Quarterly* 5, no. 1 (1983): 1–26.

Laycock, Douglas. "Formal, Substantive, and Disaggregated Neutrality Toward Religion." *DePaul Law Review* 39, no. 4 (1990): 993–1018.

Lerner, Hanna. "Constitutional Impasse, Democracy and Religion in Israel." In *Constitution Writing, Religion and Democracy.* Edited by Asli Bali and Hanna Lerner. Cambridge: Cambridge University Press, 2016.

Making Constitutions in Deeply Divided Societies. New York: Cambridge University Press, 2011.

"Permissive Constitutions, Democracy, and Religious Freedom in India, Indonesia, Israel, and Turkey." *World Politics* 65, no. 4 (2013): 609–655.

Leve, Lauren. "'Secularism Is a Human Right!': Double-binds of Buddhism, Democracy, and Identity in Nepal." In *The Practice of Human Rights: Tracking Law Between the Global and the Local.* Edited by Mark Goodale and Sally Engle Merry. New York: Cambridge University Press, 2007.

Levi, G. "On Microhistory." In *New Perspectives on Historical Writing.* Edited by Peter Burke. Cambridge: Polity Press, 1991.

Lijphart, Arend. "Constitutional Design for Divided Societies." *Journal of Democracy* 15, no. 2 (2004): 96–109.

Lombardi, Clark B. "Designing Islamic Constitutions: Past Trends and Options for a Democratic Future." *International Journal of Constitutional Law* 11, no. 3 (2013): 615–645.

"Islamic Law as a Source of Constitutional Law in Egypt: The Constitutionalization of the Sharia in a Modern Arab State." *Columbia Journal of Transnational Law* 37 (1998): 81–123.

Magnússon, Sigurður G, and István Szíjártó. *What Is Microhistory?: Theory and Practice.* New York: Routledge, 2013.

Maithripala Senanayeke Felicitation Committee. "S.W.R.D. Bandaranaike, the Progenitor of the People's Constitution." In *Maithripala Senanayeke Felicitation Volume.* Dehiwala, Sri Lanka: Tissara Press, 1972.

Malagodi, Mara. "The End of a National Monarchy: Nepal's Recent Constitutional Transition From Hindu Kingdom to Secular Federal Republic." *Studies in Ethnicity and Nationalism* 11, no. 2 (2011): 234–251.

"'The Oriental Jennings': An Archival Investigation into Sir Ivor Jennings' Constitutional Legacy in South Asia." *Legal Information Management* 14, no. 1 (2014): 33–37.

Malalgoda, Kitsiri. *Buddhism in Sinhalese Society, 1750–1900: A Study of Religious Revival and Change.* Berkeley: University of California Press, 1976.

"Concepts and Confrontations: A Case Study of Agama." In *Collective Identities Revisited (Vol. 1)*. Edited by Michael Roberts. Colombo: Marga Institute Press, 1997.

Mamdani, Mahmood. *Citizen and Subject: Contemporary Africa and the Legacy of Late Colonialism*. Princeton, NJ: Princeton University Press, 1996.

Manor, James. *The Expedient Utopian: Bandaranaike and Ceylon*. Cambridge: Cambridge University Press, 2009.

Marasinghe, M L "Ceylon: A Conflict of Constitutions." *The International and Comparative Law Quarterly* 20, no. 4 (1971): 645–674.

"Sir William Ivor Jennings." In *Legal Personalities: Volume 1*. Colombo: Law and Society Trust, 2005.

Marga Institute. *Social Image of the Judiciary in Sri Lanka*. Colombo: Marga Press, 2004.

Matthews, Bruce. "Buddhist Activism in Sri Lanka." In *Questioning the Secular State: The Worldwide Resurgence of Religion in Politics*. Edited by David Westerlund. New York: St. Martin's Press, 1996.

"Christian Evangelical Conversions and the Politics of Sri Lanka." *Pacific Affairs* 80, no. 3 (2007): 455–472.

Mazie, Steven V. *Israel's Higher Law: Religion and Liberal Democracy in the Jewish State*. Lanham, MD: Lexington Books, 2006.

Mazower, Mark *No Enchanted Palace: The End of Empire and the Ideological Origins of the United Nations*. Princeton, NJ: Princeton University Press, 2009.

"The Strange Triumph of Human Rights, 1933–1950." *The Historical Journal* 47, no. 2 (2004): 379–398.

McCleary, Rachel M, and Leonard WJ van der Kuijp. "The Market Approach to the Rise of the Geluk School, 1419–1642." *The Journal of Asian Studies* 69, no. 1 (2010): 149–180.

McConnell, Michael W. "Why Is Religious Liberty the 'First Freedom'?" *Cardozo Law Review* 21 (2000): 1243–1265.

McDaniel, Justin. *The Lovelorn Ghost and the Magical Monk: Practicing Buddhism in Modern Thailand*. New York: Columbia University Press, 2013.

McGilvray, Dennis B. "Dutch Burghers and Portuguese Mechanics: Eurasian Ethnicity in Sri Lanka." *Comparative Studies in Society and History* 24, no. 2 (1982): 235–263.

Meegama, Ananda. *Philip Gunawardena and the 1956 Revolution in Sri Lanka*. Colombo: Godage, 2009.

Moore, Mick. *The State and Peasant Politics in Sri Lanka*. Cambridge: Cambridge University Press, 1985.

Morsink, Johannes. *The Universal Declaration of Human Rights: Origins, Drafting, and Intent*. Philadelphia: University of Pennsylvania Press, 1999.

Moustafa, Tamir. "Liberal Rights Versus Islamic Law? The Construction of a Binary in Malaysian Politics." *Law & Society Review* 47, no. 4 (2013): 771–802.

Moyn, Samuel. *The Last Utopia: Human Rights in History*. Cambridge, MA: Harvard University Press, 2010.

de Munck, Victor C. "Sufi and Reformist Designs: Muslim Identity in Sri Lanka." In *Buddhist Fundamentalism and Minority Identities in Sri Lanka*. Edited by Tessa J Bartholomeusz and Chandra R de Silva. Albany, NY: SUNY Press, 1998.

Nadaraja, Tambyah. *The Legal System of Ceylon in Its Historical Setting*. Leiden: Brill, 1972.

Nadesan, S. *Some Comments on the Constituent Assembly and the Draft Basic Resolutions*. Colombo: Printed by Lake House Printers & Publishers for Nadaraja, 1971.

Nedostup, Rebecca. *Superstitious Regimes: Religion and the Politics of Chinese Modernity*. Cambridge, MA: Harvard University Press, 2009.

Nu, U. *Burma Under the Japanese, Pictures and Portraits*. New York: St. Martin's Press, 1954.

Nussbaum, Martha. *Liberty of Conscience: In Defense of America's Tradition of Religious Equality*. New York: Basic Books, 2010.

Obeyesekere, Gananath. "The Buddhist Pantheon in Ceylon and Its Extension." In *Anthropological Studies in Theravada Buddhism*. Edited by Manning Nash. New Haven, CT: Yale University Press, 1966.

"Religious Symbolism and Political Change in Sri Lanka." In *The Two Wheels of Dhamma: Essays on the Theravada Tradition in India and Ceylon*. Edited by Bardwell L Smith. Boston, MA: American Academy of Religion, 1972.

"Representations of the Wildman in Sri Lanka." In *Beyond Primitivism: Indigenous Religious Traditions and Modernity*. Edited by Jacob K Olupona. New York: Routledge, 2004.

"Social Change and the Deities: Rise of the Kataragama Cult in Modern Sri Lanka." *Man* n.s. 12, no. 3/4 (1977): 377–396.

O'Brien, Robert, and Bernard Stasi. *The Stasi Report: The Report of the Committee of Reflection on the Application of the Principle of Secularity in the Republic*. Buffalo, NY: William S Hein & Co, 2005.

Paramasivam, K, and James Lindholm. *A Basic Tamil Reader and Grammar*. Evanston, IL: Tamil Language Study Association, 1980.

Parkinson, Charles. *Bills of Rights and Decolonization: The Emergence of Domestic Human Rights Instruments in Britain's Overseas Territories*. London: Oxford University Press, 2007.

Peebles, Patrick. *The History of Sri Lanka*. Westport, CT: Greenwood Press, 2006.

Peiris, Denzil. *1956 and After: Background to Parties and Politics in Ceylon Today*. Colombo: Lake House, 1958.

Pfaffenberger, Bryan. "The Kataragama Pilgrimage: Hindu-Buddhist Interaction and Its Significance in Sri Lanka's Polyethnic Social System." *The Journal of Asian Studies* 38, no. 2 (1979): 253–270.

REFERENCES

"The Political Construction of Defensive Nationalism: The 1968 Temple-Entry Crisis in Northern Sri Lanka." *The Journal of Asian Studies* 49, no. 1 (1990): 78–96.

Phadnis, Urmila. *Religion and Politics in Sri Lanka*. London: Hurst & Co, 1976.

Preuss, Ulrich K. *Constitutional Revolution: The Link Between Constitutionalism and Progress*. Atlantic Highlands, NJ: Humanities Press, 1995.

Rahula, Ven. Walpola. "Appendix II: The Vidyalankara Declaration." In *The Heritage of the Bhikkhu*. New York: Grove Press, 1974.

The Heritage of the Bhikkhu. New York: Grove Press, 1974.

Redding, Jeffrey A. "Invisible Constitutions: Culture, Religion, and Memory: Secularism, the Rule of Law, and Sharia Courts: An Ethnographic Examination of a Constitutional Controversy." *Saint Louis University Law Journal* 57 (2013): 339–376.

Reynolds, Andrew. *The Architecture of Democracy: Constitutional Design, Conflict Management, and Democracy*. London: Oxford University Press, 2002.

Robbins, Joel. "The Globalization of Pentecostal and Charismatic Christianity." *Annual Review of Anthropology* 33, no. 1 (2004): 117–143.

Roberts, Michael (ed.). *Documents of the Ceylon National Congress and Nationalist Politics in Ceylon 1929–1950*. Colombo: National Archives Dept., 1965.

Exploring Confrontation: Sri Lanka, Politics, Culture and History. Chur, Switzerland: Harwood Academic Publishers, 1994.

"Noise as Cultural Struggle: Tom-tom Beating, the British, and Communal Disturbances in Sri Lanka, 1880s–1930s." In *Mirrors of Violence: Communities, Riots, and Survivors in South Asia*. Edited by Veena Das. Studies in Society and Culture; New Delhi: Oxford University Press, 1990.

"Problems of Collective Identity in a Multi-ethnic Society: Sectional Nationalism vs Ceylonese Nationalism, 1900–1940." In *Collective Identities Revisited (Vol. 1)*. Colombo: Marga Institute Press, 1997.

Rogers, John D. *Crime, Justice, and Society in Colonial Sri Lanka*. London: Curzon Press, 1987.

"Early British Rule and Social Classification in Lanka." *Modern Asian Studies* 38, no. 3 (2004): 625–647.

"Post-Orientalism and the Interpretation of Premodern and Modern Political Identities: The Case of Sri Lanka." *The Journal of Asian Studies* 53, no. 1 (1994): 10–23.

Rosenfeld, Michel (ed.). *Constitutionalism, Identity, Difference, and Legitimacy: Theoretical Perspectives*. Durham, NC: Duke University Press, 1994.

Rubin, B R. "Crafting a Constitution for Afghanistan." *Journal of Democracy* 15, no. 3 (2004): 5–19.

Russell, Jane. *Communal Politics Under the Donoughmore Constitution, 1931–1947, The Ceylon Historical Journal 26*. Dehiwala, Sri Lanka: Tissara Prakasakayo, 1982.

REFERENCES

Salomon, Noah. "The Ruse of Law: Legal Equality and the Problem of Citizenship in Multi-Religious Sudan." In *After Secular Law*. Edited by Winnifred Fallers Sullivan, Robert A Yelle and Mateo Taussig-Rubbo. Palo Alto, CA: Stanford University Press, 2011.

Samaraweera, Vijaya. "An Act of Truth in a Sinhala Court of Law: On Truth, Lies and Judicial Proof Among the Sinhala Buddhists." *Cardozo Journal of International and Comparative Law* 5 (1997): 133–163.

"Muslim Revivalist Movement, 1880–1915." In *Collective Identities, Nationalisms, and Protest in Modern Sri Lanka*. Edited by Michael Roberts. Colombo: Marga Institute, 1979.

Sapru, Tej B, Mukund R Jayakar, Narasimba G Ayyangar, and Jagdish Prasad. *Constitutional Proposals of the Sapru Committee*. Bombay: Padma Publishers Limited, 1945.

Schalk, Peter "'Unity' and 'Sovereignty': Key Concepts of a Militant Buddhist Organization in the Present Conflict in Sri Lanka." *Temenos* 24 (1988): 55–87.

Scheingold, Stuart A. *The Politics of Rights: Lawyers, Public Policy, and Political Change*. 2nd ed. Ann Arbor, MI: University of Michigan Press, 2004.

Scheppele, Kim L. "Constitutional Ethnography: An Introduction." *Law & Society Review* 38, no. 3 (2004): 389–406.

Schonthal, Benjamin. "Environments of Law: Islam, Buddhism, and the State in Contemporary Sri Lanka." *The Journal of Asian Studies* 75, no. 1 (2016): 137–156.

"The Legal Regulation of Buddhism in Contemporary Sri Lanka." In *Buddhism and Law: An Introduction*. Edited by Rebecca R French and Mark A Nathan. New York: Cambridge University Press, 2014.

Schonthal, Benjamin, Tamir Moustafa, Matthew Nelson, and Shylashri Shankar. "Is the Rule of Law an Antidote for Religious Tension? The Promise and Peril of Judicializing Religious Freedom." *American Behavioral Scientist* 60, no. 8 (2015): 966–986.

Schonthal, Benjamin, and Matthew J Walton. "The (New) Buddhist Nationalisms? Symmetries and Specificities in Sri Lanka and Myanmar." *Contemporary Buddhism* 17, no. 1 (2016): 1–35.

Scott, David. "Community, Number, and the Ethos of Democracy." In *Refashioning Futures: Criticism after Postcoloniality*. Princeton, NJ: Princeton University Press, 1999.

Sen, Ronojoy. *Articles of Faith: Religion, Secularism, and the Indian Supreme Court*. New Delhi: Oxford University Press, 2010.

Seneviratne, H L. *The Work of Kings: The New Buddhism in Sri Lanka*. Chicago: University of Chicago Press, 1999.

Shapiro, Martin M. *Courts: A Comparative and Political Analysis*. Chicago: University of Chicago Press, 1986.

Shastri, Amita. "Sri Lanka's Provincial Council System: A Solution to the Ethnic Problem?" *Asian Survey* 32, no. 8 (1992): 723–743.

REFERENCES

"The United National Party of Sri Lanka: Reproducing Hegemony." In *Political Parties in South Asia*. Edited by Subrata Mitra, Mike Enskat and Clemens Spiess. Westport, CT: Praeger, 2004.

Sherwood, Marika "India at the Founding of the United Nations." *International Studies* 33, no. 4 (1996): 407–428.

Singer, Marshall R. *The Emerging Elite: A Study of Political Leadership in Ceylon*. Cambridge, MA: MIT Press, 1964.

Sinhala Commission. *Report of the Sinhala Commission (Part II)*. Colombo: Samayawardhana Press, 2001.

Siriwardena, C D S. "The Idea of a Buddha Sasana Council." In *University Buddhist Annual Vol. 2*. Edited by Tilak Gunasekere. Colombo: University Buddhist Brotherhood of Colombo, 1959.

Smith, Donald E. "Political Monks and Monastic Reform." In *South Asian Politics and Religion*. Princeton, NJ: Princeton University Press, 1966.

"The Sinhalese Buddhist Revolution." In *South Asian Politics and Religion*. Princeton, NJ: Princeton University Press, 1966.

Smith, Jonathan Z. *Imagining Religion: From Babylon to Jonestown*. Chicago: University of Chicago Press, 1982.

Smith, Steven D. *Law's Quandary*. Cambridge, MA: Harvard University Press, 2007.

Smooha, Sammy. "The Model of Ethnic Democracy: Israel As a Jewish and Democratic State." *Nations and Nationalism* 8, no. 4 (2002): 475–503.

Stepan, Alfred C. "Religion, Democracy, and the 'Twin Tolerations.'" *Journal of Democracy* 11, no. 4 (2000): 37–57.

Stirrat, R L. "Demonic Possession in Roman Catholic Sri Lanka." *Journal of Anthropological Research* 33, no. 2 (1977): 133–157.

Sullivan, Winnifred F. *The Impossibility of Religious Freedom*. Princeton, NJ: Princeton University Press, 2005.

Sullivan, Winnifred F., Mateo Taussig-Rubbo and Robert A. Yelle (eds.). *After Secular Law*. Palo Alto: Stanford University Press, 2012.

Sunstein, Cass R. "Incompletely Theorized Agreements." *Harvard Law Review* 108, no. 7 (1995): 1733–1772.

Suntharalingam, C. *Eylom: Beginnings of the Freedom Struggle: Dozen Documents by C. Sunatharalingam with "Candid Comments and Criticisms by Lord Soulbury" (Pamphlet)*. Jaffna: īzam pancāyutam, 1963.

Tambiah, Stanley Jeyaraja. *Buddhism Betrayed? Religion, Politics, and Violence in Sri Lanka*. Chicago: University of Chicago Press, 1992.

Leveling Crowds: Ethnonationalist Conflicts and Collective Violence in South Asia. Berkeley: University of California Press, 1996.

World Conqueror and World Renouncer: A Study of Buddhism and Polity in Thailand Against a Historical Background. New York: Cambridge University Press, 1976.

Tamil United Liberation Front (TULF). "The Vaddukoddai Resolution." *Logos* 16, no. 3 (1977): 10–25.

Tennekoon, N Serena. "Rituals of Development: The Accelerated Mahaväli Development Program of Sri Lanka." *American Ethnologist* 15, no. 2 (1988): 294–310.

Thier, J Alexander. "Making of a Constitution in Afghanistan." *New York Law School Law Review* 51 (2006): 557–579.

Thomas, Jolyon B. *Japan's Preoccupation with Religious Freedom*. Ph.D. Dissertation, Department of Religion, Princeton University, 2014.

Turner, Alicia. *Saving Buddhism: The Impermanence of Religion in Colonial Burma*. Honolulu: University of Hawai'i Press, 2014.

Udagama, Nelum Deepika. "The Fragmented Republic: Reflections on the 1972 Constitution of Sri Lanka." *Sri Lanka Journal of Humanities* 39, no. 1–2 (2014): 81–97.

"The Sri Lankan Legal Complex and the Liberal Project: Only Thus Far and No More." In *Fates of Political Liberalism in the British Post-colony: The Politics of the Legal Complex*. Edited by Terence C Halliday, Lucien Karpik and Malcolm M Feeley. New York: Cambridge University Press, 2012.

United Nations General Assembly. *Report of the Special Rapporteur on Freedom of Religion or Belief, Heiner Bielefeldt to the General Assembly of the UN*, 2013, www.iirf.eu/index.php?id=178&no_cache=1&tx_ttnews%5BbackPid%5D=176&tx_ ttnews%5Btt_news%5D=1686 (accessed August 15, 2015).

Vaithianathan, K, and All-Ceylon-Hindu Congress. *Catholic Action and Thiruketheeswaram (Pamphlet)*. n.p., n.d.

van der Horst, Josine. *Who Is He, What Is He Doing: Religious Rhetoric and Performances in Sri Lanka During R. Premadasa's Presidency (1989–1993)*. Amsterdam: VU University Press, 1995.

Various Medical Men. *Ceylon's Uplift (Through Buddhism)*. Colombo: Lake House, 1940.

Vijayavardhana, D C. *The Revolt in the Temple: Composed to Commemorate 2500 Years of the Land, the Race and the Faith*. Colombo: Sinha Publishers, 1953.

Viswanathan, Gauri. *Outside the Fold: Conversion, Modernity, Belief*. Princeton, NJ: Princeton University Press, 1988.

Waltz, Susan. "Universalizing Human Rights: The Role of Small States in the Construction of the Universal Declaration of Human Rights." *Human Rights Quarterly* 23, no. 1 (2001): 44–72.

Warnapala, Wiswa. *Sri Lanka Freedom Party: A Political Profile*. Colombo: Godage International, 2005.

Weeramantry, Lucian. *Assassination of a Prime Minister: The Bandaranaike Murder Case*. Geneva, Switzerland: S.A. Studer, 1969.

Weerasooria, W S. *Buddhist Ecclesiastical Law: A Treatise on Sri Lankan Statute Law and Judicial Decisions on Buddhist Temples and Temporalities*. Colombo: Postgraduate Institute of Management, 2011.

Weerawardana, I D S. *Ceylon General Election 1956.* Colombo: Gunasena and Sons, 1960.

"The General Elections in Ceylon, 1952." *The Ceylon Historical Journal* 2, no. 1–2 (1952): 109–178.

Welikala, Asanga (ed.). *Reforming Sri Lankan Presidentialism: Provenance, Problems and Prospects.* Colombo: Centre for Policy Alternatives, 2015.

Whitecross, Richard W. "Buddhism and Constitutions in Bhutan." In *Buddhism and Law: An Introduction.* Edited by Rebecca R French and Mark A Nathan. New York: Cambridge University Press, 2014.

Wickramasinghe, Nira. *Ethnic Politics in Colonial Sri Lanka.* New Delhi: Vikas, 1995.

Sri Lanka in the Modern Age: A History. London: Oxford University Press, 2015.

Widner, Jennifer. "Constitution Writing and Conflict Resolution." *The Round Table* 94, no. 381 (2005): 503–518.

Wijemanne, Adrian. *War and Peace in Post-colonial Ceylon, 1948–1991.* Orient Blackswan, 1996.

Wilson, A J. "The Colombo Man, the Jaffna Man, and the Batticaloa Man." In *The Sri Lankan Tamils: Ethnicity and Identity.* Edited by Chelvadurai Manogaran and Bryan Pfaffenberger. Boulder, CO: Westview Press, 1994.

Electoral Politics in An Emergent State: The Ceylon General Election of May 1970. Cambridge: Cambridge University Press, 1975.

The Gaullist System in Asia: The Constitution of Sri Lanka (1978). London: Macmillan Press, 1980.

"Minority Safeguards in the Ceylon Constitution," *Ceylon Journal of Historical and Social Studies* 1, no. 1 (1958): 73–95.

Politics in Sri Lanka 1947–1979. London: Macmillan, 1974.

Winn, Peter A. "Legal Ritual." *Law and Critique* 2, no. 2 (1991): 207–232.

Winslow, Deborah. "A Political Geography of Deities: Space and the Pantheon in Sinhalese Buddhism." *The Journal of Asian Studies* 43, no. 2 (1984): 273–291.

Winslow, Deborah, and Michael D Woost. *Economy, Culture, and Civil War in Sri Lanka.* Bloomington, IN: Indiana University Press, 2004.

Wriggins, Howard. *Ceylon: Dilemmas of a New Nation.* Princeton NJ: Princeton University Press, 1960.

Young, Richard F, and S Jebanesan. *The Bible Trembled: The Hindu-Christian Controversies of Nineteenth-Century Ceylon.* Vienna: Inst. für Indologie der Univ. Wien, 1995.

Young, Richard F, and G P V Somaratna. *Vain Debates: Buddhist-Christian Controversies of Nineteenth-Century Ceylon.* Wien: Institut für Indologie der Universität Wien, 1996.

Zeghal, Malika. "The Implicit Shariah." In *Varieties of Religious Establishment.* Edited by Winnifred Fallers Sullivan and Lori G Beamon. London: Ashgate, 2013.

INDEX

ACBC. *See* All-Ceylon Buddhist
Congress
Adam's Peak, 108, 270
Administration of Justice Act of 1973,
167
affirmative action, 241
Afghanistan, 4
Agrama, Hussein, 214
All-Ceylon Buddhist Congress (ACBC),
50, 52, 54, 63, 66–67, 69–91,
167–168
on Buddhism Resolution, 112–114
on Buddhist privileges, 42–55
on Christianity, 225–226
Commission of Inquiry, 123
Committee Report, 78–79
on democracy, 55–56
memoranda from, 112–114
Ministry of Constitutional Affairs
and, 112
on promotional paradigm, 57
on rightful place, 107, 141–142
on Section 29(2), 54
on virtues, 112–113
All-Ceylon Hindu Congress, 235–236
on Buddhism Resolution, 118–119
All-Ceylon Moors Association,
118
Anglicans, 227–228
Anti Conversion Bill, 242
Anuradhapura, 90, 108
Asigiri branch of Siyam Nikaya, 80–83,
141, 196–197
Assisted Schools and Training Colleges
Act, 88–89
Atlantic Charter, 45–47
autonomy, 161–162, 213–214

ayurvedic physicians, 64–65
Aziz, Abdul, 124–126

Bandaranaike, S W R D, 63, 82, 90–91,
123, 132–133
assassination of, 84
Buddha Sasana Commission
appointed by, 78–79
on Buddhism, 68, 70–71, 77–78
campaign rhetoric of, 71–72
on Constitution of 1948, 67–68
constitutional reform and, 66–72
on democracy, 66, 82
election of, 67
on Free Lanka Constitution, 66–67
on freedom, 26–27
on fundamental rights, 61–62, 67–68,
70–71
on Joint Select Committee, 72–73
personal style of, 65–66
as prime minister, 61–62
rise of, 65–66
Senanayake, D S, and, 66–67
on SFLP, 66
ten policies, 71
Bandaranaike, Sirima, 91, 100,
159–160
on Buddhism, 85–87, 166–167
De Silva and, 106–107
education system overhauled by,
88–89
election of, 85
on United Front, 101–102
Bandaranaike Committee, 91
Batticaloa, 53, 119–120, 159
Berger, Benjamin, 13–14
bhikkhu, 51–52, 200, 205–209

INDEX

Bhutan, 150
Bill of Rights, 39
Bodu Bala Sena, 185
Bombay, 47
Britain
  Buddhism and, 51–52
  Ceylon and, 27–33
  colonialism of, 27, 224
Buddha, 2500th anniversary of
  enlightenment of (Jayanthi),
  69–70
Buddha Sasana, 10–19, 171–172,
  176–177, 213–214
Buddha Sasana Act, 79–80, 85
Buddha Sasana Commission, 71–72,
  77–81
  Bandaranaike appointing, 78–79
  criticism of, 80
  deliberation of, 79
  establishment of, 78
  implementation of, 84–85
  members of, 78–79
  offenses caused by, 80–81
  registration of places of worship, 78
  UNP on, 89
Buddha Sasana Commission Report,
  85–87, 123
Buddha Sasana Council Act of 1950, 79
Buddha Sasana Mandalaya, 54–55, 85,
  113–114
  branches of, 79
  creation of, 79
Buddhism, 15–16
  ACBC on privileges, 42–55
  activism and, 24
  advocacy, 90
  autonomy of, from state, 161–162,
  213–214
  Bandaranaike, S W R D on, 68,
  70–71, 77–78
  Bandaranaike, Sirima, on, 85–87,
  166–167
  battles within, 188–190
  Britain and, 51–52
  capitalism and, 179–180
  Christianity and, 56–57, 236–237
  colonialism and, 52
  competing visions of, 168–169

in DBR3, 107–110
debates over, 214–215
decline of, 50–52
defining, 168–171
democracy and, 82
foremost place of, 14–15, 143–144,
  186–187, 197–198, 239–242
freedom and, 82, 248–249
fundamental rights and, 83, 109
human rights and, 82
law and, 262–263
legal battles for, 149–154
Malalasekera on, 55–57, 90
nationalism and, 156
in 1950s, 62–65
in 1960s, 84–85
Places and Objects of Worship Bill
  and, 164
places of importance in, 170–178
promotion of, 68–70, 79, 96–97
protection of, 165–166
protection of orthodoxy, 167–170
pyrrhic constitutionalism and,
  212–216
rightful place for, 85–90, 107–111,
  115
in Sri Lanka, 7–9
as state religion, 89
territorializing, 157–159
theocracy and, 119
Theraveda, 203–206, 213–214
thought processes in, 250
traditionalist, 201–205
UNP on, 71
Buddhism Chapter, 1–8, 20, 121, 140,
  154–156, 163, 179, 264
  ambiguities in, 1–19
  Buddhist-interest litigation and,
  166–167
  consolidating, 183–187
  constitutional microhistory of,
  266–268
  development of, 104–107
  dismissals of, 264–265
  expanding, 183–187
  foremost place in, 239–240
  interpretations of, 184–185
  language of, 189

294 INDEX

Buddhism Chapter (cont.)
 meaning of, 11–19
 microhistory of, 24
 politics of, 100–104
 ratification of, 144–145
 ratifying, 20
 successes of, 99–100
 supporters of, 188–190
 Supreme Court on, 175–176
 YMBA on, 173
Buddhism Resolution, 110–111
 ACBC on, 112–114
 All-Ceylon Hindu Congress on,
  118–119
 amendments, 124
 assembly debates, 121–122
 Dharmalingam on, 133
 drafting, 110
 Federal Party on, 131–132, 135–136,
  139
 introduction of, 122–124
 language in, 118–119, 138–139
 memoranda from Buddhist groups,
  111–117
 memoranda from non-Buddhist
  groups, 117–121
 proposed amendment one, 124–126
 proposed amendment three,
  131–137
 proposed amendment two, 126–131
 Ratnam on, 135, 137
 SFLP on, 122–124
 Siyam Nikaya on, 114–115, 142–143
 translations of, 110, 132
 UNP on, 127–128
Buddhism Subject Committee, 144
Buddhist Committee of Inquiry, 113
Buddhist constitutionalism, 149–150
 in Sri Lanka, 154–156
Buddhist Ecclesiastical Law, 29–31,
  155, 205
Buddhist monks, 1. See also bhikkhu
 in courtrooms, 1–2, 261–263
 driving and, 204–205
 human rights and, 207
 laypersons and, 1–12
 legal status of, 207
 ordaining of, 79

 registering, 79
 Senanayake, D S on, 195
 Ven. Wimalawansa on, 209–210
Buddhist rights, 49–55
 implementation of, 77–81
Buddhist Socialist Republic, 112–113
Buddhist Temporalities Ordinance of
  1889, 30, 61–62
Buddhist Temporalities Ordinance of
  1931, 30
Buddhist-Hindu Committee, 230–231,
  234–236, 253–254
Buddhist-interest litigation, 155–156,
  184, 188–189, 214–215
 Buddhism Chapter and, 166–167
 Buddhist orthodoxy protected
  through, 167–170
 in Colombo, 186–187
 defining, 156
 expanding, 183–187
 idioms of, 161–162
 protection from profanation,
  178–183
 protection of Buddhist autonomy,
  161–162
 protection of Buddhist places,
  170–178
 triadic prototype, 218–219
Burghers, 9–11, 27–28
Burma, 69, 150–151

Cambodia, 69, 206
 Constitution of 2008, 149–150
capitalism, 179–180
Catholic Action, 225–226
Ceylon, 24. See also Sri Lanka
 Britain and, 27–33
 colonialism in, 27–28
 communal representation in, 31–33
 constitution-making in 1940s, 26–27
 Jennings on politics in, 64
 legal reform in, 61
 Legislative Council, 31–32
 name of, 25–26
 national dress in, 65
 in 1950s, 62–65
 in 1960s, 84–85
 Order-in-Council, 31–32, 36, 38

INDEX

295

populism in, 64–65
representation in, 31–32
riots in, 32
self-rule of, 26–27
State Council, 32–33
in United Nations, 92–93
voting system in, 103
Ceylon Catholic Union, 80
Ceylon Communist Party, 73
Ceylon Government Gazette, 140
Ceylon Harijan Union, 118–119
Ceylon National Congress (CNC),
 39–44, 59, 66–67, 102
 Declaration of Fundamental Rights,
  48–49
 INC and, 47
 Senanayake, D S, and, 44–45
 Working Committee of, 41–43
Ceylon Tamil League, 119–120
Ceylonese Tamils, 9–11
Chandananda, Ven. Palipanne,
 95–96
change, 199–200
Charities Act, 113
Charter of Fundamental Rights,
 68–69
Charter of Justice, 28
Christianity, 7–9, 113, 137–138
 ACBC on, 225–226
 adoption of, 182
 Buddhism and, 56–57, 236–237
 Code of Ethics, 229–230
 in Colombo, 181–182
 colonialism and, 217, 224–225
 conscience and, 248–249
 conversion to, 182
 Evangelicals, 29–31, 227–229
 freedom and, 248–249
 Fundamentalist, 227–229
 incorporation of, 51–53
 limiting, 231–232
 missionaries, 29–31
 power of, 226–227
 proselytizing, 182
 Supreme Court on, 182–183
 threats from, 173–174, 217
citizenship, 11–19, 205–209
 religion and, 115–117

for Tamils, 61
Theraveda Buddhism and, 205–206,
 208–209, 215
CMT. See Commissioner of Motor
 Traffic
CNC. See Ceylon National Congress
Coca Cola, 179–180
Colombo, 27, 32, 50, 64, 92–93,
 174–175, 215–216
 Buddhist-interest litigation in,
  186–187
 Christianity in, 181–182
colonialism, 5–8, 24, 128
 of Britain, 27, 224
 Buddhism and, 52
 in Ceylon, 27–28
 Christianity and, 217, 224–225
 Dutch, 224
 end of, 25–26
 Malalasekera on, 51–52
 religion and, 25–33
Commissioner of Buddhist Affairs,
 201–202
 Ven. Wimalawansa and, 203–204
Commissioner of Motor Traffic (CMT),
 190–191, 199
Common Program, 104–105
communal representation
 as abortive paradigm, 57–58
 in Ceylon, 31–33
 Ponnambalam on, 58
Communist Party, 84–85, 104–141
comparative constitutional law, 24
conscience
 Christianity and, 248–249
 conversion and, 242–243
 freedom of, 75–77, 243–245
 proselytism and, 248–249
 structure of, 247–248
consensus, 12–13
Constituent Assembly, 137–140
 changes made after, 140–144
 Subject Committees, 140–141
Constitution of 1948, 25
 Bandaranaike, S W R D on, 67–68
 contests over, 25
 enactment of, 38
 Malalasekera on, 55–56

INDEX

Constitution of 1948 (cont.)
  Ministers' Draft, 35–37
  promotional paradigm and, 37–39
  protectionist paradigm and, 37–39
  Section 29(2), 35–39, 52, 54, 60–61, 74–76, 79, 93–95
Constitution of 1972, 20, 25, 60, 154–156
  language in, 99
Constitution of 1978, 25, 154–156
  Article 9, 223, 238–239
  Article 10, 10–11, 223–224, 231–233, 238–239
  Article 12(2), 10
  Article 13(1), 223–224
  Article 13(2), 223–224
  Article 14, 223–224
  Article 14(1)(e), 10–11, 223, 232–233
  drafting of, 171–172
  elements introduced in, 171–172
  entrenched articles, 222–223, 238–239
  Thirteenth Amendment, 223
  YMBA on, 173
Constitutional Affairs Subcommittee, 106–122
constitutional law, 151–153, 255
  comparative, 24
  conflict and, 7
  conversions and, 219, 231–234, 253–256
  costs of, 5–7, 261–264
  English language and, 17–18
  language and, 17–18
  renaissance of, 17
  rethinking, 267–272
  Sinhala language and, 17–18
  in Sri Lanka, 7–8
  Tamil language and, 17–18
constitutional microhistory, 18–19, 23–24, 220
  of Buddhism Chapter, 266–268
  religion and, 264–265
Constitutional Theocracy (Hirschl), 151
constitutionalism and constitutions. *See also* pyrrhic constitutionalism
  in Ceylon, 1940s, 26–27
  conflict and, 6–7

consensus in, 12–13
  defining, 150
  discrimination and, 6–7
  as dominant form, 4
  implementation of, 147–149
  in India, 6–7
  Islam and, 150
  Jennings on, 34–35
  language in, 12–15
  law and, 2–5
  ratification, 13
  reform, 66–72
  religion and, 2–5
  revolution and, 60
  in Sri Lanka, 11, 265–272
  top-down, 152
conversions
  anxieties over, 226, 228–229
  to Christianity, 182
  conscience and, 242–243
  consolidating conflict, 234–238
  constitutional law and, 219, 231–234, 253–256
  forcible, 253
  JHU on, 233
  negative freedom and, 245–248
  outlawing, 231–232
  positive freedom and, 243–245
  problems with, 224–231
  prohibition of, 258
  pyrrhic constitutionalism and, 219
  religion and, 217–218
  unethical, 258
Cooray, J A L, 43–44, 48–49, 66–67, 73, 102
  on fundamental rights, 41–43
  on religion, 42
Court of Appeals, 192, 214

Dayaka Sabhava, 192–193
  in Court of Appeals, 192–193
  Ven. Wimalawansa and, 202
DBR3. *See* Draft Basic Resolution 3
DBRs. *See* Draft Basic Resolutions
De Silva, Colvin R., 104, 109, 121–143
  Bandaranaike, Sirima, and, 106–107
  on fundamental rights, 93

on Kandyan Convention, 128–129
on popular sovereignty, 93
on proposed amendments, 108–126
on religion, 106–122
de Silva, K M, 43
De Tocqueville, Alexis, 16
Declaration by the United Nations
1942, 45
Declaration of Fundamental Rights,
CNC, 48–49
Nehru Report and, 48–49
Declaration of Fundamental Rights for
India, 47
decolonization, 26–27
Deegawipaya Bouddha Janapadaya,
176–178
democracy, 241–242
ACBC on, 55–56
Bandaranaike, S W R D on, 66, 82
Buddhism and, 82
promotional paradigm and, 55–57
Democratic Socialist Party, 117
Democratic Workers' Congress, 117
Department of Buddhist Affairs,
186–187
Dhamma, 86, 108–109, 122–123, 163,
209–210
Dhammapada, 210
Dharmalingam, Visvanathan
on Buddhism Resolution, 133
on fundamental rights, 134
on rightful place, 133–134
Dharmapala, Anagarika, 141
Dighavapi Mahavihara, 175–176, 179,
185–186
discrimination, 2
constitutionalism and, 6–7
Donoughmore Commission, 32–33
language of, 36–37
Draft Basic Resolution 3 (DBR3),
115–117
Buddhism in, 107–110
fundamental rights in, 108
translations, 121
vagueness of, 121–122
Draft Basic Resolutions (DBRs),
102–103, 109–111
Drafting Committee, 102, 109–110

Dry Zone, 185
Dutch colonizers, 224

educational institutions, 75–76
Bandaranaike, Sirima, changing,
88–89
nationalization of, 88–89
Eelam Self-Determination and
Freedom Front, 119–120
Egypt, 4, 150–151
equality, 74–75, 111
European Union, 4–8
Evangelicals, 29–31, 227–229

Federal Party, 73, 84–85, 131, 135
on Buddhism Resolution, 131–132,
135–136, 139
Fernando, Oshan, 258
Fernando, T S, 73
First Amendment (U.S.), 6–7, 164–165,
217–218
foremost place, 175–176
of Buddhism, 14–15, 143–144,
186–187, 197–198, 239–242
in Buddhism Chapter, 239–240
rightful place contrasted with, 144
Siyam Nikaya on, 143–144
Four Freedoms Speech, 45–47
Free Lanka Bill, 43
Free Lanka Constitution, 43, 48–49, 102
Bandaranaike, S W R D on, 66–67
Free Trade Zones, 160
freedom
Bandaranaike, S W R D on, 26–27
Buddhism and, 82, 248–249
Christianity and, 248–249
of conscience, 75–77, 243–245
ICCPR on, 110
negative, 245–248
positive, 243–245
of religion, 71, 75, 110
Roosevelt on, 45
Freedom from Foreign Rule, 45
fundamental rights, 10–11, 21, 42,
68–69, 92–93. See also human
rights
Bandaranaike, S W R D on, 61–62,
67–68, 70–71

INDEX

fundamental rights (cont.)
  Buddhism and, 83, 109
  Cooray on, 41–43
  in DBR3, 108
  De Silva, C, on, 93
  debates over, 94–96
  Dharmalingam on, 134
  implementation of, 72–77
  in India, 47–49
  Joint Select Committee on,
    73
  legitimacy of, 44–47
  politics of, 91–94
  protection of, 60–61
  religion as, 39–44
  Supreme Court on, 222

Galle Face Green, 63
Geneva, 92–93
goduru gammana, 177–178
Government of India Act of 1935,
  57–58
Government of Ireland Act of 1920,
  32–33, 37–47
  influence of, 44
Gunasekera, Prins, 162–164, 167–168

Hegel, G W F, 17
Hela Kithunu Urumaya, 237–238
Hinduism, 6–7, 118–138
  in Sri Lanka, 7–9
Hirschl, Ran, 151, 156, 164, 187
human rights, 24. See also fundamental
  rights
  Buddhism and, 82
  Buddhist monks and, 207
  legitimacy of, 44–47
  religion and, 244

ICCPR. See International Covenant on
  Civil and Political Rights
ICESCR. See International Covenant on
  Economic, Social and Cultural
  Rights
Ilangaratne, T B, 122–124
INC. See Indian National Congress
India
  constitutionalism in, 6–7

fundamental rights in, 47–49
religion in, 27–28
Indian Constituent Assembly, 103
Indian National Congress (INC), 58–59
  CNC and, 47
Indian Penal Code of 1860, 29–31
International Covenant on Civil and
  Political Rights (ICCPR), 92–93
  on religious freedom, 110
International Covenant on Economic,
  Social and Cultural Rights
  (ICESCR), 92–93
International Religious Freedom Act
  (IRFA), 252–253
interreligious bargain, 99
Inter-Religious Council, 258
intrareligious bargain, 99
Iraq, 4
Ireland, 37–47
IRFA. See International Religious
  Freedom Act
Islam, 3, 6–7, 137–138, 175–176
  constitutionalism and, 150
  personal law, 29–31
  settlements, 176–177
  in Sri Lanka, 7–9
Island of Dhamma, 49
Israel, 3–4, 150–151

Jaffna Tamils, 62–63, 159
  personal law, 29–31
Janatha Vimukti Peramuna (JVP), 132,
  139
Jatika Hela Urumaya (JHU), 231–232,
  253–254
  bill of, 232–236, 242
  constitutionality of, 242–243
  on conversion, 233
  legal battle over, 248
  ratification of, 256–257
Jayewardene, J R, 64, 66–67, 74,
  160–161, 167
Jennings, William Ivor, 42–55
  on Bill of Rights, 39
  on Ceylonese politics, 64
  on constitutionalism, 34–35
  preventative paradigm and, 33–35
JHU. See Jatika Hela Urumaya

INDEX 299

Joint Select Committee of 1957, 71–77, 92–93, 133
  Bandaranaike, S W R D on, 72–73
  Draft Constitution of, 73–74, 76–77
  on fundamental rights, 73
  passage of, 73
Joint Select Committee of 1967, 97
Judaism, 3

Kahn, Paul, 13
Kalmunai Regional Council Meeting Group, 121–143
Kandy, 28–29, 77–78, 174–175
Kandyan Convention, 28–29, 94–95, 126–127
  Article 5, 28–29, 109, 123, 127, 130
  De Silva on, 128–129
  language of, 130–131
  SFLP on, 131
  United Front on, 128–129
  UNP on, 129–131
Kandyans, 29–31
  personal law, 30
Karachi Resolution, 47–48
Kataragama, 270–272
Kulatilake, S S, 123–124

labor unions, 63
language, 99
  of Buddhism Chapter, 189
  in Buddhism Resolution, 118–119, 138–139
  in Constitution of 1972, 99
  constitutional law and, 17–18
  in constitutions, 12–15
  of Donoughmore Commission, 36–37
  of Kandyan Convention, 130–131
  of law, 16
  of Ministers' Draft, 36–37
  Sinhala, 17–18
  Tamil, 7–9, 17–18
Lanka Bauddha Mandalaya, 69
Lanka Sama Samaja Paksaya (LSSP), 73, 84–85, 104–141
  on religion, 106–122
Laos, 206
laukika, 194–195, 200, 208

law. *See also* constitutional law
  Buddhism and, 262–263
  equality before, 74–75, 111
  expanded archive of, in Sri Lanka, 17–19
  Islam and, 29–31
  Jaffna Tamils and, 29–31
  Kandyans and, 30
  language of, 16
  legal life of, 221–224
  modern, 16–17
  personal, 29–31
  positive, 41–42
  pyrrhic constitutionalism and, 17–18
  Shariah, 150, 214
  Smith on, 266–267
  societal life of, 221–224
  in Sri Lanka, 156–157
Legislative Council, Ceylon, 31–32
liberalism, 161, 167, 248
Liberation Tigers of Tamil Eelam (LTTE), 156–158, 172–173, 272–273
Local Government Buddhist Organization, 69–70
lōkōttara, 194–195, 200, 208
London, 29–32
London School of Economics, 33–35
LSSP. *See* Lanka Sama Samaja Paksaya
LTTE. *See* Liberation Tigers of Tamil Eelam

Maha Sangha, 108
Mahabodhi Society, 115
Mahajana Eksath Permuna (MEP), 84–85
Mahaparinibbana Sutta, 198–201
Mahiyangana, 108
Malalasekera, G P, 50–51, 57
  on Buddhism, 55–57, 90
  on colonialism, 51–52
  on Constitution of 1948, 55–56
Malayan Constitution, 39–40
Malaysia, 3, 150–151
Malvatu branch of Siyam Nikaya, 80–83, 141, 196–197
Manor, James, 65
Maritain, Jacques, 212

300 INDEX

Marxism, 62–63, 132–133
master-narratives, 17–18
Medhananda, Ven. Ellawala, 175–176
Menzingen case, 187
MEP. *See* Mahajana Eksath Permuna
Mettananda, L H, 86
microhistory, 23. *See also* constitutional
  microhistory
  of Buddhism Chapter, 24
middle way, 112–113
Minister for Religious Affairs,
  54–55
Ministers' Draft, 35–37
  language of, 36–37
Ministry of Constitutional Affairs, 74,
  111–112, 121
  ACBC and, 112
Ministry of Cultural Affairs,
  163–164
minority rights, 57–58
Misuse of Religious Symbols and
  Expressions, 185–186
Monastic Councils, 69–70
Moor, 7–9, 27–28
mosques, 186–187
multivalent principles, 212
Munnesvaram, 270
Muslim Progressive Association of
  Kalmunai, 117
Myanmar, 206
  Constitution of 2008, 149–151
myths, 271–272

National Christian Council, 118–119
National Christian Evangelical
  Alliance, 237–238
National Christian Fellowship of
  Sri Lanka, 237–238
National Sangha Conference, 237–238
nationalism, 24
negative freedom, 245–248
Nehru Report, 47–49
  Declaration of Fundamental Rights
  and, 48–49
Nepal, 4
New Left, 101
New Zealand, 4
noble conduct, 113

Old Left, 101
Order-In-Council, Ceylon, 31–32,
  36, 38

Pali Tipitaka, 69, 203–204
Pannaloka, Ven. Pannala, 261–262
Penal Code, 29–31
People's Forum of Jaffna, 119–120
People's Liberation Front,
  132–133
Perera, Sara Malani, 186–187
Perera, Sasanka, 227–228
Pirivena Education Bill, 162–163, 165
  challenges to, 167–168
  petitioners for, 163–164
Places and Objects of Worship Bill,
  162–163
  Buddhism and, 164
  challenges to, 167–168
  petitioners for, 163
pluralism, 4–5
Police Ordinance, 29–31
Polonnaruwa, 173–174
polygamy, 164–165
polysemy, 15, 153–154
Ponnambalam, G G, 57–58, 63, 68,
  95–96
  on communal representation, 58
  on territorial constituencies, 57–58
popular sovereignty, 93
populism, 64–65
positive freedom, 243–245
positive laws, 41–42
postcolonial countries, 5–8
preventative paradigm, 25–26, 58–59
  Jennings and, 33–35
  origins of, 33–35
  Section 29(2) of 1948 Constitution
  and, 35–37
  Senanayake, D S, and, 33–35
Principles of State Policy, 106–122
Private Member's Bill, 221, 223,
  257–258
Proclamation of September 1799, 28
promotional paradigm, 19–20, 25–26,
  58–59
  ACBC on, 57
  Constitution of 1948 and, 37–39

INDEX 301

as democratic device, 55–57
origins of, 49–55
rationalizing, 81–84
routinizing, 81–84
proselytism, 113
Christianity, 182
Code of Ethics, 229–230
conflicts over, 218
conscience and, 248–249
protectionist paradigm, 19–20, 25–26, 58–59
Constitution of 1948 and, 37–39
origins of, 39–44
rationalizing, 81–84
routinizing, 81–84
Protestants, 226–227
public-interest litigation, 153
pyrrhic constitutionalism, 11, 61, 147–149, 212, 259–260
Buddhism and, 212–216
conversions and, 219
law and, 17–18
religion and, 15
sources of, 258–259

race, religion and, 27–28
Ratnam, K P, 135–136, 139
on Buddhism Resolution, 135, 137
on religion, 139–140
Reid Commission, 39–40
religion
citizenship and, 115–117
colonialism and, 25–33
conflict and, 248–251
constitutional microhistory and, 264–265
constitutionalism and, 2–5
conversions, 217–218
Cooray on, 42
De Silva on, 106–122
debating, 238–239
in European Union, 4–8
freedom of, 71, 75, 110
as fundamental right, 39–44
holidays, 29–31
human rights and, 244
ICCPR on, 110
in India, 27–28

limitations to, 113
LSSP on, 106–122
managing, 144–145
manifesting, 247–248
propagation of, 76–77
protection of, 2
pyrrhic constitutionalism and, 15
race and, 27–28
Ratnam on, 139–140
reification of, 250–251
rights, 61
social classification and, 27–28
in Sri Lanka, 4–8, 14–15
tolerance, 95–96
United Front on, 105
in United States, 2
UNP on, 89
in the West, 250
rightful place
ACBC on, 107, 141–142
for Buddhism, 85–90, 107–111, 115
Dharmalingam on, 133–134
foremost place contrasted with, 144
Siyam Nikaya on, 114–115
rights. See fundamental rights; human rights
ritual practices, 271–272
Roman Catholicism, 121–143, 224–225, 227–228
Roosevelt, F D, 46–47
on freedom, 45
Rule of Law Index, 12

Salvation Army, 237–238
Sanghadhikaranas, 86
Sapru Committee, 47–49
Sasanasanrakshaka Bauddha Mandalaya, 85–87
Saudi Arabia, 4, 175–176
Section 29(2) of 1948 Constitution, 38–39, 52, 61, 63, 74–76
ACBC on, 54
challenges to, 60–61
interpretation of, 93–95
preventative paradigm and, 35–37
revision of, 79
secularism, 137–140
separatism and, 157–159

302　　INDEX

Senanayake, D S, 40, 42–55, 63, 67–68
  Bandaranaike, S W R D and, 66–67
  CNC and, 44–45
  critics of, 63
  death of, 64
  on monks, 195
  preventative paradigm and, 33–35
  as prime minister, 62–63
  on religious tension, 34
  Young Turks and, 40–41
Senanayake, Dudley, 90–91
Senanayake, Matripala, 87
separatism, 157–159
Shariah, 150, 214
Sinhala, 7–9, 27–28
Sinhala Bauddha Sandvidhana,
  115–116
Sinhala Jathika Sangamaya, 237–238
Sinhala language
  constitutional law and, 17–18
  in Supreme Court, 18
Sinhala Only Act, 83
Sinhala Prajatantravadi Sangamaya,
  137–144
Sinhalese Buddhists, 64, 70–71, 116
Siyam Nikaya, 54, 80–83, 85–87, 90,
  95–96, 121, 141
  on Buddhism Resolution, 114–115,
    142–143
  Buddhist Sangha, 114
  on foremost place, 143–144
  memoranda from, 114–115
  monastic fraternities breaking off of,
    196–197
  on rightful place, 114–115
SLFP. See Sri Lanka Freedom Party
Smith, Steven D, 266–267
Sobhita, Ven. Omalpe, 234
socialism, 161, 167
socialist democracy, 119–120
Soulbury Commission, 38
  mandate for, 38
Sri Lanka. See also Ceylon
  Buddhism in, 7–9
  Buddhist constitutionalism in,
    154–156
  constitutional law in, 7–8

constitutional system in, 2
constitutionalism in, 11, 265–272
courts in, 1–12
expanded archive of law in,
  17–19
Hinduism in, 7–9
history of, 156–157
Islam in, 7–9
law in, 156–157
name of, 25–26
religion in, 4–8, 14–15
state ideologies, 159–161
Sri Lanka Freedom Party (SLFP), 73,
  85, 104–141
  Bandaranaike, S W R D on, 66
  on Buddhism Resolution, 122–124
  formation of, 66
  on Kandyan Convention, 131
  leadership of, 90–91
State Council, Ceylon, 32–33
Steering and Subjects Committee,
  102–103, 106–122
SUCCESS, 173–174, 184–185,
  237–238
Sudan, 4
Sumana, Ven. Nakulugamuwa,
  167–168, 185–186, 189–190
  on Buddhism, 169
  Supreme Court and, 169–170
Sunstein, Cass, 11, 98, 242
Supreme Court, 74–76, 168, 172–173
  on Buddhism Chapter, 175–176
  on Christianity, 182–183
  on fundamental rights, 222
  Sinhala language in, 18
  Ven. Sumana and, 169–170
Supreme Court (U.S.), 164–165

Tamil Congress, 84–85, 95–96
Tamil Eelam, 157–158
Tamil language, 7–9
  constitutional law and, 17–18
Tamil United Front, 68–69
Tamils, 7–9, 27–28, 57–58
  Ceylonese, 9
  citizenship for, 61
  ethnic categories, 9–11

Jaffna, 29–31, 62–63, 159
Up-Country, 9–11
Temple of the Tooth, 77–78
territorial constituencies, 57–58
Thailand, 69, 196–197, 206
Constitution, 149–150, 172
theocracy, 119
Theraveda Buddhism, 203–204,
213–214
citizenship and, 205–206
Thirteenth Amendment, 223
The Thought, Conscience and Religion
Act, 258
Tipitaka Compilation Board, 208–209
traditionalist Buddhism, 201–205
triadic prototype of the courts, 218–219
tsunami of December 2004, 175–176
tulsi leaves, 28
Tunisia, 4, 150–151

UNESCO, 185–186
United Front, 91, 100–101, 121–122,
159–161
Bandaranaike on, 101–102
on Common Program, 104–105
on Kandyan Convention, 128–129
manifesto, 100–107, 109–110
on national unity, 105
parliamentary seats of, 103
propaganda of, 104
on religion, 105
United Front Election Manifesto, 105
United Kingdom, 4
United National Party (UNP), 62–63,
73, 100–101
on Buddha Sasana Commission, 89
on Buddhism, 71
on Buddhism Resolution, 127–128
Joint Select Committee, 90–91
on Kandyan Convention, 129–131
membership of, 63–64
on religion, 89
success of, 62
unity of, 63–64
United Nations, 12–21, 44–45, 58–59,
108–109
Ceylon represented in, 92–93

United Nations Association, 92–93
United States
First Amendment in, 6–7, 164–165,
217–218
religion in, 2
Supreme Court, 164–165
Universal Adult Suffrage, 48–49
Universal Declaration of Human
Rights, 94–95, 212
Article 18, 108–109
universals, 248–251
University of Ceylon, 33–35
Chair of Buddhism at, 69
UNP. *See* United National Party
Up-Country Tamils, 9–11

Vaddukodai Resolution, 157
Veddas, 9
Velupillai Prabhakaran, 158
Victoria's Secret, 179
Vidyalankara Pirivena, 50, 195–196
Vietnam, 149–150
Vimalananda, T, 115–116, 137–144
Vinaya, 88, 199–200, 204, 208
Vinaya Pitika, 168
Vishnu, 271–272
Vivekananda Vedanta Society,
118–138
voting systems, 103

Weeramantry, C G, 210
the West, 254
religion in, 250
Wimalawansa, Ven., 191–194,
201–202, 214–215
on Buddhism, 198–200
on Buddhist monks, 209–210
on change, 199–200
citizenship and, 206, 208–209, 215
Commissioner of Buddhist Affairs
and, 203–204
Commissioner of Motor Vehicles
and, 199
constitutional microhistory and,
190–192
court decision, 209–212
Dayakas and, 202

Wimalawansa, Ven. (cont.)
  on fundamental rights, 215
  interview with, 211–212
  pragmatic Buddhism, 198–201
Working Committee of Ceylon
    National Congress, 41–43
World Justice Project, 10
World War II, 44–45

Young Men's Buddhist Association
    (YMBA), 51–53, 85–87, 142, 158,
    167–168
  on Buddhism Chapter, 173
  on Constitution of 1978,
    173
Young Turks, 39–57, 59, 66–67
  Senanayake, D S, and, 40–41

Printed in the United States
By Bookmasters